T0290052

Essential Concepts of Environmental Communication

This book draws on a broad spectrum of environmental communications and related cross-disciplinary literature to help students and scholars grasp the inter-connecting key concepts within this ever-expanding field of study. Aligning climate change and environmental learning through media and communications, particularly taking into account the post-COVID challenge of sustainability, remains one of the most important concerns within environmental communications. Addressing this challenge, *Essential Concepts of Environmental Communication* synthesises summary writings from a broad range of environmental theorists, while teasing out provocative concepts and key ideas that frame this evolving, multi-disciplinary field. Each entry maps out an important concept or environmental idea and illustrates how it relates more broadly across the growing field of environmental communication debates. Included in this volume is a full section dedicated to exploring what environmental communication might look like in a post-COVID setting:

- Offers cutting-edge analysis of the current state of environmental communications.
- Presents an up-to-date exploration of environmental and sustainable development models at a local and global level.
- Provides an in-depth exploration of key concepts across the ever-expanding environmental communications field.
- Examines the interaction between environmental and media communications at all levels.
- Provides a critical review of contemporary environmental communications literature and scholarship.

With key bibliographical references and further reading included alongside the entries, this innovative and accessible volume will be of great interest to students, scholars and practitioners alike.

Pat Brereton is a Professor in the School of Communications and is Co-Director of the Climate and Society Research Centre at Dublin City University, Ireland.

Routledge Studies in Environmental Communication and Media

Environmental Literacy and New Digital Audiences
Pat Brereton

Reporting Climate Change in the Global North and South
Journalism in Australia and Bangladesh
Jahnnabi Das

Theory and Best Practices in Science Communication Training
Edited by Todd P. Newman

The Anthropocene in Global Media
Neutralizing the Risk
Edited by Leslie Sklair

Communicating Endangered Species
Extinction, News and Public Policy
Edited by Eric Freedman, Sara Shipley Hiles and David B. Sachsman

Communicating Climate Change
Making Environmental Messaging Accessible
Edited by Juita-Elena (Wie) Yusuf and Burton St. John III

Competing Discourses on Japan's Nuclear Power
Pronuclear versus Antinuclear Activism
Etsuko Kinefuchi

Essential Concepts of Environmental Communication
An A–Z Guide
Pat Brereton

*For more information about this series, please visit: https://www.routledge.com/
Routledge-Studies-in-Environmental-Communication-and-Media/book-series/
RSECM*

Essential Concepts of Environmental Communication

An A–Z Guide

Pat Brereton

LONDON AND NEW YORK

First published 2022
by Routledge
4 Park Square, Milton Park, Abingdon, Oxon OX14 4RN

and by Routledge
605 Third Avenue, New York, NY 10158

Routledge is an imprint of the Taylor & Francis Group, an informa business

© 2022 Pat Brereton

British Library Cataloguing-in-Publication Data
A catalogue record for this book is available from the British Library

Library of Congress Cataloging-in-Publication Data
A catalog record has been requested for this book

ISBN: 978-0-367-64201-3 (hbk)
ISBN: 978-0-367-64202-0 (pbk)
ISBN: 978-1-003-12342-2 (ebk)

DOI: 10.4324/9781003123422

Typeset in Times New Roman
by Taylor & Francis Books

Contents

A–Z Audio Visual Case Studies   xii
Acknowledgements   xiii

General Appeal: Essential Concepts for Environmental
Communication   1

General Introduction 1

A   10

Access to Nature and Love of Nature: Case Study Ecotourism and
    Star Wars *in Ireland 10*
Case Study of Film Franchise, Star Wars: *Ecotourism in Ireland*
    and Skellig Michael 11
Advertising and Nature: How Environmental Issues are Projected
    in Media and PR 13
Affluence vs. Sustainable Consumption in Addressing Climate
    Change 15
Agency and Childhood Innocence in Animation: Promoting
    Environmental Activism: Case Study of FernGully *and* Princess
    Mononoke *17*
Agenda Setting and News Media Coverage of Environmental
    Issues 19
Anthropomorphism, Human Love and the Personification of
    Animals: Blackfish *22*
Anti-nuclear Modes of Environmental Thinking: Case Study of
    Chernobyl 24
Case Study of the Chernobyl Syndrome and the Rise of a Risk
    Society 27
Avant Garde Stories: Popularising Environmental Themes and
    Issues: Deseret 28

B   31

Behaviour Change Communications (BCC) and Climate
   Change 31
Blue Humanities: Increasing Carbon and Waste Emissions 35

C   38

Carbon Lock-in and Dealing with Stranded Assets:
   Communicating the Challenges 38
Circular Economy: Environmental Media, Inclusive and Just
   Transition – Snowpiercer *40*
Circular Economy Finance and Its Limitations 42
Citizen Media Engagement and Strategies Used for Effective
   Audience Reception Studies 44
Climate Literacy and Environmental Activism: Ozark *46*
Climate Markets and Cap and Trade as Practical Environmental-
   Economic Solutions 48
Cognitive Dissonance and Eco-modernism 50
Communication/Media Models Used for Environmental
   Communication 51
Community Engagement/Environmental Citizenship: 'Change by
   Degrees' 54
Conservation as an Environmental Strategy Towards Evaluating
   Wilderness: Yellowstone 55
Consumption and the Diderot Effect: Sustainable Reduction, Reuse
   and Recycle 59
Coronavirus: Health and Effective Communication of Climate
   Change – Contagion *61*
Creative Imaginary Used to Explore Solutions to Climate
   Change – Documentary 2040 *64*
Critical Theory and Environmental Communications 67
Critique of Historical Western Consumer Capitalism – *Case Study*
   of A Christmas Carol *69*

D   71

De-growth: Radical Solutions for Climate Change Stability 71
Democratic Deficit: From Techno-fix to Gaia – *The War*
   Narrative 73

E   78

*Ecological Modernism and Sustainable Development: Our
   Common Future in Crisis 78*
*Eco-villages – Case Study of Cloughjordan: An Irish Transitional
   and Sustainable Project 81*
Ecocriticism and the Growth of Environmental Communication 82
*Eco-materialism: Case Study of the Real Environmental Cost of
   Media Production 84*
*Education Versus Disinformation: Promoting Environmental
   Literacy 87*
*Employment Opportunities: Feeding into Environmental
   Communications HE Courses 89*
Enclosure Movement and Tragedy of the Commons 91
Energy Humanities: From Fossil Fuels to the Carbon Economy 95
*Energy Landscapes and Media Perceptions: Case Study of
   NIMBYism in Ireland 96*
*Environmental Media Risk Campaigns: Best Practice
   Protocols 97*
*Environmental Citizenship as a Model of Engaging Humans
   Around Climate Change 98*
Environmental Justice: Case Study of India 101
*Environmental Justice: A Case Study of Renewable Energy in
   Postcolonial Morocco 105*
*Environmental Justice: A Case Study of Uruguay (Victoria
   Gomez) 107*
*Environmental Justice: A Case Study of Representations of the
   Inuit Tribe in* The Terror *(Nora Doorley) 109*
*Environmental Management of the Media: Marrying
   Mindmapping and Carbon Footprinting 111*

F   115

*Fake News and Environment Communication – The Social
   Dilemma 115*
Fast Fashion, the 'Third World' and the Circular Economy 120
*Free Press Theory Versus Social Responsibility Model of Media:
   Case Study of ClimateGate 122*

G   127

    Green Transformation and Global Citizen Engagement – Green
       New Deal (Naomi Klein) 127
    Greening the Higher Education Curriculum: Drawing on the
       Power of Children's Media 129
    Greening the Media: Drawing on Scholarship from New
       Environmental Media Journals 132
    Greenwashing the Corporate and Media Industry: PR limitations
       and CSR 134
    Greenwashing Lite: Celebrity Culture and Green Product
       Placement: Down to Earth *137*

H   143

    Historical Environmental Representations of Communal Living:
       Happy as Lazzaro 143
    Hippie Counter-Culture, Active Environmental Agency and Eco-
       spirituality – Leave No Trace *146*
    Human Rights Violation and Climate Change: Who Should
       Pay! 149

I   153

    Intersectionality and Eco-citizenship: Drawing on Race, Class,
       Gender and Ethnicity Debates 153

J   155

    Jevon's Paradox, Energy Efficiency and Its Environmental
       Application: Case Study of F1 155
    Just Transition and Energy: From Fossil Fuels to Renewables –
       Peat Workers in Ireland 157

L   162

    Legal Representations of Environmental Agency: Case Studies of
       Dark Waters *162*
    Linguistic Discourse and Ecocriticism – Naming the Crisis! 165
    Literary Tropes for Representing Low Carbon Futures 169

M 171

Mediatisation of Climate Change with a Focus on Environmental
  Concerns *171*
Media Coverage of Climate Change Debate: Triggers for
  Promoting Environmental Literacy *172*
Multi-level Perspective (MLP) Analysis of Climate Change *174*
Museums and Curating Exhibitions as a Model for
  Representations of Climate Change *175*

N 178

Native (Invader) Species: Representations and Effects on Bio-
  diversity *178*
National Capital as a Business Response in Dealing with Climate
  Change *179*
Nature Based Solutions – A Life on Our Planet *181*
NIMBYism (Not in My Back Yard): Case Study of Renewable
  Energy (Windfarms) *187*
Non-Conventional Environmental Activism: A Case Study of
  Woman at War *190*

O 193

Organic Signifiers of Communicating with a Natural Ecosystem –
  Tree of Life *193*
Overton Window and Making Radical Political Environmental
  Decisions *194*

P 196

Pastoralism as a Model for Human's Love of Nature in Literature
  and Film *196*
Peak Oil and 'Keep it in the Ground': Contested Environmental
  Debates *197*
Petrofiction, Petrochemical Emissions: Reaching Dangerous
  Limits *198*
Posthumanism and Ecological Thinking *199*
Postmodernism and Climate Change Communication *201*
Population Overshoot: Our Ecological Footprint and Loss of
  Biodiversity – Downsizing *203*

Q   208

Queer Theorising and Nature: New Modes of Imagining Gender –
Brokeback Mountain *208*

R   211

Regenerative Soil and Overcoming Desertification: Case Study of
Kiss the Ground *211*
*Religious Fanaticism and Romanticisation of Nature: Case Study
of* A Hidden Life *213*
Renewable Energy Debates and Critiques: Case Study of Planet of
the Humans *216*
Risk Society and Climate Change 222

S   224

*Sensory Big Data and Art: Communicating through the Five
Senses 224*
*Shock Doctrine and Pandemics: As a Precursor for the Climate
Crisis 226*
Sixth Extinction and Environmental Disasters 227
*Slow Violence and Poverty: Lack of Equity in Representing
Environmental Scholarship 229*
*Social Media and Climate Change Communication: A Tool for
Innovation! 231*
Spiritual Representations of Environmental Agency – First
Reformed *232*
*Sustainable Communication and Environmental New Media
Research 237*
*Sustainable Development Goal 12 – Responsible Consumption and
Production 238*
Sustainability Accounting (Dr Aideen O'Dochartaigh DCU) 239

T   242

*Tipping Points Around Climate Change Transformation –
Audience Research 242*
*Transdisciplinary Research (TDR) and Environmental
Communication 245*

U   247

    Utopian Environmental Messaging: Lessons from Hollywood and Guides to Young People 247

V   250

    Veganism and Promoting Environmental Values Through Celebrity Endorsement 250

W   253

    Water Documentaries as Public Service Announcement (PSA) – Irish Water Conflict 253
    Case Study – Water Public Service Announcement (PSA) 257
    Weather Documentary Scholarship: Mediating Climate Change Effects and Public Opinion 261
    Westerns Reflecting Deep Environmental Issues and Nature's Revenge – Wild River *263*
    Wind Energy: Storytelling, Renewable Energy and Community Adaptation 266
    World Bank (The) and Developing Effective Financial Environmental Communication 270

The Future of Environmental Communications: Overcoming Anxiety   273

    Overview: The Great Derangement 273
    Realos vs Fundis: Green Growth vs De-growth 274
    Environmental Communications and the Future 275

A–Z Audio Visual Case Studies

2040 (2019) – Damon Gameau   64
A Christmas Carol (2019) – adapted by Stephen
    Knight, Dir. Nick Murphy   69
A Hidden Life (2019) – Terrence Malick   213
A Life on Our Planet (2020) – BBC and book version
    by David Attenborough   181
Blackfish (2013) – Gabriella Cowperthwaite   22
Brokeback Mountain (2005) – Ang Lee   208
Chernobyl (1999) – Craig Mazin (creator)   24
Dark Waters (2019) – Todd Haynes   162
Deseret (1995) – James Benning   28
Down to Earth with Zac Efron (2018) – and Darin Olien (producer)   137
Downsizing (2017) – Alexander Payne   205
FernGully: The Last Rain Forest (1982) – animation Bill Kroyer   17
First Reformed (2017) – Paul Schrader   232
Happy as Lazzaro (2018) – Alice Rohrwacher   143
Kiss the Ground (2020) – Joshua Tickell   211
Leave no Trace (2018) – Debra Granik   146
Ozark (2017) – Bill Dubuque and Mark Williams (creators)   46
Planet of the Humans (2019) – Jeff Gibbs and produced
    by Michael Moore   216
Princess Mononoke (1997) – Hayao Miyazaki   17
Snowpiercer (2013) – Bong Joon Ho [see also animation and
    Netflix series]   40
Star Wars Franchise (1977) – George Lucas   11
The Social Dilemma (2020) – Jeff Orlowski   117
The Terror (2018) – David Kajganich (creator)   112
Tree of Life (2011) – Terrence Malick   193
Wild River (2017) – Tyler Sheridan   263
Woman at War (2018) – Benedikt Erlingsson   190
Yellowstone (2018) – John Linson (creator)   57

Acknowledgements

This book received financial support from the Faculty of Humanities and Social Science Book Publication Scheme at Dublin City University.

Many of the references and examples used in this volume have been road-tested with our Masters in Climate Change students, together with other undergraduate media programmes at Dublin City University (DCU), following over 20 years of teaching and researching in the area. In particular, my gratitude goes to colleagues David Robbins and Diarmuid Torney who helped set up our Master's programme and our new research centre for Climate and Society. Continuous support and helpful comments were also supplied by numerous staff and academic friends across the world. Reading across so many related areas, I have only scratched the surface, yet hope to spark further engagement by students, as they develop their own thinking and critical engagement.

I hope I have done justice to several engaging websites (URLs), which were accurate at the time of writing when accessed during 2020 and 2021. Neither the author nor Routledge is responsible for URLs that may have expired or changed since the manuscript was prepared.

The entries draw on contemporary environmental reports and publications across a broad area of academic investigation.

Under COVID-lockdown, I have attended many online conferences and webinars, which have helped to frame and shape several of the entries in this introductory and broad-based student volume. This has been augmented by discussions across listservs, including for instance, *www.scorai.net*, which has provided valuable insights into various aspects of environmental sustainability and effective climate change communication.

The volume also draws on the back-catalogue of my own writings, while also featuring edited volumes published by Routledge and others, across this ever-growing environmental field of study; including *Pietari Kääpä's Environmental Management of the Media: Policy, Industry, Practice* (2018); Antonio Lopez's *Ecomedia Literacy; Integrating Ecology and Media Education* (2021), Ken Hiltner's edited volume *Ecocriticism, The Essential Reader* (2015), alongside Mike Hulme's edited Student Primer, *Contemporary Climate Change Debates* (2020) – all of which and many more besides have been heavily drawn on for this A–Z primer.

I have gratefully included summary overviews of areas I have little specialist knowledge; including from my recently graduated PhD student Victoria Gomez on Environmental Justice and Uruguay, Nora Doorley on the Inuit tribe featured in the TV drama *The Terror* (2018–19), alongside a summary of Sustainability Accounting by Aideen O'Dochartaigh (DCU Business School), together with overviews of publications on eco-modernism by Declan Fahy, as well as Trish Morgan and Brenda McNally, who have carried out insightful reports for the Environmental Protection Agency (EPA). I have also learned a lot from communication workshops with the Environmental Protection Agency (EPA) as well as the Local Authority Water Program (LAWPRO).

Thanks to my dear friend and mentor Michael Doorley, who has read early drafts of most of these entries and given valuable assistance in shaping many of them. Of course any errors, omissions or over-statements are my responsibility and for this I apologise in advance. In the open spirit in which the volume is created, I would encourage all student readers to go back to original sources where possible and develop their own critical engagement and scholarship.

To all my family, Angela, Robert, Rita and Conor who kept me grounded. The writing process was difficult and uncertain at time with COVID-19, a feature which not surprisingly permeates the whole volume. I hope these sometime cursory entries and audio-visual case studies will stimulate students to face up to the greatest existential threat of our time – a challenge which I believe environmental communication can and will play a major role in addressing into the future. Here's hoping!

References

Back catalogue of academic studies constantly referred to in this volume include:

Books

Brereton, Pat. Environmental Literacy and New Digital Audiences. Routledge 2019.
Brereton, Pat. *Environmental Ethics and Film*. Earthscan Routledge 2016.
Brereton, Pat. *Smart Cinema: DVD add-ons and new Audience Pleasures*. Palgrave Press 2012.
Brereton, Pat. *Hollywood Utopia: Ecology in Contemporary American Cinema*. Intellect Press 2005.
Brereton, Pat. *Continuum Guide to Media Education*. Continuum 2001.

Book chapters

Brereton, Pat. 'Environmental Ethics of Survival: Case Study Analysis of I am Legend and The Revenant'. In *The Ethics of Survival in Contemporary Literature and Culture*, edited Gerd Bayer *et al.*Springer Nature, Palgrave Macmillan (in press) 2021.

Brereton, Pat. 'Cultural and Visual Responses to Climate Change: Ecological Readings of Irish Zombie Movies'. In *Ireland and the Climate Crisis*, edited by David Robbins, Diarmuid Torney and Pat Brereton. Palgrave 2020.

Brereton, Pat. 'Communal Indian Farming and Food Ecology: A Reading of Timbaktu'. In Rayson K. Alex and S. Susan Deborah (eds). *Ecodocumentaries: Critical Essays.* Palgrave Macmillan 2016.

Brereton, Pat. 'Cinema, Ecology and Environment'. In Anders Hansen and Robert Cox, (eds). *The Routledge Handbook of Environmental Communication.* Routledge 2015.

Journal articles

Brereton, Pat. 'Aesthetics and Ecology: Utopianism and Fascist Aesthetics - An appreciation of "Nature" in Documentary/Fiction Film'. *Capitalism, Nature, Socialism*: 33–50. 2001.

Brereton, Pat. 'Nature, Tourism and Irish Film'. *Irish Studies Review* 14: 407–420. 2006.

Brereton Pat. 'Poverty and Environment in Films set in Africa'. *Media Development* 2: 57–61. 2009.

Brereton, Pat. 'Ecocinema, Sustainability and Africa: A reading of Out of Africa, The Constant Gardener and District 9'. *Journal of African Cinemas* 5: 219–235. 2014.

Brereton, Pat. 'An Eco-reading of Documentary/Fictional Narratives'. *Irish Studies in International Affairs* 31. 43–57. Royal Irish Academy Dublin Ireland. 2020.

Brereton, Pat and Barrios-O'Neill, Danielle. 'Irish Energy Landscape and Film'. *Journal of Environmental Media* 2(1): 101–115. 2021.

Brereton, Pat [with the late Robert Furze]. 'Transcendence and the Tree of Life: Beyond the Face of the Screen with Terrence Malick, Emmanuel Levinas and Roland Barthes'. *Journal for the Study of Religion, Nature and Culture* 8: 329–351. 2015.

Brereton, Pat and Gomez, Victoria. 'Media Students, Climate Change and YouTube Celebrities: Readings of Dear Future Generations: Sorry Video Clip'. *ISLE Interdisciplinary Studies in Literature and Environment* 27(1). 2020.

Brereton, Pat and Hong, Pat. 'Audience Responses to Environmental Fiction and nonfiction Films'. *Intersections: The Journal of Global Communications and Culture* 4: 171–199. 2014.

Culloty, Eileen, Brereton, Pat, Murphy, Padraig, Suiter, Jane, Smeaton, Alan and Zhan, Dian. 'Researching Visual Representation of Climate Change'. *Environmental Communication* 13(2): 179–191. 2019.

McDonagh, Pierre and Brereton, Pat. 'Screening Not Greening: An Ecological Reading of the Greatest Business Movies'. *Journal of Macromarketing*: 1–14. 2010.

O'Brolchain, Fiachra and Brereton, Pat. 'Learning Environmental Lessons while Facing up to Covid-19: Readings of The Andromeda Strain, Contagion and World War Z'. *Special Issue of Science Fiction and Philosophy* 4(1) 'The Day that Coronavirus stopped the world: What do we learn about Pandemics in Science Fiction Stories Special Issue'. 2021.

General Appeal

Essential Concepts for Environmental Communication

Aligning climate change through media and communications, while taking into account the ongoing post-COVID challenge of greening a recovery around environmental sustainability, will remain the most important and immediate preoccupation within environmental communications. The aim of this volume is to strive to synthesise writings and reflections across a broad range of scholarship in related fields, calling attention to provocative concepts and ideas that characterise this evolving multi-disciplinary field into the future. Each entry sets up and defines an essential or core concept and illustrates how it relates more broadly to the growing field of environmental communication. Audio-visual media examples are added where possible to illustrate the area under investigation. Entries also include some references and further reading. Overall the volume:

- offers cutting edge analysis of the state of environmental communications as it straddles across so many areas,
- presents an up-to-date debate on environmental and sustainable development at a local (Irish) and global level,
- gives an in-depth exploration of current key concepts across the environmental communications field,
- examines the interaction between environmental and media communications at all levels,
- provides a critical review of contemporary environmental communications literature.

General Introduction

This selection of loosely categorised A–Z environmental concepts and analysis help to constitute a summary overview of cutting-edge environmental literature and related examples from audio-visual media, which is coincidentally sometimes viewed through the lens of the 2020/21 pandemic. The primary aim of this ongoing research, building on over two decades of teaching and research, is focused around striving to highlight how the 'creative imaginary' of film, together with other media platforms, can speak to our expanding

DOI: 10.4324/9781003123422-1

concerns with environmental communication, situated within the context of a global climate crisis. We must recognise however that climate change is not the only global environmental risk exploited by Hollywood in recent years: one calls to mind for example often related issues such as nuclear war in *Terminator 2: Judgement Day* (1991); deforestation in *FernGully: The Last Rainforest* (1992); bioterrorism in *28 Days Later* (2002); species extinction in *Earth* (2007), population growth in *Slumdog Millionaire* (2008); ecology and religion in *The Tree of Life* (2011) and *The Life of Pi* (2012) etc.

In this limited selection of A–Z concepts and readings, I have adapted a broadly environmentally sensitive approach, which challenges and critiques the excesses of neo-liberal capitalism, the interconnections between the loss of biodiversity and increasing climate crises, while suggesting new media strategies that help promote a robust and even sometimes a radical green agenda. The selection of entries cannot even attempt to be comprehensive; students requiring a fuller glossary of key terms across the broad area might usefully for instance call on the *Oxford Dictionary of Environment and Conservation* by Chris Park (2007–11) with its very pithy definitions, alongside the *Companion to Environmental Studies*, edited by Noel Castree et al. (Routledge 2018) for longer expert academic explorations, towards teasing out many of the key concepts and themes embedded within environmental communications. With the global coronavirus pandemic, it appears much has changed in the world of late, making it hopefully easier to both contemplate and initiate political, economic and behavioural change around our climate crisis, which otherwise might have been considered impossible. One might even suggest that a *tipping point* towards promoting new modes of engagement through the assistance of environmental communication is more possible now than ever before.

More broadly, as an umbrella term, all aspects of Environmental Humanities can be co-opted towards linking environmental communications across a full range of humanities disciplines, which have become important for the growth and diversification of the field. Increasingly, Environmental Communications (EC) is being used to incorporate a broad-based inquiry that is both interdisciplinary in nature and pluralistic in its approach (see Nye et al. 2013; Rose et al. 2012; Corbett 2021). It also responds to the 'need to reframe global environmental change issues fundamentally as social and human challenges, rather than just environmental issues' (Palsson et al. 2011: 5). Environmental Humanities in its broader context helpfully also serves as a means by which fundamental concerns within the humanities – such as 'meaning, value, responsibility and purpose' (Rose et al. 2012: 1) can be brought to bear on questions of the environment 'through the deployment of a humanities mode of enquiry' (Åsberg et al. 2015). Scholars constantly affirm its overall role as being one of 're-imagining' relations between 'culture' and 'nature', while always striving to be constructive and hopeful (Rose et al. 2012). This remains a growing agenda for environmental communications over its relatively short history.

Seminal readers in the field which feed off a social science, together with a humanities approach, include Robert Cox's *Environmental Communication and the Public Sphere* (Third ed. 2013) and Anders Hansen and Cox's *Routledge Handbook of Environmental Communication* (see 2015 edition); both of which strive to encapsulate the scope of this ever-expanding field of study. Such academic studies explore a range of intersections between communications and the environment, which continue to be important, including for instance calling out the following questions:

- How do human agents respond to nature/environment?
- What accounts for the development and reproduction of dominant systems of representation or discourses of the 'environment' and what communication practices contribute to the interruption, distribution or transformation of such discourses?
- What effects do different environmental sources (e.g. media), as well as specific communication practices have on audiences?
- What are the relationships between or among communications, individual's values and beliefs and their environmental behaviour?
- In what ways do different modes of dissemination and reception of scientific or technical information contribute to the understanding of, or constitute 'knowledge' of nature or various forms of environmental phenomena?
- How do humans discursively or symbolically constitute space or place?
- How do local or indigenous cultures understand 'nature' or 'environment' and how might they convey understanding of our everyday life?
- How can the broad spectrum of commercial mainstream art, together with *avant garde* (eco)media promote such change?

All of these questions and more besides speak to the growing need for various forms of environmental and behavioural change, together most importantly with top-down systemic and policy change from governments and big business to meet the existential challenges of climate change. This introductory A–Z series of entries draw on contemporary thinking around the linkages between media and environmental discourses, as highlighted by (2020) journals like the *Journal of Environmental Media*, edited by Hunter Vaughan and Meryl Schriver-Rice, alongside *Media+Environment*, edited by environmental media scholars Alenda Chang, Adrian Ivakhiv and Janet Walker. The latter's opening editorial lays out some useful definitional and scoping parameters for future interconnections between all aspects of media and communication, while affirming the primary importance of environmental education and critical media literacy. The environment today, according to their opening editorial, is registered most commonly as a set of issues including climate change, deforestation and desertification, alongside ecological disruption, with a series of 'overshoots', including over-farming, over-fishing and over-harvesting of all resources, not to mention over-population.

Noting in turn that the discussion of all of these topics have sometimes 'tended to downplay' carbon emission patterns, alongside influences of race, class, gender and culture-based injustices that subverts the equitable working out of a just transition in securing a low carbon future. This journal's editorial further affirms that a core principle of much media scholarship focuses on how 'media are active participants in the social construction and material production of the world'. Like the media, 'environments are not inert or passive containers, mere receipts of the tool-wielding whims of our species' (Chang et al. 2019). The editors perceptively raise several other provocative questions for consideration, including where does media end and environment begin and what exactly do environments mediate and *vice versa*?

Of course, new forms of communication can constantly help towards 'rewiring the environment', as laid out by important global organisations like the 'International Environmental Communications Network' (IECA https://www.theieca.org/), together with high impact journals like *Environmental Communication*. At all times, environmental communications – together with the humanities in general – have been concerned with the 'creative imagination' and engaging with nature and natural habitats, while constantly focusing on all aspects of the so-called Anthropocene.

Furthermore, in the inaugural issue of *Media+Environment*, Lisa Perks and Janet Walker in an article titled 'Disaster media: Finding the cure of ecological disruption and moving towards social justice' (2020), calls attention to the centrality of disaster as a mobilising feature for future environmental communication. Disaster media is driven by various aspects of environmental ethics and especially ongoing concerns for climate justice (Brereton 2016). Echoing the disaster of the global pandemic, the authors call out how various forms of disaster media, which are embedded within several areas of humanities-based media and environmental studies, help to situate the importance of addressing our climate emergency:

1   Disasters cause people to rethink what 'media' are and to be content with the fact that especially during disasters, media is constantly changing and being updated.
2   Because they come to the fore during a crisis situation, disaster media help to explore structural inequalities, consequently practices of relief and reform need to happen and can be facilitated (or inhibited) by mediated means.
3   Environmental issues need to be considered in relation to the multiple temporalities of climate disruption.

Evaluating how media emerge and shape our environmental consciousness during crisis situations and at the same time cultivate attention to new modes of disaster relief and environmental justice, remains a clear focus for much environmental scholarship. Further examining audiences' cognitive and emotional understanding of climate change remains another major avenue of investigation which is explored in this volume. In a comprehensive study of environmental challenges around communicating climate change and assessing audience engagement, Leah Filho et al. (2019) sets out some clear steps towards teasing out the complex scientific information, data and models that can be applied to a more humanities-based investigation of environmental communications. These in turn specifically draw on information and knowledge from across the sciences, as well as throughout the social sciences, especially calling on economics and politics; all the while focusing on all aspects of communication.

Such scholarship constantly takes on board many of the broader challenges recognised in communicating climate change, including the:

- complexity of climate messages
- geographical distribution and focus
- variety of themes encapsulated by the umbrella term of climate change
- responsibility for climate change, from top level global organisations and governments to the 'bottom up' responsibility of individuals and local communities
- uncertainty principle, which can lead to adopting a 'wait and see' approach, inferring the real urgency of the problems are not immediately apparent
- lack of specialist reporters and media producers available in dealing with the complexities of the issues
- competing themes, recalling most especially short-term economic and other immediate concerns, and various other political issues that often take precedence over more longer-term, difficult or so-called wicked problems around climate change (Filho et al. 2019: 4).

Climate change communication programmes coupled with broad-based educational strategies in general seek to:

a   Inform people about specific risks that climate change may pose to their own surroundings, while making connection with this global phenomenon. An emphasis on doomsday messages for example is known to be far less efficient, than the alternative presentation of positive ones

b   Persuade people to engage and reflect around how the policies that their countries follow may be associated with climate change and how their behaviour may influence the global climate debate and mobilise people in general to become more involved in implementing climate change mitigation measures (Filho et al. 2019: 4).

Some constructive ways of achieving better environmental communication include:

- Avoid focusing on negative messages and using evidence of successful actions/solutions.
- Use a constructive approach, showing how facts contribute to addressing the problem. For instance, farmers might try new crops or adjust the seeding times to avoid droughts.

- Selecting the best and most appropriate tools to reach specific audiences and groups.
- Find ways to monitor progress and show incremental development.

Without doubt, political and sustained environmental transformation has to come from the top down, as well as being assisted from the bottom up. It is suggested for instance that the 'war metaphor' – used effectively during the 2020/21 global pandemic struggle – needs to be co-opted and foregrounded within our climate change discourse to help ensure all sections of society face up to the difficult challenges ahead. Furthermore, when proposing solutions, all stakeholders and interest groups need to be acknowledged and ought to be taken into account, when evaluating major climate justice issues. For instance, ongoing concerns about global inequalities have been highlighted by the dramatically uneven effects of the global pandemic, with poor and disadvantaged regions worst affected by the virus. Such inequalities will be even further dramatised by the consequences of climate change, producing more radically unequal effects across the world.

Mass media has a major role to play in speaking to global inequalities together with all forms of injustices, especially those exacerbated by our climate crisis. As concluded in my chapter in the *Routledge Handbook of Environment and Communication*:

> arguments will only have force if we physically feel them. In other words if an argument fails to generate feelings, or tap into the affective component of public engagement, then it will probably not persuade. This is why the creative imaginary of fiction is so important in mobilising and framing public opinion and the extensive power of emotions remains of primary importance in affecting audiences. Such arguments only motivate when it induces feelings, including satisfaction, pleasure, excitement, interest, anger or distress. If it generates no feelings at all, it is unlikely to be persuasive.
>
> (Brereton in Hansen and Cox 2015: 258–270)

For a fuller academic review of the contemporary literature, see Culloty et al. 2019.

Furthermore, as also affirmed in another seminal eco-reader, 'it is an ecology of connections' that we negotiate to make meanings both resonant and relevant for everyday living. In this mediated habitat for example, 'cinema is a form of negotiation, a mediation that is itself ecologically placed as it consumes the entangled world around it, and in turn, is itself consumed' (Rust et al. 2013: 1). Extensive and sometimes pithy textual readings are also used in this volume to illustrate essential concepts and help concretise applied environmental theories. Audio-visual examples vary from art-house documentaries like *Deseret* (1995), to well-examined cautionary and more commercial fare like *Before the Flood* (2016), not to mention more optimistic eco-documentaries like *2040* (2019) that speak directly to young people.

Throughout the A–Z entries, I will also use some Irish examples to illustrate the problems small countries encounter and how they can serve as a model for climate change communication strategies. Because 'everything is connected' there are constant overlaps across many of the entries, including discussion of energy landscapes, just transitions and renewable energy for example. Furthermore, highlighting for instance mineral exploration in Morocco, or the necessity for more sustainable development in India or China, call for more radical approaches to be adapted, using provocative media representations. Most notably, the doyen of nature documentary David Attenborough has to be included in any survey of the field, with so much stunning output over several decades, including his most provocative auto-biography, *A Life on our Planet* (Netflix 2020), which is extensively analysed. Meanwhile, more fictional narratives such as *Woman at War* (2018), or *Happy as Lazzaro* (2018) help to demonstrate the range and complexity of climate change issues and problems, with their innovative eco-narrative structures and expressive aesthetic formats.

Certainly, as the corpus of eco-media production expands – and it certainly needs to – this in turn will help to nurture an evolving set of storylines and creative imaginaries that extend the rubric of genres and mediated templates, designed to foreground and address an ever-expanding range of environmental issues and concerns. Furthermore, with the continuous growth in critical environmental writing and ecocriticism around media production, students and scholars are becoming more aware of salient representations and the development of environmental themes embedded in the media. All of which are foregrounded through the still expanding list of concepts and ideas examined in the pages to follow, which are designed to highlight and illustrate this growing body of work. At the same time, audiences can further learn about the ever-increasing and complex (re)presentational tensions, exposed through this wicked set of dilemmas facing the very survival of life on earth.

At the end of this expansive and interconnecting list of essential concepts – which of course is never complete and some hard decisions had to be made because of space – the A–Z listing remains coloured by the 2020/21 global pandemic, serving as a precursor to the even more challenging environmental problems facing us as a species in the decades to come. Several entries strive to tease out how this necessary rupturing of normal 'business as usual' practices can be co-opted and used to spark a necessary paradigm shift and transformation. All the while entries constantly reflect on how we as a species can actively learn from our holistic interconnecting eco-systems and face up to the ongoing climate crisis struggle.

See for instance, important anthologies which have dealt with these issues, including Ken Hiltner's (2015) aforementioned *Ecocriticism: The Essential Reader*, together with Scott Slovic's (2010) *The Third Wave of Ecocriticism: North American Reflections* among others, all mapping out the current phase of our evolving discipline. But, as affirmed in the Routledge *Encyclopaedia of Ecocriticism* and also in the comprehensive series of essays in the *Companion to Environmental Studies* (Castree et al. 2018), alongside several glossaries and other publications like Joni Adamson et al.'s *Keywords for Environmental Studies* (2016), or the ever-expanding Cambridge and Penguin 'green ideas' environmental series, there is an urgent need to move away from European-American centric analysis and alternatively focus on various developing regions across multiple genres. This includes a focus on problematising related issues, such as the preponderance of eco-masculinity and 'white messiah' narratives, together with the growth of multicultural and more reflexive queer ecocriticism. One might specifically also call attention to the emergence of more radically framed post-colonial, anti-racist modes of ecocriticism, not to mention animality-based studies, which has been around since 2000.

Most recently the development of applied ecocriticism, alongside more advanced audience research techniques has begun to expand the field, with special issues of important environmental and literary journals like *ISLE* (see issue edited by Alexa Weik von Mossner et al. in 2020) developing a fruitful debate. Furthermore, a so-called fourth wave of environmental scholarship has slowly evolved, calling up new modes of investigation, including material ecocriticism, transnational ecocriticism, eco-narratology, ecocritical animal studies and information eco-processing among others. Some of these threads will be alluded to in this volume, but I must again acknowledge full justice cannot be afforded to such exciting avenues of research and this student's primer can only whet their appetite. By all accounts, the field is never static and is continuously evolving, which makes it both exciting and challenging for students and scholars to keep on board and never stop learning to engage with these ongoing challenges.

References

Adamson, Julie, Gleason, William and Pellow, David. (eds). *Keywords for Environmental Studies*. New York Press 2016.

Åsberg, Cecilia, Neimanis, Astrida and Hedrén, Johan. 'Four Problems, Four Directions For Environmental Humanities: Toward Critical Post-humanities for the Anthropocene'. *Ethics and Environment* 2015.

Brereton, Pat. 'Cinema Ecology and Environment' (258–270). Hansen, Anders and Cox, Robert. *Routledge Handbook of Environmental Communication*. Routledge 2015.

Brereton, Pat. *Environmental Ethics and Film*. Routledge 2016.

Castree, Noel, Hulme, Mike and Proctor, James (eds). *Companion to Environmental Studies*. Routledge 2018.

Chang, Alenda, Ivakhiv, Adrian and Janet Walker (eds). *Media+Environment* (2020) University of California Press. https://mediaenviron.org/.

Chang, Alenda, Ivakhiv, Adrian and Janet Walker. 'States of Media+Environment: Editors' Introduction'. *Media+Environment* 1(1). 2019.

Corbett, Julia. *Communicating the Climate Crisis: New Directions for Facing What Lies Ahead*. Rowman and Littlefield. 2021.

Cox, Robert. *Environmental Communication and the Public Sphere*. 3rd ed. Sage Publishers 2013.

Culloty, Eileen, Brereton, Pat *et al.* 'Researching Visual Representations of Climate Change'. *Environmental Communication* vol. 13. Issue 2. 179–191. 2019.

Filho, Leah, Walter *et al.* eds. *Addressing the Challenge in Communicating Climate Change Across Various Audiences.* Springer [Hamburg University] 2019.

Hansen, Anders and Cox, Robert (eds). *Routledge Handbook of Environment and Communication.* Routledge 2015.

Hiltner, Ken. *Eco-criticism: The Essential Reader.* Routledge 2015.

Nye, David *et al.* 'Background Document on Emergence of the Environmental Humanities'. *MISTRA* 2013.

Palsson, Gisli *et al. Responses to Environmental and Social Challenges for our Unstable Earth (RESCUE).* ESF Forward Look – ESF-COST. Frontier of Science. 2011.

Perks, Lisa and Walker, Janet. 'Disaster Media: Finding the Cure of Ecological Disruption and Moving Towards Social Justice'. *Media+Environment.* 2 (1). 2020.

Rose, Deborah, Bird *et al.* 'Thinking Through the Environment. Unsettling the Humanities'. *Environmental Humanities.* 1: 1–5. 2012.

Rust, Stephen, Monani, Salma and Cubitt, Sean (eds). *Ecocinema, Theory and Practice.* Routledge 2013.

Slovic, Scott. 'The Third Wave of Ecocriticism: North American Reflections on the Current Phase of the Discipline'. *New Ecocritical Perspectives: European and Transnational Ecocriticism* 1(1). 2010.

A

Access to Nature and Love of Nature: Case Study Ecotourism and *Star Wars* in Ireland

Having direct access to nature is regarded as an important prerequisite for promoting and growing to love and respect nature; be it wilderness or a more controlled manicured habitat, which in turn has been reconstituted by human intervention. There has been extensive research into the psychological health improvement gained through actively engaging with nature – a realisation that has become even more pertinent during the pandemic of 2020/21, with varying lockdowns and restrictions of movement across the world. Furthermore, as is often said within environmental communications circles, if citizens don't already hold or acquire a deep love of nature, how can they possible develop higher levels of environmental literacy, much less become willing or motivated to support more radical climate crisis initiatives.

By way of illustration of these so-called 'Love of Nature' or even 'Back to Nature' tropes, while at the same time echoing how they support explicit forms of biophilia, one can trace its lineage back through history and art. What has come to be called biophilia has been explicitly illustrated by landscape artists over the centuries, in using their art and skill to capture and represent the beauty and majesty of landscape and nature through all its complexity. For instance, the early Romantic poets, writers and artists, who became spiritually and emotionally transported by an aesthetic form of epiphany gained through communing with nature which often included some type of religious reverie. Many modern (especially so-called first-wave) environmentalists suggest that such artistic representations of close connections with local habitats and landscape, remains an essential pre-requisite for developing a deep form of environmental engagement and respect for nature.

A traditional view of the romantic 'return to nature' theme constituted and embodied a form of escapism, alongside some type of spiritual communion with nature. For instance in America one can trace a long line of romantic poets, including Walt Whitman who have fed into the growth and development of the environmental movement. Most famously of course, in the United Kingdom, the poet William Wordsworth is said to have found creative

DOI: 10.4324/9781003123422-2

release through experiencing 'wild' landscapes like the Lake District, as an antidote to the harsh social realities of urban squalor with its increasing levels of pollution, sparked by the Industrial Revolution.

Coincidentally, literary critic Jonathan Bate adds a further psychological rationale for embracing nature to explain the rise of romantic art, which directly feeds into contemporary times. Referring to the psychological theories of Sigmund Freud and the unconscious, Bate suggested that as a human species, we need 'nature for the same reason that we need mental phantasy' (Bate cited in Hiltner 2015: 88). But as Bate and others reaffirm, the problem with such a romantic view of nature and human connectivity is that it depends on individual feelings and on a receptive consciousness, not to mention having physical access to beautiful unspoilt landscape. Most crudely, it is suggested, workers on the land (alongside industrial workers suffering in stifling and oppressive factories) including more contemporary developing world countries, have little time to notice, much less enjoy their environment when compared with their richer middle and upper-class neighbours. Consequently, it has been (sometimes unfairly) suggested that only more wealthy middle-class citizens across the rich Western world have both the cultural and environmental capital to actively commune with nature; as evidenced through the proliferation of leisure-based parks.

See for instance the history of the Sierra Club, which was set up in 1892 by famous environmentalist John Muir, securing a major base in California and across all American states, with extensive membership also across several other regions. The organisation has had an important role in developing various aspects of environmental education and literacy across America, through so many of its promotional campaigns. As one slogan on its website attests to: 'Inspired by nature, we work together, to explore, enjoy, and protect our communities and the planet'. Together with conservation of wild spaces across the continent, the Sierra Club has grown in stature to take on many other related environmental issues, including biodiversity, water and land preservation, as well as addressing all aspects of the climate crisis. The organisation is dedicated to 'preservation, restoration and enjoyment' of the environment and would certainly dispute any criticism around promoting an elitist environmental agenda. Over the decades, while the global wealth divide has increased, nonetheless at the same time more and more people seek to have access to wild and unspoilt nature to escape to (see for instance an analysis of the television series *Yellowstone*). Furthermore, the growth of new modes of ecotourism and general globalised travel have revolutionised the old binaries between urban and rural, nature and culture, creating new forms of active engagement with and in nature.

Case Study of Film Franchise, *Star Wars*: Ecotourism in Ireland and Skellig Michael

As I argue in a chapter on Irish ecotourism and film (see Brereton 2021) 'A growing body of literature provides evidence that cinematic film and television drama productions can influence people's travel decisions and entice them to visit particular destinations they have seen on screen' (Bolan and Kearney 2017, 2149).

The decision by Lucas Film to turn the rocky island of Skellig Michael, off the south-west coast, into the futuristic planet Ahch-To – as recreated so far in both *The Force Awakens* (2015) and *The Last Jedi* (2017) – has already brought a huge surge in tourism. Many have asked what are the unique attributes of this small uninhabited island that appeals to such an international franchise? Monks historically started building on the island in the year 600 AD, at a period in history when it would have involved a treacherous journey on small boats called curraghs. The religious inhabitants apparently desired extreme isolation to help bring them closer to God, but such visits unfortunately were often short-lived, as they mostly died very young.

This religious mode of living constituted the ultimate manifestation of a frugal, anti-materialist philosophy, reflecting at one extreme a deep ecological form of living and communing with nature. Somewhat paradoxically, escape from modernity/civilisation and its easy comforts and luxuries continues to reflect a niche aspect of ecotourism. While the more defined appeal of a spiritual pilgrimage, seeking out areas that are untouched by any form of modern civilisation has also had a long history on this sacred site. By any measure, the UNESCO designated World Heritage site of Skellig Michael fits the bill and has become a fulcrum of global mythic engagement, all the while evoking a pure form of idyllic spiritual identification.

Unlike the co-opting of the island landscape for touristic, if not spiritual purposes, the eponymous Porg toy stands out within the *mise-en-scene* of Irish-Hollywood films – designed simply to mimic puffins and serve as a piece of explicit franchising for the film. Such iconic natural birds are found all around the island, but unfortunately became too difficult to manage, much less blot out of the cinematic landscape. Not surprisingly, there was much environmental criticism of the film's crude commodification of the simulated birds as a technical continuity solution, which in turn could be more easily visualised to fit into the diegesis of the fantasy world-view. In an interview with creature concept designer Jake Lunt Davies, it was revealed that the Porgs 'were only invented to cover up the *actual* adorable creatures that turned out to be a huge pain in the ass' for writer/director Rian Johnson. 'By law, *Star Wars: The Last Jedi* was not permitted to mess with the puffins' (www.starwars.com). The love of nature which is usually celebrated in filmic culture, can at the same time unfortunately be subverted and shown to be a poor imitation of the real experience of this revered island. Such a popular tale highlights the ambiguous tensions embedded within the mediation of a deep love of nature and how audio-visual media can (ab)use such romantic place-making for their own ends.

References

Bate, Jonathan. 'The Economy of Nature' (77–96). In Hiltner, Ken. (ed.) *Ecocriticism: The Essential Reader*. Routledge 2015.

Bolan, P. and Kearney, M. 'Exploring Film Tourism Potential in Ireland: From Game of Thrones to Star Wars'. *Revista Turismo and Desenvolvimento* 27/28: 2149–2156.

Brereton, Pat. 'Representations of a Green Ireland: A Case Study of Global Franchises Star Wars and Game of Thrones' (176–186). In Mansson, Maria, Buchmann, Annae, Cassinger, Cecelia and Eskilsson, Lena. (eds). *The Routledge Companion to Media and Tourism*. Routledge 2021.

Advertising and Nature: How Environmental Issues are Projected in Media and PR

Advertisements mirror and reflect on our human view of nature and, at the same time shapes the way we view it, often in ways that have more to do with commerce than more holistic models of environmental sustainability. While historically some nature advertising and marketing for instance can be constructed as appearing overtly prosocial and environmental – recalling the iconic American conservation and anti-litter 'Crying Indian' campaign, encouraging audiences to conserve resources and support environmental-protection legislation. Nonetheless, as Joseph Clark affirms, the most memorable and dynamic nature imagery comes from adverts that promote various forms of consumption. Advertisements that urge more consumption in the name of environmentalism, illustrate an inherent paradox around all aspects of sustainability, coupled within commodity capitalism, alongside exposing the tension embedded within commercial media and the digital communication system that spans the globe today.

Hansen and Manchin's (2008) study describe the way advertising decontextualise elements of the natural world, striping them from an ecosystem that cannot exist in isolation. For example, witnessing an exquisite green manicured landscape, as (re)presented in advertising campaigns designed to illustrate the growth of dairy farming in Ireland through national branding such as 'Origin Green' (Brereton 2019: 48–51). Such representation constantly hides and does not even allude to the use of excessive levels of artificial fertiliser, including nitrogen and other harmful chemicals, to further increase yields from dairying and grass production. Natural imagery generally appears in a sanitised and romanticised fashion within the limited aesthetic strictures and *modus operandi* of advertising. All the while, (raw) nature is reconstructed as serene, distant, or majestic – a kind of postcard image – and perceived simply as photogenic, often removed from its context, like a vividly coloured frog or bird clinging to a tree branch in many conventional nature documentaries. Many of these cinematic tropes are often included in food production imagery, together with tourism and travel across such magnificent landscapes.

Of course, we live in a finite world whose resources are placed under increasing pressure from population growth, over-consumption and exploitation, alongside other short-sighted practices. Consequently, ethical communication strategies ought to take account of cultural practices that are often celebrated unconditionally through advertising and media generally and alternatively help tease out their more critical environmental ramifications. As alluded to above, this is particularly relevant concerning the excessive growth of intensive factory farming, alongside other extractive industries, encouraging the exploitation of so-called natural capital and precious resources being constantly extracted from the earth. As many scholars have noted, advertising tends to reproduce an alternative ethic of excessive consumption being simply normative, alongside promoting a thin veneer of greenwashing; all the while legitimating environmental exploitation and long-term decay. In the worst cases, advertising plays with and exploits our affinity with and love for the natural world, while, unfortunately, simultaneously helping to destroy it. Innovative technical developments like augmented reality across media production, suggest that advertising may further help blind humans to the ongoing danger of increasing modes of consumption and e-waste.

At the same time, environmental scholars caution against uncritical evangelism regarding the positive benefits of new modes of participatory online media, including advertising, to help promote environmental activism. In spite of research on Facebook and YouTube (*see* Murdock and Brevini 2019) uncovering the advertising industry's role in promoting various forms of climate denial, the expediential growth of online media continues to make some innovative developments. With huge advertising returns and especially with the growth of online advertising, the industry should of course do more towards facing up to the challenge of protecting the environment. But at least, such advertising and PR imagery can help to kick-start global citizen's love of nature, even if the adverts themselves, either consciously or unconsciously, strive to encourage its followers to consume more.

There remains more optimism regarding the positive benefits of new media protocols. Research on fan and celebrity culture for example, together with 'do it yourself' (DIY) techniques, such as mashups, through encouraging active audience/user creation of media artifacts, can be used to break up the hegemonic and dominant pro-consumption discourses. These recuperative tensions are explored in student–audience studies around the benefits of environmental media, including PR-advertising, alongside YouTube music videos (see Brereton and Gomez 2020). In this study of higher educational and specifically student environmental and critical media literacy, we found how celebrities like Prince Ea, using his creative music and marketing/advertising skills, can create a very influential and popular YouTube video like *Sorry*. Such a video speaks to environmental issues and communicates them in a very effective manner for his large online audience. By all accounts, all types of advertising can often speak to environmental issues and ought to be studied and critiqued by environmental communications students.

References

Brereton, Pat and Gomez, Victoria. 'Media Students, Climate Change, and YouTube Celebrities: Readings of Dear Future Generations: Sorry Video Clip'. *ISLE* 2020.

Brereton, Pat. *Environmental Literacy and New Digital Audiences.* Routledge 2019.

Clark, Joseph. 'Selling with Gaia: Advertising and the Natural World'. *Ecomode.* https://www.researchgate.net/profile/Joseph_Clark11/publication/286457552_Selling_With_Gaia_Advertising_and_the_Natural_World/links/5d9d578f458515c1d3a16f6c/Selling-With-Gaia-Advertising-and-the-Natural-World.pdf. Routledge 2015.

Hansen, Anders and Michin, David. 'Visually Branding the Environment: Climate Change as a Marketing Opportunity'. *Discourse Studies* 10(6): 777–794. 2008 https://citeseerx.ist.psu.edu/viewdoc/download?doi=10.1.1.407.212&rep=rep1&type=pdf

Murdock, G. and Brevini, B. 'Communications and the Capitalocene: Disputed Ecologies, Contested Economies, Competing Futures'. *Polit.Econ. Commun.* 7(1): 51–82. 2019.

Affluence vs. Sustainable Consumption in Addressing Climate Change

Wealth and affluence are often considered as a negative driver of environmental social impacts, which scholars of sustainable consumption have shown how consumers often have little control over a range of environmentally damaging decisions, not to mention ever-expanding supply-chains, which in turn add more carbon waste into the global system. Nevertheless, citizens have control over making such consumption decisions in the first place. For instance, an insightful study by Thomas Wiedmann et al. (2020) calls for a paradigm shift in economic thinking around media affordances and sustainable consumption, which seem to be paradoxically interconnected in some ways. Historically, within Keynesian-type economic models of analysis, consumer demand drives production, which appears in direct opposition to Marxist political economics, as well as general environmental sociology. Certainly such modes of engaging with the economy can be interpreted as being largely dominated by supply issues.

A majority of academic studies nonetheless appear to agree that, by far, the major drivers of global impacts on the planet are constituted by technological changes and increasing overall levels of per-capita consumption. While the former acts as a more or less strong retardant, the latter remains an accelerator of global environmental impact. Remarkably, consumption (and to a lesser extent population growth) have appeared to outrun any beneficial effect of changes in the global-material footprint and provides a check on the overall levels of greenhouse gas emissions over time. Media and environmental communication certainly has a major role to play in explaining and publicising these inherent economic and other tensions, while at the same time seeking out pragmatic ways to resolve them.

Many environmentalists blame a narrow classical-economics model and not thinking beyond reductive GDP growth and other measures for evaluating and comparing success and good practice across the world. In particular, measuring environmental justice and equity has become centrally important. See for instance the GINI Index (discovered in 1912 by sociologist Corrado Gini), where 0 indicates total equality across populations within countries, as against 100 which signifies total inequality: Scandinavia, for example is positioned at 25, and Southern Africa at 63. This metric serves to highlight various measures of inequality within countries, while the OECD report listed in the website below helps to highlight further growing inequality between countries. Overall, income is strongly linked to levels of consumption and as expected super-affluent consumers tend to drive ever-expanding consumption norms.

As a rule of thumb, it is broadly suggested that the top 10% of income earners are responsible for between 25–43% of total environmental impacts, while the bottom 10% of income earners exert only around 3–5% of total environmental impact. Consequently, it remains unfair and certainly unjust to blame, much less treat all people equally in causing environmental damage across the planet. Basically the so-called developed North and West tend to constitute the economically rich and remain most responsible for such damage – by a long measure – compared with the Global South or so-called under-developed regions who should share less of the burden or costs of dealing with climate change. This global imbalance and call to action has to be taken up and fully recognised by the global First World, where much of the heavy lifting has to take place. This can be achieved by striving to radically reduce over-consumption and not striving simply to maintain the status quo, or adopting a so-called 'business as usual' approach, but alternatively actively 'greening' the global economic system.

Paradoxically, it should also be noted that within the laudable Sustainable Development Goals (SDGs), somewhat counter-intuitively, goal number 8 apparently aims for continued GDP growth of 3%. This in turn appears to contradict Goals 12 ('ensure sustainable consumption and production patterns'), not to mention number 13 ('take urgent action to combat climate change and its impact'). We can all learn from indigenous, alongside historical pre-industrial societies, who apparently managed to live without any appreciable levels of economic growth. One wonders, however, can such a transition be activated, much less radically modified consumption patterns be achieved, while at the same time keeping in check various modalities and levels of economic, social and cultural values, as well as most importantly political stability across the world.

Furthermore, one must also take into the equation, the often unintended consequences and implications on work, employment and population growth, or how can social and political security be maintained, while levels of inequality could be further reduced. In this vein many experts have been examining a particularly thorny problem concerning what are the consequences for changing levels of trade for the Global South, as poverty is always much nearer the surface across such precarious regions (Wiedmann 2020: 7). Of course, this necessary global rebalancing and transformation can have other positive effects also. For instance, it is suggested that using alternative green energy, such as wind and solar – as evident for instance in places like Morocco where solar became a life-saver – can be part of the solution for several erstwhile poor regions.

At all times, proposals for radical transformation have to be mandated and balanced around several polarities, including robust on the ground governance, while taking on board other concerns, including:

- Replacing GDP as a measure of prosperity with a multitude of alternative indicators and being agnostic regarding the drive towards continuous economic growth.
- Empowering people and strengthen participation in democratic processes and enable stronger, local, self-governance. For example using Deliberative Democracy models to draw upon Citizens Assemblies and Citizen Juries, can be co-opted while helping to build consensus around effective environmental and sustainable solutions.
- Strengthening equality and modes of redistribution through sustainable taxation policies, basic income provision and job guarantees by setting maximum income levels, expanding public services and rolling back neoliberal reform; all of which incidentally has been foregrounded as part of a Green New Deal across many regions.
- All the while, stronger regulation might be needed to ban certain products or reign in ecologically destructive industries that have thrived on a legacy of vested interests, lobbying and state-supported subsidies.
- Transformation of economic systems can be supported by innovative business models that encourage sharing and more giving-types of economies, based essentially on cooperation and not simply focused on outright and often wasteful competition.
- Capacity building, knowledge transfer and education, using media and advertising which needs to be re-used and repurposed etc. (Wiedmann et al. 2020: 8).

Reference

Wiedmann, Thomas *et al.* 'Scientists Warning on Affluence'. *Nature Communication* 2020. https://www.nature.com/articles/s41467-020-16941-y.pdf https://data.oecd.org/inequality/income-inequality.htm

Agency and Childhood Innocence in Animation: Promoting Environmental Activism: Case Study of *FernGully* and *Princess Mononoke*

From an environmental perspective, the concept of agency draws on the free will and active power of humans to help transform their environment and shape the future in more positive and sustainable ways. However, linking active agency to childhood innocence might seem to be somewhat of a contradiction. Childhood has developed as a socially and culturally specific phenomenon, especially in the West, with extended periods of formal education and comparatively long periods of adolescence and relative freedom. This is before the responsibility of adulthood kicks in and is heaped upon the (inno-cent) child, which in turn ensures a break between the liminal stages of childhood and adulthood. Of course, such an ostensibly clear division is gen-erally less evident in poorer societies and does not reflect historical norms of familial work practices across the world. Nonetheless, innocence and child-hood remain closely connected within (Western) literature and the arts gen-erally, encouraging undiluted and even direct connection as a consequence with 'raw nature'. From a promotional perspective, childhood innocence is constantly correlated as embodying and promoting a positive and pro-active environmental and climate action agenda.

Children's animation as a format encapsulates a useful shorthand aesthetic for appreciating innocence, alongside a more open mode of human agency, which directly connects with nature. In general, the Western world's anima-tion production houses – encapsulated by the Disney aesthetic – demonstrates a marked conservatism in its depiction of childhood identity politics and tends to favour a cute feminisation and anthromorphising of the innocence of nature (Whitley 2008). For instance, *FernGully: The Last Rainforest* (1992), directed by Bill Kroyen and based on a children's book by Diana Young, is set in an Australian rainforest in the present day and involves a young surfer called Zak who is working as a logger near a magical forest glade inhabited by fairies – all of which foregrounds a range of explicit environmental issues. Such animated films function as a sop to the idea that it is now too late for adults – already entrenched in their lifestyles and belief systems – to adopt the challenge of changing themselves (Smith and Parsons 2012: 25). In the so-called Western world-view, as represented through tales like *FernGully*, chil-dren are encouraged to believe in fairies, such as the tooth fairy etc., while the trajectory of 'growing up' always entails leaving behind these attractive fan-tasies in return for 'a realistic, scientific and economic rationalism assigned to patriarchy and progress' (Smith and Parsons 2012: 30). As the fairies diminish in significance for child audiences, likely so too might more benevolent environmental values, being directly linked to childhood. The harmless 'cute-ness' of the fairies, which spill over onto the depiction of nature itself, also becomes problematic in that, as David Whitley observed of Disney's classic *Bambi* (1942), it 'may create a barrier, making it more difficult for viewers to understand and relate to a "real" nature that has not been so carefully man-icured and stage managed as spectacle' (Whitley 2008: 3).

Alternatively, Hayao Miyazaki's highly regarded animated *Princess Mono-noke* (1997) goes back in time to 14th century Japan, where a young boy named Ashitaka is wounded and cursed by a demonised boar spirit and sub-sequently goes on a journey and quest for a cure to the West. There he meets Lady Eboshi who wants to destroy the forests to develop her destructive iron mines, which nonetheless brings prosperity to her people. The story applies elements of animism and a form of Shintoism, by calling on spirits known as Kami, who reside in the forests. Just like the forest spirit and all the fasci-nating Eastern spirits examined across his oeuvre, nature can both benefit and harm humans. In this animated tale, nature is not depicted as a soft-natured entity, but rather when humans do not respect nature it seeks revenge upon them.

This very different Japanese filmic aesthetic renders nature as sublime, while invoking more complex socio-cultural differences between childhood innocence and the interconnection between nature versus culture more generally. Miyazaki's greatest triumph, according to many scholars, is in the way he makes nature sublime rather than cute, and most significantly in rendering socio-cultural differences in all its complexity.

As signalled in various studies of *Princess Mononoke*, the film makes heroes of outsiders across all identity politics categories and blurs the stereotypes that usually define such characters (Smith and Parsons 2012: 28). The principal strength of this Japanese mode of animation, lies in asking child (and by extension adult) audiences to think about compassion for the poor and the disenfranchised, in tandem with care for nature, as per the underlying principle of environmental justice.

On the other hand, *FernGully* simply expects nature to love humans (as Crysta falls in love with Zak) and the battle to save the rainforest is refigured into a battle against a dark spirit called Hexxus, as the true malefactor (Smith and Parsons 2012: 33). Developing radical new forms of animation and aesthetic strategies, as evidenced in the oeuvre of Miyazki, helps to speak to and for both children and adults, through such powerful aesthetic and generic environmentally focused formats. But this remains an ongoing challenge for all aspects of media ecology in uncovering new ways of representing such environmental complexity, while at the same time instilling a useful audio-visual strategy for the long-term growth of the environmental movement through examining new modes of animated media.

References

Smith, Michelle and Parsons, Elizabeth. 'Animating Child Activism: Environmentalism and Class Politics in Ghibli's Princess Mononoke (1997) and Fox's FernGully (1992)'. *Continuum: Journal of Media and Cultural Studies* 26(1): 25–37. 2012.

Whitley, David. *The Idea of Nature in Disney Animation: From Snow White to WALL-E*. Routledge 2008.

Agenda Setting and News Media Coverage of Environmental Issues

Agenda setting remains a key aspect of academic journalism training and focuses on how a news organisation decides on its priorities in assessing the level of importance and significance for any given news item. There are excellent press studies of this phenomenon including James Curran and Jean Seaton's classic 1989 study '*Power without Responsibility*', together with more specific applications regarding its use of environmental stories. Focusing on

how print media for instance, together with Public Service Broadcasting television organisations – like the Irish 'Radio Telefis Eireann' (RTE) or the
British Broadcasting Corporation (BBC), among others across the world –
frame a range of environmental issues or not (as is most frequently the case) –
remains a growing area of investigation. At the same time analysing how such
environmental stories are positioned within the broad agenda of news output,
also remains of interest for academic journalistic investigation. Keeping
environmental issues high on the public radar – which is characterised in the
literature as salience – is deemed essential, if audiences are to be kept
informed and most importantly actively engaged. Essentially, stories securing
long-term traction, notwithstanding the dangers of over-exposure, can help
(eco-)citizens appreciate the need for massive transformation in policy, as well
as behaviour change, while transforming human social/cultural and political
practices in the journey towards securing a low carbon future transition.

Journalists and news editors are recognised as media gatekeepers, who
actively set the agenda and decide what to print or publish throughout any
given period. For instance, it is believed that stories positioned on the front
page of a newspaper or at the top of a broadcast bulletin are afforded greater
importance than those positioned later on in the back pages. Similarly with
regards to broadcast news, evaluating the difference between the first item on
a news bulletin that is deemed the most important, compared with the last
item, which is often considered a filler and less important for the overall news
agenda of the day, remains an ongoing challenge. Much effort is constantly
expended by lobby groups in particular to either position environmental news
at the top of the news cycle agenda, or alternatively bury such stories from
public view; all of which depend on the political/ideological affiliation of the
lobbyist. See for instance Michael Mann's *The New Climate War* (2021) for a
caustic critique of American lobbyists and strategies used to keep environmental issues low down on the media agenda. Throughout the world, it has
been demonstrated that lack of success in placing environmental stories at the
top of the news agenda, can sometimes be attributed to very active climate-
denier or anti-environmental industry forces, using all their political and
commercial muscle to effectively stifle the overall messaging (see Brevini and
Murdock 2017).

Meanwhile news media, according to Painter et al. (2018) in their analysis
of climate change coverage, shows how both the amount and nature of
environmental coverage throughout media can be understood in terms of
their underlying business model and associated editorial policy (including
their target audiences) and also in terms of their positioning vis-à-vis legacy
news media organisations.

The contraction in environmental journalism within traditional news media
has been matched by a shift from journalists to first-hand sources of information, in terms of their ability to influence the agenda and the nature of
public debate about the environment (Hansen 2020: 47). Furthermore, for
specific analysis of environmental journalism's transition into more amateur

and online media platforms, see studies by David Robbins concerning Irish environmental press (2018), alongside the blurring of boundaries between journalism and science, not to mention advocacy, explored in Brüggemann et al. (2020). The changing nature of media and communication also brings with it new forms of argumentation in the public sphere, and a need to reassess some of the classic questions embedded within environmental journalism about the construction of credibility and expertise; the use of science-focused and evidence-based argument; trust, authority and uncertainty; and rhetorical style in public debate (Gibbons 2020: 47).

For instance, Irish environmental activist John Gibbon's interpretation of the evolution of environmental journalism, notes the importance of the Climate Change Act in 2008 in the UK, but puts his finger on a major concern for all concerned. Climate and environment reporting remains unfortunately siloed and has not been brought into the mainstream of media reporting. Most significantly Climategate, discussed elsewhere, which sparked a scandal within a British research centre and was wrongly accused of misleading the public with their scientific climate data, occurring after the Copenhagen conference, sparking a setback to the growth of environmental journalism. Gibbons affirms how this was the case even though it was later proved that there was no actual collusion, much less stacking of evidence against the scientists.

Many environmental historians look back on 2007/8 as a period of 'innocence' for climate journalism, especially in the wake of Al Gore's *An Inconvenient Truth* (2006). In Britain for example, it is suggested that the world-renowned Public Service Broadcaster (BBC) is often more concerned about criticism coming from the Right rather than the Left, because of specific political, economic and other repercussions. Consequently, many left-leaning academics often accuse the organisation of being too pro-business, even right-wing in its approach to environmental debates.

Following the Paris agreement on climate change, a sense of improved international cooperation emerged regarding climate change, despite the denialism emanating especially from the Trump presidency. But as Gibbons rightly concludes, our 'collective failure to action' with the copious scientific evidence available to 'avoid catastrophe' is, 'to this author at least, by far the most important "story" of this or any other century' (Gibbons 2020: 201). With the release of a damning new IPCC report (August 2021), which paints an even bleaker picture around climate, pressure is certainly being put on communications and media organisations to find ways to keep the issue firmly in the news agenda. By all accounts, there is a major up-hill struggle to contend with, across so many areas of the planet with the global climate crisis getting more severe all the time.

References

Brevini, B. and Murdock, G. (eds.) *Carbon Capitalism and Communication: Confronting Climate Crisis*. Palgrave 2017.

Brüggemann, M., Lörcher, I. and Walter, S. 'Post-Normal Science Communication: Exploring the Blurring Boundaries of Science and Journalism'. *JCOM* 19(03), A02. doi:10.22323/2.19030202.

Curran, James and Seaton, Jean. *Power without Responsibility: Press, Broadcasting and the Internet in Britain* (1989) 7th edition. Routledge 2010.

Gibbons, John. 'The Environmental Beat: Public Confusion, Digital Media, Social Media, and Fake News in the United Kingdom and Ireland'. In *Routledge Handbook of Environmental Journalism*, ed. Sachsman, David and Valenti, JoAnn Meyer. Routledge 2020.

Hansen, Anders. 'Sources, Strategic Communication, and Environmental Journalism'. In *Routledge Handbook of Environmental Journalism*, ed. Sachsman, David and Valenti, JoAnn Meyer. Routledge 2020.

Mann, Michael E. *The New Climate War: The Fight to Take Back our Planet.* Scribe Publishers 2021.

Painter, J., Kristiansen, Silje and Schafer, Mike. 'How "Digital-born" Media Cover Climate Change in Comparison to Legacy Media: A Case Study of the COP 21 Summit in Paris'. *Global Environmental Change* 48: 1–10. 2018.

Robbins, Dave. *Climate Change, Politics and the Press in Ireland.* Routledge 2018.

Anthropomorphism, Human Love and the Personification of Animals: *Blackfish*

The Oxford dictionary, together with Wikipedia defines anthropomorphism simply as the attribution of human traits, emotions, or intentions being ascribed to non-human entities. It is considered to be a basic tendency of human psychology and is frequently used throughout audio-visual media to encourage and promote human and non-human species interaction. Meanwhile, personification is related to the attribution of human form and characteristics to more explicit concepts like national identity, emotions and even environmental characteristics such as seasons and weather, alongside representations of animals, culminating most notably across so much contemporary animated Disney output. Both anthropomorphism and personification of human traits have a long history across all cultures, with fables of anthropomorphised animals serving as main characters in storylines. Writers, dramatists, as well as the general public have also routinely attributed human emotions and behavioural traits to wild animals, alongside those that have become domesticated. Various forms of anthropomorphised representation are illustrated throughout this volume, through entries focused on the power of animation, the growth of animal rights activists, as well as other related areas of environmental debate.

For some scholars, anthropomorphism is considered as beneficial to the welfare of animals, by elevating their varying similarities to the status of humans. A 2012 study by Max Butterfield et al. for instance found that utilising anthropomorphic language when describing dogs, created a greater willingness to assist them in situations of distress. All animal welfare and charity organisations tend to draw on this strategy within their promotional material. Studies have even shown that individuals who attribute human characteristics to animals are less willing to eat them as a result. Furthermore, the degree to which humans perceive some form of innate consciousness in animals, sparks a moral concern for such creatures and remain a key marker in the growth of animal rights organisations like 'People for the Ethical Treatment of Animals' (PETA), together with more hard-line ethical approaches, espoused by Peter Singer (1975) and others. Consequently, anthropomorphism can help lead humans to both appreciate and value non-humans more, especially when they appear to display human qualities and attributes, since such similarities have been shown to increase prosocial behaviour toward such species.

Across various sciences as well as the arts and media, the use of anthropomorphic language and through using various representational norms, animals are believed to display both clear intentions and emotions. Yet biologists in particular have been warned by their scientific protocols to avoid assumptions that animals share any of the same mental, social and emotional capacities of humans, and to rely instead on strictly observable evidence. Nonetheless, the study of species in their own natural environment, as well as within captivity, is used as further evidence of similarities between humans and animals, through the growth of nature documentaries that have heralded changed attitudes to animals. In the 1960s for instance, Jane Goodall's study of chimpanzees, alongside Dian Fossey's examination of wild species, were all accused of various forms of seductive anthropomorphism. Such accusations are also constantly made, even against the nature documentaries fronted by David Attenborough that have become a global phenomenon. More discussion of this complex representational phenomenon will be evident across several entries in this volume, which are illustrated here by a reading of the documentary *Blackfish* (2013).

These various wild nature and representational strategies appear to dovetail with pet-owner's deep love for their animals and constitute a transparent mode of almost telepathic empathy between humans and their pets. Most importantly for environmental communication, such positive representations also feed into prosocial ecological debates around the need for animal husbandry and supporting alternative modes of vegetarian food consumption, both from a pro-environmental and from a species protection perspective.

Media and film scholars point to the Disney oeuvre in particular for promoting various forms of anthropomorphism, especially in their animated storylines for children, from early classics like *Bambi* (1942), which privilege uniquely 'human' conceptions of love and family values, to the long catalogue of family tales that have evolved ever since. According to many scholars (see King et al. 2010), such texts have alternatively instilled a gendered, racial and ethnic approach, across so much of their output.

This famous documentary *Blackfish* focuses on Orcas held in captivity at *SeaWorld* in America and follows an incident where a woman trainer gets killed by one of the captive creatures. Although *SeaWorld* dismissed the subsequent documentary as 'shamefully, dishonest, deliberately misleading and scientifically inaccurate' (Allen 2014), it led to a CNN television debate capturing over one million viewers on 24 October 2013. Subsequently, the channel broadcasted the documentary 24 times and with repeated viewing, clocked up over 24 million viewers in total, before it moved to Netflix where it still receives lots of hits to this day.

Generally, the orcas are often discussed in terms of a tourist attraction, as explored in Geo Takach's (2013) cultural study of anthropomorphism within tourist rhetoric. *Blackfish* certainly has made a splash, however, in America's consciousness with regards to using such natural creatures for human entertainment. This echoes a long tradition from early films' exposure of explicit cruelty to animals within circuses and other controlled environments. Most memorable in this history was that reflected in the electrocution of the famous circus elephant Topsy, which was captured on camera at the start of 1903 in New York. Such cautionary animal-protection environmental stories, according to Loretta Rowley and Kevin Johnson, at least foregrounds 'anthropomorphic anthropocentrism as a tool whereby environmental communication scholars are able to ponder what these stories tell about ourselves, while also thinking through the paradoxes of the ecological and environmental frameworks' (2018: 838). In any case such provocative eco-documentaries certainly help to keep animal welfare high in the public consciousness and need to be constantly engaged with and evaluated by environmental communication students and scholars.

References

Allen, G. 'Months After "Blackfish" Release, Controversy Over SeaWorld Grows'. *National Public Radio*. 15 January 2014. http://www.npr.org/2014/01/15/262767226/m onths-after-blackfish-release-controversyfor-seaworld-grows.

Butterfield, Max, Hill, Sarah and Lord, Charles. 'Mangy Mutt or Furry Friend? Anthropomorphism Promotes Animal Welfare'. *Journal of Experimental Social Psychology* (48): 957–960. 2012.

King, R., Lugo-Lugo, R. and Bloodsworht-Lugo, K. *Animating Difference: Race, Gender and Sexuality in Contemporary Films for Children*. Rowman & Littlefield Publishers 2010.

Rowley, Loretta and Johnson, Kevin. 'Anthropomorphic Anthropocentrism and the Rhetoric of Blackfish'. *Environmental Communications* 12(6): 825–839. 2018.

Singer, Peter. *Animal Liberation*. Bodley Head (1975) 2009.

Takach, Geo. 'Selling Nature in a Resource-based Economy: Romantic/Extractive Gazes and Alberta's Bituminous Sands'. *Environmental Communications* 7(2): 211–230. 2013.

Anti-nuclear Modes of Environmental Thinking: Case Study of Chernobyl

Chernobyl has become synonymous with nuclear disaster and ongoing fear of nuclear power, when back in 1986 – Saturday 26 April to be precise – during an electrical test, reactor 4 exploded, causing radiation fall-out to spread from this north Ukrainian regional Russian power plant across the rest of Europe and beyond. The nearby city of Pripyat was evacuated; over the years it is estimated that between 4000 and 16,000 people across Europe died as a direct/indirect result of this disaster. By all accounts this nuclear accident remains the worst in the world's history. The Russian leader Michael Gorbachev even suggested that this disaster was the main reason for bringing down the old Communist state in 1991. The accident constituted the largest release of nuclear fall-out in the history of humanity and was exacerbated by the lies perpetuated at the highest level of government, abetted by a media that wilfully engaged in propaganda and the dissemination of false information. Scientific warnings were unfortunately dismissed or suppressed, when they did not fit with the agenda of the authorities.

The powerful five-part drama series *Chernobyl* (2019) directed by Johan Renek (HBO and Sky Atlantic) stars Jared Harris as Valery Legosov, a nuclear scientist and state apparatchik whose troubled life leads him to commit suicide, just two years to the minute after these awful events in 1986. The series then goes back and forward in time, capturing the confusion of various incidents, which happened both before and after the disaster. An early *Guardian* review (7 May 2019) of the first episode wonders why the residents of Pripyat nearby were not afraid – 'something to do with soothing, communist-era propaganda and a well-trained, incurious mindset – but this probably could have been sketched out a bit more'.

The officer in charge of the plant Anatoly Dyatlov (Paul Ritter) appears largely in denial regarding his role in subsequent events, claiming he was basically following orders and trying to get a delayed test completed on the plant at all costs. In some ways the imagery and visualisation recall Andrei Tarkovsky's classic science fiction tale *Stalker* (1979), which has been extensively analysed by eco-film philosopher Adrian Ivakhiv (2013) for its depiction of a futuristic ecocidal disaster.

Each episode focuses on particular aspects of the nuclear disaster, such as the small team who take on a rookie (played by Irish actor Barry Keoghan) to systematically kill all the human pets left in the radiated neighbourhood. For animal lovers and environmentalists generally, the wholesale slaughter of such innocent pets, stay in the memory long after viewing their carcasses being dumped into a big hole in the ground and being sealed with cement. Such scenes directly echoed earlier depictions of horribly charred first-responders, including Fire-fighters whose bodies were encased in concrete coffins and buried in mass graves.

The invisible terror of radiation escaping into the atmosphere is all pervasive and evocatively represented as a spectre of anti-environmental terror witnessed throughout the series. Volunteers are depicted as natural heroes, as they successfully open the water valves of large tanks that were filled up by fire engines – believing they were helping to alleviate the problem, while actually making it worse. This is followed most tragically by using poorly protected 'conscripted volunteers' to climb onto the roof to throw the heavily charged and radiated graphite back down into the core. One poor nameless volunteer who gets his foot caught in the material and puncturing his flimsy protective clothes, is told in no uncertain terms that he has no hope of survival. Much vaunted mechanical and other types of high-tech lunar-machinery from abroad are called into play, but unfortunately are not able to function within such difficult (unnatural) conditions. Consequently, the situation required the brute force of ordinary Russian manpower, working for just 90-seconds at a time in endless relays to carry out the dirty physical work of nuclear disposal. On completion, they placed a Red Flag of honour on the roof; reminding cineastes of earlier montage sequences from revolutionary film classics by Sergei Eisenstein from a bygone era. Such excessive patriotism is echoed more crassly in a 2021 Russian retelling of the story *Chernobyl 1986* (Netflix), which is directed by and stars Danila Kozlovsky. He plays a heroic firefighter who ends up sacrificing his life for his family; involving some interesting action sequences that drive the filmic narrative.

More generally, the incident recalls fictional recreations of other nuclear disasters like in *The China Syndrome* (1979), directed by James Bridges and staring A-list actors Jane Fonda and Jack Lemmon. This was a huge hit on the big screen and directly foreshadowed the 1979 incident in a nuclear power plant at Three Mile Island in America. Such narratives illustrate the dangers of taking shortcuts and constantly cutting costs and discouraging employees, across various levels of responsibility, while also highlighting the personal dangers of speaking up as whistle-blowers, much less questioning authority in any way. All of this reflects the long-term systemic weakness of business corporations in the West – not to mention the very restrictive Russian command structure – pursuing profits (and/or success) at all costs.

Such real-life stories function as powerful cautionary tales, which makes it very difficult to fully endorse the sustainable and low-carbon benefits of nuclear power. It was little wonder that many governments who were wholeheartedly pro-nuclear, shied away from recognising, much less accepting, the lessons of this awful disasters. Alternative strategies adopted in response to the disaster, included dismissing the Russians and their energy systems, as simply using outdated equipment and procedures (which of course was also true), while affirming that such an incident could never happen in other more 'advanced' countries, such as Britain or America. This remained the *modus operandi* for some of the global reaction and official response to the accident. Nonetheless, staunchly pro-nuclear countries like Germany with a growing cohort of green-focused citizens, began to reappraise their dependence on nuclear power, leading to a final decision later to abandon nuclear energy altogether, following another major scare from Japan.

The 2011 Japanese nuclear disaster in Fukushima, precipitated by an earthquake and tsunami, has further questioned the rationale and environmental risk of using nuclear power as a solution to low carbon emissions, rather than through more conventional and less risky renewable energy methods. Soon after this incident, the German government made a major announcement in May 2011, affirming that they would shut down all their nuclear plants by 2020. By all accounts a radical environmental and political response, which has had ongoing repercussions across the region.

Case Study of the Chernobyl Syndrome and the Rise of a Risk Society

Stemming from the lack of an effective communication policy, as well as not having appropriate tools at the national level to manage a response; together with the lack of information, despair, the loss of hope and a sudden shift from total trust, to total distrust towards Government – all of these tensions and pressures have resulted in a phenomenon known as 'Chernobyl Syndrome'. Basically all of this serves to reinforce a growing fear and distrust of government which has become a growing concern. At a literary level, this phenomenon is illustrated by a number of cautionary novels including, Fredrik Pohl's *Chernobyl* (1988), Andrea White's *Radiant Girl* (2008) or Orest Stelmach's *The Boy from Reactor 4* (2013).

Meanwhile, the HBO television series *Chernobyl*, keeps life under the fallout cloud that happened in that fateful summer of 1986 in the background. Incidentally, in terms of curies per square kilometre, the radiation was worst in two regions or belts: one stretching northwest across Scandinavia, the other to the south across Slovenia, Austria, and Bavaria. To help address and frame this new form of radiation fear, a major study titled *Risk Society* was published by the German sociologist Ulrich Beck, with exquisite timing in the spring of 1986. Most recently, Adam Tooze called attention to the importance of Beck's work for understanding the recent pandemic, as well as framing the radiation incident in Russia and its effects on modern society. The dominant question, so vividly exposed by a crises such as Chernobyl – and one which finds further echoes in the 2020/21 coronavirus pandemic – according to Tooze at least, is 'how to navigate this world' and cope with new risks and climate catastrophes all the time. Media representations of nuclear power alongside foregrounding various forms of environmental risk have a major role to play in framing and evaluating the power and ethical values of such complex (energy) systems into the future.

References

Ivakhiv, Adrian. *Ecology of the Moving Image: Cinema, Affect, Nation*. Wilfried Laurier University Press 2013.

Mangan, Lucy. Chernobyl Review – Chaos Reigns in Confusing Nuclear Disaster Epic, *The Guardian*, 7 May 2019. https://www.theguardian.com/tv-and-radio/2019/may/07/chernobyl-review-chaos-reigns-in-confusing-nuclear-disaster-epic

Tooze, Adam. 'The Sociologist Who Could Save Us From Coronavirus' – Ulrich Beck was a Profit of Uncertainty. *The Big Think*. August 2020. https://foreignpolicy.com/2020/08/01/the-sociologist-who-could-save-us-from-coronavirus/

Avant Garde Stories: Popularising Environmental Themes and Issues: Deseret

Most eco-criticism of media and film explored in this volume focuses explicitly on mainstream Hollywood or documentary narratives, yet environmental communication scholars like Scott McDonald (1993) believe that more alternative art-based narrative aesthetics (often deemed difficult, and sometimes even considered slow and boring by some mainstream audiences), can help develop and support a more complex and sustained environmental agenda. Drawing on the long tradition of art-aesthetics; from Méliès and Lumière's early experimentations with new modes of cinematography, together with more contemporary styles of experimental filmmaking that employs aspects of so-called slow cinema, with their use of extended shot duration for instance; such techniques can be applied to support more sustained innovation and critical investigation of various manifestations of environmental issues and ongoing crises. Furthermore, homing in on subject matter normally ignored or marginalised by mass-entertainment film, such art-based aesthetics can help 'reinvigorate our reverence for the visual world around us and develop our patience for experiencing it fully' (MacDonald 1993: 11–12).

For instance, the creative artist's use of the long-take is one way to represent and mediate an environmental landscape and encouraging a practice of simply looking, using no voice-over narration, and at the same time appearing to counter the spectator's constant need for observation and hence calling on more effort and critical investigation from the audience (Boczkowska 2017: 124); such an innovative aesthetic strategy remains fruitful as a means of marrying disparate elements together.

These techniques can be illustrated using the eco-art documentary *Deseret* (1995), directed by James Benning. The film's title stems from the Jaredite term denoting 'honeybee' from the Book of Mormon and follows a highly unconventional structure (Boczkowska 2017: 119). *Deseret* speaks to and from a range of ecological concerns, eloquently picked out by MacDonald, made up of static shots of landscape across the American state of Utah; each tied to the duration of passages about the region and read by an actor from the pages of *The New York Times* between 1852 and 1992. The first section covers the period up to 1896, when Utah became a state (and coincidentally also when cinema began) and remains in black and white, while the second half is filmed in colour. MacDonald in an early study of Independent films maps a detailed reading of how Benning's imagery evolves (2001: 338–345), especially through its evocation of place and how such avant-garde aesthetics are best placed in developing this transformative mode of telling a complex environmental story.

In a very detailed eco-materialist reading of the documentary, environmental scholar Sean Cubitt calls upon Paul Willeman who affirms that the avant garde format starts with the question: how to understand social existence. Cubitt affirms that 'we cannot look backward for a lost utopia, nor bury the past and hope it will go away'. Especially regarding the environmental agenda 'we cannot strive for a lost union with the natural world, nor simply bury the waste products of mediation, as we do daily (waste that includes millions of kilometers of cable)'. Cubitt goes on to suggest that the challenge for an ecologically informed political aesthetic then, is not simply to convey provocative good ideas to those who need them, 'it involves tracing the political tasks of identifying the good and analysing the relations it has with the means of conveying it' (2016: 21).

Today, as at the beginning of cinema, Cubitt and other environmental scholars attest to how mineral extraction, waste attendant on the manufacture and disposal of media products, and the creation of energy to run our machinery and our media systems in many ways dovetail with the exploitation of indigenous and colonial citizens and more clearly have radically affected our rural mineral-rich landscapes.

Yet, in contrast to the work of Nicholas Geyrhalter's *Earth* (2019), which uses sophisticated cinematography and active engagement with viewers, this avant-garde aesthetic pulls in the opposite direction, using still camera shots with very low 'average shot lengths' (ASL), as well as low production values etc. Nonetheless, its commentary affords precise contextual social history of the Mormons who most notably became a dominant sect in the region and supported polygamy, alongside witnessing other historical movers and shakers from the region. While the early part of the documentary focused consistently on the extermination of indigenous natives and specific conflict, which continued up to recently with 50,000 acres of land taken from the Navaho Indians in 1958; the more contemporary periodising in the documentary focused on mining and extraction. There are so many cases of radioactive cancers alluded to and various disease with miners in particular suffering very badly as a result. For instance the Environmental Protection Agency of America (EPA) considered Utah the most toxic region for chemical waste. Finally, the documentary focuses on a close-up of a 'Welcome to Utah' sign and its slogan; 'still the right place', as it celebrated its centennial from 1896 to 1996. By all accounts the specific topographic factors of landscape is constantly framed through an environmental lens with so much despoiling of the American landscape effectively captured by this micro-study of a unique habitat.

There has been an increase in *avant-garde* evocations of environmental issues and concerns over the decades, raising the long-running debate over whether such semiotically rich and complex media is simply speaking to elites (who are already predisposed to conservational agendas and generally are considered mostly environmentally literate), rather than the so-called 'general public' and other stakeholders who need to be urgently engaged with and addressed. Alternatively, one can ask if such aesthetics can be more helpful in reformulating and bringing environmental ideas back into the mainstream, while at the same time breaking down high–low cultural divisions and thereby speaking to larger cohorts of audiences and global citizens through a language they can understand and appreciate.

According to MacDonald, the artist's fascination with the concept of 'landscape as a function of time' (116), mirrors the spirit of American transcendentalist and nature writing in their restrained eco-criticism, all of which is echoed through both visual and verbal references. Simultaneously however Benning and other artistic filmmakers, tend to question the dangers of various types of environmental preaching, preferring instead critique and open dialogue, such as in the 'carefully inserted shots of ravaged landscapes, livestock and abattoir and other evidence of human despoilment that recur throughout his oeuvre' (Zuvela, cited in Boczkowska 2017: 117). Art cinema certainly has an important and ongoing role to play in setting up innovative creative imaginaries towards communicating the nuances and complexity of all aspects of the environmental agenda.

References

Boczkowska, Kornelia. 'Where Words and Images Speak for Themselves: Landscape (Re)presentation and World-image Dichotomy in James Benning's Deseret (1995)'. *Image & Narrative* 18(2): 114–128. 2017.

Cubitt, Sean. 'Film; Landscape and Political Aesthetic: Deseret'. *Screen* 57(1): 21–34. Spring 2016.

MacDonald, Scott. *Avant-Garde Film: Motion Studies*. Cambridge University Press 1993.

MacDonald, Scott. *The Garden in the Machine: A Field Guide to Independent Film about Place*. University of California Press 2001.

B

Behaviour Change Communications (BCC) and Climate Change

As affirmed in the preface to a report on climate change; 'at the heart of global warming is a cognitive and behavioural change challenge' (Pike et al. 2010: 5). To address global warming there must be a shift in thinking and behaviour that motivates people and organisations to engage in emission reductions and climate preparedness activities, while supporting new environmental policies. But

> in order to motivate people to alter their views and behaviours related to global warming, leaders within all levels of Government, the private sector and grass-roots communities, must become aware of and utilise the fundamentals of effective climate communications, outreach and behavioural change mechanisms.
>
> (Pike et al. 2010: 5)

Moving towards a carbon neutral society will require radical social, political and behavioural change across so many junctures as the planet tries to reduce its carbon footprint to zero. In an early Irish climate change report (2012) for instance from the 'National Economic and Social Council' (NESC), lead author Jeanne Moore calls attention to extensive research and practice, which shows that understanding social and behavioural aspects remains the most important and effective strategy towards reducing emissions and combating climate change. Of course, there are many other benefits of a carbon neutral society, including for instance better 'public health, increased energy security, cost savings for households, potential job creation and better social cohesion and even quality of life'. Nonetheless, according to almost all research findings in this area, changing behaviour is neither automatic or predictable and we constantly need to transform long-term habits and values, which involve not only us as individuals, but most importantly broader top-down systems and social practices across all levels of human activity. Environmental communication plays a major role in this challenge.

DOI: 10.4324/9781003123422-3

According to Moore (2012: 7), key enablers for changing behaviour include:

- Removing barriers and making such changes both available, affordable and accessible
- The social context and social system also remain extremely important to address.
- Most especially targeting key lifestyle moments like moving house, remains a good time to make major life-style changes. By all accounts, it's always best to adopt a mixed approach to behavioural change, while using different levers such as incentives, regulation and other public benefits, to help mobilise sustainable and long-term societal change and pivot towards securing and integrating a low carbon future.

There are also other key enablers involved in changing behaviour that need to be communicated to consumers of energy and that also help to reduce our carbon footprint. These include energy efficiency and co-opting more smart metering, as well as calling on greater levels of acceptance of renewable energy; all of which remain vitally important. Furthermore, social and cultural factors, habits and routines, as well as practical, financial and attitudinal concerns, all have to be taken into account when communicating the urgent need to change behaviour and generally coping with climate change through both mitigation and adaptation measures. Key marketing and communication challenges driving effective persuasion can be leveraged by helping to form networks of stakeholders to actively engage with problems, while co-producing effective solutions. For instance regarding the huge problem of methane emissions – as a consequence of intensive agriculture – farmers need to be constantly engaged at the local level, while adopting an open and holistic approach to problem solving and behavioural change.

Environmental scholarship within the communications field continues to assert general concern about global warming, but of course real action and most especially behavioural change has to be kickstarted far beyond noble words and sentiments. 'For people, organisations or society as a whole to take meaningful action, they must feel sufficient "tension" (dissonance) between some deeply held goals or values and their current condition etc.' (Pike 2010: 5). This behavioural change dilemma has been brought into dramatic relief through the 2020/21 pandemic, which effectively constituted a type of war, with a clearly prescribed enemy. This global threat to human health, one might suggest has radically changed behavioural practices across the world and climate change communication and protocols can certainly learn from this crisis into the future.

The American Centre for Research on Environmental Decisions (CRED) http://cred.columbia.edu/ based out of Columbia University in America has provided a basic overview with regards to applying behaviour analysis using environmental media communication. The researchers note that citizens and audiences worldwide are *not* adequately facing up to the consequences of climate change. The American research centre argues that this gap has to be urgently addressed, while striving towards securing audience attention through effective framing of the importance of these issues. At the same time numerous other studies have also shown that without adequate socio-cultural support and global-level infrastructure, individual action, not coupled with top-down systemic continuous engagement, unfortunately remains ineffective.

As an illustration of this growing environmental research and highlighting a range of positions, William Rees (an expert and long-time contributor to the influential website www.scorai.net) constantly affirms across numerous listserv posts that our so-called neoliberal age transfers responsibility for eco-damage to individuals and disempowering regulatory agencies. Consequently, it could be insinuated that this lets top-level stakeholders off the hook, especially with regards to the necessity for a radical top-down approach towards supporting environmental solutions. In this regard, sometimes too much emphasis is placed on bottom-up individual culpability and overall responsibility for transformational change. Whereas, to secure the global change required in the shortest possible time period, a top-down policy and systems change strategy is required, demanding multi-dimensional structural transformation.

In crude terms, general individual life-style and behavioural changes can probably only make a *marginal* difference, while noting such heavy lifting cannot be achieved by each of us as global citizens simply acting alone. Consequently, 'ordinary citizens' alone cannot implement the broad-based carbon taxes or cap and trade systems, the resource depletion taxes necessary, much less taking on board the full social cost of pricing, rapid transit systems, even most controversially, reducing the overall population through one-child policies, all of which are needed for effective reductions in the overall human carbon-footprint. Essentially, there has to be a multilateral approach, with globally framed joined-up thinking across a broad range of stakeholders to work together over a limited period of time, which in turn assists in making the necessary changes. Environmental communication strategies can nonetheless help provide the glue to implement such broad-based radical approaches and thereby assist in securing essential behavioural change at all levels of society.

By all accounts, environmental unsustainability remains a collective problem, requiring collective and multimodal solutions, necessitating both a top-down and bottom-up behavioural transformation across various modes of production, distribution as well as taking into account both supply and demand driven modes of consumption. A major communication strategy needs to be drawn up and implemented by governments and corporations, involving powerful media networks; all designed for the common good and coalescing around sustained effort to ensure the future survival of humans on the planet.

To help support this long-term communications agenda, formal education around communicating climate issues can play a major role. For instance a study from Seth Wynes and Kimberly A. Nicholas (2017) entitled: 'The Climate Mitigation Gap: Education and Government Recommendations Miss the Most Effective Individual Actions', calls for more specific climate action in school and college textbooks and across government communication pieces. The study notes that when educational sources actually cited solutions, they constantly mentioned low-impact actions, like recycling and energy saving light bulbs, rather than more difficult life-style changes, such as avoiding meat, promoting public transport, not to mention more radical societal transformations in facing up to the climate crisis.

Posing provocative even playful challenges to existing consumer behaviour, nonetheless remains a great way to motivate people to engage in trying out (or sticking with) sustainable models or lifestyles. This is especially evident at a systemic and at an educational level, as throughout the environmental behaviour literature there is evidence that younger generations are willing to depart from current lifestyles in environmentally relevant ways. Certainly, from an educational, as well as a behavioural analysis level, this remains a good strategy and a fruitful research approach and methodology to adopt.

Such an approach is particularly helpful for environmental students to take on board, especially in uncovering further links and connections between environmental and behavioural theory and down-to-earth practices. Learning from media programmes' new modes of behavioural practices; from the so-called mundane everyday application, such as using the correct waste bins and the benefits of a clothesline, rather than carbon-intensive mechanical clothes dryer – all of these everyday practices can help set the tone for concerted behavioural change and even lead to bigger and more sustainable modes of consumption and healthy living.

At the same time, more radical and effective environmental behavioural change appears quite rare and most of the literature thereby focuses on what is *not* possible. As Bass Verplanken affirms in an engaging YouTube lecture, success in bringing about behavioural change across so many areas of life; such as getting the public to wear seat belts, respecting smoking bans and supporting congestion charges in London, Stockholm and other cities – all of these success stories can help show the way forward with regards to further protecting the environment. By all accounts, we need brave and smart politicians, as well as innovative policy makers, who can undertake some hard and unpopular decisions to start with. But this approach also needs to be matched by an effective communication strategy, towards ensuring a majority of citizens to come on board, while promoting a tipping point for global change and transformation.

Overall effective communication strategies designed to educate and encourage behavioural change remains central in dealing with climate change, together with addressing all related environmental dangers. Students and environmental communication scholars need to constantly be on the lookout for such practical solutions, while assessing their relative efficacy and helping to develop new ways of supporting radical environmental change into the future.

References

Moore, Jeanne. 'Social and Behavioural Aspects of Climate Change: Background Paper no. 3. NESC 'Ireland's Climate Change Challenge: Connecting "How Much" with "How To"'. 2012 http://files.nesc.ie/nesc_secretariat_papers/ccbg_No3_Social_and_Behavioural_Aspects_of_Climate_%20Change.pdf

Pike, Cara *et al.* 'A Guide for Practitioners'. *The Social Capital Project at the Climate Leadership Initiative.* University of Oregon. 2010 https://climateaccess.org/system/files/Climate%20Communications%20and%20Behavior%20Change.pdf

Verplanken, Bass. Behavioural psychology lecturer YouTube Presentation. https://www.youtube.com/watch?v=_nTpp_VrJvE&t

Wynes, Seth and Nicholas, Kimberly A. 'The Climate Mitigation Gap: Education and Government Recommendations Miss the Most Effective Individual Actions'. *Environmental Research Letters* 12(7): 074024.

Blue Humanities: Increasing Carbon and Waste Emissions

The term Blue Humanities was ostensibly coined by an English professor Steve Mentz, according to a summary overview of the area by John Gillis (2013). Late recognition of the close relationship between modern (Western) culture and the sea, directly feeds into environmental and eco-literature. While over half of the world's people now live within less than a hundred miles of the ocean, few today appear to have any working knowledge of the sea. In fact, more is known about the dark side of the moon than is known about the depths of the oceans. Nevertheless, large numbers of citizens have grown to at least vicariously know and appreciate the sea through art, literature and most recently nature documentaries, such as David Attenborough's highly popular *Blue Planet* series. One could even suggest that the modern novel was literally born at sea, recalling classics like *Robinson Crusoe* (1719) and *Moby Dick* (1851), not to mention explicitly environmental analysis in Rachel Caron's *The Sea Around Us* (1951). The study of classic literature, from an environmental perspective can help uncover how audiences perceive such wild places and seascapes, while constantly foregrounding the perennial necessity of imagining the creation of low-carbon futures across our oceans, as well as on-shore.

Our expansive seas and oceans sustain stable eco-systems and help extract CO_2 out of the atmosphere. Yet over the years, as Attenborough's documentaries and other scientific investigations such as *Seaspiracy* (2021) have revealed, the rich sea-life habitats have been overfished and the ongoing exploitation of oceans for gas and oil has resulted in radically reduced levels of biodiversity. Meanwhile, the earth's coral reefs are dying, apparently due to warmer waters caused by climate change, together with over-fishing. In general terms, because of increased levels of carbon dioxide in the atmosphere kick-started by human activity, there is more CO_2 dissolving into the ocean with long-term, negative consequences for the health of the planet.

The ocean's average pH (a chemical measure from 0–14; with 7 being neutral, anything higher than 7 being alkaline, and anything lower than 7 being acidic) is now around 8.1. All the time our oceans continue to absorb more CO_2, the pH measure decreases and the ocean becomes more acidic, which is very bad for future biodiversity. Since the end of the pre-industrial era in the mid-19th century, the oceans have must usefully become a major carbon sink, but in the decade from 2008–17, we've dumped into the atmosphere so much poisonous gasses from the burning of fossil fuels and land-use change, that it is 'the equivalent to 252 million blue whales', all of which the oceans cannot absorb (see further details in various scientific reports cited below). This results in radically changing the chemical-makeup of our oceans for the worse. Surface waters are now apparently 30% more acidic than they were at the start of the industrial era. Further scientific projections show that by the end of this century, 'ocean surface waters could be more than twice as acidic as they were at the end of last century, if we do not reduce our carbon emissions' (NOAA 2020; Union of Concerned Scientists 2019).

Yet, while scientifically we have grown to appreciate the evolving nature of our oceans and the harm that is befalling them, nonetheless at a human and narrative level, our oceans appear so large and robust that we find it hard to imagine their destruction. They have always been in a state of flux and appear visually adept at survival. As mere mortals, according to media scholar Stacey Alaimo, we find it difficult to map and appreciate our negative influence on our massive waterways and therefore continue to use these expansive and unknown water-ways as an easy 'dumping site of disposal' (2012: 493). Alongside carbon emissions that generally remains unseen, much has recently been made of the huge volume of visible (and invisible) plastic waste choking our oceans and upsetting our expansive flora and fauna. Not to mention the huge amount of disposed fishing nets; evidence of the growth of over-fishing across the world, which is highlighted and dramatically visualised in *Seaspiracy* (2021). This Netflix documentary provocatively contrasts the plastic problem, which all but remains complicit with the huge factory-type fishing industry and their unsustainable levels of exploitation of global fishing stocks.

Recounting the transdisciplinary corpus of Blue Humanities from an environmental perspective, while drawing on literature, history, geography, business, mythology as well as media and communication, together with more scientific factual realities of water hydrology and radical loss of biodiversity; all of these areas speak to both the complexity and interconnectivity of water and land, embedded within our holistic planet. The massive extensive ecosystems of oceans, rivers and lakes remain a site of 'liquid modernity' (recalling Zygmunt Bauman's 2005 well known concept), pulling wastes and goods together in a strange mix, all of which has a major negative effect on our future ecosystems, threatening the very survival of our planet. We need to constantly call attention to and uncover new imaginaries of our fragile life-giving oceans with its dramatic loss of biodiversity, as well as dealing with the indisputable chemical and waste imbalances that are polluting our pristine blue planet.

References

Alaimo, S. 'States of Suspension: Trans-corporeality at Sea'. *Interdisciplinary Studies in Literature and the Environment* 19(3): 476–493. 2012.

Bauman, Zygmunt. *Liquid Modernity*. Polity Press 2005.

Gillis, John. 'The Blue Humanities'. *Humanities* 34(3) June 2013. https://www.neh.gov/humanities/2013/mayjune/feature/the-blue-humanities

National Oceanic and Atmospheric Administration (NOAA). Ocean Acidification. April 2020. https://www.noaa.gov/education/resource-collections/ocean-coasts/ocean-acidification

Union of Concerned Scientists. CO2 and Ocean Acidification: Causes, Impacts, Solutions. 6 February 2019. https://www.ucsusa.org/resources/co2-and-ocean-acidification

C

Carbon Lock-in and Dealing with Stranded Assets: Communicating the Challenges

Carbon Lock-in refers to an ongoing development created by fossil fuel and energy systems that tend to pull against public and private efforts to introduce more environmentally sustainable and renewable energy technologies. There continues to be a major challenge to turn around and discontinue the current fossil-fuel-driven energy infrastructure that supports the ongoing climate crisis. Basically the world has to radically reduce its dependence on fossil fuels and stop pumping more carbon into the atmosphere, which in turn is causing so much global pollution and increasing global warming, among other disastrous effects for human survival into the future.

According to several dictionaries, the concept was first coined by Gregory Unruh in a 1999 thesis entitled 'Escaping Carbon Lock-In'. It has since gained popularity in climate change policy discussions, especially those focused on preventing the widespread growth of carbon lock-in, especially with regards to rapidly industrialising countries such as India and China.

See also various seminal papers on the topic, which convincingly argues what environmentalists have been saying for decades, namely that we cannot burn all our fossil-fuel assets, if the world is to strive to achieve low-carbon transition and face up to the challenges of climate change. However, within the global industry and energy business – not to mention communicating this challenge to a general public – this leads to worries and financial concerns around what are often described as 'stranded assets'. If fossil fuel industries and their assets are no longer acceptable or usable, and thereby become 'stranded', how does the accounting management systems and business world deal with such assets. (See also *Sustainability Accounting*.) Such a strategy is based on accountancy and balance sheet numbers from company books, rather than seeing the problem primarily from a climate emergency perspective, which unfortunately can no longer consider such assets as useful, if the planet is to survive. This remains a major concern, not just for accountants and financial, or even more environmentally driven managers, but for all involved in these profitable businesses, including pension funds and shareholder returns. Finance and

DOI: 10.4324/9781003123422-4

big business can no longer be off-limits for external engagement by all aspects of environmental communication and most importantly in laying out tangible solutions.

As Dr McInerney (a Cork University financial expert), speaking at a Royal Irish Academy (RIA) webinar on 24 June 2020 affirms, electricity across the world remains a primary beacon towards progressing the move to decarbonisation within all sectors of the economy, especially around heating and transport. From a Green financial perspective, mapping the transition of heavily dependent energy companies and corporations from reliance on fossil fuels, towards adopting more cleaner renewables, demands a robust financial and regulatory stimulus. Essentially, long-established business commitment, together with legal and other fears concerning lock-in to fossil fuels, can seriously slow down a much-needed climate and energy transition, which in turn can further drive up overall costs. The process of dealing with increased levels of stranded (fossil fuel-based) assets certainly need to be managed carefully, across the global financial world. More radically and pragmatically, one wonders how national energy systems can overcome the stranglehold of big energy corporations, apparently expecting up to 8% return on their overall investment, while at the same time helping to both kick-start and drive a radically new green system change. What levers can be used to offset the pervasive inertia around maintaining the status quo and supporting a polluting 'business as usual' approach, when a radical green transformation in industry is demanded to revolutionise the mode of production, not to mention more sustainable modes of consumption. Again environmental communication and active engagement with such energy businesses and financial protocols can help show the way forward.

For instance, in a small country like Ireland at present there is a 30-year-old coal-fired electricity powerplant based in Moneypoint, Co. Clare, which constitutes such a 'stranded asset' that needs to be either repurposed or totally decommissioned. Thankfully, on 7 April 2021, it was announced that offshore windfarms will be developed to ensure its repurposing and continued viability. Furthermore, as less (natural) gas is produced in Ireland, the expansive infrastructural network around the island may quickly become surplus to requirements, leaving another expensive stranded asset in its wake. According to McInerney (2020), what Ireland and other countries do in response to these environmental and business challenges over the next five to ten years remains critical in reaching our carbon emission targets and ensuring a smooth transition away from our dependence on fossil fuels. This dilemma is replicated in various ways across the world in all types of jurisdictions and broadly needs the assistance of media and environmental communicators to both explain and highlight the problems and potential solutions for our future survival.

References

McInerney, Celine. *Keynote Speaker on a Webinar* 24 June 2020, hosted by Royal Irish Academy, Dublin, Ireland around energy solutions to climate change.

Unruh, Gregory. 'Escaping Carbon Lock-in'. *Energy Policy* 30(4): 317–325. (1999) 2002.

Circular Economy: Environmental Media, Inclusive and Just Transition – *Snowpiercer*

The idea of a circular economy can be defined as 'a continuous positive development cycle that preserves and enhances natural capital, optimises resource yields and minimises systemic risks by managing finite stocks and renewable flows, basically regenerative sustainability at its best' (Cusack 2020). Less waste means less cost, hence it is no wonder business leaders of all persuasion remain captivated by the applicability of this model of sustainable growth across so much business practice.

The circular economy aims to reduce resource and energy use, taking waste output from the traditional linear economy and focusing on designing products and infrastructure from a more sustainable life-cycle perspective (Moreau et al. 2017). In contrast to the so-called linear economy, the circular economy looks at the full life cycle of products and especially how they are disposed of at the end of their life. New innovation practices of leasing expensive products rather than buying them and then abandoning them through environmentally wasteful 'planned obsolescence' are taken on board. Overcoming levels of waste remains a major challenge for modern industrial societies and especially with regards to increasing carbon emissions as a result. It's all about thinking and making purchasing decisions more long term and constantly thinking of what is best for the environment. Basically, this circular model starts with natural resources, which are protected and regenerated, then it shifts towards designing products and services with the minimum of waste and pollution, before finally producing life-long sustainable products and services with maximum value for all concerned.

Geneviève Ready-Mulvey and Walter Stahel in their 1977 research report for the European Commission 'The Potential for Substituting Manpower for Energy', sketched a vision of an economy in terms of loops (or circular economy) and assessing its holistic impact on job creation and general economic competition. The concept focused primarily around designing products for durability, reuse, remanufacturing and recycling; all the while keeping products, components and (raw) materials circulating in the economy. The circular economy is essentially based on three core principles: designing out waste and pollution, keeping products and materials in use for as long as possible and regenerating natural systems. Yet some critics like Kieren Mayers et al. (2021) question the core premise of such a sustainable philosophy, including noting the scientific and practical difficulty of continuous recycling of processes, much less designing for durability, as not always being guaranteed within real-life production processes.

In contrast to the so-called linear economy, the circular economy nevertheless looks at the full life cycle of products and especially how they are disposed of at the end of their life and how to build this into a process that effectively reduces waste by taking it out of the system. For instance, developing new innovation practices of leasing expensive products rather than buying them, and thereby pushing out the waste of otherwise 'planned obsolescence' in the production cycle, remains a continuing challenge for modern industrial societies. Such sustainable practices involve purchasing products through using more long-term strategies and not simply going for the cheapest short-term option. Alternatively, nature is regarded as a holistic self-regulating eco-system, while human productivity and enterprise has to think beyond short-term monetary gains and costs, to secure a long-term healthy environmental ecosystem.

Putting such green ideas to the test, the European Commission in 2020 made 318 million euro in funding available for projects in the field of climate action, environment, resource efficiency as well as supporting more sustainable raw materials. Many affirm that at least in the EU and other industrialised regions across the world, we are experiencing a paradigm shift towards transitioning to a fully functioning circular economy. Basically, this alternative production system is now regarded as necessary to offset our current wasteful linear model of 'take – make – use – discard'. By any measure, this wasteful old process is not sustainable, much less environmentally efficient, and basically it's also simply not good business practice.

Environmental crises such as cutting excessive plastic waste from the oceans and addressing biodiversity collapse, together with excessive carbon emission are all causing major public concerns. At the same time, mineral resources such as precious and heavy metals are becoming scarce, and natural capital is broadly being abused, alongside being diminishing overall. For businesses, including the ever-expanding communications and media enterprises, this means more expensive raw material and less security of supply for their overall production processes.

The notion of a circular economy can be loosely illustrated by the dystopic science fictional fantasy *Snowpiercer* (2013) directed by Bon Joon ho, drawn from the original graphic novel, which has been further readapted into a successful Netflix television series. The franchise focuses on class and other conflicts in a post-apocalyptic tale where the only human survivors of a climate catastrophe live on an ever-circulating train, precariously protected from the deep frozen landscape outside. One could push the allegorical metaphor of a long train, which is constantly moving a little further, by suggesting the self-sustaining 101-carriages train (extended in later series) traversing the planet, constitutes a fixed circle of production, consumption and re-use – all the time struggling to avoid freezing to death. Reminiscent of the science fictional climate fantasy *2012* (2009), where only the super-rich humans can afford a ticket on the few super-ships equipped to survive the planet literally being consumed by catastrophic flooding. Here also on *Snowpiercer*, only the unscrupulous rich can afford a luxury seat at the top of the train.

Meanwhile, second and 'tail' class passengers have to struggle to get enough food to survive the ordeal, as the train circumnavigates the planet on

a continuous loop. Similarly, in the 'real world', a techno-fix 'creative imaginary' solution is all that appears on the table, in return for the disastrous
abuse of natural resources leading to catastrophic irreversible climatic results.
One wonders however if such cautionary tales encourage audiences to make
the environmental connections and strive to avoid rationalising the crisis
through a 'fixed-track' register, or simply encouraging wallowing in fatalistic
dystopian conflict, recalling the much-needed frisson and pleasure of conflict;
all the while appealing to audiences, thereby encouraging even less hope for a
potentially climate frozen future.

References

Cusack, Geraldine. 'Creating Sustainable Futures through a Circular Economy'. *Royal Irish Academy Blog Series,* October 2020. https://www.ria.ie/news/science-committees-climate-change-and-environmental-sciences-committee-climate-change-blog-4

Mayers, Kieren, Davis, Tom and Wassenhove, Luk n van. 'Sustainability: The Limits of the Sustainable Economy'. *Harvard Business Review* 16 June 2021.

Moreeau, V., Sahakian, M., Griethuysen, P. and Vuille, E. 'Coming Full Circle: Why Social and Institutional Dimensions matter for the Circular Economy'. *Journal of Industrial Ecology* 21(3): 497–506. 2017.

Reday-Mulvey, Geneviève and Stahel, Walter R. *The Potential for Substituting Manpower for Energy: Final Report 30 July 1977 for the Commission of the European Communities.* Battelle, Geneva Research Centre.

Circular Economy Finance and Its Limitations

A major shift in private and public investment is needed to forge a transition
to a robust circular economy. A fascinating study by Paul Dewick et al.

> highlight the risk that progress towards a circular economy will be cur-
> tailed by strategic decisions based on contestable understanding, fuzzy
> indicators, and inadequate information. Before major industry actors
> implement internal investment standards, launch innovative financial
> vehicles, and ramp up investment, we call for more effective oversight to
> prevent the circular economy from being yet another compromised and
> ultimately ineffectual sustainability concept.
>
> (Dewick et al. 2020: 6)

In this overview article, they further illustrate how such a process is consistent with current efforts to attract private finance to help address global
challenges. For instance, 130 banks from 49 countries, representing 47 trillion
American dollars in assets, equating to one-third of the global value of
wealth, signed up to the UN Principles for responsible banking in September
2019. At the outset, this appears to be a coherent strategy to globally address
our major challenges, including more difficult environmental ones. A key

element plucked from the statement by the financial industries, highlights the need to radically reduce material flows by transitioning from linear to circular systems of production and consumption.

But there are dangers of increasing levels of empty rhetoric, even various forms of greenwashing coming to the surface, while for instance hijacking the circular economy model with attempts by oil-producing countries to envisage a 'circular carbon economy' that might be financed through carbon-trading mechanisms. Basically, there remains an ongoing danger of 'fuzzy indications and inadequate information' maintaining a top-down 'business as usual' model supporting the status quo. Consequently, there is an urgent need for closer and critical transdisciplinary involvement and metrics, which could further help shift the dial across academic studies of the circular economy that often tend to be abstract and conceptual, using single case studies and ending up lacking concrete recommendations for practitioners (Kirchher and van Santen 2019). Concerns about how well a circular economy will support strong counter-measures around environmental sustainability remain a major challenge and need to be fully investigated. Furthermore, procedures, mechanisms, and tools for social sustainability efforts across the circular economy, should also be foregrounded and included in emergent frameworks and analytic conceptions (Dewick et al. 2020: 7).

From a business and media perspective a compilation of some of the most engaging recent papers from the journal *Energies* affords useful insights into how circular economy feeds off reducing waste in all aspects of business, as well as encouraging total joined-up thinking between all sectors across the business chain of production, distribution and consumption. For instance cities as microcosms of a broad range of business practices, including media and communications, have a multitude of tools to help govern the inherent benefits of a circular economy. This can include financial assistance for best practice and alternatively helping to close down poor practice, which encourages increased forms of pollution and waste. By all accounts 'a diverse range of solutions and collaborations would need to co-exist to implement the circular economy in practice' (Palm and Bocken 2021: 5).

Such complex business and environmental policy tools need to constantly be evaluated from a critical environmental communications perspective. There certainly should be more environmental nature documentaries, alongside a growth of engaging green financing audio-visual storylines, to help tease out such complex, but engaging, strategies into the future.

See for instance a reading of *Wall Street* (1987) and its sequel *Wall Street: Money Never Sleeps* (2010), reviewed in the business chapter of *Environmental Ethics and Film* (2016), where big finance is usually critiqued for highlighting the abuse of human and ethical values back in the 1980s; 'with its prophetic recreation of the chimera of high-risk electronic moneymaking and what can simply be regarded as downright gambling that has dominated world money markets of late' (Brereton 2016: 170). The original Wall Street mediated shark Gordan Gekko – like the lizard that feeds off insects and sheds its tail when trapped – speaks to the late 2007–8 global financial crash and its lack of financial probity, much less thinking of or working for the common good. All this financial complexity and mis-management of resources was later explained and dramatised in *The Big Short* (2015).

As I argued then, Oliver Stone's radical critique and parody of the capitalist 'trading mentality suggests that most investors are dupes and that big market killings are made primarily by middlemen and brokers like Gekko, who swoops in and snaps up whole companies out from under the noses of their stockholders' (Brereton 2016: 171). The sequel focuses on the newly constituted 'clean tech' industry and renewable green energy, as further detailed in my reading (Brereton 2016: 170–178). The young heir-apparent Jake is apparently smitten by his intuitive belief in 'alternative energy' being the future, and by all accounts green finance has grown exponentially over recent years and generally had a very good press ever since. One wonders however, has anything really changed that much for the better in the meantime; the world needs to radically transform itself.

References

Brereton, Pat. *Environmental Ethics and Film*. Routledge 2016.
Dewick, Paul *et al.* 'Circular Economy Finance'. *Journal of Industrial Ecology*. June 2020.
Kirchher, Julia and van Santen, Ralf. 'Research on the Circular Economy: A Critique of the Field'. *Resources Conservation and Recycling* 151(2–3). December. 2019.
Palm, Jenny and Bocken, Nancy (eds). *Achieving the Circular Economy: Exploring the Role of Local Government, Business and Civic Society in an Urban Context*. MDPI. Basil: Switzerland. 2021.

Citizen Media Engagement and Strategies Used for Effective Audience Reception Studies

Environmental and communications scholar Brenda McNally (2020) affirms at the outset in an Irish Environmental Protection Agency report that knowledge of citizen consumption patterns is crucial in the contemporary media landscape, where the proliferation of media outlets requires nuanced communication strategies to reach targeted audiences. Overall, she discovered in her short audience study that participants wanted to see and hear more about the action and steps that government and businesses will take regarding climate change.

As is often stated, tackling climate change involves foregrounding critical social questions about energy, diet, transport, inequality, poverty and foreign policy; all of which need to be encompassed through radical social transformation associated with regime change. McNally lays down some clear paths to assist in responding to both 'the scale and urgency of the challenge' (13) and calling out societal involvement in 'the form of widespread citizen engagement with climate mitigation and energy transition' (13).

1   Investigating citizen engagement as a 'state of mind' rather than a public event or process for generating citizen support.
2   Looking at engagement as an inter-related concept involving cognitive, affective and behavioural-political dimensions (Moser 2016; Carvalho and Peterson 2012). Affective engagement is particularly significant because, as Stoknes (2015) points out, feelings and emotions drive concerns and compel us to action, especially regarding climate change.

McNally's study echoes other research like Julia Metag et al. (2017), which specifically examined whether German citizen's attitudes to climate change were related to ongoing patterns of media use. Such studies have the aim of developing and improving climate change communication messages. As frequently highlighted across so much environmental communication scholarship, these messages and frames can be categorised across six levels of concern: alarmed, concerned, cautious, disengaged, doubtful and dismissive.

Not surprisingly, the primary reason for trusting environmental messaging, according to such scholarship, can be linked to: 1) reliable sources and basically recognising communication actors as having no pre-given agenda; 2) evidence-based conclusions and not just opinion; 3) finally, the expertise and reputations of the environmental expert messengers themselves remains most important.

Surprisingly, McNally uncovered low levels of citizen trust in Local Authorities, even though they are recognised as key intermediaries for building transition pathways at the local level in the community. At the same time, participants in her study trusted traditional media in general over social media platforms. The pilot study provides a number of recommendations, which could have universal application beyond an Irish context.

Communication of climate (energy) policy for example should consider using a citizens' information network by:

- Providing a socially meaningful road map of mitigation and adaptation to climate change
- Communication should focus on multimedia information platforms, with storytelling as a key mode of communication
- Communication should address climate action information gaps as part of various avenues of community engagement.

Media coverage across all aspects, including new media, business and lifestyle reports, as well as more political-focused environmental news and features in press and broadcast media, are needed to raise public awareness, provide social and political context and in turn act as a platform for public debate and help keep the issue on the public agenda. There is a need for constantly developing new opportunities for climate citizenship and encouraging more public (sphere) action. See for instance, Juliet Schor's (2010) notion of 'plenitude' which involves working and spending less and basically creating and connecting more with people and fellow citizens across communities and society generally. So rather than promoting an ongoing fixation with frugality, austerity or even sacrifice, while still helping to manage our excessive consumption, this alternative more positive notion involves a way of life that will yield a greater sense of well-being than sticking to everyday practices around 'business as usual' (McNally 2020: 34).

Promoting tangible and effective engagement with media, while encouraging active eco-citizenship across communication campaigns, include the urgent need to address the high level of negative sentiment around climate change action and the potential for wider frustration and helplessness with respect to consumer engagement. Furthermore, communication campaigns need to address and encourage active climate citizenship by promoting collective and community responses, through an urgent desire to engage citizens with a shared social vision in tackling climate change.

Taking into account the preoccupation with the 2020/21 pandemic, McNally and other scholars note the strong link between public health and climate change, and how both areas should be framed together to maximise climate change transformation. Of course, there is always the danger that the post-pandemic environment will lead to behavioural fatigue and citizen expectation of a return to business as usual. 'Navigating the competing possibilities will require nuance and tact' (2020: 47), according to McNally, and by all accounts there is unlikely to be a one-size-fits-all message, or any singular approach towards tackling the long-term challenges of climate change.

References

Carvalho, A. and Peterson, T.R. 2012. 'Reinventing the Political'. In Carvalho, A. and Peterson, T.R. (eds), *Climate Change Politics: Communication and Public Engagement*. Cambria Press.

McNally, Brenda. 'Citizens view of Climate Action in Ireland'. EPA Report 344. September 2020. https://www.epa.ie/pubs/reports/research/climate/research344.html

Metag, J., Füchslin, T. and Schäfer, M.S. 2017. 'Global Warming's Five Germanys: A Typology of Germans' Views on Climate Change and Patterns of Media Use and Information'. *Public Understanding of Science* 26(4): 434–451.

Moser, S.C., 2016. 'Reflections on Climate Change Communication Research and Practice in the Second Decade of the 21st Century: What More is There to Say?' *WIREs Climate Change* 7(3): 345–369.

Schor, Juliet. *Plenitude: The New Economics of True Wealth*. Penguin 2010.

Stoknes, P.E.. *What We Think about When We Try Not to Think about Global Warming*. Chelsea Green Publishing 2015.

Climate Literacy and Environmental Activism: *Ozark*

Climate literacy or activism, building on environmental literacy is perceived as an individual or group effort to stand for a social, political, or environmental cause, with the aim of achieving societal change (Brereton 2019). Furthermore, pro-environmental behaviour is perceived through studies by Kollmuss and Agyeman (2002), as deliberately reducing the negative impact that an action can have on the environment (especially recycling, transport use, household consumption and the use of resources, such as energy and water). Scientific literacy encapsulates the knowledge and understanding of scientific concepts and processes required for understanding essential principles and functional concepts to secure appropriate change within the environmental system. Many scholars equate developing coherent climate literacy through climate change education, together with various modes of bottom-up activism.

Caren Cooper for instance suggests using media literacy as a key strategy towards empowering public acceptance of actively addressing climate change. To achieve this aim, we need to develop independent thinking and critical analysis by:

1   Teaching climate change as part of a continuous cross-disciplinary curricula which is grounded in environmental and climate science
2   Embedding action-learning, which is connected to local problem solving
3   Developing problem solving and critical thinking skills, while focusing on individual capacity to achieve positive outcomes
4   Introduce learners to various options to reduce individual footprints
5   Using innovative narrative techniques, visual imagery and persuasive texts (2011: 231–237).

For example recalling a case study of the Netflix series *Ozark* (see Brereton 2019: 30–32), where I illustrated how this cult series puts a new spin on 'going back to nature'. The tale sets up a complex engagement with nature and contrasts various forms of individual versus communal activism, as dramatised in the opening episode, where going back to nature literally is the only option to stay alive. The main protagonist, Marty Byrde (Jason Bateman), who at first appears to be a conventional city-based financial consultant, out of the blue is presented by his business partner with a tourist brochure espousing the rural delights of the Ozarks. The tattered paper brochure sets up the key focus of the series – which is reminiscent of the 'paradise falls' motif in Pixar's classic *UP* (2009) – this is 'a utopian environmental place were one should aim to visit and even escape to before one dies' (see Brereton 2012: 141).

Following the most unexpected violence and narrative disruption and reversal in any contemporary new series; Byrde 'weaves a story' that he will sort things out if allowed to move with his family to this 'magical' lake/forested region of Ozark. This journey/pilgrimage sets up this utopian place where all the rich come to party in the summer with access to a precious nurturing and fertile lake, surrounded by an over-hanging and protective forest (Brereton 2019: 31).

Recalling other eco-filmic narratives like *Grand Canyon* (1991) or *Apocalypto* (2006), his first vision of this utopian (*Walden*-like) space is dramatised so lovingly, as he looks down on the pristine landscape. I suggest in my reading that the storyline 'consciously strives to critically oscillate between first and second wave modes of environmental engagement and even, I would argue, insinuating various modes of eco-critical learning from its active engagement with nature and later with the local inhabitants. The American (first-wave environmental) dream was traditionally built on going out 'West' to discover a pristine natural setting to help 'grow a family' and create a new community. Such myths and perennial tropes and narrative trajectories 'continue with a critical inflection embedded within such new media formats...' (31). Environmental communication students have much to learn from an active engagement with such nature-focused storylines, while extending their environmental literacy.

References

Brereton, Pat. *Environmental Literacy and New Digital Audiences.* Routledge 2019.
Brereton, Pat. *Smart Cinema: DVD Add-ons and New Audience Pleasures.* Palgrave 2012.
Cooper, Caren B. 'Media Literacy as a Key Strategy Towards Improving Public Acceptance of Climate Change Science'. *BioScience* 61(3): 231–237. 2011.
Kollmuss, A. and Agyeman, J. 'Mind the Gap: Why do People Act Environmentally and What are the Barriers to Pro-environmental Behaviour'. *Environmental Education Research* 8(3): 239–260. 2002.

Climate Markets and Cap and Trade as Practical Environmental-Economic Solutions

So-called Climate Markets and green financial tools like Cap and Trade attempt to harness real-time market forces to help reduce carbon emissions in a cost-effective manner. Like other market-based, as opposed to more government sanctioned strategies like carbon lock-in discussed elsewhere, these tools allow the (free)market to determine a general price in controlling carbon emission – which of course has to be systematically reduced across the globe. It uses this mechanism and price point to help drive global investment decisions and hopefully spur future market innovation that will assist in reducing the overall volume of carbon being put into the atmosphere.

Cap and Trade as a financial tool essentially differs from a general carbon tax in that it provides a high level of certainty about future emissions, but not about the price of those emissions. Consequently a cap-type mechanism appears to be a preferable policy to adopt when a jurisdiction, region or country, has a specified emissions target to meet.

As implied by the term Cap and Trade, carbon markets effectively set a limit on emissions while also helping to internalise such a model, offering political and economic flexibility, along with other incentives to develop the necessary energy technology systems to address the ever-expanding climate change challenge. To strive to address such energy realignments, more broad-based Emissions Trading System (ETS), together with the tools discussed above have made great headway more recently. Using such complex economic and policy instruments to help mobilise reductions in carbon emissions requires well-versed environmental communication experts, alongside persuasive media outputs to both explain and frame the importance of such instruments as triggers for both economic transformation and behavioural change, all the while securing a low-carbon future economy.

For instance environmental scholar Mike Hume (2020) in a student friendly student reader, explores the basics of such tools, while raising the level of critical engagement and analysis. Using the binary technique of having two opposing scholars arguing for and against some contentious environmental tools like Cap and Trade and teasing out the relative benefits of the Climate Market, or more generally treating the environment as a form of natural capital. This pedagogical strategy helps students uncover tensions and potential difficulties within such new green accounting and economical models, which often remains alien to many environmental communication students. Such pedagogical strategies are certainly useful in helping to instil both active and critical learning and engagement. But at the same time these can be open to the dangers of reducing the debate to simplistic black-and-white binary oppositional positions and views.

Business, for instance, often strives to take into account any potential ethical or 'moral hazards' related to decisions made, while assessing the relative pros and cons of policy or business decision. Understanding future potential impacts of any aspect of Cap and Trade policy tools, together with taking into account environmental and other triggers, such as the 'precautionary principle', needs to be always carefully considered to help alleviate any potential 'unintended consequences'. For instance, focusing on the concept of a tipping point in supporting any major change across business/industry practices, is helpful in describing and communicating possible climate scenarios and futures. Environmental communication students ought to be able to assess the relative merits of such tools in addressing specific environmental issues, especially those that are trying to radically change the economic and tax-based system of business and governance, while striving to reduce overall carbon emissions. This might include addressing perennial questions, such as: can the social, alongside the economic cost of carbon be fully measured or calculated? Social costs can incidentally include the effect on employment, or the risk to the relative wealth of a society spurned by producing non-returning 'stranded assets', as the fossil fuel industries slowly pivots towards more sustainable renewable energy systems. At the same time much effort is needed in assessing the social, cultural, as well as the political effects of Cap and Trade and Climate Markets on both the financial apparatus of business and, most especially, across the general economy.

The most common disagreement in the literature however is between those who view climate policy as purely an economic and difficult political decision-making process, compared with others, who see climate change more broadly from the perspective of future generations, while recalling struggles over equal rights, intergenerational justice and taking on board various forms of interconnecting aspects around global justice. For instance, the measurement of the world's income is usually conceived of as an aggregate of Gross Domestic Product (GDP), and remains equivalent to about 70 trillion dollars across the planet. Consequently, evaluating 'insurance risk' in planning for any climate disaster can be assessed through measuring the potential loss of this level of growth and profit and thereby producing a 'defined cost' or balance sheet offset, as being a tangible risk for the overall security of the global system. Meanwhile, the social and long-term environmental cost of carbon and its global measurement, remains more difficult to quantify.

As is often affirmed by Humanities scholars and reiterated by environmental communication scholars, seeing such environmental and climate change issues primarily through an economic lens, remains dangerous and needs to be balanced with other perspectives. Carbon Markets, much less Cap and Trade, according to Hulme and others, ultimately fail to incentivise the structural changes in the political energy economy that are necessary for deep decarbonisation. Furthermore, it is suggested such financial tools perpetuate climate injustices and development inequalities. Propagating a type of post-political myth (see Swyngedouw 2010) reduces carbon emission to a technical-economic challenge, which apparently can be met without actively confronting the power of incumbent fossil-fuel interests. Many radical, ethical environmentalists recognise this as a cautionary prognosis. Yet one could counter that a 'both and' approach to business and carbon markets is needed by activists and environmental communicators, developed across all levels of the spectrum and acknowledge there is no 'magic bullet' or singular solution, much less a quick fix to our multiple climate crises. This is the way environmental communications can help weave, broadcast and uncover such complex economic, business and technical solutions to our carbon energy problems. All the while, leveraging on the expanding expertise of green economics, green finance, as well as green-based policy levers and tools, need to be deployed and developed through national and international governance and through general carbon regulation. Environmental communication students ought to become fully aware of such complex economic, regulatory and business tensions as they relate to climate change.

References

Hulme, Mike (ed). *Contemporary Climate Change Debates: A Students Primer*. Routledge 2020.
Swyngedouw, Erik. 'Apocalypse Forever? Post-Political Populism and the Spectre of Climate Change'. *Theory Culture and Society* 27(2–3): 213–232. 2010.

Cognitive Dissonance and Eco-modernism

Western populations in particular are often struck by a form of cognitive dissonance, which is defined as not wanting to believe what they know, especially when the price to pay for such an awareness would be the renunciation of deeply held values. Such values include the 'myth of progress' associated with endless economic growth, not to mention the challenges of critiquing (over)consumption, and excessive personal wealth, which remains so dominant as an aspiration across many parts of the contemporary world. Global citizens who eat meat, drive cars, crave more consumable goods and services, travel on aeroplanes, use fossil fuels to light and heat their house(s), yet at the same time espouse strong environmental values, can be accused of a form of hypocrisy, if not cognitive dissonance. All of these tensions feeds into concerns around what has come to be described as eco-modernism.

The concept of eco-modernism is not necessarily concerned about changing unsustainable lifestyles and institutional structures, but more about promoting social adaptation and capitalist resilience in the face of politically sanctioned unsustainability, together with growing concerns about our climate emergency (see Fahy 2020). By avoiding recognising or highlighting such inherent contradictions in response to the environmental crisis – see for instance Sally Weintrobe's analysis of 'environmental bubbles' (2021) – governments and voters secure the moral satisfaction of pretending to act on environmental issues, without the discomfort of actually doing it. What is probably missing in such debates, especially around this dominant materialist-driven belief system and mode of behaviour, is an emotional hook that catches people's attention, as well as pricking the conscience of a majority of (Western/industrialised) citizens, who unfortunately remain *de facto* hyper-consumers.

Meanwhile, personal experiences of disasters, alongside mediated eco-catastrophes can serve as a useful hook towards promoting a different path for radical transformation. Unfortunately, such provocative tipping points often come too late in the day in addressing the actions required to make the much-needed radical transformation. Instead, we are frequently left with adopting even legitimising the alternative of geoengineering quick fixes, where a majority of citizens in the end don't have to make a radical transformation to their lifestyle and instead can continue their 'business as usual' ways of living and not worry about the consequences. By all accounts the dangers of not fully facing up to our climate crisis remains an ongoing dilemma and will need constant fresh thinking and critical analysis, as well as explicit media and communication responses to help pinpoint and promote concrete solutions.

References

Fahy, Declan. 'Ecological Modernism, Irish-Style: Exploring Ireland's Slow Transition to Low-Carbon Society' (131–148). In Robbins, D., Torney, D. and Brereton, P. (eds). *Ireland and the Climate Crisis*. Palgrave 2020.
Weintrobe, Sally. *Psychological Roots of the Climate Crisis*. Bloomsbury Press 2021.

Communication/Media Models Used for Environmental Communication

As illustrated in (Brereton 2001: 37–38) communication models are used to illustrate how complex communication processes can be understood and used extensively within various academic courses. Four of the most basic and popular models include:

1   Lasswell's 1948 model, which has been extensively applied to help understand advertising/propaganda and news analysis and is easily summarised by the phrase: 'Who says what (message), in which channel (medium), to whom (receiver) and with what effect'. Basically, all environmental communication messages and texts can similarly be analysed using this simple and efficient structure, which in turn feeds into the so-called colloquially titled 'hypodermic needle' model of powerful media effects.

2   The Shannon and Weaver Model, building on basic telephony, perceives the communications process as similar to a mechanical one. The historical model explores how communication is a 'one way process'; reflecting the mathematical/engineering focus of telephony, to which it was first applied. Beginning with an information source, sending a message through a transmitter or signal. But of course, there is always some danger of 'noise' or interference, corrupting the purity of the message/signal. As with the technological magic of telephony, a receiver transmits the message, which is modulating through various technological devices, before it reaches its final destination (see Brereton 2001: 38).

3   More complex communication models include Theodore M. Newcomb's ABX model, which is triangular and subsequently favoured by audience and media sociologists like Stuart Hall, who adapted it (see Hall's seminal 'Encoding/Decoding' paper from 1973). Students often find it one of the most engaging conceptual models in helping to explain the power of media and its influence on audiences. Basically, there are three main elements, including the producers who encode meaning into a message, using the 'codes and conventions' they have at their disposal to make messages. For example, the tools a print journalist has at their disposal, remains very different from those of a documentary or film maker. Furthermore, all of this has become more complicated and extended with the rise of online media production.

    After the producers encode meaning and develop their messages, they end up producing a mediated text, which in turn can be analysed through textual and content analysis. Finally, audiences can decode the meaning of the text they read/view or otherwise consume, often in very different ways to what was encoded or intended by the producer or maker of the media artefact. Hall and other semiotic scholars talk of the creation of a polysemic text, with multiple meanings and interpretations, which audiences can make. Producers can get to know what audiences really think of the text they have produced, through various forms of feedback loops, including direct messages or simply by purchasing or otherwise accessing the (audio-visual) text. For instance, within eco-film scholarship and reception studies, much work has been carried out around gauging audiences responses, from attending screenings of the dystopic climate change science fiction and special effects film *The Day After Tomorrow* (2004, reviewed in Leiserowitz 2005).

Newcomb created a very complex yet engaging model to tease out how the 'meaning' of a text is not necessarily controlled either by the producers or makers, much less the text itself, or even the audience who consume it, but rather is floating between all three constituencies. This remains a eureka moment for many students in understanding and learning about the power and varying meaning(s) of texts. In particular, following years of teaching environmental literacy, many students are surprised when they uncover what they believe is a 'strong environmental message' encoded in the media, but may not be considered to be so by others outside the bubble of environmental education. Certainly, communication, meaning making and effective transmission of messages is no simple 'magic bullet' strategy, where all agree regarding the power, much less the overall veracity of media messaging.

4   A model that remains most popular within Science/Environmental Communications and also favoured within celebrity Fan Culture Studies is the well-known 'Two Step Flow' of Communication, conceived back in 1944 by Paul Lazarfeld et al. It is affirmed within this model that most people form their opinions under the influences of opinion leaders, who in turn are influenced by the mass media. Unlike so-called 'One Step Flow' – recalling the Hypodermic Needle effects theory earlier – in this model, ideas flow from the mass media to opinion leaders (like Leonardo Di Caprio or Greta Thunberg etc.) and from them are further mediated, amplified and disseminated out to the wider public.

Of course, there are many other complementary theories that can be used to map out the communication process system and various different even complementary approaches can be usefully called upon, while unpacking specific areas of investigation. Of course, much can be made of the process of decoding, as well as the production of messages, together with related audience reception modalities. Furthermore, all of these four models and many more besides, can be combined and amended in varying ways with regards to messaging around environmental issues and debates. All of this complexity however needs to be fully taken on board through any student engagement with, and analysis of, any form of environmental communication process or investigation.

References

Brereton, Pat. *Continuum Guide to Media Education*. Continuum 2001.

Hall, Stuart. 'Encoding/Decoding'. 1973. http://epapers.bham.ac.uk/2962/1/Hall%2C_1973%2C_Encoding_and_Decoding_in_the_Television_Discourse.pdf

Leiserowitz, Anthony. 'The International Impact of The Day after Tomorrow'. *Environment* 43(3). 41–44. April 2005 https://www.upf.edu/pcstacademy/_docs/200504_theinternational.pdf.

Community Engagement/Environmental Citizenship: 'Change by Degrees'

Encouraging all levels of communities to actively engage with climate change remains a goal of environmental communication. It also remains a starting point for environmental literacy and active media communications. In a webinar discussion (4 November 2020) on 'Local Government and Climate Change Communication', Madeleine Murray (co-founder of 'Change by Degrees' together with Dr Tara Shine in Kinsale, Ireland see https://change bydegrees.com/about-us) spoke very convincingly on how to engage with local communities around sustainability and in helping to develop locally based approaches to environmental citizenship. As with all strategies around modes of communication, knowing your audience remains essential, especially when dealing with local communities, where experts cannot be seen as even appearing to speak down to, much less preach at people. Consequently, it is essential to make complex scientific information open and accessible, while always focusing on acting locally and developing practical models for community networks. People want advice on how to actively engage with climate change and develop new modes of sustainability and this is a space and forum where the media and communications industry has a major role to play. Communities often don't realise that many projects they run or actions they take to improve the quality of life for people are in fact sustainable ones that constitute climate action. Demystifying what climate action really looks like remains a powerful environmental communications function and role that is genuinely helpful to the vast majority of people who are not climate experts.

For instance, a contentious problem like plastic waste remains a gateway issue for engaging with various forms of sustainability within communities and other stakeholders, all of which are linked to climate change. The philosophy 'Change by Degrees' is informed by the community initiative they founded in their hometown of Kinsale, Plastic Free Kinsale. If they can mobilise a town of 5000 people to reduce plastic pollution, they can change larger communities and even nations. Often stakeholder engagement, Murray believes, can adopt either the top-down broadcasting model or the dialogue-focused model, which works from the bottom up and supports listening and learning from those involved. A combination of both approaches is oftentimes most effective. Furthermore, it is important to always realise that the public is made up of many disparate publics. All the while, one needs to keep appealing to the base; as well as those opposed to change, including the disengaged, who remain potentially open to transformation. At the same time, within such community dynamics there is always a danger of too much reliance on volunteers; with fatigue coming into play and forever calling on the 'usual suspects'. Finally, community involvement and active engagement in sustainable issues need recurring and ongoing support, not just one-off resource inputs to kick-start some initiative (see Watson 2020).

As a case study, the experience of their business concept 'Change by Degree' provides lessons learned and key principles around how to develop community engagement with environmental issues. Change by Degrees emphasise the need to:

i be careful of the tone and language register used when designing a campaign. For instance, the so-called general public may not know what technical environmental terms like 'decarbonising' actually mean. Consequently it's always essential to know your audience and speak their language.

ii A key focus in any communication process remains being empathetic and close identification with the topic; while putting yourself in their shoes and uncovering what is in it for the people you are communicating with. For instance, instead of talking to mothers about climate change, it can be useful to lead with specific forms of social action, like 'protecting the kids' from car fumes at the school gate.

iii As a rule of thumb and constantly affirmed within communication manuals, it is best to connect local citizen action to global citizen concerns. Following this strategy, it is helpful if you have a 'trusted peer' to learn from. Basically, we need positive messaging and peer engagement around how change can/should make people happy and safe. Climate action should make people feel healthy, happy and safe.

Principles like these and experience from local campaigns can be extended to all aspects of climate change and should in turn feed into various media and environmental communication organisations. An example of direct communication with young people discussed elsewhere is illustrated through a case-study reading of the environmental documentary titled *2040* with its extensive use of global vox pops.

References

'Change by Degrees'https://changebydegrees.com/about-us
Watson, Clare. 'Community Engagement and Community Energy' (205–230). In Robbins, D., Torney, D. and Brereton, P. (eds). *Ireland and the Climate Crisis*. Palgrave 2020.

Conservation as an Environmental Strategy Towards Evaluating Wilderness: *Yellowstone*

Protecting the environment at all levels from macro to micro habitats remains the dominant ethos of conservation. As laid out in the World Conservation Strategy, 'it is essential for conservation to be seen as central to human interests and aspirations'. At the same time, people – from heads-of-state to various members of rural communities – will all most readily embrace demands for supporting conservation, especially if they 'themselves recognize the contribution of conservation to the achievements of their needs, as perceived by them, and the solution of their problems, as perceived by them' (1980: 47).

As Paul Shepard highlights, the growing contributions within society and the struggle to convert all 'wastes' and natural habitats into 'cultivated fields and cities' would in turn 'impoverish rather than enrich life aesthetically, as well as ecologically' (Shepard 2015) Dealing with conservation and waste remains difficult to square from an environmental perspective. Often this tension is skewed in the name of supporting the ecological value of conservation, but one where nature is reduced to a 'resource to be sustained for our own well-being' (in Shepard 2015: 64). As historically noted, 'the only reason anything is done on this earth is for people. Did the rivers, winds, animals, rocks, or dust ever consider my wishes or needs? Surely, we do all our acts in an earthly environment, but I have never had a tree, valley, mountain, or flower thank me for preserving it' (Gunn 1966: 260). This traditional and common sense, yet ostensibly anti-anthropomorphic view of human environmental thinking, still carries great force in the academy, epitomised by classical historical philosophers like Francis Bacon, Rene Descartes, Friedrich Hegel, Thomas Hobbes and Karl Marx (Shepard 2015: 65). Hence, human's conception of conservation is not primarily thinking of the inherent benefits for the planet, but rather simply focusing on human survival.

Nonetheless, according to William Cronin in his seminal text 'The Trouble with Wilderness', the single most famous episode in American conservation history focused on whether the city of San Francisco should be permitted to augment its water supply by damming the Tuolumne River in Hetch Hetchy valley, situated well within the boundaries of Yosemite National Park. But even as the fight was being lost, Hetch Hetchy became the battle cry for an emerging movement to preserve aspects of wilderness. Fifty years earlier, such opposition would have been unthinkable. 'Few would have questioned the merits of "reclaiming" a wasteland like this in order to put it to human use' (Cronon 2015: 104). Cronon continues that contemporary society need a more reflexive evolution of an environmental ethic that 'will tell us as much about *using* nature, as about *not* using it' (ibid.: 104).

See for instance an eco-reading of the classic Hollywood film *Chinatown* (1974) and Los Angeles' appropriation of water from nearby land (Brereton 2020: 6–26). As Cronon affirms the 'wilderness dualism approach tends to cast any use as *ab*-use, and thereby denies us a middle ground in which responsible use and non-use might attain some kind of balanced, sustainable relationship' (Cronon 2015: 114). Cronon provides insight for exploring this middle ground between conservation activists and other stakeholders in the community, from which humanity can uncover ways of imagining a better world for all of us. This includes

> humans and nonhumans, rich people and poor, women and men, First Worlders and Third Worlders, white folk and people of colour, consumers and producers – a world better for humanity in all of its diversity and for

all the rest of nature too. The middle ground is where we actually live. It is where we – all of us, in our different places and ways – make our homes.

(ibid.: 114)

Cronon's principal objection to the abstract notion of wilderness is that it may

teach us to be dismissive or even contemptuous of such humble places and experiences. Without our quite realising it, wilderness tends to privilege some parts of nature at the expense of others. Most of all, I suspect, many still follow the conventions of the romantic sublime in finding the mountaintop more glorious than the plains, the ancient forest nobler than the grasslands, the mighty canyon more inspiring than the humble marsh.

(114)

Prioritising different habits over others has been a constant response across so much pastoral and romantic literature, art and most recently audio-visual landscape media – not to mention the contemporary growth of urban eco-media analysis (see Murray and Heumann 2018).

Furthermore, within historical environmental literature and especially through American icons like John Muir, these romantics explicitly characterised (big) ranchers as the enemy. Ranchers, he argued, 'used the wilderness rather than experiencing or studying it. They were cut off from the universal; they destroyed it through inattention'. Ranchers became the embodiment of one side of a dichotomy, dividing the exploitation of Nature from its conventional study and protection, with indigenous peoples often left to protect historical values and ecological principles. This dichotomy forms the basis of the most well-known divide in American environmental politics; the broad divide between 'conservation' and 'preservation'. Anna Lowenhaupt Tsing in a chapter titled, 'Natural Universals and the Global Scale' suggests that histories of American environmentalism often begin with Muir's disagreement with Gifford Pinchot, who became the first head of the US Forest Service (in Hiltner 2015: 219). Such tensions have festered and mutated further into contemporary times with probably more hard-line divisions developing between urban and rural communities across America, alongside many other (so-called developed) regions across the planet. It is insinuated that across regions there are contested notions of wilderness and even what various forms of conservation actually means on the ground. Such tensions can be clearly illustrated through a case study reading of *Yellowstone*.

Case study of Yellowstone

The series began with a feature length pilot on the American Paramount Pay Channel Network on 20 June 2018 and spawned a number of successful seasons since then. In ways the televisual series is reminiscent of well-known melodramatic soaps like *Dallas* or *Dynasty* with big cowboy-hats and even bigger egos. However, the series main redeeming features include its representation of landscape encapsulated by its iconic opening credits with dark sepia tones, connotating the anti-environmental history of extraction industries and farming throughout the region. Starring A-lister Kevin Costner as John Dutton, a sixth-generation rancher/farmer whose family controls the largest contiguous ranch in the US, the series explores how he struggles to protect his Montana ranch from land developers, a local Indian reservation, as well as from the demands of America's first National Park and environmentalists, who apparently want to re-wild the landscape. The big ranch owning family of Yellowstone are initially pitted against the Native American Indians, who are ghettoised on reservations and forced to build gambling casinos to provide an income for their people. But their far-sighted leader, Chief Thomas Rainwater (Gil Birmingham), ends up seeing his erstwhile enemy as coincidentally having a similar goal; namely to keep the land protected for posterity, rather than selling out for short-term gain to a corporate investor who wants to create an artificial and leisure-based metropolis. Even the far-seeing female governor, realises that the apparent building surge of her county would lead to so many different social problems – most obviously the end of the biggest ranch in the region, which maintained stewardship of the land and foretelling how such development would lead to a proliferation of more low-paying jobs. Consequently, from an environmental and planning perspective, locals would become priced out of an exclusive and unsustainable bubble, sparked by an artificially created land and housing market explosion.

Throughout the series, the autocratic ranching family focuses on many local squabbles and nefarious even criminal dealings, as each member in turn seeks to protect their legacy. Farming land, no matter where it is situated, is primarily about ownership and control and finding ways to make it more sustainable into the longer term – but unfortunately at least in this instance such efforts involve adopting less holistic environmental strategies.

Yet at the same time the series lovingly focuses on the beautiful rolling landscape, which is usually far from media scrutiny, where land grabs earn developers billions and politicians are apparently bought and sold by the world's largest oil, natural gas and lumber corporations. For environmentalists, the rolling landscape remains the most engaging feature of the storyline, and one wonders if the series has helped in its own small way to reimagine the televisual western genre and its well-founded conventions, as it explores many very prescient nature and conservation issues for a contemporary and mainly urban-based televisual audience. Unfortunately, however, the storyline does not fully live up to expectations, being pushed too far at times, while simply striving to elongate and extend the franchise. Nonetheless, one has to admit, reviving the iconic western genre for a mass televisual audience helps to keep such rural environmental issues alive for mass audiences.

References

Brereton, Pat. 'Environmental Ethics and Energy Extraction: Textual Analysis of Iconic Cautionary Hollywood Tales: Chinatown (1974), There Will be Blood (2007), and Promised Land (2012)'. *ISLE* 27(1): 6–26. Winter 2020.

Cronin, William. 'The Truth with Wilderness: Or Getting Back to the Wrong Nature' (102–119). In Hiltner, Ken (ed.). *Ecocriticism: The Essential Reader*. Routledge 2015.

Gunn, Clare. *Landscape Architecture*, July 1966.

Shepard, Paul. 'Ecology and Man'. In Hiltner, Ken (ed.) *Ecocriticism: The Essential Reader*. Routledge 2015.

Hiltner, Ken (ed.). *Ecocriticism: The Essential Reader*. Routledge 2015.

Murray, Robin and Heumann, Joseph. *Ecocinema and the City*. Routledge 2018.

World Conservation Strategy. 'Living Resource Conservation for Sustainable Development'. International Union of Conservation for Nature and Natural Resources (IUCN) 1980. https://portals.iucn.org/library/efiles/documents/wcs-004.pdf

Consumption and the Diderot Effect: Sustainable Reduction, Reuse and Recycle

Increasing levels of resource consumption most certainly leads to climate change difficulties, including also losses in biodiversity and encouraging various forms of inequalities and poverty. There is a growing recognition and appreciation of consumption and increased development being a core driver of Greenhouse Gas (GHG) emission and this dilemma needs to be faced head on, especially as carbon is found everywhere in all our consumption practices, leading to a dramatic increase in our global carbon footprint.

In the United States, for instance, the growth of household consumption took off after 1945 following the Second World War, while trying to deal with the over-capacity of factories after the war as industry switched to consumer goods production. The predominantly white working class which had benefited from the wartime boom now became major consumers and this growth was encouraged by government investment in housing and road construction. This physical transformation is often celebrated through Hollywood representations and later the Chicago school of supply economics further legitimised what is characterised as the 'American Dream' of suburban living, conspicuous consumption and ongoing growth.

From an advertising angle, Edward Bernays (nephew of Sigmund Freud) who is recognised as the creator of modern marketing back in the 1920s, wrote about how marketing and advertising serves to make us feel good, as we consume more and feel the urge to consume continuously. Observing how many advertisements across the decades encourage consumers to 'believe in themselves', aided by purchasing products, such audio-visual media certainly assist many citizens towards vicariously increasing their self-belief. Furthermore, planned obsolescence and conspicuous consumption – often simply for the sake of it – have unfortunately become the norm, as evidenced through the excesses and growth of all types of material consumption, including, for example, fast fashion. American consumer norms were further embraced throughout Europe and beyond in the post-war period and such values served as a model for the developing world. Even communist societies like Russia and China later embraced consumerism as a means of legitimising their national growth and trajectory.

In contrast to the ongoing rise of consumer culture in the West and elsewhere, the sustainable consumption model has had a slow start, only coming to the fore in the late 1990s, encouraging citizens to put the brakes on uncontrolled consumption patterns. Frugal values have been co-opted as an effective response to our climate crisis and addressing the need to reduce overall waste and curb various human-types of global pollution. Such sustainable development values fed into the growing environmental mantra of 'reduce, reuse and recycle', which became the core philosophy underpinning the sustainable environmental movement. Rather than simply recognising the economic costs of production, which apparently drove the bottom-line rationale for consumer purchasing decisions, more recently – as evident through the UN Environmental Annual Report (UNEP) – from 2016 at least, there has been a move to recognising more intangible environmental costs around waste in particular to minimise ecological impacts on our precious planet. Extensive research over the years has highlighted how to manage and reduce consumption as a collective activity, while recognising that economic growth and consumption appear to be two sides of the same coin. But this model has to be urgently re-evaluated and alternatively be remodelled and controlled by the need for more sustainable-driven growth and (slow) development.

Within this all-encompassing model, the urge to consume and by extension produce more is encouraged by what has come to be characterised as the 'Diderot Effect'. This so-called effect draws on psychological and behavioural analysis in stating that obtaining a new possession for home making often creates a spiral of consumption that in turn leads people to strive to acquire *more* consumable products and services. As a result, citizens – as *de facto* heavily driven customers – end up buying things that their previous selves might never have needed to feel happy or fulfilled (see https://jamesclear.com/diderot-effect). This so-called effects model of consumption basically draws on the inherent psychological dilemma around the treadmill of peer pressure and various aspects of competitive consumption. Essentially, the more one has, the more individuals want! All of which begs the philosophical and ethical question, can such spurious consumption ever make us really happy?

Furthermore, technological advances also drive consumption, and by using the lens of Social Practice Theory, we recognise that consumption is constantly intertwined with technology and is also aided by media culture. Unfortunately the impact of unsustainable consumption most certainly leads to climate change difficulties, with definite losses in biodiversity and at the same time increasing various triggers for specific forms of injustice, inequalities and global poverty. There is a growing recognition of economic growth and consumption being a core driver of Greenhouse Gas (GHG) emission and this dilemma has to be faced up to head on, especially as carbon is found everywhere in all our consumption practices, leading to a dramatic increase in our global carbon footprint. But changing complex systems within the market-place and throughout general business practice remains a very difficult process.

Certainly, technology alone cannot solve our climate crisis. We also need sustained behavioural changes within consumer lifestyle – recalling models like 'back to normal' or 'gregarious simplicity' – all of which were facilitated in the past by cooperative and social-engagement models of community development. Furthermore, the difficult call to replace our high-tech computer and mobile phone technology and lifestyle with an earlier form of low-tech 'wireless materialism' remains a probably impossible challenge at present – at least for so-called high-tech media citizens in the so-called developed world. The drive towards technological progress and constant innovation makes reversion to older less sophisticated modes of technology difficult to promote much less any form of buy-in unlikely in the future. But then even if this was a runner, individual lifestyle changes in themselves are not enough. Top-down systemic changes, together with governmental intervention and policy regulation, are all urgently needed, including taking on board various models of degrowth, alongside more mainstream models of sustainable green growth, as popularised in discussions of Kate Raworth's 'Doughnut Economics'. Such tensions are passionately explored in numerous discussion threats on the Sustainable Consumption Research Action Network (SCORAI), alongside specific webinars including the 'Rapid Transition Alliance' (13 April 2020).

As constantly asserted, the role of consumption and sustainability research, include gathering new data and developing new conceptual frameworks and co-creations of new knowledge through action research with and across all types of stakeholders. Furthermore, developing policy options, while trying to influence decision makers remains an ongoing challenge for environmental communication experts. By all accounts, reducing excessive consumption remains key to long-term sustainable development and environmental sustainability. All of these drivers and impediments need to be actively addressed by environmental communications students and scholars in the challenges ahead.

References

SCORAI webinar: 13 April 2020 the Rapid Transition Alliance presented a webinar entitled 'Changing our Ways'.
Clear, James. 'The Diderot Effect: Why We Want Things we don't Need—And what to dp About it'. n.d. https://jamesclear.com/diderot-effect

Coronavirus: Health and Effective Communication of Climate Change – *Contagion*

Following the ever-expanding pandemic caused by COVID-19, there has been a debate around how the phenomenon has radically transformed many aspects of climate change communication. For instance, there is a large body of research focused on how climate will affect the locations of pathogenic microbes and vectors of infectious diseases, while other scholars focus on another threat: 'the strong possibility that new, previous unknown infectious diseases will emerge from warmer climates as microbes adapt to higher global temperatures that can defeat our endothermy thermal barrier' (Casadevall 2020: 1).

The human organism is generally protected from infectious diseases by an advanced immune system, which includes innate and adaptive physical defences. Although physical defences such as skin are well known to physicians, the role of temperature and other aspects of habitat and the general human environment is often unappreciated. Mammals are remarkable in maintaining an elevated body temperature through life. Infectious diseases incidentally are acquired from other hosts (e.g. influenza virus) or directly from the environment, usually by inhalation.

For decades, researchers have debated whether climate change has an adverse impact on diseases, especially infectious human diseases. Scholars like Khan et al. (2019) have identified a strong relationship between climate variables and groups of human diseases. Several aspects that resemble the impact of climate change on diseases, include the emergence and re-emergence of vector-borne disease and the impact of extreme weather events. Humans remain highly vulnerable to diseases and other post-catastrophic effects of extreme events, as evidenced in the expanding literature. Humanity constantly needs to understand the adverse impacts of climate change and 'take proper and sustained control measures' (Khan et al. 2019: 1).

Key global viruses and diseases that affect humans include: Malaria, Dengue fever, Lyme disease, Haemorrhagic fever, West Nile fever, Yellow fever, Ebola and most recently of course COVID-19. This virus apparently began life in bats and wet-food markets in China, before being transmitted into the human population. However there is growing speculation that it may have been alternatively sparked by medical experimentation. In any case, a direct link between the environmental loss of biodiversity and pressure on food security and hygiene has helped to promote the growth of dangerous viruses. Scientists have established a clear link between climate change and many environmental problems such as droughts, floods, heatwaves, forest fires, water and some vector-borne diseases. All of these potential disasters pose serious threats to vulnerable groups like the poor, children, pregnant women and most especially the elderly.

Finally, Khan et al. (2019) conclude that hazardous 'meteorological and weather events in combination have severe impacts on numerous infectious diseases and may increase the complications manifold. Thereby, it becomes imperative to develop relationships between climate change, pathogens, vectors, and related diseases' (15). Currently, the media across the world appears to be playing a major role in disseminating various scientific responses and solutions to the 2020–21 pandemic. Again such learning and protocols can hopefully be repurposed in varying ways while addressing the even-greater challenge of dealing with the climate crisis. Certainly with the global catastrophe of the recent pandemic, and its direct and indirect connections with climate change, needs to be extensively studied and students ought to examine various interconnections between such phenomena for future studies within environmental risk communications. The following example of *Contagion* can help flesh out and illustrate some of these issues and concerns.

Case study of Contagion

In a review by Fiachra O'Brolchain and Pat Brereton (2021), so-called pandemic films like Stephen Soderbergh's *Contagion* (2011) offers a cinematic point of reference for considering the impact of a global virus on society. It tells the story of a pandemic caused by a respiratory virus called MEV-1 in a very realistic manner. The film follows a variety of characters to provide a panoramic view of the impact of a virus on contemporary society. Thematically and stylistically, *Contagion* is a kind of sequel to *Traffic* (2000). Both movies employ a stripped-down realist visual style and hyperlink narrative to emphasise the immediacy of their topic and to show the complex relationships that link distant places and government attempts to respond to the threats against social order and public health that result as greed overwhelms the economic opportunities created by global networks. The audience initially experiences the pandemic from a domestic perspective, as patient zero Beth Emhoff (Gwyneth Paltrow) returns to her family in Chicago. Following her death and the spread of the virus, we watch as the Centre of Disease Control and various scientists and other officials attempt to understand and respond to the exponentially expanding virus.

The film utilises a hyperlink structure that cuts back and forth between the characters in the manner of movements through the internet, governed by what Lev Manovich calls nonlinear database logic (see Brereton 2012). It shows us other victims of the virus who also encountered it in the casino and are now transmitting the disease as they travel to different parts of the world (Baker 2013: 8). A vaccine is finally developed, following Doctor Ally Hextall's (Jennifer Ehle) decision to bypass research ethics norms, but not before millions have died. The film concludes by showing audiences back to Day 1 – the spill-over event which started it all. Audiences witness forests in China being cleared, forcing bats from their natural environment. One bat ends up near domesticated pigs; one of which eats fruit dropped by the bat, thereby allowing the virus to jump species. The virus jumps species once again, when the chef who prepares the slaughtered pig in a hotel in Macau shakes hands with the business woman Beth Emhoff, who subsequently becomes infected. By all accounts this remains a powerful cautionary tale, echoing our own real pandemic and effectively highlight its environmental root causes.

References

Baker, Aaron. 'Global Cinema and Contagion'. *Film Quarterly* 66(3): 5–14. 2013.

Brereton, Pat. *Smart Cinema: DVD Add-ons and New Audience Pleasures.* Palgrave 2012.

Casadevall, Arturo. 'Climate Change Brings the Spectre of New Infectious Diseases'. 6 January 2020 *Viewpoint free access Tags* 111.

Khan, Mohd Danish *et al.* 'Aggravation of Human Diseases and Climate Change Nexus'. *Institute Journal of Environmental Research and Public Health* 6 August 2019. https://journals.sagepub.com/doi/pdf/10.1177/0963662519886474

O'Brolchain, Fiachra and Brereton, Pat. 'Learning from COVID-19: Virtue Ethics, Pandemics and Environmental Degradation: A Case Study Reading of The Andromeda Strain (1971) and Contagion (2011)'. *Journal of Science Fiction and Philosophy* 4. 2021.

Creative Imaginary Used to Explore Solutions to Climate Change – *Documentary 2040*

As continuously asserted across academic studies of media and environmental communication in particular, we need more effective 'creative imaginaries' to speak to environmental problems created by our global climate crisis and help to inspire root and branch policy, and governance adjustments, alongside promoting radical and sustained behavioural change in facing these ongoing problems.

Furthermore, addressing the growing problem of climate anxiety, which permeates the world at present, we need some tangible action and more fruitful and practical solutions into the future. But how to get the balance right between mere disposable entertainment vehicles, as against educating and highlighting an otherwise depressing cautionary tale, focused on both difficult and complex environmental areas of contestation remains a challenge. Film makers and media creatives in general should probably strive towards showing the positives concerning what can be solved with existing technologies in tacking climate change, without always degenerating into constantly embracing future techno-fix solutions as the go-to solution at all times. *2040* treads this difficult line and speaks effectively with and to younger new generational audiences, as it visualises solutions to climate change.

The premise of Damon Gameau's documentary *2040* (2019) – see his 2015 debut *That Sugar Film* – is focused around being worried for the future of his four-year-old daughter and wondering what it would be like for her, especially, much later in the future in 2040. The storyline is thereby constructed as a visual essay to his young daughter, projected into the future. 'Gameau's pitch is that he has the skills to distil complex ideas into thoroughly digestible chunks'. This is where we see him creating visual innovations that 'add some bling to potentially dry subject matter' (Bukmaster 2019).

Overall, very high production values are deployed in the documentary, using an engaging narrative structure throughout. The narrative thread starts with a high level of immersive engagement and empathy through calling attention to his idealised, white nuclear family, while planting a tree as a sign of pro-active environmental activity. This is followed through and completed in the final sequence of the film's timeline (see Brereton 2020).

Some of the graphic effects displayed are very impressive; such as using his house/home as a microcosm for illustrating and exploring our planet's environmental difficulties. A domestic fridge for instance is used to highlight the melting of ice and demonstrate its effects on our habitat, as water seeps around the kitchen floor. Or simply putting logs on the fireplace; dramatising the need to stop using such destructive forms of heating. This in turn is visualised by the seepage of carbon into the air, as water is poured on the flames. On close inspection the miniature workers – providing the carbon energy – look somewhat perplexed, as their industry is being turned literally upside down. All of these aesthetic new media features and strategies echo the urgent need to turn off and overcome our fixation with fossil fuels for our everyday lives, while visually and symbolically illustrating how it pollutes and dissipates everywhere across the atmosphere.

The ark of Gameau's story is his journey, even pilgrimage of self-knowledge away from his family to uncover some pragmatic solutions for dealing with climate change. The answers he proposed are not fanciful, but always based on reality and at all times being feasible within today's technology.

Some of these innovative 'solutions' to climate change highlighted in the documentary include in no particular order of importance:

a   A small technical device – presuming its cheap to purchase – which allows so-called Third World countries like Pakistan and its dispersed major populations to take back control of their energy production/consumption. Basically, individual solar energy pads placed on their homes are linked to this simple smart device, which in turn allows them to buy/ sell energy to their community etc., thereby creating local grids servicing micro-communities.

b   Promoting ocean blue-pharma responses and reactivating our seas by supporting some form of techno-fix solution. This proposed solution involves using organic seaweed positioned near the surface of oceans to help bring the habitat back to life. This process can be carried out on an industrial scale and can in turn help re-nurture (re-wild) our seas and make this vast habitat more capable of again becoming an effective carbon sink.

c   Growing human populations are presented as a 'difficult problem'; but apparently this dilemma can also be addressed by 'educating our girls' across the world and encouraging them not to get pregnant until later in life and thereby produce less children. Nonetheless, to counter the accusation that this strategy feels like a white-saviour colonial discourse; the documentary frequently uses vox pop close-ups of several mainly black/ Asian children, who speak from the heart concerning what they want for their future. These authentic innocent voices constantly affirms the need to treat our planet better. Population growth remains a controversial issue, but since a typical family in America or Europe will likely have a much bigger impact on climate change than a much larger family in Bengal or any developing world country, it is certainly not such a clear cut issue.

d   Other more 'conventional' solutions to climate change, include the use of driverless electric cars, which are not necessarily owned by customers, but hired and leased out instead. Such a process helps towards reimagining huge amounts of space that are otherwise reserved for parked cars, with 'spaghetti junction' type urban motorways becoming disused and affording evidence of 're-wilding', with organic-type nature parks, walkways and even encouraging the growth of food production across their urban and now wasted spaces.

e   The documentary also promotes moving from big-business agri-farms, which ruin the land with artificial fertilisers and require huge amounts of grain to fatten cattle for instance, to more sustainable agriculture, which remains a common plea to the food industry. It's a misnomer that big agriculture is required to feed the world, since apparently this only accounts for less than a quarter of total global food consumption. Most food is still produced by relatively small farmers, who are part of the solution and not the problem.

f   Flight shame; the narrator calls out the downright hypocrisy of using extensive travel and flights to make his own eco-documentary, not to mention drinking coffee from plastic cups that will eventually harm the seas. However, at least by using contemporary media production best practice, Gameau seeks to 'offset' the material and resource cost of his fascinating documentary, through a range of ethical environmental solutions.

g   Gameau constantly talks of the need for behavioural change and draws on the so-called 'Doughnut model', as laid out by Kate Raworth (2017). This radical economic theory becomes the model referred to several times, as the documentary develops its hypothesis for coping with the ever-decreasing limitations of planetary boundaries. Meanwhile, other experts are literally 'down-sized' as an aesthetic strategy to symbolically put them in their place, as they provide the bespoke 'objective science' and commentary on various aspects of best practice within environmental communications and climate science.

This uplifting Australian eco-documentary seemed a long way from the awful and unprecedented bush fires burning in southern Australia in late 2019, which consumed an area over twice the size of Ireland, decimating native animal and plant species and killing a number of people in the midst of 40 degree Celsius temperatures and high winds fanning the flames. Much less recognising ongoing climate and natural disasters across the planet during

2020 and 2021, which show no sign of abating. The first-hand reality of climate change is never far from the surface and we certainly need to double our efforts in communicating all aspects of the climate crisis.

References

Brereton, Pat. 'An Eco-reading of Documentary/Fictional Narratives'. *Irish Studies in International Affairs* 1(1): 43–58. 2020.
Bukmaster, Luke. 'Review of Documentary 2040'. *The Guardian*. 4 April 2019.
Raworth, K. (2017) *Doughnut Economics: Seven Ways to Think Like a 21st Century Economist*. Chelsea Green Publishing.

Critical Theory and Environmental Communications

Such theorising was originally conceived as a form of intellectual resistance to more establishment-based political and social developments within Europe in the 1930s onwards and was instigated through the scholarly work of intellectuals like Jurgen Habermas, Michel Foucault and others. While in America the term is often simply perceived as a short-hand for various forms of left-leaning Marxism. In essence, critical theory provides a coherent form of analysis of social, political and economic life, which in turn uncovers a fuller appreciation of the ideological forces that govern individuals and everyday citizens' existence. Critics suggest that such broad theorising approaches remains somewhat crude and does not focus on the actual intricacies of individual media texts for example. Remaining preoccupied with dominant ideologically framed metanarratives, which make up the majority of media output, such theorising tends to focus on generalisable overall patterns that can be detected from a broad analysis of media output. Later so-called post-structuralists like Jacques Derrida developed a more questioning approach around such theorising, believing it to be too schematic and top-down, regarding media/communication and cultural artefacts generally.

In a 2018 study of key critical thinkers within environmental communications, Murdock Stephens highlights how scholars like Peter Sloterdijk, Bruno Latour, Slavoj Zizek and Timothy Morton, all affirm that the concept of environmental risk, urgency and science in general are tangled up with the need for political and institutional change. Furthermore, all these very different scholars, can be interrogated as actively dealing with 'the struggles between belief and doubt about climate change and the burgeoning urgency of acting to confront the ecological crisis' (Stephens 2018: 1). While the Frankfurt School used capitalism as the major object of critique, Stephens study focuses on all aspects of the climate crisis, while at the same time upholding a level of philosophical scepticism towards fixed meanings and approaches. 'The particularities of climate change as an urgent crisis offers a fresh and unique terrain for the consideration of questions within the critical traditions' (Stephens 2018: 1).

Meanwhile, Robert Cox (2007) defined environmental communications in an opening issue of the journal, *Environmental Communication*, as being a sub-field within a crisis discipline, based on conservation biology, which in turn had a clear ethical duty of care. More recently, other scholars have highlighted greater tensions within the discipline, with for instance Alison Anderson (2015) suggesting that the emancipatory struggles for social change are also central to the process of becoming critically engaged with, and demonstrating how knowledge can challenge this highly tuned practice. Most notably this approach can be perceived through

> two persistent aspects which govern environmental communication: a) focusing on the enormous environmental devastation wrought by human actions and b) suspicion that the previous tools used by environmental communication are insufficient, if not complicit, in the problems of the first aspiration.
>
> (Salvador and Clarke 2011: 243)

All of these and other framing critiques seem to be constantly caught between scepticism and emancipatory politics. For instance, before the end of the Cold War, Peter Sloterdijk in his 1988 volume *Critique of Cynical Reason*, defined the spirit of the times as one of 'cynicism or enlightened false consciousness'(5). More recently, Slavoj Zizek perceived the ecological clash as similar to the clash humanity has always fought against capital, but this time being theorised as the need to fight against attempts to privatise each of the primary resource commons – all of which are underpinned by what he characterises as a politics of anti-capitalism.

Meanwhile, for environmental scholars like Tim Morton, such reflexive debate and theorising should be welcomed in a time of crisis – recalling his seminal work *Hyper Objects* (2013), which is discussed elsewhere and which can be defined as an entity/object existing outside of the usual time and space perception that guide human life. Most significantly, using such a critical train of thought, the problem of global warming/climate change is perceived as similar to engaging with a giant reflexive (hyper)object, much less dealing with the ongoing vagaries of the capitalist project. By all accounts, environmental communicators need to take such conceptualising of planetary objects and theorising seriously, as further echoed by Bruno Latour and other contemporary critical scholars.

References

Anderson, Alison. 'Reflections on Environmental Communication and the Challenges of New Research Agenda'. *Environmental Communication* 9(3): 379–383. 2015.

Cox, Robert. 'Nature's "Crisis Discipline": Does Environmental Communication have an Ethical Duty'. *Environmental Communication* 1(1): 5–20. 2007.

Morton, Tim. *Hyperobjects: Philosophy and Ecology after the End of the World*. University of Minnesota Press 2013.

Stephens, Murdock. *Critical Environmental Communication*. Lexington Books 2018.

Salvador, Michael and Clarke, Traeylee. 'The Weyekin Principle: Towards an Embodied Critical Rhetoric'. *Environmental Communication A Journal of Nature and Culture* 3(3): 243–260. 2011.

Sloterdijk, Peter. *Critique of Cynical Reason*. University of Minnesota Press 1988.

Critique of Historical Western Consumer Capitalism – Case Study of *A Christmas Carol* (BBC 1, Christmas 2019), adapted by Steven Knight (creator of *Peaky Blinders*)

Focusing on capitalism and its effects on natural environments and ecosystems which have a long history of scholarly analysis. This reading will serve to illustrate this ongoing (Left-leaning) critique of early Industrial Revolution Britain in particular and its influences on the current climate crisis – with the expediential growth of carbon-wasteful industry that has become such a crisis dilemma of late. We can allude to such a history by looking back to popular Christian allegories written by Charles Dickens and his universal story 'A Christmas Carol', which is reconceived and rebooted for a contemporary and hopefully more environmentally literate televisual audience.

This cutting-edge BBC adaptation begins with the question not often asked by such an ever-green fairy-tale; why is Scrooge like that in the first place? It could almost be read as a post-Brexit critique of the pervasive nature of neo-liberal capitalism, with a radical new character study, while applying an innovative mode of measuring and engaging with people anchored in a specific historical period. In response to such difficult questioning, Stephen Knight (2019) 'decided to make Scrooge (Guy Pearce) a handsome man in his prime. I wanted the audience to see him and then experience his character and ask the central question for themselves'. Knight also changed the nature of Scrooge and Marley's business to reflect industrial society at that pivotal historical period, which was focused on exploiting workers in the mines and not worrying about their safety. This early 19th century form of capitalist enterprise was also involved in selling off whole industries, like textiles, simply to make a fast buck. The visualisation and haunting memories and nightmares of these exploitive industries which persist up to the present day are very well captured and visualised in this short mini-series. Consequently, this latest adaptation is an attempt, not simply to insert a contemporary political point-of-view, but to actively show how some of Scrooge's extreme views were historically rooted and 'part of the economic engine that drove an Empire'. Hence the main protagonist's flawed persona can be read as simply an embodied manifestation of the capitalist spirit of the age, which unfortunately persists right up to the present day – with dire environmental consequences.

Meanwhile, in the public imagination, Scrooge is Santa's dark reflection, a non-believer whose cynicism is trounced by supernatural agents acting on behalf of cheer and goodwill and kindness. Knight draws on Scrooge's past as a vehicle to 'explain' his psychological behaviour, which in turn is provided as a justification for his actions. His father appeared to 'sell' him for (sexual) services to the school master over the Christmas break, in return for free fees. But thankfully his sister and mother took him out of such a dreadful place. Unfortunately, the troubled boy does not appear to have learned from such experiences, especially regarding the proper treatment of others, and alternatively fits in well as a driven captain of early anti-environmental industrial enterprise. Most cynically later for instance he puts poor Mrs Cratchit (Vinette Robinson) through the moral and ethical torture of having to succumb to a pernicious 'experiment'; simply wishing to prove *all* humans have a 'price'.

Nonetheless, the long-standing Christmas, if not Christian, message is clear – while adding further environmental impact – humans need to support the greater common good and not just remain focused on their own financial success. Incidentally, as it turned out, 2020 became the year of the pandemic; which has certainly tested this binary tension between selfish industrial wealth, as against promoting the common good of the community, invoking tensions that became more prescient across the world than any other time in living memory. The adaptor's (admittedly pre-COVID) intention in creating such a provocative storyline highlights that Christmas itself should not come out of this unscathed. This cautionary tale name checks the idiotic commercialism, the fake goodwill, alongside the family pressure cooker of personal relationships – all nested into this winter festival. The erstwhile utopian dream of Christmas with its excessive consumption of food and celebration of compassion has even more importance of late, as the world faces up to wars, extreme poverty and pandemics, not to mention the ongoing climate crisis, where paradoxically more equity, kindness and at the same time frugality at all levels is required. Scrooge himself, of course, would call such worries and concern 'humbug' (Knight 2019).

This three-part series powerfully calls attention to the dark side of our modern exploitative and late-capitalist-based economy, where raw wealth and its trappings are apparently promoted and valorised, no matter what the cost. An allegorical and cautionary lesson, which has become especially pertinent in the face of the terrors of climate change, pandemics and the prospect of global financial recessions. Meanwhile, contemporary populist political leaders of the period; from Trump in America, Johnson in the UK and Bolsonaro in Brazil and others beside these, emote various permutations of 'humbug' in the face of all these catastrophic environmental challenges. Hence such evergreen Christmas fare functions most effectively as a cautionary and allegorical tale for the times we live in.

Reference

Knight, Steven. 'Meet my Scrooge'. *Sunday Times* 5–7. 22 December 2019.

D

De-growth: Radical Solutions for Climate Change Stability

Degrowth is a term that signifies radical political and economic reorganisation leading to drastically reduced resource and energy throughput. Related scholarship in this growing area of debate; critiques the (capitalist) ideology behind the dogma of regulating continuous economic growth and contributes to a critical investigation of the material, social, and ecological effects of growth, as well as uncovering alternatives to growth-based development. Essentially, degrowth asserts that it is possible to organise a transition and live well under a different political-economic system to the current capitalist-driven model. Such an alternative model supports a radically smaller resource throughput, as against remaining tied to any growth model of development.

The movement began in the early 2000s when activists in Lyon, France, mobilised the slogan D'ecroissance (Degrowth) as a form of direct action and was used for framing publications against the use of cars, consumerism and various forms of advertising. The term was explored and developed through several essays by physicist-economist Nicholas Georgescu Roegen who, in the 1970s and 1980s, developed a thermodynamic theory of economic processes. He concluded that in the long run, economic activity will inevitably decrease to a more sustainable level that can be supportive of all members of society. The concept was subsequently adapted by political activists across France, Italy and Spain, as well as other parts of Europe.

All the while, the more dominant and conventional growth paradigm refers to what most economists consider as normative and good for all society. Scholars like Giorgos Kallis et al. (2020) affirm that such economic models have become normalised, naturalised and legitimised, or using Marxist terminology, which have become hegemonic over time. Yet surprisingly this has been a relatively recent phenomenon with various consequences, including the separation and even mystification of the economy as only knowable by experts. For instance, Heinz W. Arndt's *The Rise and Fall of Economic Growth* (1984) remains a classic history of the concept of growth by British and American economists. From an ecological perspective, capitalist economies grow by using more natural resources, alongside calling on the labour of

DOI: 10.4324/9781003123422-5

workers. All in turn are used to maximise output for capitalist gain. Accelerating this process is unlikely to spare the despoilation of precious natural materials and resources. Nonetheless, so-called natural resources – like water, soil, air, together with extractive minerals especially based on oil, alongside all the combined flora and fauna of the planet – are usually not monetised as so-called natural capital in determining the 'real exchange cost' of resource (and service) production. (See *Natural Capital as a Business Response in dealing with Climate Change*.)

Growth can nevertheless become 'cleaner and greener' by substituting fossil fuels with solar or wind power, as well as replacing scarce resource metals dug out of the ground with less harmful alternatives to carbon-based products. Nonetheless, such natural substitutes still have their own resource threshold and life-cycle impacts that can alternatively have further, often unintended, environmental implications into the future.

As Kallis et al. (2020) argue, ending the use of fossil fuels is likely to reduce labour productivity and eventually limit global output. Meanwhile, solar and wind power are alternatively constrained primarily by their rate of flow and storage capacity difficulties; limitations, which are being addressed at present. Unlike fossil fuels, such energy systems are diffuse and function more like rain, wind and sunshine. An economy powered by a diffuse renewable energy flow is more likely to be an economy of lower net energy and lower output than one powered by concentrated stocks. Furthermore, land use for solar or wind also competes with the primary use of land for food production. Rare, extracted materials also continue to be required in supporting all types of economic productivity.

Abandoning so-called conventional modes of economic growth seems politically, if not economically, improbable in the current dominant western political and economic system. Yet the major transformation resulting from the 2020–21 pandemic demonstrates that such radical change and repurposing of economic activity is possible. Long-established modes of production and economic practice can radically change and relatively quickly. Nonetheless, big business and industrial-funded enterprise, together with the work of many scientists and politicians, seem to support policy and technological fixes that strive to make growth ongoing and sustainable, rather than ever considering managing systems without continuous growth, much less adapting some more revolutionary model of degrowth.

Normalising environmentally centred models of development like the circular economy – discussed in detail across several entries – infer that a fixed notion of degrowth versus all types of growth need no longer be at the centre of discussion, but can instead be linked to a range of more equitable and sustainable principles. Kallis et al. (2020) suggest that we can make gains in this area through ensuring for example that 'vital resources, infrastructures, and spaces are shared and held in common; technology (becomes) convivial and serves social purposes; resource throughput is minimized; and working hours are reduced by cutting consumption, production, and wasteful expenditures' (Kallis et al. 2020: 308). The broad-based literature around a degrowth philosophy and economic model is becoming less blue skies, and is evolving beyond a form of abstract utopian expression, while being concurrently examined across the academic and most importantly within the political spectrum. But how to harmonise ongoing debates and tensions between the polarising extremes of 'degrowth' and 'green growth' will remain a constant preoccupation over the coming years, as society strives to face up to the ever-expanding climate crisis. By all accounts, amplification of such debates by media and communications will have a major role to play into the future, but through explaining, leveraging, and alternatively promoting these very different economic possibilities, more creative futures can be envisaged.

References

Heinz, W. Arnd. *The Rise and Fall of Economic Growth: A Study in Contemporary Thought.* University of Chicago Press 1984.
Kallis, Giorgos *et al.* 'Research on De-Growth'. *Journal Annual Review* 291–316. June 2020 https://www.annualreviews.org/doi/pdf/10.1146/annurev-environ-102017-025941

Democratic Deficit: From Techno-fix to Gaia – The War Narrative

Trying to build consensus in promoting a just transition to a low-carbon future, does not appear in the short term at least to be in the interest of many in the western world. According to some political and environmental experts, such as John Dryzek and John Barry, this leads to suggestions that democratic systems and politics are not effective in making the necessary structural changes to society at large. Frustrated by this so-called democratic deficit with political disappointments building over the decades, while trying to address the challenge of climate change, many including authors like David Wallace-Wells in *The Uninhabited Earth: Life after Warming* (2019), consider technological innovation (or 'quick fixes') as being simply too late and certainly not the best hope of addressing the massive environmental problems humanity faces.

Most recently the co-founder of the multinational computer and information technology company Microsoft, and now retired multi-millionaire and global philanthropist Bill Gates has published his prognosis in *How to Avoid Climate Disaster* (2021). This readable volume outlines how new technologies can be mainstreamed, towards developing a full transition to a low-carbon future. But of course technological innovation and its limitations needs to be recognised and understood as being predominantly only beneficial for a small minority, or as a way to bypass the failures of democratic politics, while at the same time a necessary part of a process towards a sustainable low-carbon future.

Meanwhile, environmentalist James Lovelock has also helped to reframe more fruitful system thinking through his Gaia theory (1972). Lovelock believes that the Earth remains a huge self-regulating organism. Unfortunately, in his view humankind is literally not smart enough to come to grips with the ever-extending and massive problems encapsulated by climate change. As he puts it in a *Guardian* interview and review by Leo Hickman, 'I don't think we are yet evolved enough to the point where we're clever enough to handle a situation as complex as climate change'. Lovelock concludes this hypothesis by affirming that the 'inertia of humans' and the inherent weakness across a range of democratic systems of governance is so huge that you 'can't really do anything meaningful' (Lovelock 2010).

Consequently, adopting this very pessimistic stance, many concur that the climate crisis needs to be put on a permanent war footing if real change and transformation is to occur. Lovelock argues that even 'the best democracies agreed that when a major war approaches, democracies must be put on hold for the time being. I have a feeling that climate change may be an issue as severe as war' (Lovelock 2010). Unfortunately however, as we know from history, war tends to polarise opinion and ideological positions, while often ignoring issues of equality and justice, all the while demanding clearly defined enemies. For all these reasons, the war narrative remains very difficult to square with the complicated interactive nature of dealing with the sometimes slow but ever-expanding environmental problems; not to mention recognising how we as humans are ostensibly deemed the 'enemy' within such a conflict scenario (Brereton 2020: 58–59).

In recent years, scholars continue to impugn the inherent weakness and slow grinding change for the common good, using 'the sacred cow of democracy' (Westra 1993: 128). In Westra's view, liberal democracy is in part responsible for the ecological crisis, rather than being simply constituting part of the solution. It is unlikely, she argues, that the citizens of such democracies will 'freely embrace the choices that would severely curtail their usual freedoms and rights … even in the interests of long-term health and self-preservation' (Humphrey 2007: 198). Alongside other experts, she calls for a global top-down regulatory scientific-based expert commission that should have a direct role in benevolently ensuring the ecological future of life on the planet (55). It could be suggested that the global as well as national strategies called on, while dealing with the 2020/21 pandemic echo this authoritarian and scientific-driven war-strategy framework.

Consequently, the slow pace of democratic transformation could be offset by a scientifically driven form of global governance, together with the adaptation of a war-like narrative, to help ignite and communicate more direct and speeded-up responses to climate change. Somewhat surprisingly, reminiscent of Lovelock cited earlier, the renowned British sociologist Anthony Giddens (2009) makes a plea for removing climate change policy away from politics altogether and separately placing it in the hands of a more expert-oriented centralised planning process, geared specifically to achieving a number of ecological goals.

Recalling and returning in ways to Plato's call for rule by 'philosopher kings', such an authoritarian and direct approach highlights the inherent weakness of contemporary liberal democracy, substituting rule by a (hopefully benevolent) system of technocratic governance. Decoupling environmental protection from social change, certainly remains the core proposition of Giddens, who further criticises the relevance of a bottom-up environmental movement, contending that it remains overly value-oriented, instead of focused on the specific problem(s) at hand. In a view that seems to contradict aspects of his earlier writings, Giddens complains that environmentalism is grounded in 'life politics', which he defined in previous writings as being a reflexive understanding of humankind's relationship to nature (see review in Thorpe and Jacobson 2013).

Other debates around deep environmentalism and its operational efficiency, coupled with an increasing role for scientific leadership in becoming a new form of fundamentalist religious practice, have come to the fore. All the while, such high-risk strategies have several long-term consequences and call out other inherent dangers that need to be addressed, some of which can be illustrated through the application of the war narrative.

Using the War Narrative to Help Address the So-called Democratic Deficit

Over the years the war narrative has been used to build political consensus in emergencies and to promote a strong sense of patriotism, using provocative storylines that encourage identification with heroes and their heroic plights, not to mention rationing of goods and services. It is argued that war in all its manifestations – including environmental science fictional allegories like *Avatar* (2009), or at a stretch, *The Day after Tomorrow* (2004) – serve to focus attention and actively engage audiences in supporting the war effort. Basically, you are either for or against a war scenario and cannot easily stand on the fence, conscientious objectors notwithstanding. At present, living through the pandemic of 2020/21, such a war metaphor is constantly in evidence, illustrating how the crisis was framed and dealt with. This global emergency witnessed nightly on news broadcasts, concentrated on comparing how countries and its citizens were coping with the struggle, all the while recounting the casualties. The notion of being all in this together, facing a deadly enemy remained the dominant discourse across much media coverage. Sometimes however fractures appeared in this consensus, as the media tends to slip into local inflections and raising fundamental concerns around health, while being pitted against the economy and ongoing worries over global financial survival.

Meanwhile, the slow-moving climate emergency, which has been with us for decades gets pushed to the background, apparently lacking the 'life-death' immediacy of war. At any rate, recounting the limitations of democratic (deficit) politics, little appears to change in the long run. As might be crudely articulated, unlike a conventional war where opposing sides and tactics are clearly laid out, in this environmental struggle, humans are front and centre constituted as causing the problem, if not being the default enemy, and therefore the struggle remains harder to address.

Recalling for instance science fictional and virus-focused war narratives, like in well-known Hollywood films such as T*he Andromeda Strain* (1971), *Contagion* (2011) and *World War Z* (2013), which also paradoxically addresses real fears of a deadly virus and the global war-like response to such disaster. These fictional narratives foreground the potential growth of dangerous viruses and assist audiences in comprehending global environmental fears for our safety, while outlining how society might cope in the future with such difficult realities. Such globally framed conflictual narratives in turn can help viewers grasp the most important challenges facing humanity at present. But how can such war parables be further repurposed and speak to our ongoing struggles with climate change? Arts and humanities, alongside business and politics have an important role to play in helping to create more effective creative imaginaries along these lines, as well as foregrounding practical solution in dealing with such pervasive and ongoing struggles.

Promoting radical paradigm shifts in thinking is essential, alongside supporting systemic and individual behaviour change, not to mention adapting new modes of scientific and economic activity in facing up to the challenges of the climate crisis. All of these elements can be suggested and embodied through powerful narratives, and used as an effective mode of mass communication. One wonders for instance if the 2020/21 pandemic over time can serve as a cautionary forewarning and concrete exemplification of the urgent need for such radical global transformation. Can such a traumatic virus be effective in acting as a tipping point towards transforming a reluctant citizenry, who often rail against major change. When it comes to practical environmental actions that affect day-to-day living, most citizens remain somewhat reluctant in putting their shoulder to the wheel. In other words, how to avoid almost by default of returning to a 'business as usual' mode of habitual high-carbon based living, when the pandemic crisis appears to be finally overcome. At all times, the global political apparatus, recalling worries around the so-called democratic deficit, linked to the preservation of business-as-usual models, alongside education, media and the arts all need to be urgently co-opted in the fight to uncover new ways of promoting social, political and environmental transformation, while at the same time maintaining social cohesion, as the world pivots towards a low-carbon transition.

References

Brereton, Pat 'Could the War Metaphor Help Drive Behavioural Change to Tackle the Climate Crisis?'. *Profit with Purpose*. Dublin City Council. 2020.

Gates, Bill. *How to avoid Climate Disaster*. Alfred Knopf Publishers 2021.

Giddens, Anthony and Sutton, Philip. *Sociology*. Polity Press 2009.

Humphrey, Matthew. *Ecological Politics and Democratic Theory: The Challenge to the Deliberate Ideal*. Routledge 2007.

Lovelock, James. 'James Lovelock: Humans are Too Stupid to Prevent Climate Change'. *The Guardian*. 29 March 2010. https://www.theguardian.com/science/2010/mar/29/james-lovelock-climate-change

Lovelock, James. 'Gaia as Seen Through the Atmosphere'. *Atmospheric Environment* 6: 579–580. 1972.

Thorpe, Charles and Jacobson, Brynna. 'Life Politics, Nature and the State: Giddens' Sociological Theory and the Politics of Climate Change'. *British Journal of Sociology*. 2013.

Wallace-Wills, David. *The Uninhabited Earth: Life After Warming.* Tim Duggan Books 2019.

Westra, Laura. 'The Ethics of Environmental Holism and the Democratic State: are they in conflict?'. *Environmental Values* 2(2): 125–136. 1993.

E

Ecological Modernism and Sustainable Development: Our Common Future in Crisis

As science communications and journalism scholar Declan Fahy affirms in a chapter on Ireland's weak layers of eco-modernism, 'ecological modernisation, or ecomodernism, or eco-restructuring, is a theory of social change that describes the process of sustainable development' (Fahy 2020: 131). Fahy argues that 'economic development can proceed in tandem with ecological protection'. More fundamentally, such a proposition suggests that 'economic growth depends on the preservation of the environment, the material base of society, and the provider of natural resources on which human society depends' (ibid.: 131–148). This evolving concept remains totally opposed to the philosophy around de-growth or de-modernisation, which alternatively argues that the best or only way to address environmental problems is to slow down or even halt economic growth. Ecomodernism rejects such apocalyptic visions of the future and perceives environmental problems as simply challenges that can in turn catalyse systemic and productive social reform. A clear set of ideas that constitute eco-modernist thought was developed by European sociologists in the 1980s and these ideas were codified in the 1987 UN report *Our Common Future* – usually referred to as the Brundtland Report after its chair, former Norwegian Prime Minister Gro Harlem Brundtland.

This remains a landmark document in the history of sustainable development, which it defined as 'development that meets the needs of the present without compromising the ability of future generations to meet their own needs' (UN World Commission on Environment and Development 1987: 41). Written before the full realisation of climate change's consequences, its authors noted that it 'is not a prediction of ever-increasing environmental decay, poverty, and hardship in an ever more polluted world among ever decreasing resources. We see instead the possibility of a new era of economic growth, one that must be based on policies that sustain and expand the environmental resource base' (UN World Commission on Environment and Development 1987: 1).

In order for such a sustainable society to develop, eco-modernists argue that political and economic systems must be reformed along ecological lines.

DOI: 10.4324/9781003123422-6

This means all the core systems and institutions of modern society – market economies, industrial production, welfare states, agricultural production and scientific and technological institutions – must be restructured to protect their precious environment. As a large-scale theory of social change, eco-modernism examines and explains how these systems and institutions of modern societies can be reformed. As a specific political programme, eco-modernism can be regarded as direct policies that seek to conserve the environment. For the political environmental scholar John Dryzek most notably, eco-modernism aims to reform, not to replace the capitalist economic system. It aims at nothing less, he wrote (2013: 145), than 'the ecological restructuring of capitalism'.

There is a growing tension across such discussion, which is constantly referred to in several entries in this volume between so-called 'green growth', which can be characterised as a more acceptable mode of modern development, as against more radical left-leaning 'no-growth' or de-growth approaches, which call for the end of neo-liberal, much less eco-modern capitalism. Basically, those who call for degrowth believe reformism of established systems are considered too little and probably too late in facing up to the global climate emergency.

For a radical critique of eco-modernism and conventional green political approaches, John Barry (Queens University, Ireland) provides a provocative analysis in a paper from October 2020. Barry talks of himself in clear terms as a 'left-libertarian (verging on anarchist) with a normative predisposition towards non-state institutions and practices', which in turn calls attention to his very forthright green political writing and activism. At the outset of his polemical essay, Barry (2020) affirms that the system of liberal representative democracy within a market-based capitalist system is simply incapable of adequately and equitably responding to the planetary emergency we face. Most pointedly he asserts how 'the system is not broken – it is made that way'! Accepting this proposition, Barry suggests that 'we have to transcend liberal democratic capitalism' (98), without necessary clarifying the roadmap to follow, much less outlining the full implications of such a radical position, which of course is difficult to assess.

Somewhat dismissively, much of the ecological modernist project is seen as 'wishful thinking – recalling the dominance of techno-optimism, as modes of framing solutions to the climate crisis', not to mention calling up 'policy thinking within the state' (Barry 2020: 99). Recounting well-versed, but by all accounts science fiction-like proposals for carbon capture and sequestration or solar radiation, Barry cites the eccentric mega-entrepreneur Elon Musk and his dreams of colonising Mars, as being like many of these half-baked proposals – 'off the radar'. Incidentally, in July 2021 while the pandemic was still raging, there was extensive media coverage of Richard Branson's Virgin Atlantic space tourism experiment, followed closely by his rival Jeff Bezos's Amazon trip to space – which by any measure could also be characterised as 'off the radar'. At the same time for many entrepreneurial citizens, more 'down to earth' yet radical views concerning the need to transition beyond capitalism and liberal democracy can appear, albeit secretly at least, for many well-healed citizens of planet earth – off the radar.

Most pointedly and interestingly, Barry calls for accepting a plurality of voices – beyond the dominant ecological modernist approach – especially within Irish and global thinking:

- Any 'just transition' to a post-carbon, post-capital society will produce 'winners and losers', this in turn necessitates conflict across transformation process and within any sustainability transformative process.
- Furthermore, such dissent and disagreement needs to be recognised and included in any process, instead of being marginalised or suppressed.
- Oppositional, non-conformist and sometimes an outright confrontation characterisation of such non-state actors, often contain the energy and insight for greater improvement and social progress (Barry 2020: 99).

By all accounts, Barry is correct in recognising little evidence – unlike in dealing with the 2020/21 pandemic – of governments making hard decisions concerning climate change. Querying, why our politicians do heed the science regarding COVID-19, but not regarding climate change, remains an important discussion point into the future. Most environmentalists would agree with Barry that this form of cognitive dissonance is encouraged by the belief that there are no fixed, not to say easy solutions to the climate emergency/crisis, only adaptive and ongoing coping strategies and these have to be negotiated over a much longer period of time. Meanwhile, government bailouts following the shock and urgent necessity to cope with the 2020/21 global pandemic, need to be further reimagined and re-used, according to Barry and others, to help create a 'sustainable, climate resilient, post-carbon, post-growth and post-capitalist economy' (Barry 2020: 104).

Certainly much more radical thinking and reimagining of how to effectively deal with the ongoing environmental crisis needs to be fuelled by well-thought out environmental communication processes and protocols. There are unfortunately no simple Right/Left, much less ecological modernist or quick fix solutions that can address all our environmental and climate crisis concerns. Most certainly, credit needs to be given to the insightful work of Barry and others in rethinking future scenarios for dealing with the almost insurmountable challenges that need to be faced while fully addressing the climate crisis.

References

Barry, John. 'The Planetary Crisis; Brexit and the Pandemic'. *The Journal of Cross Boarder Studies in Ireland*: 97–108. 2020. https://crossborder.ie/site2015/wp-content/uploads/2020/09/Final-Digital-Journal-Cross-Border-Studies.pdf

Dryzek, John. *The Politics of the Earth: Environmental Discourses*. Oxford University Press. 2013.

Fahy, Declan. 'Ecological Modernisation, Irish-Style: Explaining Ireland's Slow Transition to Low-Carbon Society' (131–148). In Robbins, D., Torney, D. and Brereton, P. (eds.) *Ireland and the Climate Crisis*. Palgrave Macmillan 2020.

UN World Commission on Environment and Development. *Bruntland Report: Our Common Future*. United Nations 1987.

Eco-villages – Case Study of Cloughjordan: An Irish Transitional and Sustainable Project

In coping with so much negative analysis of the effects of climate change, we need practical illustrations of how to build low-carbon, resilient communities. The development of so-called eco-villages provides examples of how such communities can work in practice. The Irish rural eco-village of Cloughjordan, located in County Tipperary, provides one such case study. The village houses 55 dwellings and was initially built with a population of 100 adults and 35 children. It is now considered within Europe as one of the 23 most successful 'anticipatory experiences', showing the way to create a low carbon society.

The small community achieves this accolade by essentially integrating with the natural environment, while at the same time promoting new modes of biodynamic food production and farming. A final third of the site is devoted to woodland with 17,000 trees planted in 2011 that mainly consist of native species like Oak, Ash, Scots Pine, Birch, Rowan, Cherry, Hazel and Alder.

The eco-village supports communal work on the land and recalls the active celebration of an old-Irish mode of community cooperation called 'Meitheal'; using low-energy technologies and robust as well as sustainable forms of community living. An image showing the community building houses with wood, reminds one of the Amish community in America and fictional representations like the Peter Weir film *Witness* (1985), which was analysed in (Brereton 2011).

The eco-village also revolutionised its energy output, using a distinctive heating system powered by renewable energy sources. They also kick-started the first community supported agricultural farm (CSA), which in 2020/21 grew four acres of vegetables, as well as an acre of cereal and green manure (humus building), with over six acres left in permanent pasture. Such a communal mode of food production and consumption embodies a sustainable template for post-commodification and post-supermarket exchange of food scenarios, where the members pay a modest monthly fee per family for all their needs. For a full analysis of the pros and cons of this ongoing experiment, see a historical overview by one of its founders, Peadar Kirby (2020: 287–305).

By any measure this is a tangible model for environmental media communication students to visit and learn more about. The eco-village is focused around local food production, farming energy conservation and communal living. In modern Ireland, such practices are all but lost or forgotten. In turn this very practical example feeds off a primary environmental media concern around how to reimagine sustainable living, while making a virtue out of old, often disused rural practices, together with various modes of sustainable resilience. This often-frugal philosophy in turn helps promote a key environmental literacy message around connecting with *all* citizens, beyond the bubble of committed environmentalists and activists working in an evangelical and political way. Such a community which has an active educational agenda is essential for environmental communication students and society in general to basically touch and feel what a sustainable community actually embodies. Urban dwellers certainly need far more on the ground and organic models and 'creative imaginaries', featuring successful stories that show the way towards creating a post-carbon future.

Eco-villages embody and actively serve as a beacon of hope for a future low transitional carbon society. Reminiscent of pro-active museums or heritage centres (see entry elsewhere), including those sites that promote new forms of eco-tourism, such nature-based habitats replicate many core aspects of the paradigm shift needed in moving to a more environmentally sustainable future society.

References

Brereton, Pat. 'An Ecological Approach to the Cinema of Peter Weir'. *Quarterly Review of Film and Video* 28(2): 120–134. 2011.

Kirby, Peadar. 'Cloughjordan Ecovillage: Community-led Transitioning to a Low Carbon Future' (287–304). In Robbins, David *et al.* (eds) *Ireland and the Climate Crisis*. Palgrave 2020.

Ecocriticism and the Growth of Environmental Communication

Ecocriticism, as an academic concept and process, basically involves uncovering the environmental theme or preoccupations embedded within various forms of arts, including literature and film. It has traditionally been attached to high art and more recently popular culture including film, while frequently emphasising aesthetic, ethical and activist traditions within various societies around the world. Meanwhile, environmental communications embedded in the social sciences has tended to lean towards practical issues, manifested especially within environmental journalism, together with the sociology and historical mapping of such counter-cultural movements and their effects on society.

The term ecocriticism was first coined in 1978, and took off in the mid-1990s, as a sub-discipline within the global English literature curricula. Of course there were many earlier iterations examined in David Mazell's *A Century of Eco-criticism*, with key texts including Leo Marx's *The Machine in the Garden* (1964) and Cheryll Glotfelty and Harold Fromm's *The Eco-critical Reader*, which became a landmark in literary ecology from 1996. From a literary perspective, Lawrence Buell's *The Future of Environmental Criticism: Environmental Crisis and Literary Imagination* (2005) explores the difficulty of mapping the field, as it tries to encompass so many disparate areas.

More recent edited publications include Ken Hiltner's (2015) *Anthology of Eco-Criticism: The Essential Reader,* and Scott Slovic's (2010) *The Third Wave of Ecocriticism: North American Reflections on the Current Phase of the Discipline,* alongside the *Companion to Environmental Studies,* edited by Noel Castree et al. (2018), which remain essential overviews for students to focus on. But as affirmed in the (2019) Routledge *Handbook of Ecocriticism and Environmental Communication* – also edited by Scott Slovic et al. – there is a growing need to move away from America-centric scholarship, towards securing a broader focus across multiple genres, extended beyond eco-masculinity for instance, to include queer ecocriticism among other new fields. One might also affirm the fruitful emergence of a post-colonial mode of eco-criticism has come to the fore, together with animality-based ecocriticism, which has been around since 2000. Most recently, a radical new form of applied and empirical audience reception eco-criticism has begun to expand the field (see Brereton and Gomez 2020). Furthermore, as intimated in the general introduction to this volume, a so-called fourth wave has begun to evolve; including a proliferation of material eco-criticism, transnational ecocriticism, eco-narratology, ecocritical animal studies, ecocriticism and information processing, alongside other new innovative strands of critical investigation.

According to Slovic et al. (2019) in their introduction to the aforementioned study, for 20 years now almost, environmental communication and ecocriticism has appeared to drift apart. This split was probably due to tensions across different academic and professional groupings and agendas within universities and research centres. Certainly, one could argue, environmental communication, as a broad-based mode of investigation, should incorporate various, even contradictory, aspects of ecocriticism into its fold. In a 2021 blog from the Rachel Carson Centre in Munich Germany titled, 'Why ecocritics needs the social sciences and vice versa' (Schneider-Mayerson et al. 2021), the authors use a photograph of a train track to characterise ecocriticism and environmental communications. Both disciplines are going in the same direction and have the same aims and objectives, but appear not to overlap at any stage. While I might take issue with such a clear division, one would generally agree that ecocriticism presumes that the texts it studies has a significant impact on readers and the world at large. Nonetheless, there is a growing movement to find convergence with environmental communications – as evidenced in the special issue (27) of 'Interdisciplinary Studies in Literature and Environment' (*ISLE*), edited by these same authors in 2020 – with a call for empirical forms of ecocriticism, drawing on social science methodologies. 'We are arguing that ecocriticism ought to rely on (if not conduct) social scientific research for causal claims relating to reception, yet we are not suggesting that ecocritics should only study the impact of environmental narratives on their audiences, or that empirical approaches are more important than other forms of investigation' (Schneider-Mayerson et al. 2021). Certainly much can be learned within environmental communications, by a closer alignment with all aspects of ecocriticism, from literature as well as audio visual media, which this volume also seeks to highlight.

References

Brereton, P. and Gomez, V. 'Media Students, Climate Change, and YouTube Celebrities: Readings of Dear Future Generations: Sorry Video Clip'. *ISLE* 27(2): 385–405. 2020.

Buell, Lawrence. *The Future of Environmental Criticism: Environmental Crisis and Literary Imagination*. Wiley Blackwell 2005.

Castree, Noel, Hulme, Mike, and Proctor, James D. (eds). *Companion to Environmental Studies*. Routledge 2018.

Glotfelty, Cheryll and Fromm, Harold (eds). *The Eco-Critical Reader: Landmarks in Landmarks in Literary Ecology*. University of Georgia Press 1996.

Hiltner, Ken (ed.). *Eco-criticism: The Essential Reader*. Routledge 2015.

Marx, Leo. *The Machine in the Garden*. Oxford University Press 1964.

Mazell, David. *A Century of Early Eco-criticism*. University of Georgia Press 2001.

Schneider-Mayerson, M., Weak von Mossner, A., Malecki, W.P. and Hakemulder, F. 'Why Ecocritics Needs the Social Sciences and Vice Versa'. *Rachel Carson Centre*. 21 July 2021. https://seeingthewoods.org/2021/07/21/why-ecocriticism-needs-the-social-sciences-and-vice-versa/

Slovic, Scott. 'The Third Wave of Ecocriticism: North American Reflections on the Current Phase of the Discipline'. *European Journal of Literature, Culture and Environment* 1(1) 2010 https://ecozona.eu/article/view/312

Slovic, Scott *et al. Routledge Handbook of Ecocriticism and Environmental Communication*. Routledge 2019.

Eco-materialism: Case Study of the Real Environmental Cost of Media Production

As media and environmental scholar Sean Cubitt claims with casual poignancy, eco-politics is the last master-narrative (2005: 9). Certainly, identity differences and geopolitical struggle will mean nothing, if this planet becomes uninhabitable. Moving away from the conventional focus on gender, race and class representation, while drawing on a Political Economy approach, eco-materialism strives to access and investigate the concrete environmental impact of media practices. Basically such an approach moves from the aesthetics of showing nature through textual analysis, to evaluating the way in which cultural production, distribution, consumption and waste impact across a macro level. In various ways, this approach focuses on how the use of natural resources within the broader media and communications network, affect all aspects of the material reality of our planet. In particular, this approach calls attention to the acceleration of global warming and the institution of a new mode of ecological imperialism that ranges from mining of Congolese precious metals, to the assembly of smart technology in Chinese sweatshops, or to the dumping of toxic e-waste in Kenyan villages among others; all such material realities and postcolonial tensions call attention to the global importance for these on the ground and the implications of all for both humans and the environment. A number of short freely available documentaries have explored this expanding theme, including *Congo, My Precious: The Curse of the Coltan Mines in Congo* (YouTube July 2017); *Conflict Minerals, Rebels and Child Soldiers in Congo* (YouTube May 2012) as well as *Congo, Surviving: The Resource Curse* (YouTube 2020).

Within media studies, Alison Anderson's (1997) *Media, Culture and Environment* was years ahead of the curve, predating Naomi Klein's more recent environmental condemnation of capitalist industry in *Shock Doctrine: The Rise of Disaster Capitalism* (2007) and placing ecocriticism within the rising critical analysis of globalisation, arguing that environmentalism is a global problem that must be understood 'within the context of global capital, new systems of mass communication and the rise of consumer culture' (75–76).

Across this evolving field, Nadia Bozak's *The Cinematic Footprint* and Richard Maxwell and Toby Miller's *Greening the Media* (both from 2012) remain seminal studies in setting the historical scene for students. For instance, Bozak argues 'because its biophysical layers is so inextricably embedded within film's basic means of production, distribution, and reception, its effects remain as overlooked as they are complex' (2012: 11). Film and media unfortunately remains an energy-based art-format, though mostly intangible and invisible; consequently its uses of energy remains extensive and important in assessing their green footprint and thereby evaluating their importance for active environmental engagement.

According to Maxwell and Miller (2012: 26) media and computer technology impacts planetary boundaries, by addressing effects ('the earth's ability to provide resources, renewable or not, e.g. soils, forests, water, minerals, etc.) and sink functions/output effects (the ability of the earth's ecosystem to absorb and recycle waste from media technology's electrical and chemical products and processes') (cited in Lopez 2021: 152). By 2030, it is predicted that the global cloud, which services IT, but also is becoming more central in supporting all forms of new media platforms, will consume as much electricity as the entire country of Japan. Whereas in 2007 the carbon footprint of ICT's was tagged at 1%, by 2040 it is predicted to reach about 14%, half of the size of the entire transportation industry (Wilson et al. 2017). Environmental communications students in future decades will have to take on board such expediential material growth of energy, which will need to be placed in context with a critical analysis of the various forms of carbon emissions and measured against an ever-growing climate crisis.

Material Turn in Ecocriticism: Environmental Cost of Globalised Media Production

The concept of a 'material turn in ecocriticism' highlights the growing carbon footprint of so much media production, alongside its distribution and consumption, which drives an ever-increasing carbon footprint. As a consequence there is a major move to assess and measure the relative carbon footprint of all media products and services and try to find ways of reducing it, as well as recognising its importance in framing eco-textual analysis and debate. For instance, this can include assessing the relative scale of production and carbon costs embedded within big-budget Hollywood blockbusters, while also recognising their potential to communicate environmental messages to large audiences, as compared with low-budget art-house films for example. Such discussion has also begun to feed into environmental policy and management across all areas – both online and off-line.

This area of investigation exposes the increasing tensions embedded within environmental studies of the media, which is an industry that also needs to put its house in order from a carbon emissions perspective. Expanded as a sub-field within environmental media and ecocriticism, it draws on a top-down Political Economy approach to the environmental cost of resource usage, while examining the apparent greening of the media. Such an approach strives to take into account the full cycle of media production, distribution and consumption, while at the same time seeking to slow down overall consumption 'to listen to the world – empirically and imaginatively', which may be 'our only hope in a moment of crisis and urgency' (Swanson et al. 2017: M8).

The material reality of media and its make-up is certainly becoming more recognised in the literature. As Parikka (2015) explicitly asserts, 'it is the earth that provides for media and enables it: the minerals, materials of the ground, the affordances of its geophysical reality that makes technical media happen' (13). As we move around with our 'cell phones, all of us have a piece of Africa, China or South America in our pockets'. Certainly, the carbon footprint and materiality of our mobile phones, and our growing dependence on new digital media generally, when looked at from an environmental communications perspective, deserves urgent critical investigation. Building on an early study like *Greening the Media* (Maxwell and Miller 2012), which caustically cite how the 'tech industry narratives greenwash their environmental impacts', this specific mode of material investigation has grown at a pace. Nonetheless, such assertions cannot be left uncontested either and ought to be modulated and balanced against a range of debates and related business and media concerns. For instance, there is a danger of using such discussion to simply reaffirm a conventional Left-leaning, often dismissive ideological position that underpins and frames much media and communications critical analysis.

In my experience as an educator, this concern with the quest for more wealth and increasing levels of materialism has been raised by many mature and career-minded students wishing to work in companies and business enterprise across the spectrum of media production. Such concerns are certainly prevalent within the environmental communications meta-discipline; focusing explicitly on this 'materialist turn' that can help towards reimagining a best practice approach, which helps to break down the apparent schism felt between business drivers and the overarching environmental agenda. Whether it's the media industry and/or some other profit motivated industries; simply demonising commercial enterprises for their material abuse of resources is not always helpful however in winning hearts and minds and securing the radical transformation necessary towards addressing this ongoing environmental struggle. More environmentally sustainable, engaging, and inclusive measures and targets ought to be set, while working with *all* stakeholders across the economic sphere to push the needle firmly in the green direction.

Unfortunately, however there is no easy or quick fix, much less a purist left-green solution towards addressing all our environmental difficulties, without as many tend to believe, disrupting basic civil and economic liberties. One has to realize, as the environmental crisis escalates, the room for manoeuvre narrows and radical action and transformation needs to be stepped up even further, but within a shorter window of time. Balancing such re-engineering of businesses with a range of just-transition edicts, not to mention taking on board various other possible unintended consequences, remains a conceptual and operational challenge and a growing dilemma. The bottom line is the urgent need to assess how to manage the global transformation necessary for a future low-carbon transition.

References

Anderson, Alison. *Media, Culture, and the Environment*. Rutgers University Press 1997.

Bozak, Nadia. *The Cinematic Footprint*. Rutgers University Press 2012.

Cubitt, Sean. *Ecomedia*. Rodopi 2005.

Klein, Naomi. *Shock Doctrine: The Rise of Disaster Capitalism*. Allen Lane an Imprint of Penguin Book 2007.

Lopez, Antonio. 'Expanding Ethics to the Environment with Ecomedia Literacy' in Frau-Meigs, Divina *et al.* (eds) *Handbook of Media Education Research*. Routledge 2021.

Maxwell, Richard and Miller, Toby. *Greening the Media*. Oxford University Press 2012.

Parikka, Jussi *A Geology of Media*. University of Minnesota Press 2015.

Swanson, Heather, Tsing, Anna, Bubandt, Nils and Gan, Elaine. 'Introduction: Bodies Tumbled Into Bodies'. *Arts of Living on a Damaged Planet: Ghosts of the Anthropocene*, edited by Tsing, Anna, Swanson, Heather, Gan, Elaine, and Bubandt, Nils. University of Minnesota Press 2017.

Wilson, C., Hargreaves, T. and Hauxwell-Baldwin, R. 'Benefits and Risks of Smart Home Technologies'. *Energy Policy* 103: 72–83. 2017.

Education Versus Disinformation: Promoting Environmental Literacy

As Greta Thunberg pronounced in a speech to British MPs in April 2019, 'avoiding climate breakdown will require cathedral thinking. We must lay the foundations, while we may not know exactly how to build the ceiling' (cited in *The Guardian* 23 April 2019). What better way to lay firm foundations in this growing field of investigation, than developing robust modes of basic environmental education, which supports broad-based interactive curricula at all levels.

Unfortunately, environmental education itself probably always has been a cultural and political battlefield. There is an ongoing struggle between educationalists who wish to uphold the status quo and experts, led by the science of climate change, who advocate a more equitable and sustainable future. There are no easy answers or worked-out resolutions to such tensions. This struggle is not only evident in the extremely polarised and populist hot-bed of American culture and politics, but it also rages at different levels of intensity, especially in educational institutions across the world. In particular, we have seen a well-funded and organised campaign of disinformation and misinformation turned at both the nations' educators and the news media, with the goals of actively sowing doubt in the population (Oreskes and Conway 2011; Farrell 2016).

At the most basic level, climate change education must be able to affect change at a scale commensurate with the problem, especially as it extends over the coming years. Unfortunately, for example, American formal schooling remains a mishmash of agendas with only some regions spending large amounts of educational time on it and other places not teaching about climate change at all (Henderson et al. 2020).

Climate change remains a collective action problem and needs to be dealt with by many different kinds of people and stakeholders, working across various scales of influence. Meanwhile, research in the area and across the world is only slowly emerging, lagging behind other domains of social science research (Henderson et al. 2020). For instance, there is growing research around how children or young people think and conceptualise differently than adults, especially when it comes to climate change (Brereton and Gomez 2020). Meanwhile, political ideology is consistently one of the major drivers of climate change perception (McCright et al. 2016), and this is apparently true regardless of direct personal experiences with weather extremes precipitated by climate change.

Increasingly, academic scholarship is recognising and emphasising that climate change education should be both holistic and included in cross-curricular projects, which in turn seeks to marry STEM (science, technology, engineering and maths) and the social sciences and humanities, or as the British Academy now characterise as SHAPE (Social Sciences, Humanities and the Arts for People and the Economy). As many scholars in the field affirm, information on its own is not enough to create real and permanent change. In other words all strands of communication need to be co-opted in promoting increased environmental literacy and active engagement with the challenges of climate crisis.

For example, the renowned scholar Maxwell T. Baykoff (cited in Henderson et al. 2020; Baykoff and Ostness 2019) insinuates that usage of climate change comedy and humour can be appropriated for instance to:

- increase salience of climate change issues by exposing audiences to new insights
- offer new routes to 'knowing' about climate change through experience/ emotion
- help increase accessibility of a complex, often distant, long-term set of issues
- engage new audiences by disarming defences through laughter
- increase retention of climate change information through effective story telling
- provide relief amid anxiety-producing evidence of causes and con-sequences of CC
- bridge difficult topics, overcoming polarised discussions through often-entertaining/non-threatening ways.

At all times, as many environmental educational studies affirm, it is time for climate change education to jump into civic life by being more directly engaging with local, regional, state and national governments. Climate change educators are uniquely positioned to serve as a bulwark to help pivot society between broad curricular development and its implementation in the field and across this ever-changing environmental and political minefield.

References

Baykoff, Maxwell and Osness, Beth. (2019) 'A Laughing Matter, Confronting Climate Change through Humour'. *Political Geography.*

Brereton, Pat and Gómez, Victoria. (2020) 'Media Students, Climate Change, and YouTube Celebrities: Readings of Dear Future Generations: Sorry Video Clip'. *ISLE: Interdisciplinary Studies in Literature and Environment* 27(2) 385–405. https:// doi.org/10.1093/isle/isaa021

Carrington, Damien and Walker, Peter. 'Greta Condemns UK's Climate Stance in Speech to MPs'. *The Guardian* 23 April 2019. https://www.theguardian.com/envir onment/2019/apr/23/vacant-seat-for-may-as-party-leaders-meet-greta-thunberg

Farrell, J. (2016) 'Network Structure and Influence of Climate Change Counter-movement'. *Nature Climate Change* 6(4): 370–374.

Henderson, Joseph and Drewes, Andrea *et al.Teaching Climate Change in the US.* Routledge 2020.

McCright, A.M., Dunlap, R.E. and Marquart-Pyatt, S.T. (2016) 'Political Ideology and Views about Climate Change in the European Union'. *Environmental Politics* 25: 338–358.

Oreskes, N. and Conway, E.M. *Merchants of Doubt.* Bloomsbury 2010.

Employment Opportunities: Feeding into Environmental Communications HE Courses

Various avenues for further employment of environmental communication graduates draw on growing areas of work around sustainability, science and the broader communications industry, including those areas focused on policy, governance and legal professions, as well as education, training and community engagement. All of these interconnecting areas are added to by ongoing research and academic development, focused around the challenge of dealing with both multi- and trans-disciplinary approaches required to tackle our growing climate crisis. As often affirmed within Higher Education, teachers have to train students for future work and jobs that have not been developed or even imagined as of yet. Many in the field of media and communications especially rail against crude instrumentalist pedagogy and explicitly vocational training. Frequently media software, technology and even protocols, which are used today in the industry, become outdated by the time students find themselves working in the media industry (see Starosielski and Walker 2016). Hence reflexive pedagogical approaches speak of teaching and developing critical and reflexive principles of engagement with the industry, which always remains current. Such future-proofed employment possibilities can be grouped into a number of broad categories, as collated throughout the following broad examples.

Sustainability professionals – include potential opportunities foregrounding the role of a green champion or ambassador, corporate sustainability manager, total quality management director, community change agent, sustainability coordinator or social entrepreneur, feeding off a range of related skillsets. Policy entrepreneur, green city planner, triple-bottom line economic developer and policy entrepreneur, which can further evolve over time from these core meta-environmental discipline areas. These in turn can be bolstered by a sustainability researcher, ecological economist, sustainability social scientist, or human–natural systems modeller. Furthermore, this rich seam of possibilities incorporate aspects of the functions of an innovation intermediary director, sustainability venture capitalist, as well as a green technology entrepreneur. All of these are necessary as industry and commerce pivots towards a greener and more sustainable future model of development.

Law and government – including policy advisors, modellers, legal and cross-country experts helping to uncover comparative analysis of various forms of green finance and also learning from other legal and business best practice regimes across the world, as countries strive to move towards a low-carbon transition.

Education, Training and Research – noting the urgent need for more teachers across all levels of formal education, from Primary to Third Level. Teachers need dedicated training to gain expertise across the growing field of Environmental Communication to help teach new generations of citizens and uncover new ways of communicating the ever-changing environmental issues and dilemmas facing into the future. Higher Education in particular needs more full-time researchers and specialists, helping to discover new creative toolkits and solutions, while effectively communicating environmental issues, as we face into even more challenging times ahead.

Communications and Science – these include for example the development of a specialist journalist role and dedicated audio-visual storytellers, who can critically deal with the complex nature of such global wicked climate problems, alongside environmental communication officers across all areas of industry and service industries. These in turn can be augmented by activists in NGOs and dedicated officers within political organisations who can speak to these broad areas – as all organs of governance hopefully strive to imagine and help to achieve a low-carbon energy transition. Climate change scientists need ongoing support to help effectively communicate their complex and long-term data-driven messages across a range of stakeholders, as societies strive to face up to the challenges ahead. Furthermore, there is a need for 'creatives' across all aspects of audio-visual production fields; from so-called legacy media (film, television and press) to a growing cohort of online, short-form and video games media specialists, to help produce innovative new environmental media content.

Note, of late, funding agencies for media production are beginning to demand more quality assured and low-energy green production, which is further driving the radical transformation of the industry. For instance the ALBERT initiative in the UK has developed a Carbon Calculator for assessing the environmental sustainability of media productions, which is becoming normalised even mandatory across many regions. More and more media production companies, like here in Ireland, we have co-opted the software package for a local market using an umbrella organisation 'ScreenGreening'. Over time, support for such new green initiatives in promoting environmental sustainability protocols will hopefully lead to more green and sustainably driven jobs within the media industry.

References

Starosielski, Nicole and Walker, Janet eds. *Sustainable Media: Critical Approaches to Media and Environment*. Routledge 2016.

Enclosure Movement and Tragedy of the Commons

The tragedy of the commons builds on what is conceived as an economics-based problem in which all individuals apparently are encouraged to use up and consume more natural resources – often at the expense of other (competing) individuals – leading to a global depletion of resources. The concept was originally formulated by asking what would happen if every shepherd (or farmer), acting in their own self-interest were allowed to graze their flock on a commonly contracted field. This inherent tension is evident across so many generic Westerns in particular, which often involve conflict over scarce resources like water and good grazing. If one farmer or rancher selfishly wants to control all the water rights to a river and does not accept that others also need access to water, then this leads to conflict and can end in tragedy. Certainly, if everybody strives to act in their own selfish interest, it results in harmful over-consumption; basically all the grass is eaten and the water is used up to the detriment of everyone else in the neighbourhood or commons.

This phenomenon can be traced through British history back as far as the Norman Conquest, when knights and overlords began to gain control over the numerous local commons land; the notion of a 'commons' basically constituted the contract a community of people made with their local natural system. According to Gary Snyder, by the 15th century the landlord class, working with urban mercantile guilds and government offices, increasingly fenced off village-held land in common and turned it over to private interests. The Enclosure Movement was further backed up by the big wool corporations, who found profits from sheep to be much greater than that coming from more mixed (and sustainable) farming. The wool business, with its extensive exports, presented an early example of industrially driven agribusiness that unfortunately had a destructive effect on the soils and at the same time ended up dislodging peasants from the land.

The arguments for enclosure of land in England, including obvious benefits of efficiency and higher production rates in particular, ignore however various social and ecological effects that unfortunately, over time, served to cripple sustainable agriculture across some regions. The enclosure movement was stepped up again in the 18th century, when between 1709 and 1869 almost five million acres were transferred to private ownership – constituting one acre in every seven within the UK. After 1869 however, there was a sudden reversal of sentiment for this project, characterised by the 'open space movement', which ultimately halted enclosures and managed to preserve land, via a spectacular lawsuit against the lords of fourteen manors, such as in the Epping Forest. As a media analogy, this complex tension over land and resources can be repurposed and evidenced within the evergreen franchise focused on the tale of Nottingham forest and the myth of Robin Hood, who fought for the ordinary people in opposition to the controlling land-lord class.

Historically, leading scholars like Karl Polanyi (2001) argue that the enclosure movement, beginning in the 18th century created a population of rural homeless who were forced in their desperation to become the world's first industrial working class, as they migrated to the big towns and cities. In hindsight, it can be argued that the enclosure movement had tragic consequences, both for the human community and for natural ecosystems (Snyder 2015: 73).

Elsewhere, the takeover of commons land across the European plain began about five hundred years ago. Nonetheless, up to one-third of European land has remained in public hands and was never privatised. A survival of the commons practice in Swedish law for instance, allows anyone to enter private farmland to pick berries or mushrooms, to cross on foot and to camp out of sight of the house. Most of these former commons land is now under the administration of government land agencies (Snyder 2015: 74).

Meanwhile, across the United States, as fast as the Euro-American invaders forcefully displaced the native inhabitants from their own type of traditional commons, the land was opened for exploitation to the new settlers. In the arid West however, much land was never even homesteaded, let alone patented.

The native people who had known and loved the deserts and blue mountains were scattered or enclosed on reservations, and the new inhabitants (miners and a few ranchers) had neither the values nor the knowledge to take care of the land. Consequently, an enormous area was *de facto* designated as part of the public domain within the Forest Services, the Park Services, and the Bureau of Land Management formed to manage it (Snyder 2015: 74). Much of this public state 'wild' land coincidentally served to promote the growth of the environmental movement in America, through organisations like the Sierra Club in particular.

Other global examples include the colonialisation of West Africa and contemporary dilemmas over fishing (not forgetting more long-term systemic difficulties caused by a deep history around colonial exploitation), which has dramatically effected the local population, who depend on ocean fishing to survive. This situation is most vigorously evidenced in the 2021 Netflix documentary *Seaspiracy*, highlighting the growing problem of over-fishing across the world. As a consequence, the 'richest' global (communal) stocks of fishing coincidentally congregate off the West African coast. For many years now, apparently big Chinese, European and other factory boats fish 'illegally' off this fertile seascape and have ended up decimating the fish stocks. The growing counter-tradition of postcolonial sea-pirates, explored in *Captain Phillips* (2013) and analysed in Brereton (2016: 47–48), outlined the precarious nature of survival for such indigenous fishermen, who were forced to take on new industrial forms of 'global capitalism' with their giant container ships, who are exploiting the seascape as a commons, which is indicative of increasing levels of globalisation. *Seaspiracy* also illustrates how such coastal regions are exploited by these international fishing fleets, leading to a global tragedy of the commons, which is not only affecting biodiversity, but further exacerbating the climate crisis.

Post-colonial Enclosures, Eco-land Management and Cheap Nature

Postcolonial literary scholar Jason Moore remains an important writer in this area of research and perceives the so-called end of 'cheap nature' as the reassertion of external 'limits to growth'. Moore highlights what he calls 'four cheaps: labour-power, food, energy, and raw materials' and argues that 'today's mode of capitalism has exhausted the historical relations that produced cheap nature' (2014: 288). The appropriation of unpaid work, including what can be characterised as 'free gifts' of nature, together with the exploitation of wage-labour form a dialectical unity, remaining a continuing ecological problem. The world-ecological limit of capital is capital itself, Moore claims, which has had a long history of overcoming seemingly insuperable barriers to revive ever increasing accumulation. For early modern modes of materialism, the point was not only to interpret the world but control it. To make ourselves as it were 'the masters and possessors of nature' (Moore 2014: 51).

A historical workable solution to these problems of scarce natural resources was of course to secure more colonies and thereby access new frontiers to further control (cheap) resources. Consequently, over the centuries, the so-called 'limits to growth' dilemma (Meadows et al. 1972) were not necessarily external, but rather derived from an exhaustion of natural resources, most especially through soil erosion, mining and other forms of extraction, together with all forms of over-exploitation of labour. All the while, the rise of capital launched a new way of organising nature, mobilising for the first time a metric of wealth, premised on labour productivity, rather than simply land productivity.

Historically, Marx and Engels critically analysed the fertility of the soil and how it could 'act like an increase in fixed capital' (see Bellamy Foster's (2013) scholarly analysis of the notion of 'metabolic rift' and environmental/colonial exploitation of soil erosion over history, using an early example of the Irish Famine in the 1840s). The English (and later global) agricultural revolution developed precisely on this basis, by ostensibly cashing in on more permanent pasture farming, which produced more nitrogen (Overton 1996). This is similar, in certain ways, to environmental legacies of the American mid-west, leading up to the Dust Bowl disaster in the 1930s and witnessing soil literally blowing away, having been overused and abused through intensive farming methods. All of these nature and environmental tensions have unfortunately continued unabated ever since. By most measurements however, the problems have got much worse, as big agribusinesses and increased levels of industrialisation of natural exploitation have developed at an expediential rate. The Tragedy of the Commons has never been more important than today and environmental students need to be fully aware of such prescient historical analysis, as they engage with and undertake a deeper understanding of the urgent need for sustainable management of all natural resources, if we are to survive into the future.

References

Brereton, Pat. *Environmental Ethics and Film*. Routledge 2016.

Foster, Bellamy. 'Marx and the Rift in the Universal Metabolism of Nature'. *Monthly Review* 65(7): 1–19. 2013.

Meadows, Donnela H. *et al.The Limits to Growth: A Report for the Club of Rome's Project on the Predicament of Mankind*. Universe Books 1972.

Moore, Jason. 'The End of Cheap Nature Or: How I Learned to Stop Worrying about "the" Environment and Love the Crisis of Capitalism'. In Suter, Christian and Chase-Dunn, Christopher. (eds) *Structures of the World Political Economy and the Future of Global Conflict and Cooperation*. LIT 2014.

Overton, M. 'Agricultural Revolution in England: the Transformation of the Agrarian Economy, 1500–1850'. *Agricultural History Review* 44(1). 1996.

Polanyi, Karl. *The Great Transformation*. Boston-Beacon Books 2001.

Snyder, Gary. 'The Place, The Region, and the Commons' (77–96). In Hiltner, Ken (ed). *Ecocriticism: The Essential Reader*. Routledge 2015.

Energy Humanities: From Fossil Fuels to the Carbon Economy

Energy Humanities represents various new perspectives and different methods for scrutinising and understanding environmental politics. See for instance *Carbon Nation* (2014) by historian Bob Johnson, who teases out how energy was owned and controlled and how it was governed through policy, alongside how it formed the basis of culture and political power. Johnson argues that consumers, business elites and policy makers ignored our reliance on fossil fuels and their associated environmental and human costs, and unfortunately have embraced the 'carbon economy'. At the same time much policy discussion tended to ignore increasing accidents at work, much less the exploitation of labour, and the general devastation of landscapes, among other environmental disasters.

Many environmentalists, including Vaclav Smil (2018) talk of the world's true universal currency being the wealth of natural systems. Energy Humanities in particular seeks to redress this neglect and places both monetary and other forms of value on all aspects of nature and the global national ecosystem. Furthermore, the emergent field of energy humanities also shows communication scholars new perspectives and different methods for scrutinising and understanding environmental politics. In doing so, both media and art generally can spur the imagination of researchers, illuminating different social realities and experiences that researchers can explore more systematically.

Political economic analysis on the other hand, functions as a powerful way to understand energy systems. Yet this approach has often been neglected within environmental communication; as compared to the vast number of studies grounded in quantifiable social science or the language-focused approaches, including rhetoric or discourse analysis.

Communication researchers have started to tease out what potential democratic futures look like, while drawing on concepts like energy democracy. As Timothy Mitchell affirms in *Carbon Democracy* (2013), we need to rethink relations between humans and non-humans and most especially how to reimagine our relationship with energy and oil as the planet pivots towards low-carbon renewable energy and fuels.

Divisions around energy transition are therefore influencing decisions about what kinds of societies we will inhabit into the future. Amid such changes, dialogue across society that cuts across ideological lines and social circumstances can help identify and decide on common goals and shared future plans, as well as overcoming fragmentation and policy divisions.

> This is a fundamentally democratic process, one that communication researchers can help describe, facilitate, explain, critique, and evaluate, to help ensure the process operates with accountability, scrutiny and engagement to help ensure we are citizens and not subjects in our energy futures.

(Fahy 2020: 5)

Engaging with all aspects of Energy Humanities remains a focus for environmental communication students as they learn to uncover linkages across so many otherwise discrete fields of study.

References

Fahy, Declan. 'Review of Energy Humanities: Insights for Environmental Communication': 712–716. 2020.

Johnson, Bob. *Carbon Nation: Fossil Fuels in the making of American Culture.* University Press of Kansas 2014.

Mitchell, Timothy. *Carbon Democracy: The Political Power in the Age of Oil.* Verso 2013.

Smil, Vaclav. *Energy and Civilisation: A History.* MIT Press 2018.

Energy Landscapes and Media Perceptions: Case Study of NIMBYism in Ireland

As affirmed in a journal article on 'Irish Energy Landscapes' (Brereton and Barrios-O'Neill 2021), the invisibility of energy itself requires some type of an avatar to make it more real. An expert in the field, Patrick Devine-Wright (2014) for instance, explores how most citizens seem to look at electricity networks as being simply 'cables and wires' rather than being constructed by human beings and organisations. One way governments have sought to make energy systems more visible has been through in-home visualisation tools, such as smart meters which have become very prevalent across the western world in particular. But even these, while effective in the short term, perhaps due to financial incentives in the form of savings, remains ineffective nonetheless in shaping understanding or behaviour across the longer term (Strengers, 2011).

Certainly, the difficulty of communicating both the specific, domestic and personal, as well as the networked, complex and regional (or even global) energy picture, remains just one problem faced by those hoping to communicate the complexity of energy systems (Strengers, 2011). Broadly there remains strong public support across many jurisdictions for alternative energy solutions, as evidenced by extensive international opinion polling since the 1970s. But at the local level in Ireland for example, there is often controversy and public opposition, where so-called NIMBYism – a moniker for the 'not in my backyard' mentality – becomes a point of focus and contention. In such a construction, backyard becomes a signal for one's immediate 'local landscape'. 'NIMBYism' gestures at an attitude of self-preservation over the greater good; recalling the idea that while energy transitions must occur somewhere, they should not be local, or visible, to the local person concerned.

While it may have genuine applicability in some cases, NIMBYism is no doubt overused as a way of caricaturing the attitudes and beliefs of residents to local energy development needs, much less other environmental developments; some of which are likely to have valid and complex reasons for resisting local energy transitions (Clayton et al. 2015). Nonetheless, for environmental communicators to map out and encourage various alternative forms of deep time communication with regards to environmental agency – including dealing with renewable energy projects – the general public has to be encouraged to see beyond their local-partisan stakeholder selves and both recognise and embrace more global and community-driven energy protocols. Environmental communications has a major role to play in promoting and critically evaluating new forms of renewable energy landscapes (see Brereton and Barrios-O'Neill 2021) and developing ways of encouraging audiences and citizens to embrace a low-carbon energy future.

References

Brereton, P. and Barrios-O'Neill, D. (2021) 'Irish Energy Landscape and Film'. *Journal of Environmental Media* 2(1): 101–115.
Clayton, S., Devine-Wright, P., Stern, P.C., Whitmarsh, L., Carrico, A., Steg, L. and Bonnes, M. (2015) 'Psychological Research and Global Climate Change'. *Nature Climate Change* 5(7): 640–646.
Devine-Wright, P. (ed.). (2014). *Renewable Energy and the Public: from NIMBY to Participation*. Routledge.
Strengers, Y.A. (2011, May) 'Designing Eco-feedback Systems for Everyday Life' (2135–2144). In *Proceedings of the SIGCHI Conference on Human Factors in Computing Systems*. ACM.

Environmental Media Risk Campaigns: Best Practice Protocols

An environmental communicator should be able to present clear and simple recommendations adapted to the audience in question and not hide behind scientific language and uncertainties. Christian A. Klockner characterises these attributes using the following adapted strategies:

- Media channels are very different in their structure, audience and needs. The most promising channels need to be carefully selected and a successful environmental media campaign needs to be tailored to them.
- New media and social media in particular offer possibilities that cannot be fully utilised without changing from traditional to new media campaign styles, affording audiences a more active role.
- Analysing the characteristics of an environmental risk helps predict how important citizens will perceive this projected risk.
- People tend to dissociate the risk associated with their own behaviour from the risk of global environmental problems. Reconnecting personal behaviour to the specific environmental problem should be part of the focus of the campaign, and concrete behavioural advice should be disseminated.

- An environmental risk communicator should be aware that risk perception is socially constructed and risks affecting people or things are perceived differently.
- Increasing people's perception of a threat is not enough to motivate them to change their behaviour. It is necessary to provide them with effective and manageable options for coping behaviour; otherwise maladaptive coping mechanisms can occur.
- Complex social processes can both amplify and attenuate perceptions of a risk. Being aware of and monitoring them is crucial to avoid difficulties.
- Media will always pick up on controversy. Environmental communication should anticipate potential counter-arguments and try to immunise their communications protocols proactively.
- Media campaigns need to be well timed and tailored to specific journalists, who should in turn be selected carefully.
- For media campaigns that run over longer times, careful planning and time to communicate, on being presented with new pieces of information is necessary (Klockner 2015: 143–144).

In his comprehensive study, Klockner recalls the use of hotel towels as a simple case study. Initially, many hotels who wanted to save energy costs around cleaning towels used an international campaign to entreat customers to 'please help us save the environment and reuse your towels'. This campaign was effectively changed however to 'the majority of our guests reused their towels' which was more effective (Klockner 2015: 170). The bottom line is that environmental interventions requiring behavioural change need to be tailored to specific situations and target groups; and they also need to be carefully pilot tested. (In other entries, including Greenwashing and PR, see various critiques of such campaigns.)

References

Klockner, Christian A. *The Psychology of Pro-Environmental Communication: Beyond Standard Information Strategies.* Palgrave Macmillan 2015.

Environmental Citizenship as a Model of Engaging Humans Around Climate Change

Environmental citizenship has become an influential concept in many different arenas, such as economy, policy, philosophy, corporation management and marketing. The power of citizenship can also be better exploited and established within the field of education (see Goldman et al. 2020).

Promoting this type of citizenship can be defined as encouraging 'pro-environmental behaviour in public and in private'; all of which is 'driven by a belief in fairness of the distribution of environmental goals' (Dobson 2010: 6). Such a model of environmental citizenship could help to develop a more sustainable society and world, with the subsequent transformation of the values, beliefs, attitudes and behaviour of individuals who see themselves as part of global environmental politics. Of course, there are many related concepts attached to this proposition, drawing on for instance 'environmental citizenship (Dobson 2010), green citizenship (Barry 2017), ecological citizenship (Jagers and Matti 2010) and sustainability citizenship' (Hadjichambis et al. 2020: 8) – all of which have not been clearly distinguished or delineated in the literature. Much more definitional scholarship is required, however, in the future to help tease out all these various permutations.

Many scholars argue that the ultimate goal of environmental education should be to develop student's ability to act as informed and empowered eco-citizens. For instance, 'Kerr (2000) differentiates between "passive and historical" and "active and critical" forms of citizenship education. While Johnson and Morris (2010) focus on political, social, self and praxis, which in turn represents the component elements of critical citizenship education' (Hadjichambis et al. 2020: 8).

There are at least three types of citizens (not including a range of anti-social modes of non-active citizenship):

1   Citizens who are personally responsible and obedient to laws and acts responsibly, but do not actively question the norms of society.
2   Citizens who are participative, but tend to act as individuals.
3   The socially responsible citizen, motivated by a concern for social justice and who can identify obstacles, which need to be overcome to attain a fairer society and cooperates with others in enacting change (cited in Hadjichambis et al. 2020: 20).

Environmental citizenship most especially recognises the importance of justice (especially gender justice), alongside social sustainability. In general, across western democracies, citizens with higher levels of education tend to agree with the need for global citizenship, supporting the protection of human rights and also in prioritising various global aspects of environmental responsibility. Young (1984 cited in Hadjichambis et al. 2020 24) for instance, identifies four clusters of problems where the notion of global citizen obligations would apply:

1   Commons that belong to all – e.g. climate systems like the Antarctic wilderness.
2   Shared natural resources – extended areas beyond national boundaries, such as rivers
3   Transboundary externalities – such as acid rain areas, which bleed across boundaries
4   Linked issues, such as cutting down air travel and its effects of livelihoods etc.

In 2015 the UN adopted a new key document, 'Transforming our World: The 2030 Agenda for Sustainable Development'. Its primary aim is 'to end poverty and hunger everywhere; to combat inequalities; to protect human rights and provide gender equality; to build peaceful, just and inclusive societies and ensure lasting protection of the planet and its natural resources' (UN 2015). It also resolved to create conditions for inclusive and sustained economic growth across all areas.

Currently citizens and communities across the world are forced to find ways of overcoming the challenge of over-consumption together with the fundamental restrictions of planetary boundaries that are essential to sustain human civilisation. All the while, environmental communication scholarship continuously asks, how can (environmental) citizens, alongside environmental communications actively assist in this ongoing challenge?

Persuading people to become fully fledged environmental citizens, while building on environmental literacy is crucial towards supporting an ever-expanding list of difficult environmental issues. It is becoming a necessary condition for embedding all aspects of sustainability and has been identified for example as one of the EU's core priorities. Education for Sustainability (EfS) is often considered, across many educational systems (see UNESCO 2009) to be an integrative concept of environmental education, where the ecological direction is more strongly supplemented with social, cultural and economic aspects. In the age where some of the planetary ecological limits have already been exceeded (now accepted by science), the education of environmental citizenship remains most important in understanding what these circumstances mean within areas that affect individual health and all other aspects of society.

Key competencies for securing effective environmental citizenship, which naturally feed into media and communication evaluation of 'best practice' protocols include:

- critical analysis, establishing interrelationships between social, economic and environmental aspects from the local to global level
- sustainable use of resources and prevention of negative impacts
- ethical principles of personal, local, national and global scales
- active participation in community processes, enhancing environmental protection through environmental and social change (Hadjichambis et al. 2020: 156).

So much can be gleaned from such a checklist that in turn can be directly ascribed to various forms of environmental communication best practice protocols. From most pointedly affirming all aspects of ethical values, to encouraging active participation with environmental communication; all the while encouraging critical evaluation of the sustainable use of all resources. Certainly such an initial checklist presents a good starting point for students towards collating and framing the broad range of environmental communication discourses that need to be deployed in facing up to and addressing our climate emergency.

References

Barry, John. 'Citizenship and (Un)sustainability and Green Republican Perspectives'. Gardiner, Steven M. and Thompson, Allen (eds.) *The Oxford Handbook of Environmental Ethics*. Oxford University Press 2017

Dobson, A. 'Environmental Citizenship and Pro-environmental Behaviour – Rapid Research and Evidence Review'. *Sustainability Development Research Network*. 2010.

Goldman, Daphne *et al.* 'Education for Environmental Citizenship and Responsible Environmental Behaviour' (115–135). In Hadjichambis, A. *et al.Conceptualising Environmental Citizenship for 21st Century Education*. Springer 2020.

Hadjichambis, A. *et al.Conceptualising Environmental Citizenship*. COST Springer 2020.

Jagers, S. and Matti, S. 'Ecological Citizens: Identifying Values and Beliefs that Support Individual Environmental Responsibility among Swedes'. *Sustainability* 2(4). 2010

UN. 'The 17 Goals'. 2015. https://sdgs.un.org/goals

UNESCO. '2009 UNESCO Framework for Cultural Statistics'. 2009 . http://uis.unesco.org/sites/default/files/documents/unesco-framework-for-cultural-statistics-2009-en_0.pdf

Young, O. *International Governance: Protecting the Environment in a Stateless Society*. Cornell University Press 1984.

Environmental Justice: Case Study of India

While traditional media, including newspapers continue to thrive in India, many commentators assert that environmental concerns are usually simply an afterthought. Most notably however, the horrific 1984 Union Carbide gas leak in Bhopal stands out, remaining one of the world's worst industrial disasters. The local government has affirmed that over 15,000 people died indirectly over the years from the disaster, caused by the American multinational chemical company (Taylor 2014). The tragedy ended up changing, in many ways, how the environment was covered across the world throughout the media, as a major news story.

Environmental journalism has a tremendous task of informing, educating and challenging the status quo reflecting this poor environment record, using its public service investigation brief. Consequently the media's role remains significant, whereas newspapers are perishing in many parts of the world and losing their power, they still continue to thrive in India and invariably have a huge role to play in the coming years in promoting all aspects of environmental activity. Furthermore, over time with increasing levels of internet penetration, scholars predict that new digital media formats will also have a major role to play in the region.

The arrival of such new media technology has also brought a flicker of hope to the environmental journalism landscape in this very populated region, because more individuals can go on to report environmental issues through social media platforms, without having to wait for traditional media to take a stand. Of course, the flip side of this is that there is so much material online, it becomes difficult to evaluate the provenance and value of so much output that is uploaded for public dissemination. Certainly getting information remains so much easier, but at what cost.

In an analysis of the energy needs coupled with India's environmental health (see Mishra and Das 2017), apparently the situation has never looked bleaker. For instance, taking into account increasing levels of polluted air, water and soil, rapidly disappearing green cover, biodiversity loss, alongside coastal regions despoiled by plastic and a lingering fear of more environmental destruction to come. Echoing this position, back in 2014 New Delhi was named by the World Health Organization (WHO), as the most polluted city in the world, a situation that has improved little since then.

Climate change remains the most pressing global issue, despite the emergence of multiple additional global crises, including the COVID-19 crisis, refugee crisis and financial crisis (Wurzel et al. 2021: xlv), India like many regions has had a complex relationship with various aspects of climate concern. The 2015 Paris Agreement most notably was based on a bottom-up approach, requesting that states like India put forward voluntary pledges in the form of Nationally Determined Contributions (DNCs). In a study by Kirsten Jorgensen, titled 'India: from climate laggard to global solar energy leader', it is suggested that within such international climate negotiations, India (like many other countries it must be said) has for a long time been perceived as a nay-sayer, unwilling to commit to climate mitigation goals and persuading fellow developing countries to do the same. India, in turn, has counter-argued that because industrialised countries have generated the problem of climate change, they should solve it, by reducing gas emissions (GHGE) at home and providing funding for emission reductions in developing countries (Jorgensen in Wurzel et al. 2021: 45).

Jorgensen goes on to summarise that India faces a complex 'climate trilemma' that makes the formation of consistent domestic climate policy preferences difficult, all of which has shaped the country's domestic climate process and international negotiated strategy. Due to the massive size of its population and the rapid growth of its economy, India remains one of the world's three largest global carbon dioxide (CO_2) emitters, even though its per capita emissions are among the lowest in world comparison (see Dubash 2019). High poverty rates in India are accompanied by low per capita electricity consumption, among other factors, approximately 300 million people still lack access to electricity supply.

Alternatively, in America for instance, the per capita energy use remains at least ten-fold higher compared to India. Consequently, the related 'growth first' thinking holds that India's most important priority, as a former British colony and developing country, should be towards extensive industrial and services development and poverty reduction, which in turn should not be hampered by emissions reduction goals (Wurzel et al. 2021: 48).

Many scholars in other parts of the world also call for an 'alternative, transformational approach to development' which would involve innovative 'ways of thinking about things and ways of acting on them' (Agarwal 1992: 153). Furthermore, by failing to explicitly confront such political economy issues, ecofeminist analysis, for instance, is often called upon as a unifying critique towards aligning such developing regions. For instance, see references to the concept of 'ecology of the poor' or the notion of 'popular ecology' developed by Guha (India) and Martínez Allier (Spain), who also worked in Ecuador for a long time, encapsulating 'a third way of being an environmentalist'. Such scholarship requires much more space and foregrounding across global political and environmental responses to help tease out contrasting sustainable solutions for all.

On the ground, Bina Agarwal, in an insightful article on the limitations of conventional eco-feminist discourse 'The Gender and Environmental Debate: Lessons from India' (1992), suggests that similar to much of Asia and Africa, a wide variety of essential items are collected by rural households from the 'village commons' throughout India and from forests for everyday personal use and sale – including food, fuel, fodder etc. Recalling studies from the 1980s, it is suggested that for the Indian poor, the village commons account for between 9–20% of their total needs. Furthermore, it is estimated that over 30 million people in India totally depend on local forests for food. Allegorically, if not in reality, only the rich can afford to dig deep wells, while the poor need such resources to be more freely available in nature, or otherwise suffer the consequences if they are not. All the while, it is women and children – especially from poorer classes/castes – who suffer the most from all types of environmental destruction.

Such proposals regarding new modes of environmentalism was born out of observing ecological conflicts on the peripheries across the world and today there remain many cases that illustrate this new reality. For instance, Allier and his team at the Autonomous University of Barcelona, mapped all these ecological conflicts, where the movement of environmental justice across its version of the 'ecology of the poor' can be traced (see https://ejatlas.org/). Students from across the world should uncover their own real-world examples and explore how these various conflicts have been communicated to the wider world.

Chipko Movement: A Case Study

In India, indigenous environmental groupings like the Chipko movement (meaning to embrace or hug – 'embeds the notion of human-nature solidarity') have become notable towards illustrating specific aspects of environmental justice. Such a movement has been 'ground-breaking in the history of the environmental protest movement', according to Usha Sundar Harris (2019: 129). The protest movement is mainly known for the agency enacted by women forest dwellers of the sub-Himalayan region, who embraced the trees in order to protect them from commercial exploitation back in 1974. 'The hill people of the Garwahi district maintained the traditional eco-balance while using local resources for food and shelter and ended up forming a human chain around their beloved trees when a timber company came to cut them down'. Such a movement, as explained by Harris, was a result of years of 'grassroots organisation by Gandhian activists who dispersed to rural India after independence, teaching communities about sustainable livelihoods and forest protection' (ibid.: 129).

But as in all these indigenous debates and conflicts, one wonders who is really listening? As Harris strongly affirms – 'participatory environmental communication invites diversity of voices, values and beliefs, as well as cultural perspectives. It uses a wide variety of media forms and communication channels such as face-to-face communication, folk media, traditional and new media'. While

> many young people are leaving traditional ways of life to live and work in urban areas and losing interest in old ways. This distance means that old ways of knowledge exchange, where elders in the community progressively taught the young about traditional knowledge are no longer possible.
>
> (Harris 2019: 169)

Such movement of people and related environmental tensions are echoed across the world. See for instance my reading of *Happy as Lazzaro* in another entry.

At the same time, in spite of all the developments with new online media as a powerful tool for communicating and responding to climate change, it has been found for instance after the 2004 Tsunami in Aceh, Indonesia and again even during Hurricane Sandy in New York in 2014, that face-to-face communication is the most powerful during a crisis. More recently, in some very severe flooding events in Germany and across Europe (and China) during July 2021, it was noted that analogue local flood alarm systems had been disconnected and replaced by more high-tech digital software resulting in more casualties. Furthermore, mapping such communication information flows 'makes visible the patterns of communication that only local people are aware of within a community' (170). Depending on high-tech digital alarm systems is not always the most effective for local communities, reminding us that disaster communication planning, including all aspects of climate change responses, requires a 'both-and', belt-and-braces, approach to environmental health and safety.

India alongside China and other vast regions of the world which have much less published scholarship within Environmental Communications literature, will certainly help shape the future of our discipline. Much more research needs to be carried out towards bringing together the complex array of cultures and regions across the world with their varying issues and local

difficulties. Environmental students need to find new ways of actively engaging with and learning from such global case studies as they build up their
own knowledge and skill-sets.

References

Agarwal, Bina. 'The Gender and Environmental Debate: Lessons from India'. *Feminist Studies* 8(1): 119–158. 1992.
Dubash, N. *India in a Warming World: Integrating Climate Change and Development.* Oxford University Press 2019.
Harris, Usha Sundar. *Participatory Media in Environmental Communication: Engaging Communities on the Periphery.* Routledge 2019. https://www.theatlantic.com/photo/2014/12/bhopal-the-worlds-worst-industrial-disaster-30-years-later/100864/
Mishra, M. and Das, N. 'Coal Mining and Local Government: A Study of Talcher Coalfield of India'. *Air, Soil and Water Research* 10: 1–12. 2017.
Taylor, Alan (2014, 2 December) *Remembering the Bhopal Indian Disaster.*
Wurzel, R., Andersen, M.S. and Tobin, Paul (2021) *Climate Governance Across the World: Pioneers, Leaders and Followers.* Routledge.

Environmental Justice: A Case Study of Renewable Energy in Postcolonial Morocco

Africa remains central to the global environmental crisis for a number of
reasons, according to a study by Ibrahim Saleh.

> Africa is vulnerable towards major climate disturbances, especially with
> the weak capacity of African societies to respond to the gravest climatic
> disruptions, such as the deforestation levels of ten percent measured
> between 1990 and 2005, which is more than half the recorded global
> shrinkage.
>
> (2015: 140)

Not to mention centuries of slavery and exploitation of rich natural
resources that have left a difficult legacy across the world. 'But it is almost
impossible to clearly understand, much less try to resolve the increasing ecological crisis in Africa, without resolutely dealing with problems within
society. Economic, ethnic, cultural, and gender conflicts, among many others
in Africa, lie at the core of the most serious ecological dislocations we face
today, apart from those that are produced by natural catastrophes' (2015:
140–141). As in all continents, there is no 'typical' region or country and it is
therefore difficult and dangerous to make any generalisations. Consequently,
this Moroccan case study simply skims the surface of one region in the north
of this vast continent.

At a more regional level, almost all of Moroccan raw energy (fossil fuels
etc) is imported, yet currently the country is striving to radically change this
dependency and achieve carbon neutrality, with massive solar energy plants

being installed. The country situated on the northern plains of the African continent even has plans to become the largest producer of solar energy in the world. At the same time, according to a number of surveys (see Broue 2020), Morocco holds 77% of the world's total phosphate reserves and is the world's largest phosphate exporter, making up over 90% of its GDP. Mining for copper and silver constitutes about 10% of the country's GDP and these mines are situated in very poor region, where inhabitants are directly exposed to environmental and health risks related to the mining industry.

But such colonial and mining-extractive issues are seldom addressed by the Western media at least, much less are taken up by global politicians, unlike the country's efforts to invest in renewable energy projects, which has received widespread media and environmental attention. According to a 2014 national census, it should be noted at all times that over 50% of the people in this region live below the poverty line. The silver mining company SMI and its subsidiary Managem, which manages the mine are certainly culpable in not supporting broad levels of equity and social justice. In particular, SMI (Societe Metalvrgique D'Imider) remains a huge silver mining company based in Imider village and Igoudrange in Southeast Morocco. The Berger community in the region have actively spoken out after many years of toxic waste being produced. Many protesters have spent over a decade camping on a hilltop on the Great Atlas Mountains, protesting against the fallout through human disease and natural despoilation. For a powerful illustration of the effects of extractive industry, see the 2019 art-house documentary *Earth*, directed by Austrian director Nickolaus Geyrhalter (reviewed in Brereton 2020). At one stage in 2011, the protesters turned off the water reservoir system connecting with the mine located in Mount Alrbran.

Globally, of course mining is a major cause of environmental damage and displacement of indigenous peoples, as evident across other regions of Africa and throughout the world. Most especially in this region, the aforementioned Amazigh (Berber) community led an eight-year campaign against the silver mine that was draining their water reserves and destroying their agricultural land. In their long campaign against the mine operators, the Berbers eventually received official approval from UNESCO, who designated their local historical irrigation system as being unique in Africa. Together with undertaking active resistance there was also an innovative use of art/media to get their message across, as documented in a study by Usha Sundar Harris, titled *Participatory Media in Environmental Communication* (2019). Furthermore, a local activist short documentary *300KmSouth* (2016) – shown at COP22 in Marrakesh – includes images of trees that were witnessed flourishing again in this otherwise desolate habitat.

As explained in the documentary, the local Berber community paid a voluntary stipend to maintain their ongoing struggle and support the activists. Witnessing a very old method of local democracy and even signalling the potential application of democratic modes of deliberation was certainly innovative. Drawing on global community struggles, the documentary's trailer calls attention to this visual mode of active engagement. Berber inhabitants formed a large circle almost every week to listen to updates and work together as communal citizens to make various decisions. Such mediated case studies illustrate how the arts in general can be deployed as a form of local celebration around environmental resistance. But measuring the relative effectiveness of such artistic projects is another matter. Much can be learned from a broad range of environmental activist examples like these across the world. The arts and community engagement in particular needs to be constantly examined and investigated with regards to how they speak to environmental issues. All the while, teasing out the most effective methods to use in the struggle towards better environmental sustainability, remains an ongoing challenge.

References

Brereton, Pat. 'An Eco-reading of Documentary/Fictional Narratives'. *Irish Studies in International Affairs* 31: 43–57. 2020.
Broue, Fadoua. 'The Mining Industry in Morocco: A Policy Paradox that Leaves People Far Behind', 27 May 2020.
Harris, Usha Sunder. *Participatory Media in Environmental Communication: Engaging Communities in the Periphery.* Routledge 2019.
Saleh, Ibrahim. 'Climate Crisis in Africa' (139–151). In *Media and the Ecological Crisis.* Ed. Maxwell, Richard, Roundalen, Jon and Lager Vestberg, Nina. Routledge 2015.

Environmental Justice: A Case Study of Uruguay (Victoria Gomez)

Uruguay is a leading country in the shift to renewable energy (Kirby and O'Mahony 2018), covering 97% of the internal consumption of electricity. Wind turbines constitute two-thirds of the energy sources, while nuclear energy was considered over a decade ago, but was discounted in the end. However, the economy of this relatively small country in South America is heavily based on agri-industrial production, all the while challenging core environmental protection goals. Nowadays the country is one of the world's largest food producers per capita, supplying food for about 28 million people – nine times the country's population. It is a traditional Uruguayan assertion that the cow population is more numerous than the human population and the country's exports have historically been concentrated on products derived from livestock, and, more recently, grain agriculture and forestry.

Nonetheless, methane emissions are not part of the public conversation (Gómez 2021; Climate Promise 2021), much less the successful policy of investing heavily in renewable energy. Furthermore, climate change evaluations are not backed by increased levels of climate literacy, even within government officials (Stuhldreher 2020). Generally, the 'Feeding the World' label of its agri-exporting role is just starting to be contested by the vegan and vegetarian generational agenda and pushed by young activists. Reminiscent for instance of Norway and oil extraction (Norgaard 2011), it seems that high levels of environmental awareness is coupled with a rarely criticised key traditional industry – no matter how much it contributes to the environmental crisis. At the same time, pulp mills pollution, resulting from the forestry industry (Sannazzaro 2011), together with chemicals used in grain agriculture (Santos et al. 2012; Gómez 2021) are perceived as serious environmental risks. These concerns are expressed in various socio-environmental conflicts and through the activism of environmental organisations (*Friends of the Earth, Fridays for Future Uruguay*).

Historically, economic and social inequalities remain a predominantly post-colonial challenge across Latin America, where environmental protection targets are usually discussed in contrast with basic economic needs. This tension appears when looking at public opinion surveys (i.e. Latinbarometer or LAPOP), while at the policy level, it tends to be solved by prioritising economic and even social justice targets. Furthermore, social scientist Eduardo Gudynas (Uruguay) promoted the notion of 'progressive neo-extractivism' to refer to the Latin American phenomenon of preserving the world-system role of commodity providers, through non-limited extraction of natural resources, despite the spread of left-wing politicians in power who had initially committed to an environmental agenda (Gudynas 2010). As a result, socio-environmental conflicts persist in the territories (Temper et al. 2015), not only involving peasants and indigenous groups (see for instance the film *Daughter of the Lake*, 2015), but also urban inhabitants (Anguelovski and Martínez Alier 2014). Maristella Svampa (Argentina) proposes an eco-territorial approach to neo-extractivism that acknowledges the language of Latin American socio-environmental movements, such as 'Sumak Kawsay' (Good Living) and Rights of Nature (Svampa 2019). In Uruguay, this trend is best represented by the 2009–15 conflict around large-scale iron mining during the ruling of the progressive president's Tabaré Vázquez and José Mujica. The extractive project 'Aratirí' was promoted by the government, but finally rejected as a result of the grassroot movement beginning in rural communities. Street demonstrations were used along with various mediated forms of protest and advocacy (see for instance the YouTube documentary series *Otras Voces por la Tierra*, 2014). The resistance was kick-started by scientists and intellectuals, leading to a public controversy (Gómez 2013; López Echagüe 2017).

References

Anguelovski, I. and Martínez Alier, J. 'The "Environmentalism of the Poor" Revisited: Territory and Place in Disconnected Glocal Struggles'. *Ecological Economics* (102): 167–176. 2014.

Climate Promise. *Climate Perception in Uruguay*. UNDP 2021.

Gómez, V. *Tracks of a changing world: an approach to online discussions over environmental issues in Uruguay*. IAMCR - Fundación Comunica 2013.

Gómez, V. *Mediations of Environmental Risk: Engagement of Young Audiences in Uruguay and Ireland*. DCU 2021.

Gudynas, E. 'The New Extractivism of the 21st Century: Ten Urgent Theses about Extractivism in Relation to Current South American Progressivism'. *Americas Program Report* (21): 1–14. 2010.

Kirby, P. and O'Mahony, T. 'Development and Sustainability in the Global South: Different Routes to Transition and a Sustainable Society' (173–200). In: *The Political Economy of the Low-Carbon Transition*. Palgrave Macmillan 2018.

López Echagüe, C. 'El caso del Proyecto Aratirí de minería a cielo abierto en Uruguay: análisis de una controversia científico-tecnológica'. *Revista Iberoamericana de Ciencia, Tecnología y Sociedad* 12(36): 107–137. 2017.

Norgaard, K. *Living in Denial: Climate Change, Emotions, and Everyday Life*. MIT Press 2011.

Sannazzaro, J. 'Controversias científico-públicas. El caso del conflicto por las 'papeleras' entre Argentina y Uruguay y la participación ciudadana'. *CTS: Revista iberoamericana de ciencia, tecnología y sociedad* 6(17): 213–239. 2011.

Santos, C., Oyhantcabal, G. and Narbondo, I. *La expansión del agronegocio agrícola en Uruguay: impactos, disputas y discursos*. Congress of the Latin American Studies Association 2012.

Stuhldreher, A.M. 'Cambio climático en la región Noreste del Uruguay: clivajes en las percepciones de los actores territoriales'. *Opera* 27: 181–191. 2020.

Svampa, M. *Neo-extractivism in Latin America: Socio-environmental Conflicts, the Territorial Turn, and New Political Narratives*. Cambridge: Cambridge University Press 2019.

Temper, L., Del Bene, D. and Martínez Alier, J. *Environmental Justice Atlas*. 2015. [Online] Available at: http://ejatlas.org [Accessed 1 August 2018].

Environmental Justice – A Case Study of Representations of the Inuit Tribe in The Terror (Nora Doorley)

The impact of European imperialism on Indigenous communities and the cultural and economic forces that drove this process continue to resonate in contemporary western attitudes to natural habitats, especially in the way in which the urge to map and exert control over nature tends to ignore the symbiotic relationship between the Indigenous inhabitants and their home environments. AMC's television adaptation of Dan Simmons' novel, *The Terror,* explores precisely this theme in its fictionalised depiction of the infamous 1845 Franklin expedition. The goal of the expedition, commanded by Captain Sir John Franklin, was to locate the Northwest Passage and navigate a course through to the Pacific Ocean from the Atlantic via British colonial territory in the Arctic, thereby shortening trading routes to China and India from the west. Success in this mission would have earned Franklin and his crew of 129 men international renown, but fortune eluded them, and they disappeared.

Over ten episodes, the series charts the transmogrification of 'an adventure for Queen and country' into a horror story culminating in the death of all but one of the men – Captain Francis Crozier, known to the Indigenous inhabitants as Aglooka. Beyond its appeal as a supernatural thriller, *The Terror* provides for a thematically rich exploration of colonial and ecological discourses, as seen in the representation of Inuit culture and the troubled relationship of the men to an environment that is unforgiving to the unwelcome.

Analysed through the lens of survivalist themes, *The Terror* (2018) is a show that juxtaposes a group of foolhardy adventurers eager to map out the surrounding wilderness against an Inuit community whose respect for nature coupled with an awareness of its capacity for brutality deters them from such recklessness. The Netsilik Inuit, who lie at the heart of this story, possess a detailed knowledge of the area north of Hudson Bay, which enables them to cope in ways that those unfamiliar with the environment cannot. 'This place wants us dead', says Crozier to Franklin as he attempts to convey with urgency the increasing likelihood of entrapment in the ice. Crozier's sober warnings about the unsustainability of their mission fall on deaf ears, however, and Franklin, who permits idolatry of empire to cloud objective judgement, instead chooses to place his faith in the guiding spirit of Rule, Britannia! to divine an entrance to the Passage.

Given that the drama can ostensibly be viewed as a cautionary tale about imperialist hubris and man's blind faith in his superiority over nature, it is no surprise that when the ice solidifies, so too does their fate. The natural world responds with resistance to the lofty ambitions of conquest displayed by the argonauts, employing self-preservation in the face of potentially destructive outside forces and denying intruders the right to sustenance. Indeed, the Tuunbaq – described by the Inuit as a spirit that dresses as an animal – may be interpreted as a personification of the hostile landscape, leaving carnage in its wake and contributing significantly to the crew's death count. British hegemony over nature is not a hierarchy the Tuunbaq accepts. It is a creature 'bound to no one at all', and so, when an Inuit elder serving as its shaman and sole human interlocutor is fatally wounded by the gunfire of an Englishman, all previously imposed restraints on its behaviour cease to exist.

Central to the show's narrative is the shaman's daughter, a young Inuk woman named Silna. Unlike Simmons' portrayal of Silna in the novel, her screen counterpart has a voice, and by extension, a perspective. The decision taken by *The Terror*'s showrunners to provide Silna with a voice of her own demonstrates a willingness to nurture sympathy among audiences for the personal circumstances of her character and to present the experience of colonial subjugation from a Native viewpoint. Her frustrations about the psychic harm inflicted on her home as a result of the expedition's presence are keenly felt, and up until episode six – when she cuts out her tongue to appease the unruly Tuunbaq – she is pointedly vocal about them, questioning the men on what she perceives as self-destructive impulses: 'Why do you want to die?' The hardship Silna endures over the course of *The Terror* arguably points to the wider issue of western contempt for Indigenous communities, not to mention the parasitic quality of all imperial pursuits.

The colonial drive to map and control nature, as shown in The Terror's provocative ecological allegory, still persists today. The 21st century Arctic is a hotbed of geopolitical tensions, which sees global powers competing over natural resources and exploiting the region's minerals and fisheries at the expense of Indigenous communities and with little care for the fragility of the landscape. In the context of an impending climate catastrophe, and with the planet's fate hanging in the balance, the sustainable modes of living practiced by Indigenous tribes like the Inuit should serve as an example to the rest of the world. If the wonder of this place is to be preserved, then everything depends on its protection.

References

Burgan, Michael and Dwyer, Helen. *Inuit History & Culture*. Gareth Stephens Publishing 2011.

Eschner, Kat. 'Tales of the Doomed Franklin Expedition Long Ignored the Inuit Side, But "The Terror" Flips the Script'. 6 April 2018. https://www.smithsonianmag.com/arts-culture/heres-how-amc-producers-worked-inuit-fictionalized-franklin-exp edition-show-180968643/.

MacKenzie, Scott and Westerståhl Stenport, Anna. *Films on Ice: Cinemas of the Arctic*. Edinburgh University Press 2016.

MacKenzie, Scott and Westerståhl Stenport, Anna. 'The Polarities and Hybridities of Arctic Cinemas'. *Oxford Handbooks Online*. April 2019. https://www.oxfordhandbooks.com/view/10.1093/oxfordhb/9780190229108.001.0001/oxfordhb-9780190229108-e-8

Moore, Fiona. 'Comparing Colonialisms in Dan Simmons' Novel The Terror and its Adaptation'. *Academia*. n.d. https://www.academia.edu/40129260/Comparing_colo nialisms_in_Dan_Simmons_novel_The_Terror_and_its_AMC_adaptation

Stern, Pamela R. *Historical Dictionary of the Inuit*. Scarecrow Press, Inc. 2004.

Environmental Management of the Media: Marrying Mindmapping and Carbon Footprinting

This entry draws heavily on the scholarship of Pietari Kääpä (2018) who has carried out extensive interviews with senior media executives across film and television, as they try to steer their expanding industry toward becoming more environmentally sustainable and reducing their carbon footprint. At the same time the media industry needs to produce more provocative environmentally driven content and programming – especially those with a Public Service Broadcasting remit – in taking on the challenge of actively communicating the climate crisis.

For a long time scholars like Richard Maxwell and Toby Miller (2012) have argued that the media industry, together with the growth of communications and ICT, alongside all digital media companies are all complicit with regards to the proliferation of electronic waste and radically increasing their carbon footprint. This is further evident with so much technological obsolescence across interconnecting communications ecosystems. Sean Cubitt's *Ecomedia* (2005) was one of the first studies to focus on these material concerns, outlining not only many of the natural materials that go into media production, exhibition, distribution and consumption, but also initiating scholarly discussion that focused on the related environmental footprint of digital media. Cubitt's work emphasises the notion that those studying the media cannot simply concentrate on texts and textual analysis, but also need to take into account the variety of contextual factors that underpin media production. Later, another media and environmental scholar, Adrian Ivakhiv, takes up this point by suggesting the focus of critical media analysis would need to be on 'things, processes, and systems that support and enable the making and disseminating of cultural texts' (Ivakhiv 2007: 19).

Using sustainability as a clear benchmark and approach, Cubitt provides a productive explanation for evaluating the balance between the material base of production and the (anthropocentric) management of the industry, which needs to be fully understood and appreciated. This involves the difficult challenge of making 'the media more committed to sustainability' and 'to sustain the very media we use' (Cubitt 2017: 14).

For a broader media perspective of this environmental transformation, see also Hunter Vaughan's analysis of the use of water in the classic musical *Singin in the Rain*, published in *Sustainable Media* (2016), where he evaluates

> Hollywood's green conscience to this point is a marketplace conscience, torn in conflicting directions by the forces of economics, industry, and public image. Recognising the economic benefits of sustainable practices, studios have begun to tighten the efficiency and renewability of their raw material use, foregoing however any radical industrial change or empirical critique of the environmental ramifications of film production, and to avoid governmental regulation of its practices.
>
> (27)

Taking on board many of these general observations, Kääpä produces a useful grid of the whole media system, which all environmental media scholars and communication industry insiders ought to take on board. These include:

a   Regulation of the industries:

- domestic media regulations concerning the industry's environmental responsibility (i.e. laws imposed by government ministries for environmental and cultural concerns, adoption of these into media practices)
- environmental frameworks of regulation (concerning issues such as energy usage, recycling standards, chemicals, metals, and trade in hardware)

- industrial affiliations with NGO's (cooperative partnerships with organisations like Greenpeace to promote sustainability and green effectiveness)
- self-regulation (establishment of often voluntary best practice protocols for specific media sectors, economic initiatives to subsidise the adaptation of environmental strategies).

b The organisation of labour

- management strategies – promoting sustainability from top down and bottom up
- employee protocols – organisational rules on implementing green directives, tactics on motivating employee sustainability
- environmental HR – green runners, eco-supervisors, and other roles designed to oversee sustainability in organisations
- training workshops – coordination of sustainability training from external or intra-organisational sources.

c Resources

- production pathways – the role of traditional and digital media technologies in media production, resourcing materials
- carbon pricing – ways to improve or circumvent existing legislation by drawing on 'green taxation'
- digital data – awareness and regulation of the methods of digital data flow and storage
- production protocols – procurement of subsistence, equipment, waste management, travel; approaches to the sharing economy.

d Networking

- industry initiatives – documents focusing on policy; the use of best practice guides to normalise sustainability
- workshops – participation at seminars and workshops organised by industry organisations (BAFTA and the roll out of a Carbon Calculator etc.)
- consultancy organisations – the role of commercial ventures devoted to developing sustainability policies
- organic linking – networks between individuals and collaborations from a grassroots perspective (Kääpä 2018: 7–8).

Within environmental media scholarship there has continued to be a focus on texts and textual analysis, but as Kääpä and others rightly affirm, we need to explicitly focus on the impact of content, or what is called 'the brainprint'. Basically, while content dominates much eco-media analysis there is less interest in the carbon footprint produced by such media production and output. Probably, it is not surprising that most studies from industry and the academy have focused on the ability and responsibility of the media to communicate for and about the environment, rather than 'looking inside the hood' of the finished production and assessing its specific carbon footprint. For instance, BAFTA in Britain estimates that a single hour of television drama produces 13.6 tonnes of CO_2, which is equivalent to approximately four times the size of an individual's annual CO_2 footprint. As in all businesses, both public and private organisations, the constant question raised focuses on how sustainability and the media business can co-exist productively (Kääpä 2018: 10).

Certainly, much further work is needed to develop a robust integration of protocols of effective media management, sustainability and active environmental engagement into the future. The media industries remain probably the most important sites for such productive engagement with both mindmapping and in helping to promote mass behavioural change with regards to environmental transformation. At the same time, as a growing and interconnecting industry, it constantly needs to reduce and control its total carbon footprint, as media industries converge, integrate and evolve over the coming critical decades in helping to support the future survival of the planet.

References

Cubitt, Sean. *Ecomedia*. Rodopi 2005.

Cubitt, Sean. *Finite Media: Environmental Implications of Digital Technologies*. Duke University Press 2017.

Ivakhiv, Adrian. 'Green Film Criticism and its Futures'. *Interdisciplinary Studies in Literature and Environment (ISLE)* 15(2): 1–28. 2007.

Kääpä, Pietari. *Environmental Management of the Media: Policy, Industry, Practice*. Routledge 2018.

Maxwell, Richard and Miller, Toby. *Greening the Media*. Oxford University Press 2012.

Vaughan, Hunter. '500,000 Kilowatts of Stardust: An Ecomaterialist Reframing of Singin' in the Rain' (23–37). In Starosielski, N. and Walker, J. (eds) *Sustainable Media*. Routledge 2016.

F

Fake News and Environment Communication – The Social Dilemma

Fake news is a form of propaganda or mistruths that consist of deliberate misinformation spread by the media and especially focused around digital social media. Often sensational headlines are used to mislead the reader, while exaggerating the importance of the story being presented. Of course, intentionally misleading fake news is different from satire or parody, which is intended to amuse, but not necessarily mislead. Media scholars in particular worry that fake news can undermine serious journalism and media coverage and can deflect attention away from the truth of the news story under investigation. Especially with regards to the seriousness and difficult theme of climate change, several layers of fake news can be deployed, especially recalling various facets of climate denialism, which can have major effects on getting across the seriousness and long-term consequences of climate change.

While the notion of post-truth – similar to fake news – remains a deep problematic political and cultural condition embedded especially within the new media ecosystem. This in turn has global ramifications for environmental communications, as well as for all forms of media ecology. By locating the roots of the phenomenon in the trust crisis suffered by liberal democracy and its institutions, Gabriele Cosentino (2020) argues that post-truth serves as a space for festering ideological conflicts and geopolitical power struggles that are reshaping the world order. While fake news or so-called post-truth has been of concern for a long time, this phenomenon has become more prevalent of late and is exacerbated by the proliferation of new online platforms and the development of social media, coupled with the growth of active user engagement across all digital spheres of communication. The growth of such new-media platforms serves to polarise audience usage and responses. Furthermore, feeding off untrustworthy content and sourcing can amplifying news and the potential for disinformation, which in turn drive up conflicting agendas.

A fascinating piece in the *Boston Review* (Callison and Slobodian 2021) pronounces how viral films such as *Plandemic* and *Hold-Up* (2020) – with an estimated audience of over 9 million and 6 million respectively (on YouTube),

DOI: 10.4324/9781003123422-7

describe the pandemic as a pretext for global elites to roll out a thorough-going transformation of everyday life. With regards to the climate emergency there has been a long history of 'deniers', with overt if not covert media opposition to scientific pronouncements regarding the seriousness of the crisis. This is particularly evidenced by ClimateGate as discussed elsewhere, demonstrating how online media can sow the seeds of dissent through some form of conspiracy. It would appear there is strong evidence of extreme alt-right groups pushing climate-denialism, including new forms of conspiratorial fake news. By all accounts, unfounded questioning of the legitimacy of all forms of democratic politics and governance, appear to be in the ascendent.

For instance, academic reports during 2020 focused on a radical German grouping 'Querdenker' who voted Green and Left in previous elections and explore how these movements can be contrasted with Trump's 'Save America Rally's' and the subsequent unfounded lawsuits and pronouncements that the 2020 American election was fake and illegal. All of these global incidents were allegedly pushing a form of constitutional rights of 'Free Press' and spurious concerns about press censorship into the public arena. Meanwhile, the environmental crisis gets more pressing all the time and is sometimes lost in such low-level media frenzy concerning fake news debates. From an environmental perspective, one must also worry of course how such radical disruptive movements affect the global political struggle to instigate change across all our behaviour-patterns, as we face the most pernicious global struggle to protect our planet from ecocidal disaster.

Surprisingly, up to half of the social media audiences researched in several surveys, confirm they 'mostly distrust' the internet posts they come upon about science (Pew Research Centre 2017). Basically it would appear 'society is drowning in a sea of unmoored opinions and values', with Rush Holt (2019) Chief Executive of US Advanced Science, together with several environmental communicators, arguing that 'democracy requires a citizenry that is informed' (433). Yet despite the spread of fake news, the positive potential for the internet at the same time is enormous. (See for instance the African website www.oxpeckers.org or examine the journalistic writings of Carey Gillam, author of *Whitewash: The Story of a Weed Killer, Cancer and the Corruption of Science.*)

Most academic media and communication commentators affirm that the key goal of all journalists is basically to follow the facts and bring truth to light. Yet recently for instance data scientists have documented how fake news can spread across Twitter's users, through what they call 'propaganda bots' (in Sachsman and Valenti 2020: 85; see Mann 2021 for American political examples), all of which has been exacerbated by the phenomenal Twitter outputs of ex-President Trump. While at a more local and defined business level, one could examine the work of Sharon Lerner on 'Teflon Toxic', focused around dumping by the chemical company DuPont (2015–18) which was published in *The Intercept*. The American Environmental Protection Agency (EPA) had fined the company over 16 million dollars in 2006 for covering up years of health hazards infringements. Then in 2017 the company agreed to settle thousands of legal claims for 671 million dollars. This environmental story is effectively illustrated in the Hollywood film *Dark Waters* (2019) discussed elsewhere in this volume. The mass media, in spite of dangers around fake news, has a major role to play, as illustrated through the following cautionary tale.

A Case Study of the Power of Online Fake News: The Social Dilemma (2020)

The Netflix documentary has proved very popular since it first appeared online, with many contributors being 'ex-employees' of the giant media tech companies and calling out warning against the online platform's inherent dangers – basically seducing susceptible young people in particular. For instance, Roger McNamee affirms 'on the record' that Facebook's algorithms favour content that emotionally engages its captive audience. This preoccupation around 'manipulation' and the inherent unique power of a new media platform dominates a majority of the documentary. It focuses on two case study exemplars of young 'addicted' archetypical users, who are apparently badly affected by the influence of such powerful online media platforms. One is a typical, high-consuming media user, being a young girl who is lacking confidence and is literally 'blasted' by a huge amount of spiteful responses from fellow students, alongside so-called online 'friends'. Incidentally, as noted in the documentary, the only other industry, which calls its customers 'users', is the drug industry!

Many of these posts really hurt this otherwise 'fictional constructed person', as she is shown sitting alone in her bedroom contemplating her lack of a true authentic identity, outside of the '*Black Mirror*' (referencing the cult television series) of her 'smart' phone, through which she makes and keeps contact with the world. All of which foregrounds a hyper-mediated landscape and a purely digitised means of engaging with the world. Researchers, including child psychologists and sociologists, often suggest that this is unhelpful for teenagers who are actively engaging with such powerful and manipulative media formats during their formative years. Reminiscent of old fashioned media manipulation theories, this critical analysis infers that young audiences in particular are perceived as being victimised, having no power/agency within such vicarious new media engagement.

In the documentary, viewers are also 'connected' with an archetypical late-teen boy, who is totally addicted to his phone for all his activities and engagement. When his mother creates a test for him to go 'cold turkey' for a week and give up his phone, the boy finds it impossible. Meanwhile, the advertising bots – personified as human agents – effectively use every psychological trick at their disposal to get their customers/clients to (re-)click and connect with their paid-for advertising services. Various insidious tricks and motivators are used to get the imaginary boy back into the 'game and get hooked up'.

The intensity of the barrage of messages and pernicious modes of advertising – as with the young girl cited earlier – becomes too much for the boy to cope with. He cannot distinguish between what is useful or not. Soon he becomes hooked on various fake news sites and is seduced by outlandish 'conspiracy theories' – which incidentally is often signalled as an explanation for the rise of climate deniers, much less anti-vaccine followers, during the recent pandemic. These media-like drugs apparently help him to feel important and different, while coaxing him into more real-life dangerous activity, including attending an anti-establishment demonstration. Here he gets arrested, together with his big sister trying to protect him. Recalling such cautionary ('teacherly') incidents, it is worth carrying out detailed analysis of the documentary and its strategies towards demonising such online media platforms, as simply enticing its users to be hooked on the platforms through free software.

Customers/users or subscribers end up becoming 'click-bait' for advertisers to prey on them for all types of marketing and other monetised strategies. As the old adage goes, if something is free which *we* are using, then it is often *we* who are being 'sold to advertisers' to pay for such services. The online digital media ecology is certainly far from a benevolent natural or egalitarian system and seeks to engage its users in the process of creating winners and most certainly lots of 'losers'.

For instance, CNBC 'Facebook Rebuts: The Social Dilemma!' (2 October 2020) by Todd Haselton and Jessica Bursztynsky, focused on how social networks use algorithms to keep (susceptible) people coming back, while also addressed how global tech-companies have apparently influenced elections, ethnic violence and even affected rates of depression and suicide among some viewers. As a consequence, some interviewed on the programme announced they were deleting their Facebook and Instagram accounts. Meanwhile, Facebook of course rebutted such accusations, affirming that 'rather than offering a nuanced look at technology, it gives a distorted view of how social media platforms work to create a convenient scapegoat for what are difficult and complex societal problems' (Haselton and Bursztynsky 2020).

Regarding alleged Russian intervention in American elections for instance, much less rejecting the importance of environmental issues by giving a platform to climate deniers like Trump and others, Twitter and other online media platforms quickly moved to censor such popular 'cash cows', once Trump lost power. By all accounts Twitter and Facebook were said to have 'served as President Donald Trump's digital megaphones' and were widely blamed for 'polarising political opinion, normalising extremism and mobilising violent protest' (Thornhill 2021). But then as history shows, the medium is often blamed for the message. Nonetheless, a pivotal point occurred when such media savvy icons became toxic and even too extreme for a libertarian media ecology.

Facebook and other multinational IT media companies have taken some steps to secure the integrity of all [future] elections, such as banning new advertisements the week prior to the election and banning those who seek to delegitimise the election. However, the constant self-serving assertation that online media platforms such as Facebook, Google, Twitter and others were not designated as broadcasters or media producers, was not enough to let them off the hook of curating, managing and controlling their massive online content. Constantly enunciating the assertion that they are simply a 'free to air' platform provider, and thereby taking no responsibility as a publisher or (public service) broadcaster for that matter and thereby having to take responsibility for what is posted on their platform.

Alternatively, audiences much less global citizens expect and probably demand too much from their online media portals. In particular, as environmental communicators, we are primarily concerned with the dangerous rise of fake news around climate change. Yet at the same time, any strategies that can mobilise public opinion towards both recognising, accepting and actively dealing with the crisis, is becoming a major responsibility and challenge for all media platforms. Both legacy media and digital online media need to put their shoulder to the wheel and actively address the enormous difficulties around climate change and facing up to the growing emergency.

Incidentally, other new media global players like Apple – at least according to those constantly in the firing line, such as its competitor Facebook – can be regarded as even more complicit in their strategies around securing customers and hooking app-users through their Apple store. It should be noted that the Apple corporation is the first private corporation to reach a market value of two trillion dollars (Preston 2021: 76). Such debates are tied into customers losing some of their freedoms, at least according to an industry expert Eric Benjamin Seufert. But of course what use are freedoms, if we don't have a planet to be free in!

Seufert (2020) affirms for instance that Apple's app-tracking transparency technology does not provide real consumer choice. The Freemium App economy is targeted at personalised advertising and calls up some major issues. 'If Apple wants to provide customers with real choice around how their data is collected and used, it should explain why their data is collected and used, and for what purpose'. The reality is that the data used to personalise advertisements by most online platforms is benign, and most importantly boring, Seufert concludes in his provocative piece.

In any case, online media will continue to have a major role to play in reflecting political and business as well as entertainment agendas for young people and all citizens alike. However, its combined global power needs to uncover more innovative and radical ways of using this power for protecting our planet and helping to reduce our carbon footprint, before it is too late.

References

Callison, William and Slobodian, Quinn (12 January, 2021) 'Thinking in a Pandemic: Corona Politics from the Reichstag to the Capital'. *Boston Review* https://bostonreview.net/politics/william-callison-quinn-slobodian-coronapolitics-reichstag-capitol

Costentino, Gabriele. *Social Media and the Post-Truth World Order: The Global Dynamics of Disinformation*. Palgrave Macmillan 2020.

Curran, James and Seaton, Jean. *Power without Responsibility: Press, Broadcasting and the Internet in Britain*. Routledge 1997.

Gilliam, Carey. *Whitewash: The Story of a Weed killer, Cancer and the Corruption of Science*. Island Press 2017.

Haselton, Todd and Bursztynsky, Jessica. 'Facebook Rebuts: The Social Dilemma, A Popular Netflix Drama'. *CNBC*. 2 October 2020. https://www.cnbc.com/2020/10/02/facebook-rebuts-the-social-dilemma-popular-netflix-documentary.html.

Holt, Rush. 'Democracy's Plight'. *Science* 363(6426): 433. 1 February 2019. https://epic.org/people/rush-holt/

Lerner, Sharon. 'The Teflon Toxin: How DuPont Slipped Past the EPA'. The Intercept. 20 August 2015. https://theintercept.com/2015/08/20/teflon-toxin-dupont-slipped-past-epa/

Mann, Michael. *The New Climate War: The Fight to Take Back our Planet*. Public Affairs 2021.

Pew Research Centre. 'Science News and Information Today'. 20 September 2017. https://www.pewresearch.org/science/dataset/2017-pew-research-center-science-and-news-survey/

Preston, Paschal (ed). 'Decoding the 'Social Dilemma'. Guest Editor of special Section with several reviews of Jeff Orlowski's film: 'The Social Dilemma'. (Distributor: Netflix). Reviews published in *The Political Economy of Communication* 8(2). 2021.

Sachsman, David B. and Valenti, JoAnn Myer. *Handbook of Environmental Journalism*. Routledge 2020.

Seufert, Eric Benjamin. 'App Tracking Transparency Does not Provide Real Consumer Choice'. 18 December 2020. https://mobiledevmemo.com/att-does-not-represent-real-consumer-choice/

Thornhill, John. 'The Tech Platforms are not Entirely to Blame for Washington Unrest'. *Financial Times* 7 January 2021.

Fast Fashion, the 'Third World' and the Circular Economy

Many student projects are kick-started by addressing the abuses of 'fast fashion'. Fast fashion supports cheap clothing – often sourced and manufactured in 'sweatshops' by poor usually female employees in India and other parts of the developing world and such products are mostly sold to Western customers in very large volume. Many big western-clothes-branded retailers have been accused of exploitation and this has led to more reactionary responses to such unethical practices. Boutique and anti-fast fashion brands have become popular, together with a massive increase in second-hand clothes and the reuse and upscaling of quality and environmentally sustainable clothing products. All the while, the health, provenance and climate justice implications of such a global industry is constantly being called into question. This highlights the environmental cost of making and dying garments, alongside the often substandard working conditions and low income of many producing the garments in the first place, who tend to live in poor developing regions.

In a very useful webinar hosted by the Institute of International and European Affairs (IIEA), together with the Environmental Protection Agency (EPA) to celebrate Earth Day on 22 April 2021, Inger Andersen, who is the director of UN Environmental programme since 2019 and for 30 years has been working on developments in Africa and 15 years in the World Bank, provided a very engaging keynote speech on all aspects of the economy, including fast fashion, together with the benefits of the circular economy. Basically, she affirmed that moving to a circular economy is critical for all countries with so much disposable packaging and throwaway sources, including the latest digital gadgets that keep driving us. Essentially, we need to look at the full life cycle of products, while promoting a resource efficient economy and a resilient society. Within the literature, the use of a robust circular economy is often considered a core response towards dealing with the environmental dangers of fast fashion, alongside other carbon wasteful industries.

Anderson (2021) spoke for instance of how the 2020/21 pandemic has caused lots of difficulties, but how we need to face up to a combination of more long-term crises – especially the climate crisis; the biodiversity crisis and nature; and the pollution crisis – which are all intricately interconnected. Consequently, we need a global economy that is entirely circular. All three crises have devastating economic and social impact and are accelerating our overall planetary crisis. And of course these crises always affect the poor more than other sections of society. We have unsustainable models of production and consumption – not least within fast fashion where western society in particular throws away so much scarce resources. Apparently, the clothing industry globally produces more greenhouse gasses than even air transport. Like many environmentalists, she calls out the need for a global model of collecting and recycling, and most importantly not using the developing world to basically 'get rid of waste' from the rich Western world. This remains a major challenge and one which environmental communication students and scholars need to be actively highlighting and addressing. For example, Cambodia's textile industry produces over three-quarters of the world's dyes and has a major influence on their natural habitats. All of society needs to urgently accelerate transition to a circular economy and not simply export our First World waste.

But of course circularity as it applies to fashion and other industries, is not an easy fix or panacea for a broad range of global difficulties. We need a whole of society approval, to initiate and demand the move to circularity and sustainable consumption and to deliver on the Sustainable Development Goals (STG), which are globally recognised but need to be urgently acted upon. Recalling ethical debates around how we used to have 'sweat shops' or various forms of slavery in the West; apparently Andersen notes 'we' wanted and strove to end such unjust practices. Now we need to be equally radical and home in on the need for a just global economy. But of course regarding Fast Fashion, not to mention various other forms of digital media e-waste, we still need to rethink our circular economy models and support a just transition for all our global citizens.

References

Andersen, Inger (the director of UN Environmental program since 2019), for a very useful webinar, hosted by the Institute of International and European Affairs (IIEA), together with the Environmental Protection Agency (EPA) here in Ireland, to celebrate Earth Day on 22 April 2021.

Free Press Theory Versus Social Responsibility Model of Media: Case Study of ClimateGate

Free Press or the Libertarian media model favours private ownership of media, which envisages its main purpose as being to inform, entertain, sell, and at the same time serve as a watchdog (or acting as a 'Fourth Estate') while protecting general public interests; all the while keeping governments and powerful stakeholders in check. The theory is based on the primary belief that every citizen has the right to information and protection of their welfare for the common good – which also extends into a holistic environmental common sphere. Furthermore, the theory also perceives public/citizen(s) as rational enough to decide what is inherently good or bad and thereby the press's role should involve not restricting or becoming too heavy-handed regarding censorship of ideas or responses as a consequence.

Using this broad approach, one could argue that 'Climate Deniers' – even though only representing apparently around 3% of *bone fide* scientists, for instance – should be given a representative if not equal voice to put across their oppositional point of view. While cynically it is recognised that media organisations basically 'love conflict', as it serves to build ratings. Hence including climate deniers in any debate 'spices up the discussion' and apparently can help to build larger general audiences. This ongoing debate continues with (public service) broadcasters in particular striving to maintain their objectivity and impartiality by recognising and affording a platform for such minority dissenting voices. However, environmentalists and climate activists perceive this apparent 'free press' rationale as neither fair or even tenable in the long-term struggle to transform the planet. It would appear that several public service broadcasters, such as the BBC and others, have now accepted that this so-called Libertarian free press logic does not justify affording deniers the unhelpful oxygen of free publicity.

Other more authoritarian models of media control do not have the luxury of such libertarian debate as evident across so-called 'repressive regimes' like North Korea, China, Russia, or Afghanistan (where the Taliban have retaken the country, following a controversial withdrawal after a 20-years' war in response to the 9/11 attacks on America); as well as many other African and other regions. Such regions tend to ensure journalists and media outlets are kept on a tight leash – not just regarding environmental reporting – and are often forced to support and endorse national government edicts. Somewhat crudely these modes of media ownership and control are often set up and contrasted with the so-called Social Responsibility model, which supports the long-established liberal ethos of public service broadcasting. Media organisations like the BBC embody these core principles, where the 'Public Good' is considered as the most important set of values, positioned above the financial or commercial imperative of simply maximising audience figures and increasing advertising profits and other revenue streams. In reality however, many media and communication scholars would rightly contest such crude polarities and divisions, highlighting hard evidence of ever expanding political-ideological tensions and conflicts across environmental or other issues, which constantly flare up across different regions and communities.

Nonetheless, embedded in their DNA almost, Public Service Broadcasting (PSB) actively support deliberative and democratic processes, recalling the roots of Western broadcasting media institutions across canonical academic studies of press and broadcast media (see for instance Curran and Seaton's seminal study *Power without Responsibility* 1997). Such organisations continue to embody the role of investigative and public watchdog for the protection of all citizens. Crudely, the so-called 'Fourth Estate' recalls the historical evolution of mass media in France and the rise of Republican values, where the media as an estate was constituted as a balancing power block between other powerful estates such as government, judiciary and the Church. Consequently, broadcast television media was designed to help protect democratic rights and responsibilities of individual citizens, against all forms of oppressive power or other legal constraints put upon them. With the crisis of our global environmental dilemma, the need for robust and challenging (PSB) journalism is demanded more than ever, to stand up to hegemonic powerful establishments and businesses (if not also deniers), as well as global corporations who often simply want to protect the status quo and do not consider the urgent necessity to address the climate crisis.

Contemporary debates especially with the proliferation of so much new/online media, continue to focus on what is or is not in the 'public interest'; all of which remains highly contentious, as particularly evident across a broad range of environmental issues and debates. Whether its Carbon Taxes, the Green New Deal, Public Ownership of Natural Resources, GDP growth, Degrowth or reducing overall Consumption – these are all highly contentious issues and debates, which feed off fundamental ideological divisions that have been part of the media DNA since it first evolved. Environmental communication's marshalling of empirical evidence and strategies for coping with such a range of issues do not have simple solutions, demands extensive critical awareness and robust assessment of evidence to uncover appropriate media responses to such problems. In the end such dialogue will help to sustainably negotiate the issues and come up with appropriate strategic and long-term responses.

Case Study of Climategate

For instance, America's constitution guarantees the rights of free speech, and journalists might appear on paper at least to have greater rights of public expression within such a regime. But unfortunately viewing figures and profits continue to drive public media protocols, with money and financial interests appearing to dominate the news agenda. Thankfully, there have been notable examples of the free press fighting back and flexing its considerable ethical muscles. Recalling for instance the 1970s Watergate Scandal, which lead to the impeachment of President Nixon, on uncovering corruption at the highest level of political office. Such incidents stand out as key bell-weather markers of the importance and power of the media to help promote political and economic transparency – including calling out incidents of environmental corruption – and effectively support the common good.

Environmental scandals, most notably the so-called 'Climategate' incident (2009) in the UK, stands out as a media story pushed into the public arena for very different reasons. Initially, the incident served to discredit some scientists with the apparent illicit publication online of scientific data dealing with the spread of climate change. But much later such allegations were proved wrong. Nevertheless, it would appear some damage was done to the reputation of a few well-known scientists. To get a flavour of this important story, see for instance Lucy Mangan's *The Guardian* article from 14 November 2019, which analysed the Channel 4 documentary on the affair *Climategate: Science of a Scandal*.

The Climategate incident was based on the true story of an anonymous hacker who stole and shared thousands of emails between scientists at the Climatic Research Unit (CRU) based at the University of East Anglia in the UK. These hacked emails were seized on by assorted sceptics and deniers and used to cast doubt on the scientific accuracy of our climate crisis and global warming generally. Mangan goes so far as to assert that further damage was also done by an 'uncritical media that leaned into the storm'. The CRU director Phil Jones in particular came under intense scrutiny, yet two independent inquiries and a Government Select Committee all exonerated him, together with the CRU of all accusations. Nonetheless, according to several commentators, the scandal helped towards contributing to the lack of success of the 2009 Copenhagen Climate COP and fed off more unfortunate incidents of denial rhetoric around climate change that cluttered up the mediasphere for a time.

Studies by Ramon and Pearce (2020) argue that there were three norms that set the foundation of Climategate and escalating it to the level of a scandal:

- using scientific consensus to justify climate policy
- that openness is fundamental to validation of scientific knowledge
- that the public was conceived as passive recipients of scientific knowledge rather than participants in dialogue.

By all accounts the 'oxygen of publicity' of the media can be used as a double-edged sword in the struggle to speak to the ongoing catastrophic challenges of climate change, not to mention the future survival of humans on the planet. Environmental scientists often complain that they simply want to report their findings and are not specifically trained to deal with the machinations of the media apparatus. Meanwhile, investigative journalists and commercial news outlets are often trying simply to uncover some angle or contradiction that conflicts with the findings to frame their resultant news headline and thereby make their story more interesting. Basically, media news outlets have to compete with other media organisations in communicating such global stories and consequently strive to make their story as appealing and conflict-driven as possible. All the while news outlets tend to believe as a first-principle of commercial media practice that controversy ('if it bleeds it leads' approach) can produce larger audiences.

Furthermore, powerful forces who want to maintain the status quo can use a range of nefarious means at their disposal to fight the sometimes amateurish communication strategies of the poorly funded 'official' environmental lobby groups. But the pendulum remains unbalanced when pitted between a well-funded, professional and long-term media strategist organisation. For example, one can easily see the tensions between a PR organisation who wants to promote the fossil-fuel industries continuing and/or diversifying into renewable energy, as against a poorly funded, less-professional and more short-term range of activists, who often cannot give such stories the time needed to develop them properly. It is easy to predict who secures the greatest traction and extensive media coverage.

Nonetheless, promoting environmental discussion through constant repetition and salience remains a core mission for instance of the left-leaning UK newspaper *The Guardian*. This position is geographically illustrated by promotional comments, tagged following various review pieces cited from this newspaper during 2020 and 2021.

> *The Guardian* recognises the climate emergency as the defining issue of our times. That's why we have pledged to give climate change, wildlife extinction and pollution the sustained attention and prominence they demand, as a core part of our journalism.
>
> At this pivotal moment for our planet, our independence enables us to always inform readers about threats, consequences and solutions based on scientific fact, not political prejudice or business interests. This makes us different. And we are equally determined to practice what we preach: we have divested from the oil and gas sectors, renounced fossil-fuel advertising and committed to achieving carbon neutrality by 2030.
>
> We believe everyone deserves access to information that is fact-checked, and analysis that has authority and integrity. That's why, unlike many others, we made a choice: to keep *Guardian* reporting open for all, regardless of where they live or what they can afford to pay. Our work would not be possible without our readers, who now support our work from 180 countries around the world.

References

Mangan, Lucy. 'Climategate: Science of a Scandal Review – the Hack that Cursed Our Planet'. *The Guardian*. 14 November 2019. https://www.theguardian.com/tv-and-radio/2019/nov/14/climategate-science-of-a-scandal-review-the-hack-that-cursed-our-planet.

Ramon, S. and Pearce, W. 'Learning the Lessons of Climategate: A Cosmopolitan Moment in the Public Life of Climate Science'. *WIREs Climate Change* September 2020.

G

Green Transformation and Global Citizen Engagement – Green New Deal (Naomi Klein)

Environmental communicators need to examine various ways of ensuring attitudinal and behavioural change that supports a radical new green agenda, especially taking into account growing concerns for personal health and well-being as we struggle for our environmental survival. All these areas need to be framed and actioned through the core values of fairness and solidarity across the world. Uncovering robust and transparent ethical models for dealing with disadvantaged and vulnerable social groups and communities most affected by the drive towards a low-carbon future has to be a number one priority. While persuading citizens to replace wasteful everyday practices and modes of consumption with environmentally friendly habits is essential in this ongoing struggle to address our climate and health emergency.

Consequently, we badly need behavioural change and long-term commitment, trust, social acceptance and buy-in from people, communities and organisations across the spectrum. This can be achieved by developing effective new strategies to help induce change and transformation, including innovative recommendations and incentives that take account of differences between regions, countries and even continents.

Such radical transformation around citizen and consumer behaviour can be facilitated through co-opting all forms of media, communications and broad-based education. As the following case study of America illustrates, actively using the tools of citizen science, applying observation and monitoring across a range of environmental problems, can in turn help build new forms of civic engagement and social innovation towards addressing the climate emergency.

Naomi Klein's (American) Response to the Climate Crisis

In a new introduction to a revised edition *On Fire: The Burning Case for a Green New Deal* (2020), the internationally renowned environmental journalist Naomi Klein calls attention to the raging pandemic, which has

DOI: 10.4324/9781003123422-8

trust the entire globe into an era of rapid and radical change. Radical changes to our individual habits, expectations, and routines. Radical changes to government and fiscal policy. Radical changes to the relationships between powerful nation states. And radical changes to the natural world around us – from sudden drops in air, water, and noise pollution to abrupt shifts in the behaviour of countless wild species.

(xiv)

Most notably Klein, like many other worried environmentalists, calls out the necessity of major behavioural change around air transport and travel generally alongside supporting less meat consumption to help address the problem. Furthermore, as also alluded to in this volume, she ponders if major companies and governments can carry out such radical 're-thinking' and system change for a 'global pandemic', then 'why not for green jobs, like planting trees, remediating polluted land, and building energy-efficient affordable homes? Why can't stakeholders at all levels be paid to retool their skills to shift from high-carbon sectors to zero-carbon ones?' (ibid.: xix).

While fully recognising the importance of an all-encompassing radical Green New Deal, especially in America, such commentators allude to the often quoted criticism that climate change is somehow being used as a Trojan horse, designed to abolish capitalism and replace it with some kind of eco-socialism. The scientist who is famous for his 'hockey stick' graphs of climate change, Michael Mann (2021), further reinforces this interpretation with his scathing critique of the rise of climate denialism and how well-funded, fossil-fuel industries are using various nefarious strategies to disrupt the drive to support urgent carbon reductions. The analogy of a watermelon for instance is used by Mann, which is green on the outside but red inside, to help illustrate the fear of socialism being brought to the fore by adopting a green agenda. This often unacknowledged fear is also fully illustrated in Larry Bell's *Climate of Corruption* (2011), which argues that climate change 'has little to do with the state of the environment and much to do with shackling capitalism and transforming the American way of life in the interests of global wealth redistribution' (Klein 2020: 72).

While some climate change activists demand an end to all forms of dangerous trade, others, 'more judiciously demand simply an overhaul of the reckless form of "free trade" that governs every bilateral trade agreement and the World Trade Organisation' (ibid.: 85). Of course, dealing effectively with our climate crisis demands that we consume less, but as Klein pithily affirms 'being consumers is all we know'. Overall, climate change is not just a problem that can be solved simply by changing what we buy – 'a hybrid instead of an SUV, or some carbon offsets when we get on a plane. At its core, it is a crisis of overconsumption by the comparatively wealthy, which means the world's most manic consumers are going to have to consume less, so that others can have enough to live' (Klein 2020: 122).

Yet some 'de-growth' environmental commentators however remain far less optimistic regarding the inherent benefits of such a Green New Deal, no matter what it is called. There is also some evidence of late in America and elsewhere of simply avoiding using the tagline Green New Deal because of objections to its inherent left-leaning politics and philosophy. In spite of its apparent 'top-down' strategizing and not always taking into account the inherent complexities of life on the ground across the world, the policy package certainly strives to promote sustainable results. It nevertheless appears however that such broad based green political strategies remain the only coherent approach for most Liberal-Democratic systems, as the ongoing herculean struggle and ideological tensions between so-called 'degrowth and green growth' forces continues to be played out.

The key challenge for environmental communications scholarship includes bringing audiences and citizens along while facing up to the challenges ahead and encouraging all citizens to make governments and corporations take on their even greater responsibility for the protection of our planet. Klein, Mann and several other environmental commentators in their ongoing writings have signalled some important ways for global citizens to learn about and help kick-start global transformation, while ensuring transparency and becoming much more proactive in the pursuit of a low-carbon transition.

References

Klein, Naomi. *On Fire: The Burning Case for a Green New Deal*. Penguin 2019 (see 2020 ed.)

Bell, Larry. *Climate of Corruption: Politics and Power behind the Global Warming Hoax*. Greenleaf Books 2011.

Mann, Michael. *The New Climate War: The Fight to Take Back our Planet*. Scribe 2021.

Greening the Higher Education Curriculum: Drawing on the Power of Children's Media

Many left-leaning critics remain worried that Higher Education has 'become a service for sale, even more ready to hire itself out to governments or multi-nationals' (see Illich cited in Waks 1991: 57). Such concern call to mind current efforts to 'green the curriculum', designed according to some critics as simply aiming to service the needs of industry and commerce. But of course the reality is not as simple or as clear cut, with educational scholarship suggesting that greening the academy must also assist in 'interrogating the liberal arts disciplines'. Such an ongoing process

> does so pedagogically, to explicate the qualitative difference between capitalist (and related oppressive forms of) disciplinary "greenspeak" on the one hand, and the disruptive democratic types of ecological disciplinarity that move beyond mere speech, and to which we must now transition by any means necessary, on the other.
>
> (Fassbinder et al. 2012: xvii)

By all accounts, the domination of 'sustainability as a science', together with feeding off 'sustainability as (encapsulating) justice and equity', has strongly come to the fore. This echoes an inaccurate representation of the reality of sustainability as 'an amorphous trans-disciplinary subject area, speaking to all forms of environmental issues that have heretofore been studied in separate departments'. But now, more than ever, such discourses need to be brought together in the academy, since as is constantly affirmed across environmental communications, 'everything is connected'. A study of the area by Fassbinder et al. (2012: xx) rightly affirm that Higher Education should draw on more traditional scholars like John Dewey (1897) and revolutionaries like Antonio Gramsci (long-embraced by critical media studies scholars), while at the same time recognising that 'every crisis is also a moment of reconstruction' in which 'the normal functioning of the old economic, social, cultural order, provides the opportunity to recognise it in new ways' (Hall 1987 cited in Fassbinder et al. 2012). This proposition is certainly appealing during 2020/21, as the world continue to face the global challenge of climate change, while being alternatively consumed by a totalising struggle of a deadly, global pandemic.

Such a global tension and crisis can be harnessed also through Higher Educational initiatives. For instance, in an ongoing partnership, encapsulated by the American based 'Academy for a Social Purpose in Responsible Entertainment' (ASPIRE); much work is being harnessed around designing ways to create media-based capstones and service-learning opportunities (Rice 2017: 38). One can usefully frame the objectives of ASPIRE to include various aspects of environmental education, together with all forms of educational literacy in dealing with the ongoing climate crisis. All of these attributes and core activities are particularly designed for liberal arts undergraduates and its successes can be repurposed as we move towards facing up to prescient global environmental disasters.

Audio-visual training across Higher Education, as constantly alluded to in this volume, can play a key role in this global challenge, by helping citizens to tease out both the realities of various environmental sustainability crises and suggesting imaginative solutions to deal with them. See for instance the ongoing University of California, Los Angeles (UCLA) Grand Challenge, with its campus-wide promotion of sustainability efforts, which ought to be replicated across all educational campuses aiming to promote environmental praxis. Furthermore, much more innovation is required across their media and communication courses, much less environmental ones, to help ensure sustainable use of resources. For example, in a useful practical filmmaking example, students shared selected files through a Google Drive forum created especially for the course and then uploaded rough-cuts of their work to this site. With massive strides made towards more effective online teaching and learning, radically expanded by the way, in having to pivot to online teaching during the 2020/21 pandemic, environmental communications and extensive new online forms of media literacy can be harnessed at all levels of the educational spectrum, as students and educators strive to promote innovative online learning. Environmental communication as an evolving pedagogical set of practices and investigations most certainly needs to be at the vanguard while learning from such innovative practices and case studies.

Case Study of Children's TV and Environmental Media Education

Alongside mainstream Higher Educational media production and environmental communications courses are facing up to the challenges ahead, concurrently professional media approaches to children's education have also evolved to meet these challenges. For instance, a comprehensive study by Sharifi et al. (2019), outlines a strategy aimed 'to design a model for children's TV education using a cognitive approach to environmental education. Children's television is now used as one of the most important means of distance learning'. This comparative study continues by suggesting that the main areas of environmental education on television that feed into new production methods includes:

Teaching natural geography and the dangers of manipulating nature
Focus on individual diseases caused by non-observance of nature
Teaching basic and simple concepts of sustainable development
Teaching about the planet, (especially with regards to air and soil)
Waste recycling learning and entertainment and cleaning the environment
Campaigning around the environment and using interactive techniques, as well as forming social networks in the media, as well as promoting cooperation
Developing positive sensitivity for issues and discourses, while seeking sustainable management of the environment.

(Sharifi et al. 2019: 85)

Educational (environmental) programmes on television usually aimed at children are often considered to be based on the following generic factors:

a   Stimulus sending and receiving. Attention is based on comprehensibility of the content, alongside the measures deployed in the programme. For instance, music, special effects, camera movement and narration are among such measures used.
b   Perception and short-term memory; looking to the pattern of information processing by humans, after the data is received and recorded in the sensory memory, and when it enters the short-term memory.
c   Transfer of such information and audio-visual experiences to long-term memory (Sharifi et al. 2019: 92).

According to the so-called information-processing approach towards knowledge and learning, there are numerous educational steps suggested, including: promoting attention, becoming aware of goals, relating to previous knowledge, providing materials for learning and organisational cues, while encouraging students to react and dialogue and always providing effective feedback to them (cited in Sharifi et al. 2019: 86). At the same time, emotions remain a powerful source of behaviour and cognition as recognised through so much scholarship. Within children's educational pedagogy and also in media education generally, games and gaming are frequently considered the most important tool for children's programme-making, alongside experiencing creativity and being rooted in culture, language and geography. Levels of gamification can of course be modulated to suit all levels of academic ability and towards cogently addressing the active co-creation of critical environmental learning. Incidentally, while primarily focused on younger children, it is aften affirmed that gaming strategies also appeal to teenagers and especially Higher Educational students, as well as the general public, who can all learn through media and gaming structures (see Brereton 2019).

Audio-visual media remains a powerful and potentially critical art form and communications medium for sharing information, which can be co-opted as part of various educational programmes to prompt active engagement around prescient environmental questions and debate. This is especially true; one might suggest in building on the shock of the pandemic of 2020/21 and uncovering ways around how to use online media and environmental education into the future. Combining screenings, alongside virtual or face-to-face talks and seminars, such an educational programme, can be co-opted using a broad range of factual and fictional narratives to generate discussion and broaden understanding of the science, research and skillsets underpinning our most important environmental issues, while further coping with future pandemics, not to mention other global seismic impacts on the educational system.

References

ASPIRE website http://www.aspirelab.info/

Brereton, Pat. *Environmental Literacy and New Digital Audiences*. Routledge 2019.

Dewey, John. 'My Paedagogic Creed'. *School Journal* 54(January) 1987:77–80.

Fassbinder, S., Nocella, A. and Kahn, Richard (eds.) *Greening the Academy: Ecopedagogy through the Liberal Arts*. Rotterdam: Sense Publishers 2012.

Rice, Andy D. 'Non Fiction Video Practice as 21st Century Liberal Education: The ASPIRE Experiment in UCLA'. *Journal of Film and Video* 69(3): 38–53. Fall. 2017.

Sharifi, S.D. *et al.* 'Designing a Model for Children's Education through TV with a Cognitive Approach for Environmental Education'. *Quarterly Journal of Environmental Education and Sustainable Development* 7(4): 83–102. Summer 2019.

Waks, Leonard J. 'Ivan Illich and Deschooling Society: A Reappraisal' (57–73). *Europe, America, and Technology: Philosophical Perspectives. Philosophy and Technology*. Springer 1991. pp. . doi:doi:10.1007/978-94-011-3242-8_4

Greening the Media: Drawing on Scholarship from New Environmental Media Journals

Film and media scholars have constantly drawn attention to the need for various forms of 'greening the media' (Maxwell and Miller 2011; Vaughan

2019; Vaughan et al. 2020), 'eco-media' (Cubitt 2005; Rust, Monani, and Cubitt 2015), or 'sustainable media' (Starosielski and Walker 2016). In a recent 'material turn' towards recognising the physical cost of producing and distributing media at all scales and levels, not to mention the waste produced as a result of media production, the environmental communication field no longer can afford to ignore the physical and digital materiality of film and media technologies in themselves across these ever-expanding industries. These global industries incidentally need high levels of extractive components and materials to facilitate such growth, alongside increasing levels of energy consumption to support more global media usage, not to mention the mass (digital) media's direct effects on global climate change.

An entire cycle of film and media scholarship have more recently focused on and shaped these evolving issues; with several new academic journals already mentioned in the volume's introduction, including the open access *Media+Environment* journal, together with the *Journal of Environmental Media* – both launched at the end of 2019 – to help increase academic environmental engagement across cognate disciplines. Furthermore, by focusing on climate-related physical disturbances, such as glacial melts, sea-level rise, species extinctions and atmospheric warming among other issues, environmental media scholars have expanded the scope of the field. See the overview discussion in the introduction to this volume of this new research, including questioning the material and physical make-up of media industries, together with practices of mediation across all media platforms (Peters 2015; Ruiz 2018; Jue 2020).

Such broad interconnecting and transdisciplinary work encourages critical thinking for instance around 'disaster media in relation to geological time (Parikka 2015), measuring cinematic carbon footprints (Bozak 2011), analysing the use of video game play and scientific research paradigms (Chang 2019), as well as programmable earth interfaces (Heise 2008; Gabrys 2016), alongside evaluating the direct wiring of media into various aspects of nature (Schwoch 2018)' (Parks and Walker 2020). The interdisciplinary openness of contemporary film and media studies to such investigations has prompted scholars to engage with and across a broad range of scientific fields, such as geology, meteorology, biology, and oceanography among others. This broad-based approach can help tease out the process of how media can participate in, produce knowledge about, and themselves materialise climate-related disasters and practices that call attention to, while at the same time being complicit and even directly implicated in various forms of environmental planetary destruction. All of these strategies help to support the ongoing greening of the media.

References

Bozak, Nadia. *The Cinematic Footprint: Lights, Camera, Natural Resources.* Rutgers University Press 2011.

Chang, Alenda Y. *Playing Nature: Ecology in Video Games*. Minnesota University Press 2019.

Cubitt, Sean. *Ecomedia*. Rodopi Press 2005.

Rust, Stephen, Monani, Salma and Cubitt, Sean. Ecomedia: Key Issues. Routledge 2015.

Gabrys, Jennifer. *Program Earth: Environmental Sensing Technology and the Making of a Computational Planet*. University of Minnesota Press 2016.

Heise, Ursula K. *Sense of Place and Sense of Planet: The Environmental Imagination of the Global*. Oxford University Press 2008. https://mediaenviron.org/

Jue, Melody. *Wild Blue Media: Thinking Through Seawater*. Duke University Press 2020.

Maxwell, Richard and Miller, Toby. 'The Environment and Global Media and Communication Policy' (467–485). In Mansell, Robin and Raboy, Marc. *The Handbook of Global Media and Communication Policy*. Blackwell Publishing Ltd 2011.

Starosielski, Nicole and Walker, Janet. *Sustainable Media: Critical Approaches to Media and Environment*. Routledge 2016.

Parikka, Jussi. *A Geology of Media*. University of Minnesota Press 2015.

Parks, Lisa and Walker, Janet. 'Disaster Media: Bending the Curve of Ecological Disruption and Moving Towards Social Justice'. *Media+Environment* 2(1). 2020.

Peters, John Durham. *The Marvellous Clouds: Toward a Philosophy of Elemental Media*. University of Chicago Press 2015.

Ruiz, Rafico. 'Iceberg Economies'. *Topia: Canadian Journal of Cultural Studies* 32 (February): 179–199. 2018.

Schwoch, James. *Wired into Nature: The Telegraph and the North American Frontier*. University of Illinois Press 2018.

Vaughan, Hunter. *Hollywood's Dirtiest Secret: The Hidden Environmental Costs of the Movies*. Columbia University Press 2019.

Vaughan, Hunter et al. *Journal of Environmental Media*. Intellect Press 2020. https://www.intellectbooks.com/journal-of-environmental-media

Greenwashing the Corporate and Media Industry: PR limitations and CSR

In the article 'Greenwashing Revisited', Peter Seele and Lucia Gatti begin by questioning if greenwashing is 'a concept describing companies using misleading communication or is it constructed in the eye of the beholder?' (2017: 239). Greenwashing remains a major concern with regards to many businesses and organisations, as well as states striving to rebrand themselves using environmentally sustainable agendas. While some strategies are transparent and coherent, others are often facile and a product of PR and marketing, designed to paint over some environmentally unsustainable work practices. Furthermore, many environmentalists in trying to change the mindset of the general public, seduced by a global popular entertainment culture are often mesmerised by the public celebrity profile and power of the media industry to assist in this challenge. Conventional legacy media for instance, including television, press, and cinema, together with the phenomenal growth of online media and various digital platforms have revolutionised the media and communications industry.

Sometimes we also forget that media services remain part of a globally controlled media network of interrelated commercially driven corporations, who are often deeply implicated in and susceptible to maintaining a fossil-fuel, energy-driven system. Such well-established 'business as usual' industrial norms – whether coincidentally or not – are also being used to build and support much of our harmful modern industrial economy. At the forefront of these greenwashing fears of course is the advertising industry, which often supports and feeds back into promoting all types of media production that can be regarded as complicit in supporting anti-environmental and regressive modes of production/consumption. For instance, in a useful business study from 2012, it was found 'that green-washing (discrepancy between green talk and green walk) has a negative effect on financial performance and green-highlighting (concentrated efforts of the talk and walk) has no effect on financial performance' (Walter and Wan 2012: 227). This study concludes that once firms are identified as succumbing to being 'greenwashed' – they are viewed as 'untrustworthy, manipulative and opportunistic' (ibid.: 231).

For a more mainstream audience, the varying levels of complicity with a greenwashed agenda are teased out in Sharon Beder's *Global Spin: The Corporate Assault on Environmentalism* (1997), where she summarises the situation at least from within a post-1970s sensibility that 'we've been clobbered'. Corporate America has formed unprecedented alliances and set up industry groups and disguised public media groups to help regain its lost legitimacy and to ensure that its viewpoint dominated discussions and even suggesting solutions to environmental issues.

By 1990, Beder reported that 'the big US firms are spending about 500 million a year on PR advice about how to green their images and deal with the opposition'. Furthermore, the wider media industries themselves are often complicit in such greenwashing strategies. Using one left-field example for instance, James Lindheim, director of Public Affairs Worldwide at Burson-Marsteller in London, advised the chemical industry to 'build a therapeutic alliance with the public'. Cynically affirming that 'once the bond of trust is established, true therapy can begin and factual information can be transmitted' (Buell cited in Beder 1999: 169–192).

Such double-talk modes of greenwashing (or fake reporting for that matter can be reapplied to any corporation) paint a very disturbing picture of the role of big business towards explicitly hiding, much less even acknowledging, the environmental dangers ahead. In media terms, these tensions are dramatically illustrated in a (fictional) case study of chemical giants like DuPont, as represented by the eco-film *Dark Waters* (2019), which is textually analysed elsewhere. While Bruce Harrison in *Going Green: How to Communicate Your Company's Environmental Commitments* (1993), pragmatically recognises and affirms the pervasive need to value green community activists to help consciously improve all aspects of business practice.

Basically, once market research found consumers willing to pay more for 'green' products and natural (organic) foods, the market has developed exponentially ever since (see Prothero and McDonagh 2014). This can be further appreciated and illustrated with regards to the most corporate PR driven nuclear industry. The American Nuclear Society, for example, has produced a kit which tells children about the beneficial uses of nuclear technology and attempts to describe the problem of waste disposal in harmless terms. Most critical media analysis highlight any form of blatant PR intervention or use of mistruths. This strategy is also evident in similar slick on-site tours of Sellafield in the UK for instance (see Kenny 2003). Such complicit tensions are most effectively dramatised in the HBO classic five-part series *Chernobyl* – discussed elsewhere in this volume – which helps to highlight and critique such secretive if not blatantly greenwashing strategies.

Meanwhile, the expediential growth of Corporate Social Responsibility (CSR) strategies within big companies especially, designed to paint a caring public face for organisations wanting to appear in touch, and at the same time connect with values beyond the bottom line of profit margins, have had a long scholarly history of study and investigation within business studies. Certainly, environmental communication students for example could learn a lot by comparing CSR online statements and reports across a range of multinational organisations in comparison with smaller scale companies, who have much less time and resources to assert their erstwhile green credentials.

While taking issue with the binary definition that Greenwashing is either on or off, present or absent, I would contend that the phenomenon is more complex and evolving over time, all the while displaying varying levels of culpability and influence. We nonetheless need to always call out certain malevolent features when they come to the surface, as well as understanding how they are deployed and insinuated into a contemporary business ecology. At one extreme, Naomi Klein's polemical environmental study *On Fire* (2020) for example speaks of her Jewish background and calls out various abuses of Green politics and what she regards as insidious forms of greenwashing, which were apparently used by the Israeli state in their promotion of 'green values'. According to Klein, the Jewish National Fund (JNL) under its slogan 'turning the desert green' boasts of having planted 250 million trees in Israel since 1901, many of them unfortunately are non-native to the region (2020: 151).

Furthermore, Klein calls out a growing contemporary manifestation of what she considers a pernicious form of greenwashing; recalling the erstwhile benign policy and phenomenon of carbon offsetting. Indigenous people from Brazil to Uganda apparently, as illustrated in her study, are finding that some of the most aggressive land grabbing is being done by conservation organisations supporting a form of carbon offsetting (Klein 2020: 152).

The dangers of greenwashing have to be constantly acknowledged and balanced against all aspects of climate justice and equity regarding the burden of facing up to the environmental challenges ahead, while at the same time avoiding having the poorest in our communities suffering, because of the radical need for change to meet global carbon targets. All of this so-called greening of the planet remains a critical balancing act. Environmental challenges and proposed solutions which stand accused of being tarnished by greenwashing, need to be constantly measured against and linked to all aspects of climate justice and transparent ethical values, as well as taking into account other dangers, while always being guided by the precautionary principle.

References

Beder, Sharon. 'Public Participation or Public Relations?' (169–192). In Martin, Brian (ed.) *Technology and Public Participation. Science and Technology Studies.* University of Wollongong 1999. https://herinst.org/sbeder/envpolitics/publicpart.html#.YaaLBvHP1p8

Harrison, Bruce. *Going Green: How to Communicate Your Company's Environmental Commitments.* McGraw-Hill 1993.

Klein, Naomi. *On Fire: The Burning Case of a Green New Deal.* Penguin 2020.

Kenny, Colum. *Fearing Sellafield.* Dublin: Gill and MacMillan 2003.

Prothero, A. and McDonagh, P. 'Sustainability Marketing Research: Past, Present and Future'. *Journal of Marketing Management* 30(11–12): 1186–1219. 2014.

Seele, Peter and Gatti, Lucia. 'Greenwashing Revisited: In Search of a Typology of Accusation Based Definition Incorporating Legitimating Strategies'. *Business Strategies and the Environment* 26(2): 239–252. 2017.

Walker, Kent and Wan, Fang. 'The Harm of Symbolic Actions and Green-Washing: Corporate Actions and Communications on Environmental Performance and their Financial Implications'. *Business Ethics*: 227–242. 2012.

Greenwashing Lite: Celebrity Culture and Green Product Placement: *Down to Earth*

A popular tabloid series like *Down to Earth* starring Zac Efron (Netflix 2020–21), which foregrounds green and environmental issues can be read as an illustration of a *lite* type of greenwashing, coupled with a form of environmental PR, designed simply to promote green-tinged products and services sponsorship. In this eco-reading and analysis, I strive to take issue with our current academic and environmental fixation with 'pointing the finger' at all forms of business and corporate sponsorship, especially regarding what can be considered environmentally driven magazine-type media promotions.

Greenwashing concerns are constantly recalled through future imaginaries. While academic scholars like Todd (2004) and others pragmatically suggest 'environmentally conscious consumers demand a deep level of ecological commitment and responsibility from corporations and thus green entrepreneurs must sell the environmental ethics of the company, not just the eco-friendly nature of their products' (92). This may be true for most green-tinged corporations, even completely excessive science fictional ones like 'Leisureland', visualised in the fantasy futuristic eco-film *Downsizing* (2017), which is discussed elsewhere in this volume. But in the very act of 'selling' their (green-tinged Corporate Social Responsibility) ethics, corporations can also promote a *de facto* view of environmentalism that necessarily includes more production and even consumption. Certainly such paradoxes around consumption and environmental (conservation) values need to be constantly excavated and unpacked, as this film cautiously strives to address.

Meanwhile, one might also query *Down to Earth*'s bespoke ethical values as a travel programme with some obvious product placements throughout each episode. (See the program's corporate sponsors listed here: https://downtoearthza cefron.com/—.) Consequently, at the most fundamental level of investigation, one might question if the series could be classified as a greenwashing stunt for its sponsors to appear more environmentally friendly then they actually are!

The series seems to have been inspired by Efron's friend, Darin Olien, who is a 'back to nature' type of person and guru of healthy living and superfoods. Each light-magazine-type episode is sprinkled with lots of easily digestible 'facts', such as humans can live up to three weeks without food, but only three days without water. In the first episode, the two friends meet up with a (wine-like) connoisseur of water, who provides them with a 'tasting session'. Basically, our expert insinuates that most purchased bottled water is little better than tap water. 'Good water' needs to include a number of minerals, rather than being overly purified. Incidentally, the tasters apparently loved the Australian heavy water, alongside the British Hilton brand, while the Spanish Vichy sparking brand was also well liked and appreciated. One wonders, if such promotion of specific brands might encourage viewers to drink such expensive water products – a natural resource which is usually free – and thereby functions as product placement advertisements.

For the rest of the episode, the team travelled to France to 'experience' how water remains part of a great food culture. All of which could certainly be underscored as an eco-touristic and PR advertisement for *Eau de Paris*, who control the public water supply in Paris. On arrival in the region, Olien speaks of the necessity of hydrating after flying such a long distance from America (the presumed 'centre of the world'!) and illustrates the benefits of literally, if not figuratively, 'connecting with the earth'. Apparently, audiences discover that our Circadian Rhythms (or internal human clock, which can be upset by jet lag) needs to be put back into alignment after such debilitating long-haul flights. Such an imbalance apparently can be alleviated by walking barefoot on the earth, and basically becoming re-grounded with the magnetic field of the planet. Certainly, some wry fun is had regarding such a 'scientific' proposition, as they run barefoot through the grass.

Later, on driving up to the French capital in an expensive car, wearing smart casual clothes, our celebrity presenter demonstrates why he remains so popular in the media/film industry. Apparently, Efron has the rare skill of being able to 'tear up' and become emotional on demand when on screen. What a valuable skill to have in the creative media – echoing in ways the free-flowing and constructed nature of such a (scripted) performance, as displayed in such a popular online series.

Finally, they witness the sights of Paris, together with its free water supply, which in many ways is considered better than America, as it does not include so much chlorine; keeping it more 'natural' and healthy for the general populace. Furthermore, a council official informs the team that like other EU cities, Paris is also striving to get rid of all wasteful plastic bottles, by providing free water for all its citizens and visitors alike.

All of this light environmental discussion and analysis, outlining the importance of fresh water as a civic amenity – much less cutting the use of plastic bottles – probably remains interesting for a general uninitiated audience, who otherwise might have little concern for such natural resources. But then adopting a strange mode of associational logic, the episode's trajectory jumps forward to Lourdes in the south of the country, essentially to taste the 'spiritual water', which can apparently produce miracles. One assumes for many of Efron's secular young followers, this so-called spiritual water can be dismissed as simply harnessing a placebo effect. Nevertheless, Zac seems to buy into the religious power of group prayer, especially in witnessing and actively engaging in a daily ceremony of light, held at night, while parading through this sacred pilgrimage site. The evocation of a desire for miracles and espousing the general Catholic belief system are dealt with well enough, especially for a broad-based secular and young audience, who probably know little of such experiences, much less its underpinning belief systems. In many ways such an engaging strategy echoes and dovetails across eco-touristic modes of representing exotic forms of travel, consumption and spirituality, witnessed in similar magazine-like travel programming. The series follows an unashamedly tabloid format in its approach to knowledge, while calling up environmental, cultural, and even spiritual nuggets of experiential learning along their travels.

This first episode ends with some general statistics focused around how the earth is made up of 70% water, while humans constitute 60% of this precious natural liquid. Efron pronounces his final teacherly message: 'We have one earth – let's make it last'. But surprisingly, he does not make it clear if he is simply talking about water and or all the other scarce resources necessary for life on the planet, which underpin an environmental agenda. The episode nonetheless calls out our need for precious natural resources, which are needed to sustain our life as a species, and hence foregrounding our desire to secure sustainable levels of production and consumption.

The second episode consumed in the same viewing period, is encouraged through the enticing affordances and protocols of digital platforms like Netflix. Basically, if you don't escape immediately from the online series, on getting a glimpse of Costa Rica and its natural beauty, the casual onlooker is hooked. Apparently 50,000 to 70,000 Americans are living in this idealised natural habitat in South America. The top storyline teases and invites the viewer to vicariously witness a place where education and schools have no (unnecessary) tests and no homework – simply encouraging pupils to question everything and always challenge received ideas. What more radical educational model could one imagine! Furthermore, it's an ex-pat's haven to escape from the pressures of civilization, while supporting an engaging, affordable and healthy lifestyle.

Audiences are introduced into a commune and its well-developed eco-village, focused around healthy and sustainable living. The founder talks of how they 'merge where they live with what they eat'. Most memorable for outside audiences of course is seeing them eating a living plant from which chocolate is made. This delicacy simply grows naturally in the region – reminiscent of the children's fantasy franchise *Charlie and the Chocolate Factory*.

Viewers also witness a practical application, supporting the smallest ecological footprint possible, by constructing their fantastic houses with lots of materials that exist naturally and which are freely found in the region. All of this appears somewhat idealised, environmentally sustainable and certainly uncomplicated from an outsider Western perspective. Furthermore, audiences are introduced to a communal garden, being the hearth of their idealised society. Note, unlike a more objective and balanced public service type (broadsheet-like) documentary, we do not hear any concern or dissenting voices. One presumes, even within such a broad-based and open community, there *must* be some tensions or disagreements.

Anecdotally, as once affirmed by a member of a local eco-village in Ireland and discussed elsewhere, when asked to sum up the pros and cons of their community: 'the best thing are the people ... the worst thing is also the people'. How normal tensions and frustrations are resolved would constitute an interesting, if minor sub-story to be uncovered, as part of such an exploration of this idealised community. Instead, however, to maintain a surface tabloid-like and specifically one-note representation of the region, the natives and/or ex-pats are represented from the start as *de facto* and unconditionally embracing a radical green world-view, while remaining typecast and exoticized for the viewers. This is inferred when Zac first spies the community from the boat and appears excited, thinking they were all wild, enticing females with long hair!

Getting rid of human waste using an anaerobic digestion system and joking about such techniques, again reminds audiences of constant references to the natural benefits of their bounteous food harvest and at the same time recalling sustainable modes of consumption. All of these practices remain the antithesis of synthetic fast-food production and consumption protocols across the world. Furthermore, actual screen time is given over to the radical education model being rolled out, with one (well-trained) child affirming for the camera how 'you get to choose your destiny'. Environmental and local-based critical modes of education remain the top priority within such an idealised community.

Across this heavily forested region, the team also visit an animal sanctuary and discover how they deal with wild species affected by increasing human population, many of whom become entangled in electricity wires, often causing serious injury. It is insinuated that by giving financial donations to an animal charity, this helps to appease the film-makers (eco-)tourist conscience on their short-stay visit. Nevertheless, at least audiences get a vicarious and quick glimpse of how 'wild nature' can show the way towards new and more eco-sustainable modes of living and consumption.

Yet by all accounts, such a tabloid magazine programme and series remains far too simplistic and idealised in its approach, constantly feeding off exotic modes of construction of these natural habitats, as it seeks to promote new forms of ecotourism for its younger, unconnected online/Netflix audience. All of which is sparked by the celebrity affirmation at the start of the series around how he (Efron) always finds 'escape into nature' as his preferred mode of unwinding from the stresses of (civilised) American living.

Such a magazine programme is not speaking to the conventionally educated 'environmental community' bubble, but then this is probably not its intended audience. Instead, as I have illustrated in *Environmental Literacy and New Digital Audiences* (2019), recalling other so-called lite greenwashed documentaries such as the hugely successful franchise *Top Gear*, together with James Mays' *Big Ideas* (80–85), we need more mainstream and populist voices like Efron's; all speaking to an environmental agenda from varying perspectives and especially addressing and connecting with the much larger non-environmentally driven mainstream audiences.

More recently May's colleague and anchor Jeremy Clarkson has produced a hit with *Clarkson's Farm* (2021, Amazon Prime), where the erstwhile boy-racer and here-to-fore anti-green celebrity, takes on the responsibility of running a farm – albeit not being dependent on it for his livelihood, unlike so many real farmers. In many ways, such populist series can do more towards promoting environmental issues than many right-on environmental experts and more explicitly environmentally driven texts. Even if there is a real and present danger of some aspects of greenwashing, promoting even more consumption, while supporting big corporations, I would counter-argue that such risks are probably worth it, if larger audiences become more aware and informed as eco-citizens of their growing environmental responsibilities and complexities regarding the issues under investigation. At least the seed of green thinking and expression can be sown, especially for viewers who probably just happen to come upon such targeted celebrity-driven YouTube magazine programmes.

Nonetheless, at the same time, various explicit and pernicious modes of even light forms of greenwashing ought to be constantly called out by students and environmental communication scholars. Communication and educational programmes must not shy away from their ethical responsibilities towards unpacking the meanings and business implications of such commercially driven programmes. Mass media industries and digital online platforms, including Netflix and YouTube, are all striving to make documentaries that interest audiences, which can include promoting a broad, green-based agenda.

Such a move towards more green-tinged programming and product placement has become popular of late. This will probably result in a proliferation of celebrities either 'jumping on the bandwagon' of green thinking and indulging in alternative living, especially with the paucity of productions following the 2020/21 pandemic. Nonetheless, as long as some explicit and tangible form of active engagement and environmental learning occurs and most importantly, if such programmes help to provide a pipeline and space for more reflective 'hard hitting', anti-greenwashing narratives to come to the fore, then such easy going, disposable magazine programmes can serve a useful purpose.

Finding an audience of potential eco-citizens for such innovative environmental genres to get made across the tightly knit and commercially driven media production landscape, remains a global challenge. Consequently, we should accept – if not always embrace – such magazine style, light environmental programming, or at least acknowledge their (small) role in promoting environmental literacy and education. All the while, students and critics must always remain aware of the danger of crass simplicity and encouraging audiences to simply feel good about themselves, while letting such celebrities get off lightly, while promoting their own self-serving model of communing with nature. See also, for example, discussions around fast fashion and food documentaries.

References

Brereton, Pat. *Environmental Literacy and New Digital Audiences.* Routledge 2019.
Todd, Anne Mare. 'The Aesthetic Turn in Green Marketing: Environmental Consumer Ethics of Natural Personal Care Products'. *Ethics and the Environment* 9(2). 2004.

H

Historical Environmental Representations of Communal Living: Happy as Lazzaro

Reminiscent of the long and troubled history of colonialism and exploitation across the world, environmental history has an equally long pedigree and specific preoccupation around mapping out various scales of injustice across the planet for much of the history of human habitation. This field was founded on conservation issues, but more recently the discipline has dealt with the growth of urban society and cities and the dominant need for sustainable development. The field has also become more multidisciplinary, drawing on social history as well as natural sciences to explore the complex, historical interrelationship between humans and their natural habitat, including how they conceive of nature, through attitudes, beliefs and values at all levels. To illustrate the breadth of this ever-evolving disciplinary field, I will use a historically framed Italian movie, which focuses on evolving tensions between a predominantly feudal mode of rural existence, as against a more alienating form of contemporary urban living.

While focusing on historical issues around human selection and justice, this historical allegory certainly speaks to contemporary concerns around our environmental crisis and provides an art-house exposition of effective environmental communication, drawing on postcolonial, historical and injustice tropes. Such representations draw on a long history from feudal to contemporary urban modes of living, while always learning from the past, as cogently set up by Pope Francis' evocative environmental pronouncements in one of his earlier pronouncements:

> Human beings are themselves considered consumer goods to be used and then discarded. We have created a "throw away" culture which is now spreading. It is no longer simply about exploitation and oppression, but something new. Exclusion ultimately has to do with what it means to be a part of the society in which we live; those excluded are no longer society's underside or its fringes or its disenfranchised – they are no longer even a part of it.
>
> (Pope Francis 'Evangelii Gaudium' art.53 Nov. 2013)

DOI: 10.4324/9781003123422-9

Directed by Alice Rohrwacker and starring Adriano Tardiolo, the historically based film focuses on an unceasingly kind, Italian peasant and his family who are constantly exploited by a tobacco Baroness, while working as indentured servants on the land. At first, according to Peter Bradshaw's *The Guardian* review, everything in the film 'could be happening around the end of the 19th century', but in many ways the themes explored remain contemporary to Italian society and culture. The film is set in a remote village called Inviolata (meaning inviolate or pure), where an innocent boy meets the Baroness's son Tancredi who wants him to help stage his own kidnapping.

Such feudal modes of hand-to-mouth existence still characterise much of the developing world and speak to ever-present concerns over human value and environmental justice across the planet today where human exploitation and excessive resource extraction from nature's bounty remains the norm. Calling attention to such long-term historical, ethical and environmental injustice, is probably sufficient for audiences to engage with and learn from this allegorical tale.

Meanwhile, this eco-filmic narrative allegorically calls upon themes of social repression, economic exploitation and marked abundance of nature, which is later contrasted with the more soulless landscapes and extractive environments of contemporary urban industrialisation. Rich people are represented as purely materialistic in a throw-away culture, while the poor are left ignorant and powerless. Money and wealth remains a dominant corrupting element throughout, which is both universal and timeless, and the (environmental) root of the loss of human values is predetermined apparently by not being close to the land. Consequently, the fictional landscape of the film incapsulate a mixture of time periods, alongside various political, social as well as cultural clusters of values.

At the same time the corrupt Baroness De Luna has some deep, if worrying psychological insight into the frailty of human nature, as relayed in one memorable speech to her son that roughly suggests:

> Human beings are like animals. Set them free and they realize they are slaves locked in their own misery. Right now, they suffer, but they don't know. I exploit them, they exploit that poor man. It's a chain reaction that can't be stopped.
>
> (Hans 2019)

Many reviewers interpret the historical period, much less the character of Lazzaro, as more of an idea, or even a blank slate for audiences to project what they want onto his character. For instance, Peter Bradshaw's aforementioned review in *The Guardian* (2019) perceives the story as a pastoral enigma and an attack on exploitable Feudal snobbery, through the innocent representation of the main protagonist. One can further read the film as a tale of reincarnation, whose hero is a cross between two figures from the Bible – Lazarus and the Christ child. Ostensibly, the story pays homage to Olmi's eco-classic *The Tree of Wooden Clogs* (1978), while focusing on a remote Italian community of around 50 people who are trapped in sharecropping and serfdom working on a tobacco plantation, while knowing no other form of living.

However, the final act of the film moves even further away from its ostensibly historical roots, with a Magic Realist twist, as the community eventually moves away to the city. A move which is emblematic of an ongoing developing world (and also First World) phenomenon, with many poor, rural people migrating to the city to find greater prospects, but often ending up being swallowed up and sometimes becoming worse off than they were originally. Furthermore, here in this historical and allegorical fantasy, everyone grows old, cynical, crooked and defeated, but Lazzaro stays as innocent as a child and remains in a 'state of grace' echoing something other-worldly and spiritual in his character. His apparent rebirth, like the biblical Lazarus is closely associated with the power of nature. While the serf-like workers appear no happier in the big, dirty city, where they are ostensibly free, while unfortunately encountering a whole new set of insidious injustices and cruelties. The Master/Slave mentality and mode of economic control has cheapened everyone, as they eke out a marginal living. As noted with regards to the official end of slavery in America for instance, injustice and inequality live on through various forms of pernicious new modes of inequalities, right up to the present day. On a broader scale, all of these intersectional tensions and injustices have to be ameliorated if not resolved – including gender, class, alongside race and ethnic inequality – if environmental justice and harmony is to firmly take root.

Throughout the film, celebration of primitive modes of communal rural living and basic low-technological modes of agriculture remains engaging in its representation, while also showing the benevolence and fecundity of nature. Audiences get to witness raw nature in its most primal state, as it is romantically and lovingly worked on by its local tied community, who are at the same time systematically exploited in their employment by a local Baroness – recalling her barbed, if insightful, analysis cited earlier. The romantic idyllic notion of enjoying earthy work that brings the worker closer to the land, is very much called into question here. For instance, recalling the Dust Bowl and the displacement of poor soil due to 'over-farming' across middle America – as recounted in John Steinbeck's 1939 classic *The Grapes of Wrath* that was quickly turned into a successful film directed by John Ford (1940). Or more specifically, echoing the harvesting of tobacco, which has further references in the Oscar winning *Out of Africa* (1985). All of these examples highlight how precious land can be destroyed through such a pernicious and soil-hungry cash crop, provoking so many environmental and exploitative overtones (see readings in Brereton 2013).

Incidentally, the dominant motif of a wolf who roams the landscape looking for food has further echoes of the representations of a primal animated alpha-hunter, witnessed in among other tales *Fantastic Mr Fox* (explored in

Brereton 2016). Similarly, in *Happy as Lazzaro* there is a clear sense of awe and respect for the wild animal, as the mythical wolf wakes the boy from his near-death fall and apparently follows him into the city. Finally, the allegorical animal leads our hero – or at least his soul – out of this inhospitable landscape to conclude this enigmatic tale.

But of course, wild nature remains fully alive, even in this otherwise inhospitable city-space, as our hero has learnt to recognise so many precious plants and their properties that can be used for food and human sustenance. Humans can survive severe hardship by acquiring the appropriate environmental knowledge and adapting the right attitude towards their habitat. Stealing and scavenging is not the only answer or response to moving to the city. But unfortunately, there appears to be no clear recuperation for the displaced community from the pernicious influence of their old modes of oppression. Somehow their authoritarian and oppressive system back in their rural existence afforded 'order and control' to their life, allowing space and time to actively commune with nature, while never being able to foster longer term harmony and a deep connection with nature. Most importantly however, unlike a benevolent counter-cultural 'back to nature' commune, this unequal hierarchical and historical structure of power inequality and control did not foster a necessary surfeit of ethical or social justice, which is essential if harmony is to be restored between humans and nature.

References

Brereton, Pat. 'Eco-cinema, Sustainability and Africa: A Reading of Out of Africa (1985), The Constant Gardener (2005) and District 9 (2010)'. *Journal of African Cinema* 5(2): 219–235. 2013.

Brereton, Pat. *Environmental Ethics and Film*. Routledge 2016.

Bradshaw, Peter. 'Happy as Lazzaro Review – Magic, Enigma and a Dark Journey'. *The Guardian*. 3 April 2019. https://www.theguardian.com/film/2019/apr/03/happy-as-lazzaro-review-alice-rohrwacher-adriano-tardiolo-nicoletta-braschi

Hans, Simran. 'Happy as Lazzaro Review – Mesmerising Magic Realism'. *The Guardian*6 April 2019. https://www.theguardian.com/film/2019/apr/06/happy-as-lazzaro-review-alice-rohrwacher

Pope Francis. *Evanvell Guadium* art. 53. November 2013. https://www.vatican.va/content/francesco/en/apost_exhortations/documents/papa-francesco_esortazione-ap_20131124_evangelii-gaudium.html

Hippie Counter-Culture, Active Environmental Agency and Eco-spirituality – *Leave No Trace*

Hippy counter-culture basically rejected the conventional mores of mainstream American life, especially with regards to its preoccupation with conspicuous materialism and sexual conformism. Drawing on the Beat movement from the 1950s and radical writers like Alan Ginsberg and Jack Kerouac, this dispersed and loosely defined movement actively opposed involvement in the Vietnam war (1955–1975). Furthermore, many so-called hippies adapted vegetarian diets based on using unprocessed foods and often practiced holistic forms of medicine. Some even ended up as drop-outs from society, foregoing regular jobs and stable careers. They promoted non-violence and 'make love not war' became a common slogan of the movement. Cult films like *Easy Rider* (1969) embodied many of their values, reaffirmed a permissive yet still patriarchal attitude towards women. As explored in *Hollywood Utopia: Ecology in Contemporary American Cinema* (2005), *Easy Rider* embodied the 'ride into nature', codified as a metaphor for the escape from urban oppression into the 'freedom' of self-discovery (Brereton 2005: 104).

Social historian Timothy Miller, argues that during this period hippies were reacting to 'an emotional pressure cooker' within American society, which in turn caused 'widespread mental illness and even compulsive violence'. Because of a deep running cultural malaise 'the rational alternative', as the Hippies saw it, was 'simply to drop out' (Miller 2011: xviii). Recalling the renowned scholar Herbert Marcuse, who described this countercultural movement as the 'only viable social revolution' of the period, arguing that despite their disinterest in Marxism, the hippies still had a revolutionary impact on society. This impact has continued to the present day and has contributed to major cultural transformations around environmental thinking. One could argue the movement also inspired and road tested various types of communes, such as contemporary transition towns, eco-villages and even farmer's markets. In turn these have morphed into many green alternative ways of living and lifestyle patterns. The cultural and representational complexity of the hippy legacy will be analysed through a case study of *Leave no Trace*, which foreground many of these evolving counter-cultural values and speak to their direct relationship to environmental concerns.

Leave No Trace – A Contemporary Back-to-Nature Environmental Parable

The pessimism of the environmental and psychological analysis of an avant-garde tale like *Safe* (1995) which was analysed in Brereton (2005), remains in stark contrast with the more optimistic and innovative Hollywood film *Leave No Trace* (2018). A term and mantra used for the global scouting movement, which seeks to inculcate environmental values in all its young members. Directed by Debra Granik, who earlier produced the evocative *Winter's Bone* (2010), the film explores a more realistic and sometimes nostalgic evocation of a form of hippie environmentalism, brought to life by provocative performances from Ben Foster as Will, who is a military veteran suffering from post-traumatic stress disorder, and a father to his younger daughter Tom, played by Thompasin McKenzie. The storyline pushes the stereotypical counter-cultural and environmental agenda into the mainstream. Basically, the father and daughter live a kind of 'radical Thoreau-guerrilla existence', or at least a more unconventional hippy one in a huge public park in Portland, Oregon. By all accounts, *Leave no Trace* paints a more hopeful and realistic environmental space than for instance *Safe*.

Certainly, according to Peter Bradshaw's (2018) *Guardian* review,

> there is an attractive humility and restraint at work, a quietism. No scenery-chewing, no fireworks, no obvious scary Colonel-Kurtz (from *Apocalypse Now*) stuff with Will, or obvious teen rebellion histrionics from Tom. Neither appears concerned with what the future holds for them, nor when Tom should really be getting a tent of her own – let alone meet other people of her own age.
>
> Following questioning by social workers and some crude yes/no psychological testing, this incident remains one of the few intrusions into their otherwise solitary life in nature. Yet, at the same time such an intrusion functions as the only time in the story they have to consciously and objectively examine their lives – a form of exploration, which remains the totalising focus in *Safe* (see review in Brereton 2005). Perhaps as Bradshaw asserts in his aforementioned review, 'not having to think about yourself, not having to shoulder the burden of relentless neurotic self-examination is part of what their way of life is about' (13 May 2018). Such personal forms of examination is encouraged through modern technology, such as mobile phones and especially via the endless mirroring of self through online social media which is so pointedly critiqued in the 2020 documentary directed by Jeff Orowski, *The Social Dilemma*, discussed in detail elsewhere. Escaping into nature is not necessarily just about communing with nature and embracing its biophilic pleasures, but also functions as an escape from having to constantly examine the shallowness of self and modern society's ongoing fixation with discrete and individual identity formation.

The closest the father–daughter unit get to an idealised hippy community is through their encounter with an aging caravan trailer community in the forest. Their hard social and psychological lives have been marked out on their faces, but still appear content and accepting of what life has thrown at them. The great character actor Dale Hickey (Dale) in particular stands out in her marginal role; she refuses to take money from her new inmates and even leaves food on a tree in the woods for a 'deep outsider' soul, who apparently has not been seen for years. Like in her helpful probing of Tom's state of mind, Dale instinctively assumes all is fine, since the food always disappears. This loosely based community serves as a mid-way house for those wanting and needing to escape the strictures of established (urban) society, but still requiring some human contact. At night, like many back-to-nature communal camps, they sing and drink to pass the time. What more could one ask for in learning to develop a close connection with and in nature. The daughter realises this is a social and communal life worth living and can no longer face the perils and loneliness of isolated survival with her dad. The romantic notion of solitary living at one with nature is very much tested and called into question throughout this tale. Unlike *Safe* which questioned the false sense of community a counter-cultural experiment might bring, *Leave no Trace* posits the continuing need for human contact, even when striving to escape into nature.

Getting the balance right through escaping into nature and recognising our growing preoccupation with alternative visions of the 'good life', for both psychological and bodily security, as families strive to do the right thing in making such a big decision has remained a dominant trope across such literature and audio-visual media. All of which is driven by a deep environmental preoccupation, almost along the lines of 'making frugality sexy' and living a more sustainable life in close harmony with nature. Such teacherly narratives need to become more ubiquitous and normalised, as well as being revalued and not simply exoticised as a minority pursuit of strange hippie-types. These allegories and storylines highlight the pervasive tension across such environmental learning in rediscovering or through co-existence with and in nature; all the while striving to fight against consumptive-driven models of living that are literally producing a catastrophic tipping point in the ongoing struggle to alternatively save our planet.

Such back-to-nature allegories are very powerful in highlighting the environmental tensions exposed through living our conspicuous consumptive and usually urban-based lifestyles, and certainly speak to audiences desiring change, by dramatising sustainable alternatives that lead to the environmental 'good life', which in many ways becomes a prerequisite for addressing a range of climate problems. In conclusion, a key tension revolves around whether we should simply concentrate on responding to climate change at an individual level, as suggested by several 'back to nature' narratives like *Safe* alluded to earlier, or alternatively calling on strong bonds of community expressed in *Leave no Trace* which are required to bolster a human-centred interconnection with nature. These so-called hippy counter-cultural narratives are helpful in fleshing out such social and cultural history, while addressing ever-present environmental tensions. See also several other related hippie narratives like *Captain Fantastic* (2016) or the Oscar winning *Nomadland* (2021), which in varying ways deal with escape to nature themes in contrasting ways.

References

Bradshaw, Peter. 'Leave No Trace Review – Deeply Intelligent Story of Love and Survival in the Wild'. *The Guardian*. 13 May 2018 https://www.theguardian.com/film/2018/may/13/leave-no-trace-review-debra-granik

Brereton, Pat. *Hollywood Utopia: Ecology in Contemporary American Cinema*. Intellect Press 2005.

Miller, Timothy. *Hippies and American Values*. University of Tennessee Press 2011.

Human Rights Violation and Climate Change: Who Should Pay!

Can climate change debates also be characterised as a form of human rights violation, or alternatively are climate change rights constituted as a proxy for aspects of human rights? Such tensions remain part of many debates addressed across a very student-friendly environmental communications and ethics primer, edited by Mike Hulme (2020). Certainly, climate change presents a large-scale, serious and accelerating threat to the security of basic rights. The long-developed 'polluter pays' principle (PPP), which permeates much ethical and policy thinking in the field, basically posits that those who have done most to cause climate change, as a consequence ought to do the most to prevent their actions from violating the basic environmental rights of present and future populations. Such climate justice first principles have directly fed into much of the policy discussions across this fraught area, including the Paris Climate Agreement (2015), while striving to ensure the rich polluting Western world pay their fair share rather than putting even more pressure on the fragile poorer developing world, where of course the greatest harm in the future will be done and in areas that contain the least culpable and economically deprived populations.

Such radical thinking, pulls against traditional isolationist nationalist politics, with hegemonic rule and control by some 'richer' states, who strive to club together to either maintain the status quo, or at least ensure the least-worst option for the future of the planet is stacked in their favour. All the while, more multilateral approaches using fresh innovative and radical thinking is badly needed. This in turn has to be underpinned by climate justice for all people on the planet, while at the same time ensuring the maintenance of more sustainable bio-diversity across all regions of the planet. Of course, this underpinning philosophy is built on the ever-adaptable principles of 'everything being connected' and focused around how planetary health remains constituted by a delicate balance across several interconnecting holistic systems that have to be kept in constant harmony.

Of late, environmentalists talk of how the so-called Anthropocene period heralds a rupture within the modern imaginary, while calling for new modes of thinking. Systemic policy and operational change using international human rights legislation can provide effective remedies to further address global climate change impacts, such as sea-level rise in small island development states, much of which is caused by greenhouse gases emitted by China or the USA, alongside other large emitters. Furthermore, successful carbon emissions reduction also lie in the hands of non-state, rather than state actors in doing what they can to avoid catastrophe. Since climate change or the term global warming gained political saliency in the late 1980s, it has been predominantly viewed in holistic terms as a major 'tragedy of the commons' dilemma, extended onto a global and planetary scale.

By all accounts, as affirmed by a global report published in 2017, breaking up (with fossil fuels) is hard to do. At least a 'proactive state approach involving legal strictures and human rights can at least begin the process' and help get us as a human species through this dilemma. This study estimated that just 100 companies in the fossil-fuel industry (and its products) were responsible for 71% of all industrial GHG emissions produced since 1998

(CDP 2017). Adopting a radical shift towards greater legal obligations within contemporary society and using the strict 'polluter pays' principle, demands that these 100 major international companies and many others besides, have to be forced to urgently make the low-carbon transition and embrace radical transformation for the very future of our planet. Of course, the ideological struggle continues around who should specifically pay for such transition; with many large energy companies apparently expecting up to 7% return on investment in switching to renewable energy sources, while at the same time presuming that their so-called 'stranded carbon-based assets' will be refinanced by governments and international organisations, rather than having to take a financial hit on their historically polluting investments. Teasing out the risks associated with increasing the engagement of global corporations in climate mitigation, and working out what are the best ways to anticipate and reduce such financial risks, remain a core preoccupation across much analysis and discussion.

Climate legal experts have been grappling with these tensions and demands for many years now. For example, in a chapter by Sadhbh O'Neill and Edwin Alblas titled 'Climate Litigation, Politics and Policy Change: Lessons from Urgenda and Climate Case Ireland' (cited in Robbins et al. 2020), the authors tease out the landmark successful 2015 Dutch legal case with its order for the government to reduce its greenhouse gas emissions by 25% before the end of 2020. Meanwhile in Ireland, a successful case was also taken by the Irish Environmental Non-governmental Organisations (ENGO) that was able to call on broad public appeal for its 'Climate Case' against the national government. Legal argument focused on the Irish government's

> failure to comply with national, international and human rights law, by adopting a National Mitigation Plan that failed to set Ireland on a pathway aligned with the latest climate science, as articulated by the Intergovernmental Panel on Climate Change (IPCC) and international and European Union law.
>
> (Robbins et al. 2020: 58)

While these two case studies demonstrate how legal instruments can have great power in promoting climate and human rights, the authors nevertheless conclude that

> while litigation is a powerful instrument in the advocacy toolkit, by itself it is unlikely to sufficiently effect the emission reductions that are recommended by the IPCC. As such it is vital that ENGO's and civil society continue to push for climate action.
>
> (in Robbins et al. 2020: 70)

Certainly, across the world, legal instruments are being added to the growing arsenal of climate action tools and are helping to secure added legitimacy to the climate struggle, building on a long history of more conventional human rights legislation. But much more needs to be done in this area as it applies specifically to environmental communications and scholarship.

References

Hulme, Mike (ed.). *Contemporary Climate Change Debates: A Students Primer.* Routledge 2020.

Robbins, D., Torney, D. and Brereton, P. (eds.). *Ireland and the Climate Crisis.* Palgrave 2020.

CDP 'New Report Shows Just 100 Companies are Source of Over 70% of Emissions'. 10 July 2017. https://www.cdp.net/en/articles/media/new-report-shows-just-100-companies-are-source-of-over-70-of-emissions

I

Intersectionality and Eco-citizenship: Drawing on Race, Class, Gender and Ethnicity Debates

Intersectionality is a theoretical framework for understanding how aspects of a person's physical, social and political (e.g., gender, race, ethnicity, class, sexuality, religion, occupation, physical appearance, disability etc.) coalesce, to create unique modes of discrimination, in contrast with all forms of privilege and domination within and across society. Adding environmentalism to this mix, while further characterising personal identity and politics, remains an important new mode of engaging with identity and political values.

However, at its most fundamental level, it must always be appreciated that intersectionality identifies advantages and disadvantages that are felt by people, due to a combination of factors. For example, a black woman might face discrimination from a business that is not simply due to her race (because the business do not discriminate against black men), nor distinctly due to her gender (because business per se does not discriminate against white women), but which might be due to a unique combination of such factors. Most certainly, connecting racial or sexual discrimination together with various forms of environmental injustice across the planet, remains an important new set of matrices and a useful prism to draw on to provoke active engagement across a wide range of debate and analysis.

Historically, for instance intersectionality broadened the lens of the first waves of feminism, which largely focused on the experiences of women who were both white and middle-class, to also include the different experiences of women of colour, alongside women who are poor, immigrants and from other minority groupings. This grouping of intersectional matrices could be further extended to also include a range of environmental disadvantages, including food, water and shelter being in short supply. Intersectional feminism aims to separate itself from 'white feminism', by acknowledging the broad range of women's different experiences and identities across the planet. Furthermore, by pushing such categorisation to further include environmental issues, through for instance eco-feminist discourses, which has been a major spur for the growth of environmentalism (see Brereton 2005), this in turn can support radical new modes of thinking and analysis.

DOI: 10.4324/9781003123422-10

In essence, intersectionality is a qualitative analytic framework developed in the late 20th century that identifies how interlocking systems of power affect those who are most marginalised in society – including in environmental terms – and takes these relationships into account when working to promote social and political equity. Consequently, those groups who are environmentally disadvantaged can also be added to the mix and be used as a bulwark against a common appreciation of environmental values being predominantly linked with (white) middle-class privilege.

Certainly, adding attributes of intersectionality – race, class, gender, ethnicity etc. – to the broader environmental justice agenda is essential, where climate justice and poverty remains a clear division within and across the growing climate emergency. This has become a growing area of research and scholarship that environmental students are particularly exercised around. Such tensions have also become a major research and practice-based approach towards supporting a robust climate justice and equitable low-carbon transition. Environmental justice and equity for *all* citizens remains the biggest challenge facing humanity – bigger probably than slavery, poverty and even global disease – and this broader environmental crisis needs to be faced head on and resolved in an equitable manner. Without ensuring issues of poverty, slavery, disease and all forms of human injustice and inequality are fully addressed and integrated into robust solutions to the climate crisis, global environmental issues will not be resolved and may even be made worse in the longer term. See also Human Rights Violations and Climate Change entry.

Reference

Brereton, Pat. *Hollywood Utopia: Ecology in Contemporary American Society.* Intellect 2005.

J

Jevon's Paradox, Energy Efficiency and Its Environmental Application: Case Study of F1

It is suggested using this model for an increase of efficiency in resource use will, as a consequence, generate further increases in resource consumption, rather than a potential decrease. Such a paradox in turn can for instance challenge the sustainability development goals (SDGs), since it questions the dominant philosophy behind energy policies striving for improvements in fuel efficiencies. This phenomenon is illustrated later in a case study of Formula 1 (FI) professional racing. There is a constant need to recognise the so-called 'rebound effect', which basically asserts that the prospect of further increased consumption more than cancels out the energy saved as a consequence of an efficiency-drive process. However, such effects may be less relevant or applicable now, than back at the height of the Industrial Revolution, when the notion was first mooted in 1865 by a 29-year-old Englishman, William Stanley Jevons, on publishing a book titled *The Coal Question*.

In this study, Jevons argued that the bonanza of so much coal production would not continue to have the same effect over time. At that time the British Empire depended on its generous endowment of coal to drive the Industrial Revolution, but it was believed that this precious resource was rapidly depleting. In ways, this form of natural exhaustion is reminiscent of later times concerning extractive fossil-fuel industries and growing fears around 'Peak Oil'. Such concerns help to assess the prospect of depleted reserves of oil around the world, which might drastically affect the modern oil-based global economy. Consequently, there have been increasing calls for energy efficiency and greater levels of sustainability to help offset reductions across these natural energy reserves. But Jevons' thesis essentially presents a counter-argument to such worries and concerns by claiming that 'it is wholly a confusion of ideas to suppose that the economical use of fuels (or any natural resource for that matter) is equivalent to diminished consumption. The very contrary is the truth' (cited by Owen 2010).

David Owen, in a useful overview piece on the topic in *The New York Times* (2010) titled 'The Efficiency Dilemma: If Our Machines Use Less

DOI: 10.4324/9781003123422-11

Energy, We Will Use Them More?', provides some insightful examples to illustrate how the so-called economical and sustainable use of fuel in particular, results not necessarily in diminished consumption, but rather in an overall increase in demand. Nevertheless, energy efficiency has been historically labelled the 'Fifth Fuel' (after coal, petroleum, nuclear power and renewables); and considered by some experts, as being almost a cost-free tool for accelerating a transition to a green-energy economy. In 2007 for instance, the United Nations Foundation (UNF) wholeheartedly adopted such a proposition, saying that efficiency improvements constituted 'the largest, the most evenly geographically distributed, and least expensive energy source', while at the same time claiming to have got rid of over 1.1 gigabits of greenhouse gasses annually in America.

Taking one simple example cited by Owen (2020), the World Economic Forum report, 'Towards a More Efficient World', noted how 'the average refrigerator sold in America today uses about three quarters less energy than the 1975 average, even though it is 20% larger and costs around 60% less'. Certainly, most households in hot climates would probably regard refrigeration as essential. One wonders however, in spite of so much effective advertising and promotion, can the same be said for the exponential growth of the mobile phone, computer technology and the ever-expanding media industry, which produces so much carbon energy waste. At the outset, one might expect all of this technological efficiency and innovation appears incontestable, and presumably it should end up reducing the total amount of energy consumed on the planet. But unfortunately this does not take into account human habits and rituals, with homes surprisingly increasing their use of refrigeration for example (as well as air-conditioning – not to mention media and computer gadgets), by having *more* technology in their homes, including the continued use of older and environmentally unsustainable products and services. Consequently, energy use and consumption actually continues to rise rather than decrease in the long run.

Certainly, the link between innovation, efficiency and sustainability is not necessarily as one-directional as one might first imagine. For example, 'looking at society's thermodynamic foundations, sustainability is based on a dynamic balance of two contrasting principles regulating the evolution of complex adaptive systems: the maximum entropy production and the maximum energy flux' (Giampietro et al. 2018). Hence the constant rhetoric around efficiencies and economic sustainability as a one-size-fits-all solution, unfortunately is not as simple, much less as clear-cut, as initially envisaged.

This situation can be explained and illustrated through a case study around gauging fuel efficiencies within the automobile industry. Such efficiencies of course remain desirable, even if they do not significantly reduce total greenhouse gas emissions (GHG). For example, the popular sport of Formula 1 (F1) racing, at least for some critics, constitutes a hyper-masculine/gas-guzzling and dangerous activity, which over the years has been used as an advertisement and promotional tool, for automobiles and fast driving generally. Film narratives, from road movies to action adventure, continue to sell the visceral excitement of driving fast cars and travel generally, which of course pulls against the ongoing need for more sustainable carbon-reducing technologies. Yet surprisingly in various press releases, FI and its engineering affiliates announced a radical plan to become carbon neutral as soon as 2030!

Ray Galvin's decision to use FI qualifying sessions to measure the rebound effect from changes in average speed was surprising to all. Yet there was some precedence referring back to 2014 with the evolution of what was called Formula E, and which kick-started an initiative that foregrounded all aspects of sustainability, specifically calling for long-term electrical research into battery improvement. One could be hopeful that the oil-wasteful FI sport essentially might put limits on excessive fuel consumption. But how such re-engineering will play out into the future, especially as the broader industry moves into producing and promoting only safe and sustainable electric vehicles remains open to debate. What effects will such a transformation have towards dramatically reducing the overall transport carbon budget, much less assessing the implications of these processes being rolled out into the massively lucrative globalised transport industry sector? Basically, one wonders will this radical change help to reduce the total carbon footprint, or simply make the industry more acceptable (even dare I say greenwashed) within the public mindset, as citizens struggle to adapt and embrace the prospect of a low-carbon future. For the automobile – as well as the high-tech media and other fossil fuel-based industries – there is so much to be done towards addressing our climate crisis and most certainly environmental communicators and campaigns have a major role in helping to effectively document and even promote this necessary transition towards securing a zero-carbon emissions future.

References

Giampietro, Mario and Mayumi, Kozo. 'Jevons Paradox: The link between innovation, efficiency and Sustainability'. *Front Energy. Res.* 6(26): 2018.

Owen, David. 'The Efficiency Dilemma: If Our Machines Use Less Energy, We Will Use Them More?'. *The New York Times* 13 December 2010.

Jevons, W. Stanley. *The Coal Question: An Inquiry Concerning the Progress of the Nation, and the Probable Exhaustion of Our Coal Mines.* Macmillan and Co. 1865.

Just Transition and Energy: From Fossil Fuels to Renewables – Peat Workers in Ireland

Moving from fossil-fuel energy production to a renewable energy model across the world, usually means that many workers in these traditional, often manual, labour-based industries either lose their jobs and/or have to quickly retrain and re-equip themselves to meet the changing market requirements. This is true whether its oil, coal, peat or some other extractive and high-carbon industry. Just transition, as a broad term highlights the financial and other personal detrimental effects on a local population, while struggling to make such a paradigm shift across work and general industrial practices. All the while embracing the green philosophy that our planet must urgently transition into a low-carbon future before a crisis point is reached. People who suffer because of such transition should be 'fairly compensated' and adequately retrained in an equitable and ethical manner – whether it's the so-called developing global population and countries, where so much mineral extraction occurs, alongside taking into account traditional energy workers in Europe or America and across the world. However, managing and operationalising this mammoth task will require huge planning and resource reallocation. As the energy or extractive industry sector in particular (which can also include farmers and others working on the land) pivots towards a more environmentally sustainable and low-carbon energy future, managing this transformation both equitably and sustainably, requires a globalised, yet reflexive system of toolkits, alongside imaginative communication strategies.

To take one small example of an imaginative proposal to cope with energy transition around peat extraction in Ireland. In a progress report (April 2020) Kieran Mulvey, Commissioner for such a 'Just Transition' in Ireland, recommended the setting up of a Climate Change Centre to document and help kick-start the transition of the bogland regions in the Midlands – an area that has increased levels of unemployment and poverty as a result of the peat extraction industry coming to a close. Of course, an educational-led Climate Change Centre for the region would need to get the balance right between local, national and even international support and buy-in, while coalescing with all agencies to secure overall engagement with such an initiative. At the same time marrying entertainment and education aspects of the project needs to be considered, through for instance using both pre-recorded, online, as well as live interactive exhibits, which remain the dream of many environmental communication and educational practitioners. Ideally, such a centre ought to also speak to various related aspects of environmental injustice, including race, class and gender divisions, alongside broader urban-rural divisions, as well as inter-generational tensions – all the while supporting a robust and inclusive Just Transition.

This is reflected in the European Union's science research protocols (see Novitzky et al. 2020), which constantly affirm the need for active public engagement through gender equality, open access, ensuring ethical frameworks and governance. Such a Climate Change Educational Centre, if it was to ever get off the ground, should also strive to ensure engagement with all aspects of open innovation, co-creation of knowledge and research, open science and supporting a general openness to the world at large. These attributes and core ethical values, moderated through the lens of environmental sustainability, can help to guide any environmental project and specifically steer such an ambitious long-term, media-driven exhibition space.

Like other liminal energy regions across the world, bogland remains a contentious environmental space in Ireland. It is one of the most endangered ecosystems in the country, as well as heretofore, one of the most important industrial resources in the region. To date, several reports estimate over 92% of boglands have been excavated for fuel or damaged through urban development. The treatment of bogland in many ways reflects the larger and problematic character of environmental attitudes in Ireland, which tend to hinge on utility (e.g. employment) rather than long-term sustainability and this bears out through Ireland's industrial energy policy on every level. As a major semi-state organisation Bord na Mona has for decades been charged with excavating the bogs for energy consumption, but the company is currently charting a radical new future, as it develops a green-tinged and more sustainable operational strategy (see Brereton and Barrios O'Neill 2021).

Any Just Transition project strives to set out a series of economic and social interventions needed to both secure and at the same time shift economic and social activity in a region that was dependent on an extractive industry for jobs, towards more sustainable activities related to a regenerative economy. Consequently, in line with the objectives of achieving EU climate neutrality by 2050, through an effective and fair manner, the European Green New Deal proposed a Just Transition mechanism, including a fund to ensure that no one is left behind from such a transition. Such a scheme's considerable resources, among other sources of revenue, might be leveraged in seeking to promote:

- rural tourism, enterprise development, rural towns, broadband
- basic services targeted at hard-to-reach communities, rural youth
- protection and sustainable use of waste water resources, local biodiversity, renewable energy (Mulvey 2020: 21).

Meanwhile, a Climate Action Fund (secured under Project Ireland 2040) is committed to support initiatives that contribute to a low-carbon and climate-resilient future, while achieving Ireland's climate and energy targets in a cost-effective manner. Most notably, Bord na Mona, after a radical transformation of its operations, now intend to develop various green projects around re-wetting and rehabilitating the bogs to increase their sequestering of carbon capability, which in turn will require some of its employees to be redeployed. The semi-state company has also implemented a 1.6 billion euro renewable energy, resource recovery and recycling business, to assist in such a radical redirection of its operations. Furthermore, developing new ventures in aquaculture, herbs and birch as well as water activities remains a high priority of late.

This fractured and highly depleted boglands region is also looking to Higher Education and various partners to help research future peat-land usage through a Green Eco-Sustainability hub. Such an environmentally driven reimagining process is already underway with converted bog-scapes across the whole island, designed to help promote new modes of ecotourism. For instance, one project has been brought to fruition within the Lough Boora Discovery Park (in County Offaly), which remains a hidden gem in the region. All of these initiatives could be further explored and amplified through the physical manifestation of such a research centre initiative.

But environmental communications experts are also well aware of possible inherent conflicts embedded in such a project; in particular looking to Bord na Mona with its radical new green-tinged business plan and its Corporate Social Responsibility agenda, and assessing the efficacy of its transformation from a so-called 'brown to a green' business mindset. Such a strategy can easily call to mind associations that are tinged with various types of green-washing. For many decades the semi-state company was committed to extraction of peat and 'despoiling of the landscape', at least from an environmental perspective. Consequently, some critics rightly question the rationale for the organisation's reframing of its *modus operandi* towards supporting a more wholesome (green) operational mandate. This radically revised business strategy can thereby be easily critiqued as a text-book illustration of large-scale greenwashing of the industry. As with all fossil fuel corporations who switch to renewable energy futures, such concerns need to be responded to directly and transparently, if the overall environmental communication message is to be successfully transmitted to all stakeholders. Effective media engagement and good communication strategies are essential towards helping to evaluate such industry transformation.

Once these concerns are adequately addressed however, then Just Transition funds and grants are required to help leverage a broad range of environmentally friendly projects designed to support both sustainable short and long-term objectives, alongside other local initiatives. Such initiatives can help give back so much to these very disadvantaged regions, while also promoting new forms of green-based enterprise development and innovative ways of conceptualising energy and employment. Whether it is coal workers in Poland or America, oil workers in the Middle East or, on a much smaller scale, peat workers in Ireland, a Just Transition model has to be comprehensively formulated and worked out over the longer term to ensure equitable solutions are co-created with all stakeholders, especially those directly affected on the ground. Certainly, such a green transformation remains a major challenge across many transitionary extractive energy regions of the world. But if this challenge is addressed and faced head on, using the skills of environmental communications, these nature-depleted and socially deprived areas and habitats, together with its local citizens can be treated fairly and justly.

References

Brereton, Pat and Barrios O'Neill, Danielle. 'Irish Energy Landscapes'. *Journal of Environmental Media* 2(1): 101–115. 2021.

Mulvey, Kieran. Climate Justice and Irish Bogland, Interim Draft Report. 2020. http s://www.gov.ie/en/press-release/06b7f-just-transition-progress-report-is-published/
Novitsky, Peter. 'Needed: Tougher Ethics, Policies in EU Research Projects'. *Science/ Business.* 9 July 2020. https://sciencebusiness.net/framework-programmes/viewpoint/ needed-tougher-ethics-policies-eu-research-projects

L

Legal Representations of Environmental Agency: Case Studies of *Dark Waters*

The legal route is becoming more significant in overcoming various environmental conflicts, whether it is assessing Just Transition rights or citizen rights explored in earlier entries, while encouraging the maintenance of non-polluted habitats or environments. Environmental legislation and legal methods can hold governments to account in facing up to securing a safe low-carbon future. Securing the physical health and safety of citizens through taking legal actions against big polluting corporations have had a long history within literature and film. In this illustrative case study we focus on a powerful Hollywood example, which sets a high benchmark for active environmental engagement and human pro-active agency.

In researching for Todd Haynes' earlier film *Safe* (1994), as an illustration of hippie environmental culture, he found this 'beautiful' quote from a cancer patient who believed that 'humans would rather accept culpability than chaos'. In many ways, as I argued elsewhere, *Safe* serves both as an elucidation and a critique of Ulrich Beck's seminal analysis of post-industrial society where new dangers and risks are ever-present and must be faced and accommodated through legal or other actions, if the human species is to survive (see review in Brereton 2005: 173–178). Meanwhile, Haynes' more recent film *Dark Waters* (2019) addresses the effects of environmental pollution more directly from a legal procedural perspective in his fictionalised recreation of this real-life environmental story.

Mark Ruffalo – a long time environmental activist in his own right – plays a corporate defence lawyer Rob Bilott who usually defends big business chemical companies and who thankfully finds his moral compass and switches sides to defend a small farmer in a rural community, who has been poisoned by chemicals in the local water course. His client Bill Camp plays the disgruntled farmer Wilbur Tennant whose animals are dying of horrible diseases, like in an Old Testament allegory. Yet nobody appears willing to recognise such injustice, much less help this poor farmer. In this 'David versus Goliath' story, the evil corporation is embodied by the well-known chemical giant

DOI: 10.4324/9781003123422-12

DuPont who kick-started a huge pollution problem through a synthetic polymer substance called Teflon, which was discovered by one of their scientists and initiated a revolution in home cooking. Recalling adverts like; 'choose a pan like you choose a man', or even a British advert for the product, 'it's what's on the inside that counts'. All of these adverts seek to illustrate the synthetic product's unique if paradoxical properties and embody a good example of the power of marketing and branding within the media.

Basically, at a corporate level, by not taking on board the precautionary principle, much less other ethical concerns around unintended consequences (see Brereton 2016) – not to mention the more subjective fears of environmental illness, explored in Haynes' earlier drama *Safe* – this real-life corporation remains criminally culpable. Such malevolent corporate governance does not even appear to recognise, much less respond to the environmental and human consequences of their ongoing industrial actions. A Pandora's Box of dangerous poison is unleashed, basically because of such chemical and synthetic scientific innovation by the company. On discovering that there were real and potentially catastrophic health issues to contend with, both consciously and literally the company buried the evidence, so that their corporate responsibility would remain minimised. This incontestable ecocidal form of corporate governance and practice had to be exposed by the narrative – recalling other similar legal eco-tales like *Erin Brockovich* (2000) – and effectively demonstrates how nature and human welfare have to be protected at all costs.

Ruffalo, who also co-funded the project, is sometimes accused of pontificating and preaching with regards to his long-term commitment to climate change activism. Like a charismatic priest, such knowing (and self-righteous) agency can be dismissed as simply preaching to the converted. While the storyline follows a very conventional path, the final act finds its unique voice, leaving a powerful impression on audiences.

Furthermore, there are visual moments in the film that interestingly feed off the director's art-house credentials. Haynes captures and paints the corporate world of Cincinnati with its shiny surfaces, skyscrapers and anodyne landscapes, in contrast with the dark foreboding of a rural landscape and local town Parkersburg (West Virginia) under the shadow of DuPont. Consequently, there is no need to labour all the sponsorship and other (legal) contributions the company has made to help legitimise and ingratiate themselves into the fabric of the locality. So many company services and buildings are plainly listed on hoardings, as he drives slowly through the neighbourhood. The community obviously depend so much for their livelihood on such corporate benevolence, hence not surprisingly most citizens remain supportive and even protective of their local employer.

As highlighted in the opening sequences of the film, the dark polluting water on the farmer's land is set up like a science fiction horror trope and back-story with local kids illicitly swimming there at night. Their teenage excitement in communing with nature is suddenly upset by a patrolling company boat who unceremoniously forces them out of the water and sprays some unknown liquid on the contaminated water – presumably to get rid of the evidence. Basically, nurturing, refreshing, and otherwise healthy, life-giving nature is literally turned on its head, all because of financial greed and the malevolent anti-environmental stance of such a big corporation in protecting their guilty secrets. Investigative reporting of all types are tipped off by these otherwise everyday routines. Especially in this filmic version of events, DuPont is characterised and foreshadowed as a malevolent spectre, on actively misusing such natural resources to effectively hide the evidence of their toxic chemical waste.

It's a classic but hopefully rare story of the polluter trying to ignore their corporate responsibility and illustrating how the official and legal system – much less the investigative aspects of media coverage in highlighting the story – has to eventually stand up to such pernicious corruption, while affirming an environmental first principle; the polluter (should) pay. But of course, corporate big business has all the financial clout and other necessary resources at its disposal to fight such ethical claims and can actively overcome any environmental protection lawsuit. Media investigation further explore how the fragile legal system is abused and can slow down and even potentially overturn such universal ethical and environmental edicts.

Like many heroic media stories of personal endurance and struggle, the dogged legal investigator only comes to the truth through a painfully slow process, while methodologically and literally unpacking the (hard) evidence. Basically, as constantly affirmed within the core principles of the classic Hollywood narrative, the truth will out, but only if one looks hard enough. However, attempting to secure a water-tight legal conviction is another matter. The official Environmental Protection Agency (EPA) – in America at least – allegedly had no teeth at the time and were beholding to big corporations like DuPont. Nonetheless, in 2005 with the legal evidence available from this investigation, the company paid over 16 million dollars to EPA for concealing the toxicity of the chemicals used back as far as 1981. Furthermore, according to a comprehensive *New York Times* article by Bryan Schutmaat from 2016, DuPont had dumped over 71,000 tons of the dangerous chemical (PFOA or C8) into Dry Run Landfill beside the farm, which in turn seeped into the water table and affected the whole neighbourhood. As in all branches of life, especially with regards to businessmen and scientists (not to mention media), there needs to be a robust system of checks and balances, with greater levels of transparency and accountability underpinning legal due process to expose such environmental injustice. All such controls can help ensure ethical and environmental justice is maintained and all aspects of nature is protected.

So it takes a more tenacious lawyer, willing to take a cut in salary and spend his whole waking life – to the detriment of his family – investigating such malefice, or at least teasing out what could be construed as amoral practices and thereby uncovering the full facts. The emotional toll is cranked up so high in some key scenes, you almost want to cheer, or literally scream at the screen. Similarly, in facing up to all aspects of climate change concerns, the media using various modes of storytelling to uncover new ways of appealing to the common good and support the development of close bonding between humans in 'doing the right thing' for society and the community, as against succumbing to base profit or other selfish motives. All of these challenges tend to be mediated, at least within Hollywood, through 'white messiah' figures, or sometimes less obvious mainstream heroes, who are driven to 'do the right thing' and face up to protecting our precious nature and habitats.

Meanwhile, the human cost to those at the receiving end of such injustice is enormous, with the poor farmer who initiated this class-action losing almost all his cattle and his livelihood. The erstwhile steward and protector of the land has little to look forward to, receiving no support from those around him. Ordinary citizens are shown as weak and afraid, while not being able to face up to the huge chemical-based corporation. Audiences recognise the palpable fear in the big rough farmer's eyes, as he tries to keep his small business going, while unfortunately ending up getting cancer, alongside his wife. Thankfully as a fitting eulogy to his noble life and death, the lawyer paints an emotional heroic elegy for this non-educated steward of the land, who alone stands up to oppression, while knowing all the time that the legal system would never let him win without a huge personal fight. All climate struggles and activists can certainly learn from this powerful real life storyline.

References

Brereton, Pat. *Hollywood Utopia: Ecology in Contemporary American Cinema*. Intellect Press 2005.
Brereton, Pat. *Environmental Ethics and Film*. Routledge 2016.
Schutmaat, Bryan. 'The Lawyer Who became DuPont's Worst Nightmare'. *New York Times*. 6 January 2016. https://www.nytimes.com/2016/01/10/magazine/the-lawyer-who-became-duponts-worst-nightmare.html

Linguistic Discourse and Ecocriticism – Naming the Crisis!

Kjersti Flottum in *The Role of Language in the Climate Change Debate* (2019) focuses on key linguistic themes that frame traditional scholarly analysis of print media's engagement with climate change, which include 'linguistic polyphony, lexical choices, metaphors, narration and framing' (1). Many of these research approaches outlined in a 2014 paper titled 'Linguistic Mediation of Climate Change Discourse', affirm that 'current debate reveals some discrepancies between the claims and evidence presented by climate science and the "stories" circulating in the media, among politicians and ordinary citizens. In this, language plays a crucial role' (Flottum 2014: 7).

As many cultural and environmental scholars assert, climate change is not just a scientific and measurable problem but also calls on so many aspects of social, political, ethical, cultural and communication debates, while both framing and assessing the problem and providing possible solutions (see Hulme 2009, 2013). The central importance of linguistic and discursive approaches using various ways of constructing stories, remains embedded in these media debates (see Nerlich et al. 2010). While most effort has been afforded to the linguistic analysis of words used in scientific reports and media articles, less focus has been afforded to more complex audio-visual modes of communication with regards to the evolution of the climate change narrative (see Culloty et al. 2019).

At least five components are highlighted in this traditional print-based linear process of communication around climate change (Adam 2008):

- initial situation: human beings apparently having lived in harmony with nature
- complication: carbon emissions increased dramatically since 1990 and causing serious climate change
- re-action: the UN organises scientists (COP's) to discuss action on climate change
- outcome (resolution) though the negotiating countries have not yet reached any binding agreement of measures to undertake
- final resolution: accepting there is a serious threat and taking the problem 'seriously'.

For instance, a close analysis of high-level reports like the 'Overview: Changing the climate for Development: World Bank's World Report' (World Economic Forum 2010), affirms from the start that economic growth is necessary to reduce poverty and remains at the heart of strategies towards increasing resistance to climate change in poorer countries (7). Over the years, such paradoxical analysis constantly blames climate change for hindering (economic) growth. While the report urges the world to be 'climate smart' and to find solutions without affecting 'our ways of life too much'. This tension remains an ongoing and for some an impossible challenge to face up to.

Meanwhile other linguists talk of how language change represents various forms of ecological change. Discursive experts like Norman Fairclough (1995: 199) have helped call attention to three-dimensional discourse and analysis, from textual analysis to practical analysis. Examining the socio-cultural practice around discursive and social processes remains essential. All the while, environmental stories embodied through the broad range of oral and written, alongside audio-visual media reports, need to be carefully analysed to assess their influence and effectiveness. This is exemplified through a growing range of studies of environmental organisations like Greenpeace (Zelko 2017).

A comprehensive overview set out in a chapter in the *Routledge Handbook of Ecocriticism and Environmental Communication* (Slovic et al. 2019) explores various modes of linguistic analysis, including the growing (linguistic) discourse of anthropocentrism, alongside other textual modes of explicit ecological engagement. More prosaically, such linguistic dexterity continues through so many forms of discursive engagement in the media. From greenwashing industrial processes of mass production of food, using effective advertising and branding – such as referring to 'Chicken McNuggets' for the 'coagulated ball of pink flesh slurry that was once a living creature' is a case in point. Alternatively, images of free-range animals, across so many advertisements are constantly deployed. Instead of calling out the reality of otherwise cruel factory farming methods, which is normalised across so many modern agricultural practices. Such representations and advertising campaigns seek to greenwash and frame these linguistic protocols using a wide range of strategies.

Coupled with freely used words like 'green', 'fresh' or 'natural' to connotate healthy and organic food production in advertising, while further exploring how 'green images' are constantly being used to reinforce many otherwise (un)wholesome production methods. Other random examples include using the term 'landfill', instead of calling a waste-disposal site a 'dump'. Not to mention the replacement by American and other Western officials of the term 'global warming' with 'climate change', because the latter term was considered less 'provocative' and more 'direct', or recalling moves by environmentalists to rename the growing environmental crisis as either a 'climate emergency'; 'climate catastrophe'; 'climate breakdown' alongside other renaming events. Hence linguistic dexterity in naming and/or spinning more positive PR connotations to industrial processes and defining areas of pollution or climate disruption, remain common place and need to be faced up and explored from an environmental communications perspective at all times.

Linguistic dexterity and manipulation of language in calling out a range of 'mental images' of climate change is also further reworked through the use of visual images, as linguistic short hand for clarifying specific meanings. Most pointedly, the move from using smoke stacks to denote global pollution, or the ubiquitous image of a polar bear trapped on a small floating ice-cap comes to mind. Stephen Lewandowsky and Lorraine Whitmarsh in a short, open-access piece titled 'Climate Communication for Biologists: When a Picture Can Tell a Thousand Words' (2018), talk of how images, together with well-chosen words, can nonetheless help to provoke a tipping point around effective communication engagement within mass audiences.

Lonie Jooubert (2020) in a further review piece on the power of images, 'War of Words: The Language of the Climate Emergency' cited in *The Daily Maverick* asserts:

> If anything put the sternum punch back into the climate story, it must be the iconic photograph of the charred body of a Joey – a "teenage kangaroo" – snared in the strands of a fence that blocked its escape from a raging wildfire during the recent conflagration sweeping across South-Eastern Australia.

The explicit image of the animal burnt alive, certainly serves as a counter to the often 'cute' animal stories used to address and speak to climate change.

Most prescient, in going back to still images and the power of print media, one can examine various environmental articles from *The Guardian*, including for example on 17 May 2019, when the editorial provocatively assert – 'Why the Guardian is changing the language it has used about the environment' by Damian Carrington. So many names have been ascribed to this phenomenon, from climate crisis to global heating, while more recently preferred terms such as climate emergency, crisis breakdown, or global heating, all of which are favoured over global warming in effectively communicating the issues.

Basically, as Katherine Viner senior editor-in-chief of *The Guardian* affirms, climate change sounds rather passive and gentle, while the scientists are alternatively informing us it is certainly a real and present danger and a catastrophe for humanity. Hence we need more sustained and stronger language around the climate crisis to effectively get the message across. Many environmental communication commentators call out the veracity and popularity of the Swedish activist Greta Thunberg who talks of climate emergency, ecological breakdown, ecological crisis and ecological emergency. These specific terms have become some of the most salient modes of expression of our ongoing climate emergency.

Nevertheless, the use of language protocols within such climate change discourse remains hotly debated. For a fuller understanding of the construction, the interpretation, and the circulation of climate knowledge and claims, linguistic and discursive analysis should be undertaken by all students, as intrinsically affirmed by environmental communications through 'collaborating with both social and natural sciences in truly integrated and inter-disciplinary approaches' (Flottum 2014: 20).

References

Adam, Jean-Michel. *La linguistique textuelle. Introduction à l'analyse textuelle des discours.* Armand Colin. 2008.

Colloty, E., Murphy, P., Brereton, P., Suiter, J., Smeaton, A.F. and Zhang, D. 'Researching Visual Representations of Climate Change'. *Environmental Communication* 13(2): 179–191. 2019.

Fairclough, Norman. *Media Discourse.* Edward Arnold 1995.

Flottum, Kjersti. 'Linguistic Mediation of Climate Change Discourses'. *Asp.* 65: 7–20. 2014.

Flottum, Kjersti. *The Role of Language in the Climate Change Debate.* Routledge 2019.

Hulme, Mike. *Why We Disagree About Climate Change.* Cambridge University Press 2009.

Hulme, Mike. *Exploring Climate Change through Science and in Society.* Palgrave 2013.

Jooubert, Lonie. 'War of Words: The Language of the Climate Emergency'. *The Daily Maverick.* 27 January 2020. https://www.dailymaverick.co.za/article/2020-01-27-war-of-words-the-language-of-the-climate-emergency/

Lewandowsky, Stephen and Whitmarsh, Lorraine. 'Climate Communication for Biologists: When a Picture Can Tell a Thousand Words'. *PLOS Biology* 16(10) 9 October 2018. https://journals.plos.org/plosbiology/article?id=10.1371/journal.pbio.2006004

Nerlich, Brigitte, Koteyko, Nelya and Brown, Brian. 'Theory and Language of Climate Change Communication'. *Wiley Interdisciplinary Reviews: Climate Change* 1 (1), 97–110. 2010.

Slovic, Scott *et al. Routledge Handbook of Ecocriticism and Environmental Communication*. Routledge 2019.

World Economic Forum. 'Overview: Changing the Climate for Development: World Bank's World Report'. https://www.weforum.org/reports/financial-development-report-2010

Zelko, Frank. 'Scaling Greenpeace: From Local Activism to Global Governance'. *Historical Social Research* 42(2): 318–342. 2017.

Literary Tropes for Representing Low Carbon Futures

As poet W.H. Auden famously wrote 'poetry makes nothing happen' in and of itself, the outside-the-box thought experiments of literature – alongside other media formats, as constantly asserted in ecomedia analysis – can nonetheless offer unique resources and examples for activating concern around creative thinking concerning the planet's environmental future. But by themselves, creative depictions of environmental harm are unlikely to free societies from lifestyles that depend on radically transforming ecosystems. Nonetheless, reflecting on works of imagination may prompt intensified concerns about the consequences of such choices and suggest more environmentally sustainable alternatives. This remains the key hope and challenge for the development of environmental media.

Some key aspects to consider regarding environmental links to literature include the following:

- Ecocriticism has developed into an increasingly worldwide movement. First of all through a commitment to preservationist environmentalism, while the second stage is marked by a more sociocentric environmental ethics, attaching special importance to issues of environmental (in)justice, to collective rather than individual experience as a primary historical force and concern within works of imagination, and (increasingly) linked to the claims of a global or planetary level of environmental belongings.

- Accompanying and influencing the trajectory just described has been a diversification of ecocritical interests from its original concentration on Anglo-American romantic literature to include indigenous and other minorities into the mix.

- Interest in the possibility of alliances between scientific and humanistic methods of inquiry was crucial in catalysing ecocriticism as a sub-discipline and has continued over time, although it has been sharply criticised, especially by those who view institutionalised 'science' as contributing to today's environmental problems.

- Ecocritics initially privileged modes of literary representations as being realistic reflections of the natural world
- A keen interest in differential experience and perception of environment especially through analysis of gender issues
- Ecocriticism shares interest in redefining humans' relationship to other species (Buell et al. 2011: 420).

Greg Garrard further notes how many eco-critics – within literature studies in particular – tend to cling rather uncritically to 'the assumption of indigenous environmental virtue' as a corrective to runaway modernisation, thus laying themselves open to the charge of perpetuating the nostalgic myth of the 'ecological Indian' and essentialising pure visions of nature. A charge which could also be levied against my often recuperative eco-textual analysis of mainstream Hollywood narratives over the last two decades. Scholars, especially those dealing with complex environmental issues and themes, all need to be constantly aware of the dangers of such binary contestations.

Reference

Buell, Lawrence, Heise, Ursula K. and Thornberg, Karen. 'Annual Review of Environment and Resources'. *Literature and Environment* 36: 417–440. November 2011.

M

Mediatisation of Climate Change with a Focus on Environmental Concerns

Concepts like 'mediation' or 'mediatisation' – defined as how media relates to other media and the real world – are currently used in environmental studies literature to capture how processes of communication transform society and help to shape large-scale relationships. Mediatisation was first applied to explore media's impact on political communication and to explain other effects with regards to democratic modes of politics. The Swedish media researcher Kent Asp (2007) was the first to speak of the mediatisation of political life and used the term 'mediated politics' to describe how the media have become a necessary source of information and a bridge between politicians and those in authority, compared with those who are governed. According to Asp's understanding, politics are mediated when the mass media are the main or the only source of political information, through which it may influence or even shape people's conceptions of political reality. Such mediation has a major role in both foregrounding and legitimating the central importance of our climate crisis as a core focus of political engagement and activity. Asp's theoretical assumptions that mass media may influence and mobilize current political ideas through mediatized rituals have been adopted by various communication scholars.

This concept has evolved to focus not only on media effects, but also on the interrelation between the change of media communication on the one hand and socio-cultural changes on the other, all of which are part of our everyday communication practices and our communicative construction of reality. Mediatisation research investigates the interrelation between media communicative change and socio-cultural change. While media does not necessarily directly cause a range of transformations across politics, economics, education, religion or institutional systems, it can nevertheless highlight and even showcase a way forward. An example of a study mobilising mediatisation theories would be one interested in how various aspects of media informs the ways environmental crises and/or protests are presented, while facilitating active communication between individual bodies and a shared understanding

DOI: 10.4324/9781003123422-13

of environmental activists and future crises. Such a model further aims to analyse how such knowledge transfer and practices are moulded by the media and how these are staged in ways that help to increase their influence and engagement across a broad range of audiences.

References

Asp, Kent. 'Fairness, Informativeness and Scrutiny: The Role of News Media in Democracy'. *Nordicom Review* Jubilee Issue: 31–48. 2007.

Media Coverage of Climate Change Debate: Triggers for Promoting Environmental Literacy

Media coverage of international climate change issues can in various ways influence public opinion, alongside promoting active forms of engagement (Flora et al. 2014). Yet the direct impact of media power remains a contested area of investigation and generally has been considered highly dependent on various ideological predispositions or motivations (Nisbet et al. 2013; McCright and Dunlap 2011).

Factors which can be used towards categorising large swathes of American public beliefs for example, according to studies such as Wonneberger et al. (2020), tend to focus on assessing attitudes and bespoke behaviours relating to climate change, global warming beliefs, issue involvement, policy preferences and of course resultant behaviour patterns. As frequently asserted, such responses are often broken into at least six categories:

- the *alarmed*, who are fully convinced of the reality and seriousness of climate change and want to take action immediately
- the *concerned*, who apparently make up the largest group, yet are not fully engaged with taking any form of direct action
- the other three categories which apparently constitute a crude breakdown of American values and behaviour patterns, include the *cautious, the disengaged* and *the doubtful.*

All of these apparently discrete categories represent different stages of understanding and acceptance of climate change and can help to map a response towards dealing with the crisis. All the while the type and strength of motivation has been found to vary, mainly due to individual differences and contextual factors. These variations can include strongly held attitudes, alongside high levels of knowledge and involvement, which can alternatively trigger defence motivations to reinforce these predispositions (Strickland et al. 2011). Alternatively, negative forms of issue engagement can further trigger more defensive motivation, leading to a disconfirmation bias (Kunda 1990). Meanwhile, other less engaged segments of the population appear driven by defensive motivations, which might not lead to high-accuracy motivations or even being actively engaged. Specifically, this appears to be the case for complex issues and triggers like climate change, where the academic literature suggests 'low-accuracy motivation can help to balance much needed resource commitment and accurate engagement' (Chaiken et al. 1989).

Furthermore, as found across various other studies, part of the less engaged student population did not appear to change their beliefs, attitudes, or intentions, or at least did so in a negative direction (Flora et al. 2014). Thus, such findings indicate a mix of indifference and reinforcement of pre-existing negative attitudes towards the issue, which was assessed via their relative levels of environmental literacy (Wonneberger et al. 2020: 179; Brereton and Gomez 2020).

As a rule of thumb, in comparing information seeking behaviour across climate-change audiences, segmentation analysis has revealed, not unexpectedly one supposes, that more engaged and environmentally literate segments of society are more actively looking for information about climate change in the media (Metag et al. 2017; Roser-Renouf et al. 2015). However, the less engaged cohort may be less inclined to pay attention to media coverage about the issue, rendering potentially effective situations of high exposure to climate change information less likely (Wonneberger et al. 2020: 180). Their findings further indicate that media effects are therefore segment-specific and also that exposure to event-specific media coverage can often evoke unhelpful defensive motivations, which in turn can trigger a confirmation bias for those with stronger opinions and beliefs. While higher exposure levels seem to contribute to a disconfirmation bias for the least engaged segment (such as the doubtful). These tendencies seem to confirm the common-sense view that media coverage mainly reinforces pre-existing attitudes (e.g. Stroud 2010 cited in Wonneberger et al. 2020: 187).

Nevertheless, as left-leaning media and audience studies and scholarship affirm, going back to Marxists like Antonio Gramsci in the 1970s, the media apparatus is never fully fixed or solely on the side of the dominant ideological systems or orthodoxy. Similarly, audiences across the full spectrum, as evident across several other entries, can hopefully learn and adapt to the environmental agenda, while stepping out of their erstwhile normal behaviour patterns of values and beliefs. Such opacity of media messaging, together with evaluating specific audience influences and effects, remains an ongoing avenue for the future of environmental communication engagement and increasing levels of critical literacy.

References

Brereton, Pat and Gomez, Victoria. 'Media Students, Climate Change and YouTube Celebrities: Readings of Dear Future Generations: Sorry video clip'. *ISLE Interdisciplinary Studies in Literature and Environment* 27(1). 2020.

Chaiken, S., Liberman, A. and Eagly, A.H. 'Heuristic and Systematic Processing within and Beyond the Persuasion Context' (212–252). In Uleman, J.S. and Bargh, J.A. (eds) *Unintended Thought*. Guilford Press 1989.

Flora, J.A., Saphir, M., Lappé, M., Roser-Renouf, C., Maibach, E.W. and Leiserowitz, A.A. 'Evaluation of a National High School Entertainment Education Program: The Alliance for Climate Education'. *Climatic Change* 127(3–4): 419–434. 2014.

Kunda, Z. 'The Case for Motivated Reasoning'. *Psychological Bulletin* 108(3): 480–498. 1990.

McCright, A.M. and Dunlap, R.E. 'The Politicization of Climate Change and Polarization in the American Public's Views of Global Warming, 2001–2010'. *Sociological Quarterly* 52(2): 155–194. 2011.

Metag, J., Füchslin, T. and Schäfer, M.S. 'Global Warming's Five Germanys: A Typology of Germans' Views on Climate Change and Patterns of Media Use and Information'. *Public Understanding of Science* 26(4): 434–451. 2017.

Nisbet, E.C., Hart, P.S., Myers, T. and Ellithorpe, M. 'Attitude Change in Competitive Framing Environments? Open-/closed-mindedness, Framing Effects, and Climate Change'. *Journal of Communication* 63(4): 766–785. 2013.

Roser-Renouf, C., Stenhouse, N., Rolfe-Redding, J., Maibach, E. and Leiserowitz, A. 'Engaging Diverse Audiences with Climate Change: Message Strategies for Global Warming's Six Americas' (368–386). In Hansen, A. and Cox, R. (eds) *The Routledge Handbook of Environment and Communication*. Routledge 2015.

Strickland, A.A., Taber, C.S. and Lodge, M. 'Motivated Reasoning and Public Opinion'. *Journal of Health Politics, Policy and Law* 36(6): 935–944. 2011.

Wonneberger, Anke *et al.* 'Shifting Public Engagement: How Media Coverage of Climate Change Conferences Affect Climate Change Audience Segments'. *Public Understanding of Science PUS* 29(2): 176–193. 2020.

Multi-level Perspective (MLP) Analysis of Climate Change

Recessions and pandemics certainly remain as shocks to the system, which create dramatic changes and have a major effect on communicating climate change most especially. To enable such multi-level perspectives and mapping of climate change to evolve, it takes a lot of time and effort to understand the various tensions and debates within the field. Such tensions can include the framing of sustainable market values or limitations around planetary boundaries, alongside taking into account the influences of technological substitution and in particular where the new replaces the old, producing regime transformation and hopefully new ways of thinking around potential solutions. For instance, it is suggested various forms of re-alignment and de-alignment of systems have been created by the COVID-19 virus, leading to de-stabilising within the normal function of global society, yet at the same time allowing for niche innovation to emerge into the future.

Basically, system rules shape markets and stimulate long-term levels of innovation and this can feed into major climate change policy decisions. For instance, as discussed elsewhere, contemporary German politics and societal attitudes were radically influenced by the Japanese Fukushima nuclear incident (2011). Yet research by Bird et al. (2014) found that public concern about climate change in Australia reduced following the accident, at the same time as public support for nuclear power declined. While Poortinga et al.

(2013) also observed changes in public attitudes towards climate change in the UK as a result. Surprisingly in Japan itself, public acceptance of the reality of climate change appeared as high after Fukushima, as before. This suggests that whilst the accident has affected Japanese attitudes to nuclear power, this did not extend to attitudes to the broad spectrum of climate change. Hence making direct correlations between major events like this accident, much less mapping a clear connection between climate change behaviour and the power of audio-visual media, always remains contentious.

Nonetheless, whatever way you look at it, the climate crisis, much less nuclear concerns like this, certainly appeared to constitute an existential threat across many regions. Similar to the Russian nuclear incident in Chernobyl explored elsewhere, one explanation posited was that unfortunately the Japanese did not have the latest or the best technology to deal with the crisis. Germany however recognised such a disaster as an existential threat for their energy industry which sparked a major change of policy direction. Hence, co-opting and diffusion of green policy decisions can be recognised as a multifaceted process, beyond single development or causal sparks and incorporating multiple innovations around whole systems change. By any measure, the power of media communication in framing and shaping citizen responses remains a key aspect in this pivotal change as nations uncover more environmentally sustainable ways of dealing with crises and striving towards a low-carbon future.

References

Bird, D.K., Haynes, K., van der Honert, R., McAneney, J., Poortinga, W. 'Nuclear Power in Australia: A Comparative Analysis of Public Opinion Regarding Climate Change and the Fukushima Accident'. *Energy Policy* 65: 644–653. 2014.

Poortinga, W., Aoyagi, M., Pidgeon, N.F. 'Public Perception of Climate Change and Energy Futures Before and After Fukushima Accident: A Comparison between Britain and Japan'. *Energy Policy* 62: 1204–1211. 2013.

Museums and Curating Exhibitions as a Model for Representations of Climate Change

Museums are seldom mentioned with regards to environmental communication, as they appear fixed and localised, focusing on addressing their targeted stakeholders – often specifically from an arts and heritage perspective. But recently much more mediated artifacts and installations have been added to museums and their repertoire of events which help to illustrate the growing interconnectivity between museums and all aspects of media and communication. Most typically this dovetails specifically with environmental communication, across specialist science communication galleries, together with environmental and heritage institutions. Curating appropriate media items for such installations remains a core preoccupation for a range of environmental communication strategies and can be characterised under the following broad areas:

- Drawing on a range of perspectives, ideas, scales and disciplines to form their own conclusions. Yet museums must also establish their own opinion within these contested spaces.
- Climate change is multi-scalar in space and time and needs to be represented in museums (as well as across media in general) in a similar way.
- Need to build new relationships with new audiences, going beyond existing audiences (see Cameron et al. 2013: 20).

Drawing on the experience of curating a climate-change museum exhibition, we can learn ways to draw on people's imagination to help innovate and propose new directions for themselves and others. Climate change is constantly perceived to be distant (psychologically) in terms of its temporality, geography, uncertainty and socially (Spence et al. 2012). People can be inspired for instance by 'hatred and by fear', museums can alternatively focus on 'promoting inspiration towards positional social and environmental outcomes, connecting personal satisfaction and fulfilment with a wider public good' (Cameron et al. 2013: 21).

Henry McGhie (2018) for example in a report for Manchester Museum, all but proposes an idealised, yet also common-sense manifesto around what museums should do (which in turn could be added to various forms of innovative new media), while effectively communicating big and complex issues like climate change:

They should not allow themselves to be irrelevant to society.
They should acknowledge that what they do normalises people's views on what is acceptable.
It is not enough to aim to connect people with the museum, but also with the world.
It should have a wealth of resources to contribute positively to climate change.
It should make connections between private lives and wider world culture
It should explore the past, present and possible futures.
It should develop a vision of a better future – all of which are essential for media also.
It should explore individual pictures bigger than themselves, while framing discussion.
It should keep abreast of research and related topics.
It should aim for a deep approach, and risk exploring deep, cultural experiences.
It should not be dependent on commercial/neo-liberal marketing systems to show the way.
It should be upfront regarding what it holds as important in the real world.

Furthermore, reminiscent of all good Public Service Broadcasting (PSB) television and mass media generally, museums should base all its major decisions on robust, critically informed, reflexive information. Certainly, the usual 'best practice' rules apply, inferring that museums should 'strive to be honest and trustworthy, delivering serious information with the utmost sensitivity. Yet they should always strive to both challenge and appeal to all types of people' (see Cameron et al. 2013: 21).

Collaboration between artists, museums (alongside media industries and environmental education), together with the general public most importantly, allowing for the co-creation of new understandings, and supporting access to alternative sources of knowledge and experience that might not otherwise be possible. All forms of environmental communications can learn from such a curated model of public engagement and how museums ideally at least might speak to their audiences.

References

Cameron, F. *et al.* 'Representation Climate Change in Museum Spaces and Places'. *WIRE's Clim Change* 4(1): 9–21. 2013.

McGhie, Henry. 'Manchester Museum Report: Evaluating the Nature Conservation Mission of Museums'. 2018. http://www.curatingtomorrow.co.uk/wp-content/uploads/2020/01/McGhie-HA-2018_Evaluating-the-nature-conservation-mission-of-museums.pdf

Spence, A., Poortinga, W. and Pidgeon, N. 'The Psychological Distance of Climate Change'. *Risk Anal.* June, 32(6): 957–972. 2012.

N

Native (Invader) Species: Representations and Effects on Bio-diversity

As affirmed in an 'environmental science' website Yale Environment 360 online listed below, invasive species often happened historically as part of a colonial enterprise, where 'exotic' plants and animals were brought back from the colonies as part of a trophy from what was considered an exotic landscape. Of course, many did not thrive in their adapted habitat, because of a lack of appropriate food or unhelpful climate conditions. But others adapted very well and some wreaked havoc on the new habitat and over time became an invasive species. More recently for instance fish species have been introduced to the Great Lakes for sports fishing, with no recognisable negative effect. While for instance zebra mussels imported, for example into the Great Lakes, rapidly covered submerged surfaces, clogging up water intake at treatment facilities and power plants. Removing such invasive species costs an estimated 500 million dollars annually in this region alone.

A key factor that makes any type of invasive species thrive, is a lack of predators in the new environment. See, for example, in Ireland when grey squirrels were introduced as a present for a large, landowning family. Predators apparently preferred the native red squirrel and consequently the grey squirrel thrived on the island, growing to dominate the country's ecosystem and habitat up to the present day. Similarly, the barbed goat grass, when it was first introduced into western America, surprisingly thrived in spite of poor soil. Apparently, most animals did not like its taste and consequently the goat grass become dominant throughout California, which probably contributed to wildfires in the region.

With thousands of species on the move as the climate changes, many scientists say that the dichotomy between native and alien species has become an outdated concept and that efforts must be made to help migrating species adapt to their new habitats. Basically, it's no longer helpful to have such a clear distinction and division between nature and conservation anymore. Nature documentaries have constantly explored this phenomenon and usually supported increased biodiversity from various perspectives. Of course, if so-called alien species are upsetting the ecological balance, then such an influx is

DOI: 10.4324/9781003123422-14

usually demonised and efforts to regain the pre-existing balance are encouraged. But this so-called balance is not an easy equation to stick to. Most notably, see globally successful nature documentaries, especially those fronted by David Attenborough, which are extensively discussed elsewhere. Evaluating levels of biodiversity and so-called threats from invading species remains an ongoing global concern, which environmental communication scholars and students need to be constantly engaged with.

Natural Capital as a Business Response in Dealing with Climate Change

Natural Capital or ecosystem services, as they are sometimes called, can be defined as the world's stocks of natural assets that include geology, soil, air, water and all living things on the planet. It is from recognising this so-called natural capital that humans derive a wide range of materials and (free) services, often called 'ecosystem services' that basically makes human life possible. The most obvious ecosystem services derived from nature, includes the food we eat, the water we drink and the plant materials we use for fuel, together with building materials for shelter and natural medicines to cure our ills, alongside other natural resources that are extracted from the planet. There are also other less visible ecosystem services, including the essential and protective systems of climate regulation and natural flood defences afforded by mountains and other topographical features like forests, the huge amount of carbon stored in our oceans, on our land and peatbogs, as well as the 'free' pollination of food crops provided by various insects. Putting a monetary value on such natural resources and services forms part of a re-oriented sense of green accounting and thinking, which has become popular in recent years. This constitutes an evolving re-monetising strategy to help highlight the necessity of adequately supporting and evaluating the primary importance of protecting nature, which is literally necessary for our very survival.

Yet, for those who are not fully aware of such geo-systemic realities, nature and our planet is only perceived through a very narrow (anthropomorphic) lens, as being literally 'free' to exploit in whatever way humans want, with no apparent negative consequences. For example, some farmers might use precious soil to grow crops, without necessarily recognising the eventual reduction in soil quality, which can in turn lead to a loss of food production capacity through over-exploited soil.

Natural habitats and their resultant accumulation of capital underpin our global wellbeing and prosperity, providing life-giving value and security, alongside resilience with regards to the long-term effects of climate change. All humanity relies on natural resources, especially water, soil, food and shelter, together with a broad range of other resources. Both big and small businesses rely on the benevolence of nature for (raw) essential resources; including water, land and natural fibres, all forms of extractive metals, together with oil, which drives our fossil-fuel industries, as well as other necessities that keep us alive. Yet according to the 'Financing Nature Report', it is estimated that in 2019, the world only spent around 124 billion US dollars per year on activities that benefit nature and its protection worldwide. While this figure is increasing year on year, such a figure is certainly not near enough to compensate, much less adequately address, the catastrophic bio-diversity loss of natural capital and related climate-change difficulties that the world is facing.

Furthermore, as Ben Constable Maxwell (2020: 13) affirms with regard to dealing with recovery after the 2020/21 pandemic, 'we need to recognise that the resilience of our economic system is ultimately dependent on the natural ecosystem and that our financial analysis needs to be directly informed by this interconnectedness. Maxwell continues how this relationship is a delicate balance, as 'many of these services are finite, if not carefully managed' and basically how it is much easier to survive if 'we recognise the value of natural capital and nurture rather than deplete it' (ibid.: 13).

Even on a 'selfish' or short-term balance-sheet level, protecting nature and biodiversity is worth it from a purely financial perspective, as well as from an insurance perspective, since on aggregate the global capacity of nature actively helps prevent climate change, water crises, biodiversity loss and global diseases, even pandemics. Some researchers and reports go so far as to suggest that the cost/benefit analysis of investing in natural capital projects far outweigh any level of initial outlay. For instance, when measured against environmental return on investment, the long-term, cost-benefit analysis can be assessed, according to some reports by as big a factor as 5:1.

There are also numerous other potential risks for businesses that dramatically counter their hesitancy or inactions, yet unfortunately facilitates the overall loss of biodiversity and natural habitats. All of which results in increasing costs, together with other operational and liability risks, affecting supply-chain continuity, as well as mitigating against any sense of predictability in business operational practices and securing overall regulation. All aspects of business need to take on board these greater financial risks into the future.

Environmentalists nonetheless constantly rail against the prospect of 'buying into the monetary trap' of re-assessing *all* natural capital explicitly and only in monetary and measurable terms, implying of course that all aspects of nature can be evaluated and measured in such human-centric ways. Alternatively, arguing that nature is immeasurable and affirming how no finite price can be put on such 'services' in turn helps to reinforce an essentialist notion that tends to add mystique to the power of nature to control our destiny. But on balance, if such balance-sheet modelling and crude valuing of natural services assists in the global debate and leads to greater business intervention towards re-establishing greater levels of biodiversity levels and increased carbon capture using natural resources like forests and land etc., then probably it's an economic and financial strategy, which is worth taking on board.

References

The Nature Conservancy. 'Financing Nature Report'. n.d. https://www.nature.org/en-us/what-we-do/our-insights/reports/financing-nature-biodiversity-report/
Maxwell, Ben Constable. 'Unlocking Business Potential'. *Profit With Purpose*. Dublin City Council: 10–14. 2020.

Nature Based Solutions – A Life on Our Planet

It is often affirmed that to affectively address climate change, nature together with a full range of natural solutions in particular have to be adopted. This magnus opus documentary helps to frame many essential threads in dealing with biodiversity loss and climate change. Nature-based solutions are essential towards securing our future. Yet in stark contrast the extensive and ongoing loss of biodiversity has put a huge strain on our planetary ecosystems. The famous television broadcaster and naturalist David Attenborough has presented such environmental issues and tensions in a clear and concise way, echoing his long back-catalogue of popular audio-visual documentaries seen by millions on television screens across the world.

The opening of this one-off special described as an autobiography, remains both provocative and insightful across so many discursive levels. The camera focuses on grim shots of a derelict city, with Attenborough walking through the decaying buildings, witnessing scattered books on the floor and some strange graffiti on the walls. Wondering where this site might be from, audiences are quickly informed that it is in fact Pripyat, a Russian city near Chernobyl that was home to over 50,000 inhabitants. On 26 April 1986 the area became suddenly uninhabitable because of a nuclear explosion at the nearby power plant. Within less than 48 hours of the accident the city was totally evacuated. No human has officially lived there since. (See review in this volume of the Netflix television series *Chernobyl* (2019) that deals with the disaster from a dramatic and organisational, risk-management perspective.) The accident basically resulted from bad management and human error, and was – according to Attenborough – probably the most costly mistake in human history.

But the true tragedy of our time, Attenborough affirms in his hypnotic and dulcet tones, is the loss of our planet's wild places and its related destruction of biodiversity. As the 'ultimate' nature-based solution, we rely entirely on this finely tuned natural ecosystem for our very human existence. Yet the way we humans live on earth now is eradicating our rich layers of biodiversity to dangerous levels of decline. It too will lead to what happened in Chernobyl, only worse, pronounces our trusted narrator. What more dramatic and provocative use of the ultimate destructive 'creative imaginary' – recalling Tim Morton's iconic 'hyper-object' – could one call upon in setting up such a cautionary storyline.

Further adding to the drama, the story is narrated by the celebrity profile of probably the greatest ever nature documentary personality, as he (finally) focuses his considerable communication and scientific skills on the precarious and interconnecting biodiversity and climate crises. Attenborough continues in almost a confessional and autobiographical mode: this film is my 'witness statement' and constitutes his vision for the future. Announcing that he is 93 years of age, his long screen-life is used to recall his most extraordinary back-catalogue of film and nature documentaries, presented by him, over the years. They are used to both frame and punctuate this 'final' witness statement and underpin his most heart-rendering environmental and teacherly mini-documentary. The ark of the narrative structure is focused around him as an old but sprightly man, looking back over his years as a natural historian and communicator. He reminisces through snippets of audio-visual material garnered from the BBC archives and other series, captured while travelling around the globe to represent wild nature for mass audiences, who watched in the safety and comfort of their living rooms.

A structuring and temporal device of showing the passing of time and linking this with the earth's ever-increasing human population is used to both punctuate and underscore his long screen life, alongside the earth's symbiotic history of humans and natural biodiversity. David Attenborough was born in 1926 when the human population was just 2.3 billion in total. It was a very different world then, where the human species had little understanding around how the planet really worked. The field he entered in later life was called natural history. As a child he loved exploring his local area in Middlesex (now part of greater London) and observing the fossils, some of which were 180 million years old. One can read the planet's long history in this way – every 100 million years or so, something catastrophic happens through a mass extinction event. All forms of evolution have been undone by these awful disasters. These dramatic events and disasters have happened five times in the four-billion-year-old history of planet Earth. The last time was the end of the dinosaur era – when a meteorite crashed into the earth, killing over 75% of all species. Life had no option but to rebuild from scratch. Attenborough argues that the human species is facing a major catastrophe again, but one which we can do something about, if we act quickly.

For 65 million years up to our current time, the Holocene has been the most stable epochal period in the Earth's history, with only about 1% variation in temperature. This has allowed nature to grow and stabilise, building immense forests and creating balance in the atmosphere. Meanwhile, nature has locked away (harmful) carbon into various natural habitats – characterised as carbon sequestration. This has provided a major environmental support for the planet, while increasing and extending all aspects of biodiversity. Increased biodiversity also brought stability to the planet, coupled with reliable natural rhythms, created through the seasons. Attenborough goes so far as to pronounce that this was our 'Garden of Eden', during the so-called Holocene period. We invented farming and used the seasons to produce crops. Our intelligence changed the way we would evolve, all the while drawing on the power of innovative ideas and human ingenuity. While some critics might accuse Attenborough of embracing a 'white messiah' complex, speaking through a well-healed, Western-centric, Judeo-Christian and Liberal mindset, one can forgive him these limitations in communicating such vital messages. Nonetheless, one hopes his successor's will speak from a broader spectrum of the human race, while reflecting more diverse groups of people.

Incidentally, such a transformation may be evidenced in a much smaller 2021 production by the BBC, serving as a useful antidote to this big-budget, Attenborough, nature documentary vehicle. All the while affirming the global environmental message, yet delivered by an 'alternative' voice of a disabled black presenter. Titled *Climate Change: Ade on the Frontline* this new BBC magazine series is headed up by the very engaging Lagos-born Paralympian, Ade Adepitan. Ade appears more than willing to travel to the remotest regions of our world and tentatively walk on foot with his crutches, or is seen pushing his wheelchair; all of which somehow helps to (metaphorically at least) visualise the worrying story of climate change, in a more provocative and engaging manner and certainly is not targeted simply for a minority disabled audience.

Meanwhile, Attenborough affirms with religious zeal in his own autobiography how 'nature is our biggest ally and our greatest inspiration'. Scientists and environmentalists for a long time now have asserted that life on our planet needs to be in balance with nature. Our only option of course is taking on the challenge around how we as a human species can be sustainable and also become part of nature.

Then fast-forward to our current times and the year 1954, when Attenborough was in his 20s, which coincided with the development of global air travel. Through endless travel across the world, he witnessed the free bounty of nature. Of course, such new forms of nature documentary and our modern media landscape could not have developed either, without such growth and innovation. After World War Two in particular there was an expediential progress in developing more technology to make life easier to travel to make such programmes. It seemed like nothing could limit our progress, as we developed more and more. By 1960 the world's human population was 3 billion. The African plains and its wild landscape was regarded as endless and unlimited with huge herds of wild animals roaming freely around. In 1968 with the Apollo Space mission, humans saw our pristine 'blue marble' sphere as planet Earth for the first time, provoking a rediscovery of a fundamental environmental truth: that humans depend on the natural world for their very existence.

Later in 1971, on a visit to New Guinea he observed a so-called 'primitive' Hunter Gatherer tribe in the forest. They were an indigenous people who lived sustainably in their self-contained habitat and would probably continue like this forever, if simply allowed to by the outside world. By all accounts, the nature-media industry can be critiqued for making the world 'smaller' and bringing the 'exotic' into our living rooms, often without much contextualisation. Such seductive, nature-based media can be read as also culpable as a contemporary and distasteful mode of cultural imperialism, including a Western-centric form of nature colonisation. Of course, at a material level, the Western world demanded more resources from (wild) nature and thereby needed to encroach on more and more untapped regions of our planet to secure scarce resources to help sustain our ever-growing and voracious consumption-driven population. Incidentally, such stark tensions and conflicts are at least allegorically illustrated through the popular eco-blockbuster science fictional fantasy *Avatar* (2009).

Then by 1978 the still growing population had reached 4.3 billion. In the 1970s, Attenborough presented his *Life on Earth* series, which was shot in over 39 countries, travelling approximately 1.5 million miles. Such a resource-taxing, audio-visual media feat calls to mind the paradox of producing resource-expensive nature documentaries that have an extremely high carbon footprint, while paradoxically often railing against excessive carbon-based consumption. Incidentally, all this is set against the contemporary drive to measure and reduce the carbon footprint of all media programmes in the BBC for example, as outlined by BAFTA and its Albert Carbon Calculator discussed elsewhere.

Most noticeably, Attenborough concedes some animals were harder to find for the series. As illustrated for instance in his most recent BBC series *A Perfect Planet* (2021), where a short segment at the end of each episode is devoted to the herculean efforts needed in trying to capture some rare footage of exotic creatures. This strategy echoes the Susan Sontag thesis around how the camera has replaced the hunting rifle in capturing such a trophy or memory of one's exotic travels. For example, in one early episode audiences witness the effort used to photograph the endangered species of a small herd of wild Bactrian camels hidden in the Gobi Desert. Wild nature is most certainly in retreat.

Meanwhile, in this short but very powerful historical natural auto-biography, Attenborough focuses on the ravages of whale hunting, as he had witnessed decades before the awful carnage of marine life being destroyed through excessive human fishing and hunting. Consequently, blue whales have become nearly extinct. This has been called to attention by environmental activists including members of Greenpeace, with their small boat trying to force big industrial harvesting boats to stop butchering the whales, in a dramatic David-versus-Goliath struggle. Making people aware of and supporting a love of the natural world became the prime objective of all his campaigning work. By this time the human population has doubled, compared to when Attenborough was born.

By the end of the 1990s, Borneo's extensive natural rain forests were reduced by over 50%. A key problem within such regions was the replacement of natural ecosystems with a monocultural palm oil industry, which necessitated cutting over 3 trillion trees and consequently destroying over half of all the rainforests. All of which is instigated for a product that is used simply to complement and streamline so many Western food products, and consequently it was in high demand by the food processing industry. As we have discovered to our determent, no natural ecosystem is secure – even one as vast and bountiful as our oceans, which envelops well over half of the surface of our planet. Echoing and referring to another of his series, *The Blue Planet* (not to mention the more blunt 2021 Netflix eco-documentary *Seaspiracy*), which was filmed in the late 1990s and of course also became hugely popular across the world.

By 1997 the population rose to 5.9 billion, while almost 90% of the large fish in the sea were destroyed through over-fishing and such stocks unfortunately have not been replenished. Coral reefs are dying by turning white, mainly because of the oceans warming, as we have lately discovered. In 1993, *Life at the Freezer* focused on the warming of arctic summers and some years later in 2011, his series *The Frozen Planet* was aired. Explaining climate change so well for mass audiences, Attenborough narrates how the planet is unable to absorb all the heat, with 1% warmer seas and reducing ice shelf at the poles. Around 40% reduction in the total ice on the planet in less than 40 years means that we are heading for disaster. Our impact on the precarious ecosystem of the planet is now global. The assault on the planet has affected the very foundations of our living world. We have most especially overfished and over-farmed our habitats to a very critical level; doubling overall levels of pollution, while reducing the size of our total fresh water by over 80%. We have replaced the 'wild' with a controlled and 'tame' landscape.

Incidentally, taking into account such radical transformation and species depletion and other related pressures, one can easily deduce how all this can further help spark the probability of harmful viruses skipping into the human food chain, as evident with the COVID-19 pandemic. All in all, the wild animal population has decreased by over half in his lifetime, which remains a shocking statistic to contemplate. Hence it is no exaggeration to conclude his statistical evaluation by summarising: 'we have destroyed the non-human world'.

Using a melodramatic close-up of this celebrity nature presenter looking down and depressed, remains the only logical, if clearly emotional, response to such heavily weighted statistical analysis. Like in a confessional mode of revelation, Attenborough slowly reiterates: this is my 'witness statement'. 'Global decline is happening now and at scale'. Yet as environmental communicators, we realise that despair and hopelessness are not useful in actively turning the dial regarding behavioural change. Instead we need hopeful solutions, based on a clear road map for the future. But before he can even suggest possible solutions, Attenborough has to highlight and reiterate even more starkly the current scale of the problems. Hence the voice-over commentary switches gear again and pronounced with a more measured tenor of conviction: 'but it does not end there'.

In 2020 the global population is now a staggering 7.8 billion. While scientists predict that by the 2030s the Amazon rainforests (the 'lungs of the planet') will be all cut down, producing huge carbon releases from the land.

Then, by the 2080s, there will be a global food-production crisis, assisted by the over-use of precious soils. Our weather is already becoming more unstable. By the 2100s a large part of the earth will be uninhabitable, leading to a mass extinction event. The security and stability of the Holocene and basically our 'Garden of Eden' will be lost!

By any measure he has become an evangelical climate campaigner – yet only relatively recently has he explicitly called out climate change as a clear and present danger, recalling the success of his plastic pollution surge and mediated global influence following a section in *The Frozen Planet*. Remaining a pragmatic optimist, the environmentalist affirms that 'we can fight back'. Replaying a speech he delivered in 2018 at the Poland Intergovernmental Panel on Climate Change (IPCC) where he pronouncing that 'we have to fight back … no one wants this to happen'. Looking for clear solutions, he calls out; 'So what do we do'? Answering this perennial question, he suggests, it's straightforward and staring us in the face. 'Recreate our biodiversity – the very thing we depend on. It's the only way out of the crisis we are in: '*Re-wild the world*'!

Beyond such generalities and as an emotional call-to-arms for the environmental movement, Attenborough also provides some more concrete nature-based assertions and solutions including:

- Population control, (considered a toxic topic for many environmentalists) using the example of Japan with its higher standard of living, and noting how their national birth rate has fallen and how the country's population has now become stabilised. People choose to have fewer children. In the West many of us are living longer, leading to higher populations overall. As a 93-year-old himself, he echoes what is often asserted, namely that the trick is to raise *everyone* across the world out of poverty, while also getting girls to stay in school longer.
- Renewable energy has to become the norm and we need to phase out fossil fuels. He illustrates this with a case study of Morocco, which apparently is now a major supplier of solar energy. (See discussion elsewhere of mining and pollution in Morocco, as an antidote in fleshing out this positive environmental story.) Basically, it's crazy when you think of it that our Banks and Pension funds still support the fossil fuel industries. This imbalance and stupidity have to end.
- Oceans are a critical ally in our battle to secure our future. We need to repopulate our oceans with life and this can be a win-win situation with targeted approaches rather than over-fishing.
- We must radically reduce the area we farm. The quickest way to do this is to change our diet. The planet cannot support billions of meat-eating humans. We can cut the land we use by half, if we become vegetarian!
- Great examples such as the Netherlands are highlighted in supporting very intensive vegetarian production.

- Reversing the land grab for human and animal food is essential. There is an ongoing need for much of the so-called 'free land' to be effectively reforested. In turn, this can help lock-in carbon and also become a centre for increasing biodiversity.

Following a powerful narrative strategy of linking the introductory sequence of this short documentary and re-splicing it again into the conclusion, helps create a book-ended, circular, closed loop of connectivity. This strategy affords some clear hooks for audiences to connect with and embrace. By reframing the opening sequences around the derelict city, following the nuclear disaster of Chernobyl, the programme uses a most evocative illustration and 'creative imaginary' around how we as a human species can actively learn from our mistakes.

Viewers are shown real-life physical evidence of how aspects of nature, through the introduction of wild animals and wild flora and fauna have come back of their own accord to this radiated space, deep in the heart of Russia. Nature has recolonised and repurposed this desolate space without any human interference on its own. Like so many science fictional narratives, like *I am Legend* (2011) or uplifting eco-documentaries like *2040* (2019) – see also an extensive reading of this documentary in this volume, which also uses bullet-point modes of solutions and highlights how the natural rewilding of cities can provide a beacon of hope into the future.

Such hopeful uplifting messaging and quick-fire environmental lessons are essential if mass audiences and concerned citizens are to discover the positive energy and productive strategies needed to fight such a long-term battle over the existential crisis of the century. Environmental communicators at all levels can use such evocative media narratives as part of their arsenal in their challenging work concerning the precarious future that we are all facing into.

References

Attenborough, David. *A Life on our Planet: My Witness Statement and Vision for the Future*. Penguin 2020.

NIMBYism (Not in My Back Yard): Case Study of Renewable Energy (Windfarms)

The concept of NIMBYism is frequently used in environmental communications to refer to research around renewable energy and wind energy, where public opinion is generally in favour of this form of sustainable technology, but often not when proposed installations are sited close to their own neighbourhoods. Such a proposition asserts that people are willing to accept changes in society, including a transformation into renewable energy, as long as they do not directly impact them in an actual or perceived negative way.

Recalling a study I was involved in which focused around the perceptions of Wind Farms for a European funded COST network (European Cooperation in Science and Technology) Doctoral Training Summer School (2017). This workshop illustrated that there remains a big communications deficit with regards to understanding the range of objections to the development of 'clean' wind and solar power across Europe and the rest of the world. Environmental journalists talk of encouraging communities to move to clean energy as being the best way to achieve a low-carbon future and to unlock citizen's renewable energy potential. For instance, 'Friends of the Earth' (www.foe.ie) – 1 of the 100 organisations that signed up to a position that embraces alternative energy, envisions Ireland as a nation of energy citizens who will plan, generate and distribute energy for the benefit of their communities. But how to transcribe these ideals into a viable reality on the ground, remains a challenge and demands very broad ranging multi-disciplinary strategies and activities.

One oft-quoted belief cited by John Barry et al. (2008), suggests that wind farms are considered a form of 'pollution', being either characterised as 'matter out of place', or simply dismissed as more suitable for other EU countries. Furthermore, historical and cultural analysis calls upon long-established, deep-seated, anti-colonial discourses to explain the hardening up of resistance in Scotland (alongside Ireland and other regions) to these forms of renewable energy sources – echoing in particular how the land was 'cleared' and sacrificed for early manifestations of nature exploitation and colonisation, through energy harvesting throughout the centuries.

Furthermore, according to Barry and others, windfarms are perceived in some quarters as the 21st century version of William Blake's description of factories as 'dark satanic mills', which were viewed as despoiling England's 'green and pleasant land'. Such binary positions and romantic evocations of landscape also echo discussions of Ireland with its predominant touristic and nostalgic sensibility that further feeds off a postcolonial mindset.

At a stretch, windfarms can be negatively perceived and considered as a form of 'enclosure', while reflecting the 'privatisation of the commons' (Barry et al., 2008: 81). In trying to reframe ongoing tensions between renewable energy and economic growth and commercialisation, at least rhetorically, if not practically, much emphasis is placed on the importance of 'sustainable development' that came into vogue in the late 1980s. This framing is particularly understood and appreciated through the lens of policy discourse and involves what has come to be known as 'ecological modernization' (Barry et al., 2008: 81).

Meanwhile, an anti-windfarm stance is framed as depicting 'giant' turbines destroying areas of beauty and tranquillity and turning the 'rural' landscape, or specific areas of 'wilderness' into an outdoor industrial production plant for electricity generation. For instance, the Irish Tourist board (see Bord Failte, www.failte.ireland.ie) can influence the future of planning applications for wind projects, since tourism is considered essential for the economic welfare of the country. Consequently, one might presume that tourists surveyed would have a very negative attitude towards the construction of windfarms across the island. Yet surprisingly, at least anecdotally, through extensive tourist research carried out over recent years, it was discovered that tourists and visitors apparently did not really care about the presence of such windfarms across the landscape (Bevk et al. 2017).

A key conundrum for environmental communication scholars remains focused around how positive media representations of such alternative energy solutions can assist in this process of low-carbon energy transformation. According to environmental scholar Patrick Devine-Wright (2005) who has worked extensively in this area, the growing literature around public perceptions of a wide variety of renewable energy resources, including wind energy, has presented a striking divergence of approaches. One wonders how such perceptions have evolved and changed within different regions and are there comparative modes of analysis to be gleaned across different energy landscapes and countries. In general, there remains strong public support, at least in principle, for alternative energy solutions. Nonetheless, at the local level, there is frequent controversy and public opposition – often reduced to being categorised as a form of NIMBYism – in addressing the introduction of different energy technologies, from both a social, economic and a particularly cultural context. Furthermore, several other key communication questions are also raised throughout the literature, including:

- What tangible supports exist or are seen to exist amongst the public for a switch to wind energy from more conventional fossil-fuel based resources?
- What physical or environmental characteristics are linked to negative perceptions of wind farms?
- Do those living closest to a wind farm have the most negative attitudes?
- Do negative attitudes to a wind farm lessen over time?
- Does NIMBYism in itself explain wind farm opposition?
- Does local involvement in wind farms help to increase public support? (Devine-Wright, 2005: 126).

All the while, political and popular support for wind farms constantly vacillates, depending on the political, cultural and social temperature of public opinion in particular localities. This situation can become especially toxic – as illustrated by an American documentary *Windfall* (2010) – when there was much public opposition and no measure of compromise appeared to satisfy the various stakeholders. Surprisingly there are relatively few fictional or even documentary representations of renewable energy sources, such as wind turbines in the UK or Ireland. Yet it is easy to appreciate how reconsideration of landscape might lead to alternative constructions of justice and equity, which is explored in a 2021 paper 'Irish Energy landscapes' and illustrated by wind and other forms of Irish energy landscapes (see Brereton and Barrios-O'Neill 2021).

To ensure effective roll-out of cleaner alternative energy solutions across the world requires robust environmental communication strategies and transparent engagement with local communities. All the while, remaining cognisant of the dangers of simply perceiving wind and solar energy as a panacea for all our climate crisis – see the Michael Moore produced documentary *Planet of the Humans* (2019) discussed elsewhere, alongside other entries on wind energy. There remains however a lot to be achieved around communicating the necessity of green energy and supporting civic society, which needs much more active engagement at all levels in addressing and tackling the climate crisis.

References

Barry, J., Ellis, G. and Robinson, C. 'Cool Rationalities and Hot Air: A Rhetorical Approach to Understanding Debates on Renewable Energy'. *Global Environmental Politics* 8(2): 67–98, May. 2008.

Bevk, T., Martinez, N.M., Brereton, P., Lasosevi, M. and Peri, M. 'Iterative Digital Photo-Based Assessment for Rural Landscape Perception: A Small Experiment from County Wicklow, Ireland'. *Journal of Digital Landscape Architecture* 1(2): 18–27. 2017.

Brereton, P. and Barrios O'Neill, D. 'Irish Energy Landscapes on Film'. *Journal of Environmental Media* 2(1): 101–115. 2021.

Devine-Wright, Patrick. 'Beyond NIMBYism: Towards an Integrated Framework for Understanding Public Perceptions of Wind Energy'. *Wind Energy*. 8: 125–139. 2005.

Non-Conventional Environmental Activism: A Case Study of *Woman at War*

Conventional environmental activists are often stereotyped as middle-class, (white) left-leaning conservationists, who have both the time and the financial resources necessary to be concerned about their environment. Of course, this categorisation does not correspond with the growth of younger more passionate activists – like Greta Thornburg and the Friday Strike Demonstrations – alongside a range of NGO activists from the ranks of Greenpeace, Friends of the Earth and more recently Extinction Rebellion, who often do not fit into any neat category or grouping. Representing non-standard approaches, such 'progressive' examples of environmental activists need to be part of the broad scope of environmental representation, designed to help ensure more strands of society and citizens, which are mobilised and help feed into this growing movement. Representing non-conventional activists in this struggle can serve to highlight the growing scope for more radical engagement, which encourages mainstream audiences to recognise and engage with such a global struggle that needs to be fired up over time. A small-scale Icelandic fictional film *Woman at War* (2019) can help illustrate some of these aspects and concerns (see Brereton 2020).

Icelandic director Benedikt Erlingsson and cinematographer Bergsteinn Bjorgulfsson wonderfully capture the pure beauty of this magical country with their dry Green Goddess eco-narrative. Starring Halldora Geirharosdottir as Halla, who according to Mark Kermode in his review in *The Observer* combines 'the athletic physicality of Tom Cruise's Ethan Hunt with the kaleidoscopic character depth and subtlety of Liv Ullman or Greta Garbo' (5 May 2019). Halla is certainly like Artemis, the Greek goddess of the wilderness, as she burrows into the earth at times to find solace and avoid capture.

This gentle understated tale references many other eco-films, including the Oscar winner *The Revenant* (2015) – not withstanding its comparatively much larger budget – and its more everyday take on using sheep's hide rather than a bear's to disguise herself in hiding from authorities on carrying out radical environmentally driven acts. Kermode further asserts how it puts a 'DIY twist on *Mission: Impossible* riffs, presenting its life-or-death struggles in thrilling offbeat fashion'. More generally references to Robin Hood archetypes are also called to mind; albeit being a middle-aged and middle-class underdog, who strives to attack the system and 'do the right thing'. With her bow and arrow literally slinging shots at a high-voltage power wire, such 'creative imaginaries' of climate-change rebellion against a fossil-fuel driven energy company remains memorable.

Or alternatively hiding from capture inside a flock of sheep, alongside recalling the iconic and romantic act of total submersion underwater to avoid detection by a drone; all of these images certainly stay with the viewer. Environmental admirers who are either radical activists or most likely not, can enjoy the simplicity of using an arrow shot to take down the high-tech surveillance drone and finally punching it to a pulp, together with the natural way the character overcomes extreme cold by becoming totally submerged in the famous hot springs on the island.

Following an art-house strategy of using diegetic music – also surprisingly evident in the quirky comedy *There's Something about Mary* (1998) – the soundtrack is performed live within the romanticised landscape and evocative *mise-en-scene* of this Icelandic paradise. Basically, the music functions as both a motif and as a chorus, reflecting her professional background. In her screen day job, Halla is a choir leader, supporting the construction of a positive vision of society that encourages citizens to stand up and pull together to maintain the long-term benefits of community.

But, of course, the status quo and oppressive system cannot allow her to win through her anti-capitalist and pro-environmental stance; especially recalling the (criminal) act of hijacking electricity stations. Energy systems are always ring-fenced as untouchable (natural) natural assets, which are essential of course to sustain economic development. Humorously, the Icelandic government is supported by both America and Israel no less, in hunting this lone (comic) terrorist. I was particularly taken with the co-opting and use of umbrellas and other everyday objects, like her environmentally friendly bike, to assist in her political activism – with recurring echoes of real-life student violence/demonstration and their symbolic use of umbrellas across Hong Kong most recently in its struggles against closer ties with China.

As in all appealing human interest stories, she is in no sense simply a one-dimensional environmental activist. For instance, we discover Halla has put in an application to adopt a child and later somewhat surprisingly learns that she has been successful in adopting a four-year-old orphan from Ukraine. While some critics might cynically consider this sub-plot as an illustration of an eco-feminist discourse being subverted by sentimental versions of mother-hood, one could counter this somewhat surface reading, with a more positive environmental interpretation. Contrasting environmental activism with extreme modes of spiritual revere; audiences are introduced to her sister, who has vowed to enter into a nunnery for the sins of the world, but who selflessly swaps a future of prayerful incarceration to enable her activist sister to serve the common good, while at the same time supporting such an orphaned child.

Yet even this fantastic twist of fate and self-sacrifice is not an easy ride, much less a conventional conclusion to the storyline. While taking the child out of Ukraine on a bus, during an extreme flooding event (aggravated by climate change, one presumes), they literally have to exit the vehicle and pre-cariously walk across high flood water to reach safety. Such imaginary cir-cumstances is reminiscent of so many iconic, real-life migrant journeys, sparked by environmental and other political incidents, captured on our tele-vised news feeds. The metaphorical/allegorical struggle to address climate change remains ever-present and needs to be taken seriously. One might sug-gest, such a heroic, but small-scale narrative and creative imaginary narrative helps provide its audience with new and innovative ways to perceive how citizens might assist in this environmental struggle.

References

Brereton, Pat. 'An Eco-reading of Documentary-Fictional Narratives'. *Irish Studies in International Affairs* 31: 43–57. 2020. Royal Irish Academy Dublin Ireland.

Kermode, Mark. 'Woman ar War Review – The Mother of All Green Goddesses'. *The Guardian*. 5 May 2019. https://www.theguardian.com/film/2019/may/05/woman-at-war-review-benedikt-erlingsson-icelandic-eco-comedy

O

Organic Signifiers of Communicating with a Natural Ecosystem – *Tree of Life*

Richard Powers won the Pulitzer Prize for *The Overstory* (2018) a monumental account of how tree history and human history are intertwined, although they operate on enormously different time scales. Powers notes that 'attempts at successful inter-species communication, by means of either science or spiritual awakening, tend to place those able to communicate and translate on the brink of insanity in the eyes of others' (Pusse and Downes 2020: 1). At the same time trees and forests are often considered as recreational spaces for eco-tourism and serve as a pristine landscape for going 'back to nature'. For instance, Australian philosopher Glenn Albrecht established the term 'solastalgia', as a combination of nostalgia, lost solace and desolation, connected to a lost place and a culture formerly in harmony with an unspoiled natural environment (Pusse et al. 2020: 10).

Much literary analysis of trees stresses the secret value of humankind's persistent constructions of nature solely in terms of what Freud famously termed the 'family romance' (e.g. mother/earth, father/sky, family/tree) etc. This generic correlation is extended into media and film. For example, scholars like Colin Carman likens the act of viewing a film to that of moving through a forest, which is not, for him, a 'static' physical entity, but instead a moving picture. Like the sea, the forest defies both language and photography, since it 'cannot be framed'. For example, the oak tree standing tall outside the O'Brien family home in Waco, Texas in *The Tree of Life* is meant to contrast with another tree with its roots set in concrete at the base of Jack O'Brien's office building in the city. Both of which explicitly serve as an objective correlative for Jack's detachment from nature in an urban environment (Carman 2018: 637).

At a more explicit semiotic level of analysis, a reading of the abuse of chemicals in the DDT scene – showing children following a machine spraying (lethal) chemicals on the ground – further affirms the film's ecological credentials (see reading in Brereton and Furze 2014). As affirmed in several studies, Terrance Malick's film presents a nuanced and complex audio-visual

DOI: 10.4324/9781003123422-15

narrative that foreground a complex range of environmental and spiritual motifs, which certainly speak to an art-house audience and affirms a very deep form of biophilia and human-spiritual connectivity with and in nature.

References

Brereton, Pat and Furze, Robert. 'Transcendence and The Tree of Life: Beyond the Face of the Screen with Terrence Malick, Emmanuel Levinas, and Roland Barthes'. *Journal for the Study of Religion Nature and Culture* 8(3): 329–351. 2014.
Carman, Colin. 'Tree Worship and the Oedipal Ecology of The Tree & The Tree of Life'. *ISLE* Summer25(3): 630–651. 2018.
Powers, Richard. *The Overstory.* Norton and Co. 2018.
Pusse, Tina-Karen and Downes, Rebecca (eds) *Madness in the Woods: Representations of the Ecological Uncanny.* Peter Lang 2020.

Overton Window and Making Radical Political Environmental Decisions

The concept of the 'Overton Window' (Lehman 2010) has recently attracted notice as a metaphor for understanding policies and behavioural change that are considered viable within political and by extension environmental communication discourses. Embedded in this concept is the notion that promoting a position on climate change, which currently seems extreme (i.e. outside the window of acceptability), may nevertheless help to shift or nudge mainstream opinion in the preferred direction. It could be argued therefore that the weaponising of language and various terminology around a perceived climate change tipping point is necessary, since a more dramatic visualisation of the impending crisis may in turn shift (the Overton Window) to a position more favourably disposed to concrete and reliable mitigation policies. Consequently, it is suggested that a broad range and spectrum of environmental organisations can help shift the dial towards a greener direction. These include establishment bodies like the American West Coast conservation movement, The Sierra Club, as well as Friends of the Earth, Greenpeace etc., all of which can be combined with more provocative, yet nonetheless pacifist contemporary organisations such as Extinction Rebellion (EX), together with even more radical animal rights organisations like People for the Ethical Treatment of Animals (PETA).

Alexa Weik von Mossner (2021), for instance, provides a useful analysis of two radical environmental activist documentaries: Jerry Rothwell's *How to Change the World* (2015) – focusing on the birth of *Greenpeace* and its development of 'mindbomb' communication strategies – and Marshall Curry's *If a Tree Falls* (2011), which chronicles the rise and fall of the *Earth Liberation Front* and its tactics of ecotage. She argues how such documentaries straddles the line between ostensible objectivity and sympathetic advocacy for the individuals they portray. All the while, as Keith Makoto

Woodhouse (cited in Weik von Mossner 2021) together with Weik von Mossner affirms, such radical forms of environmentalism are confronted by two central questions that might be summarised as follows:

- what kind of actions are permissible in the name of protecting the environment?
- what kinds of action will successfully raise public concerns or conversely, turn public opinion against the activists?

For instance, one founding member Paul Watson was regarded as too radical for *Greenpeace* so he was ousted in 1977, going on to develop *EarthForce* and then *Sea Shephard Conservation Society* – which was an anti-whaling pressure group that was critiqued for its violence against property and people. Meanwhile, another radical American-based organisation *EarthFirst* opened the door for even more radical offspring, such as *The Earth Liberation Front* (ELF), which is documented in *If a Tree Falls*, recounting how the organisation came to prominence in the mid-1990s. The organisation was considered so radical at the time, the Federal Bureau of Investigations (FBI) labelled them as domestic terrorists in America.

In many ways such environmental activist documentaries demonstrate how a broad range of approaches, feed into changes in attitudes and approaches that help to demonstrate the Overton Window concept. Adding various forms of radical engagement into the mix can help to widen public debate around societal action and ethical values regarding contentious environmental issues. As with all forms of activism, there is no fixed or consensual mode of engagement for all environmentalists to follow. See also the entry on *Linguist Discourse and Ecocriticism – Naming the Crisis!* together with categorising of communication strategies, which need to be adeptly deployed in all cases. Such variations are also witnessed in 'conventional' politics and across ideological debates. Hence it is useful to have a range of potential options in moving the dial towards successful solutions and tipping points for general citizen buy-in with regards to the huge struggle over the climate crisis into the future.

References

Lehman, Joseph. 'An Introduction to the Overton Window of Political Possibility'. Mackinac Centre of Public Policy. 8 April 2010. https://www.mackinac.org/12481
Weik von Mossner, Alexa. 'Rhetoric of Ecology in Visual Culture From Mindbombs to Firebombs: The Narrative Strategies of radical environmental activist documentaries'. *RRS Rhetoric* 8(2). 2021.

P

Pastoralism as a Model for Human's Love of Nature in Literature and Film

In the 1964 touchstone work *The Machine in the Garden*, Leo Marx advanced the now commonplace argument that pastoralism is foundational for the quintessential American experience of historical expansion, with the Anglo-colonisers originally perceiving North America as literally a new Eden to be explored. One wonders however, if contemporary audiences are satisfied in the same way by such historical modes of pastoralism, as the binary urban/rural divisions no longer clearly hold true across so much contemporary environmental analysis.

Alexa Weik von Mossner in her insightful summary of literary environmentalism (2020: 1) argues that how 'writers feel about specific places and what their literary representations of those places might do to the feelings of readers was a keen interest of so-called "first wave" ecocriticism'. According to Greg Garrard, this was marked by a tendency to celebrate nature and human–nature relationships rather than necessarily querying them as abstract concepts like biophilia and others discussed elsewhere. Jonathan Bate's *Romantic Ecology* (1991) remains a typical example, exploring ecocriticism's long-standing engagement with the romantic tradition and its celebration of human emotions toward actively engaging with nature. This is further echoed by Lawrence Buell's claim in *The Environmental Imagination* that American nature writers such as Henry David Thoreau and John Muir, presented 'a deeply personal love and reverence for the nonhuman', which over time led 'to a deeply protective feeling for nature' (1996: 137).

Meanwhile, Ursula Heise's *Sense of Place and Sense of Planet* (2008) argues that ecologically oriented thinking must come to terms with feelings around place and placelessness. More recently, so called 'eco-critical waves' tend to privilege all planetary spaces, both rural and urban. For instance, in a practical illustration of the continuing relevance of the concept of pastoralism, repurposed into an urban space, Robin Murray and Joseph Heumann call attention to so many urban-based filmic narratives that also evoke a romantic-nature sensibility. This phenomenon is explored in their 2018 volume *Ecocinema and the City*.

DOI: 10.4324/9781003123422-16

Either way, on a narrative level, the residents of our contemporary, mainly urban-based, human population do not necessarily find refuge from the ills of civilisation in the countryside; probably because there is no longer a pristine countryside to escape to. Instead, some aspire to travel to outer space in a spaceship that combines the splendours of shopping malls, alongside the convenience of conventional cruise ships. One would almost instinctively agree with Murray and Heumann's conclusion that the popular animated science fictional tale *Wall-E*'s artificial environment, can be read as anathema to the restorative qualities of romantic pastorals, a trope, which continues to have echoes in the eco-blockbuster *Avatar* (2009). Nonetheless, I would argue all forms of pastoralism continue to have an abiding hold on contemporary society across the world, as evident through so many entries in this volume.

References

Bate, Jonathan. *Romantic Ecology: Wordsworth and the Environmental Tradition.* Routledge 1991.

Buell, Lawrence. *The Environmental Imagination: Thoreau, Nature Writing and the Formation of American Culture.* Harvard University Press 1996.

Heise, Ursula. *Sense of Place and Sense of Planet.* Oxford University Press 2008.

Marx, Leo. *The Machine in the Garden: Technology and Pastoral Ideal in America.* Oxford University Press 1964.

Murray, Robin and Heumann, Joseph. *Ecocinema and the City.* Routledge 2018.

Weik von Mossner, Alexia. 'Affect Emotion and Ecocriticism'. *Ecozon@.* 2020 https:// ebuah.uah.es/dspace/bitstream/handle/10017/45731/affect_von%20mossner_ecozon% 40_2020.pdf?sequence=1&isAllowed=y

Peak Oil and 'Keep it in the Ground': Contested Environmental Debates

The term Peak oil is used to denote a belief that global oil reserves will become exhausted. However, such fears have abated in recent years, as the finite nature of oil production and supplies appears somewhat contested, not to mention the growth of new forms of energy extraction such as fracking. Echoing much early environmental scholarship on the subject, cultural environmentalist Mike Davies concludes his analysis with a sobering evaluation that a transitionary post-carbon economy is unlikely to have been realised by 2030 and that 'the convergent effects of climate change, peak oil, peak water and an additional 1.5 billion people on the planet will produce negative synergies, probably beyond our imagination' (Davies 2010). Drawing on such worrying analysis, one could affirm that there are so many environmental challenges and tipping points ahead of us – even if peak-oil is not as prescient as predicted. Of course, even if there was more oil in the ground or under the sea, fossil fuel extraction still has to be stopped to reduce our carbon output, as reflected in the 'keep it in the ground' movement. It remains difficult however to perceive how all of these crises can be addressed, much less resolved, without dramatic ruptures to all of our long-established systems.

Long-time, environmental campaigners like Bill McKibben, form part of a broad-coalition of environmental activists and NGO's who firmly believe in the need to 'keep it in the ground' and strive to fight global corporations and 'business as usual' with regards to the dismantling of the fossil-fuel industry. As affirmed by the 'keep it in the ground' website and so much environmental media coverage, fossil-fuel production must enter a managed decline immediately, and renewable energy must be advanced to swiftly take its place, but always in the context of a just transition.

References

Davies, Mike. 'Who will Build the Ark'. *New Left Review* 61. January/February. 2010.
Keepitintheground website. Open Letter to World Leaders. http://keepitintheground.
   org/ www.365.org

Petrofiction, Petrochemical Emissions: Reaching Dangerous Limits

The term petrofiction was first coined by Amitav Ghosh (2014) to explore literature's (and by extension audio-visual media) representation of the potency of oil and fossil fuel, generally. Alternatively, planning for a low-carbon future without such precious natural resources draws upon much innovation in thinking and practice by scientists, NGO's and think-tanks. Incidentally, the late sociology and media scholar John Urry for instance believed that reminiscent of the petrochemical industry, the 2011 Fukushima nuclear accident almost overnight make a worldwide nuclear energy programme less likely. Of course commentators argued that the Chernobyl accident of 1986 provided similar incentives for a previous generation, though such direct correlations are probably unlikely. Likewise, Urry argues that the Deepwater Horizon blow-out in the Gulf of Mexico in 2010, reduced the possibility of rapidly extending deep water oil and gas drilling (Urry, 2013: 203). But with ongoing Artic exploration, together with other fragile regions of the world being affected, such assertations are far from uncontested.

Urry usefully however talks of the green shoots of a powered-down future. But one wonders can environmentalists be really so optimistic. While the average UK family takes only six days to use a barrel of petroleum, the comparative figure is three days in North America and Australia, thirty days in China and India, and over a thousand days in some parts of Africa (Urry 2013: 205). Urry provides a pie-chart to help visualise these global injustices around energy usage. But as in so many environmental documentaries and publications, one wonders if such graphs simply reinforce the requisite Western guilt, or alternatively help to reaffirm what is considered *de facto* normative, across the world. Uncovering how to provocatively and effectively visualise climate change for a mass audience remains a key dilemma for all strands of environmental communication.

For instance a dystopic future is clearly evident within so many science fiction, energy-driven stories, even recalling (hyper) documentaries such as *Detroit: The Last Days* (2010). Its population reduced to 750,000, this futuristic tale shows rusting hulks of abandoned car plants, empty freeways, blackened corpses of burnt-out houses, alongside trees sprouting from the tops of deserted skyscrapers. Essentially over half of the children are living below the poverty line, and almost half of the adult population are functionally illiterate. Meanwhile, over a quarter of the inner city of Detroit has been reclaimed by 'nature' (reminiscent of Attenborough's foregrounding of a re-wielded city in Chernobyl in *A Life on our Planet* 2020), with many gardening projects reappropriating land for collective primitive agriculture, where anyone can harvest the crops grown. A new form of public commons is thereby created in such a fantasy; while Detroit appeared as an otherwise 'modern' city and is described as a forgotten place; a striking testament to the potential end of the car industry itself, which is umbilically connected to the growth of the oil industry. This decline which begun in the 1970s and 1980s, creating such a dystopic (future) metropolis, reminds me in ways of the lost cities of the Mayan civilisation – which might further extend to many of the erstwhile rich oil-producing nations of the world. This well-honed image corresponds with the ever-growing 'collapse of civilisation' narrative, foregrounded for instance in Mel Gibson's *Apocalypto* (2006), which has been explored in *Environmental Ethics and Film* (Brereton 2016: 60–64).

References

Brereton, Pat. *Environmental Ethics and Film*. Routledge 2016.
Gosh, Amitav. 'Petrofiction and Petroart'. 27 August. 2014. https://amitavghosh.com/blog/?p=6441
Urry, John. *Societies Beyond Oil*. Zed Books. 2013 (and see his earlier volume *Climate Change and Society*. Polity 2011).

Posthumanism and Ecological Thinking

This area aims to examine the changing status of subjectivity and of agency that is formed by the complex relations between nature, technology, science and cultural theory, through examining growing trends in framing many interconnecting areas. Ecology is here understood not in terms of a human-centred, romantic closeness to nature, but as a radical remapping of traditional Humanities' focus of knowledge and engagement. Posthumanism is now well established as a critical discourse within the humanities and the social sciences, due to major contributions of critical thinkers like Michel Foucault, Donna Haraway, Katherine Hayles, Gilles Deleuze and Rosi Braidotti among others. Although it seems difficult to have a common definition of the posthuman as a concept associated with different ideas, frequently the term is adopted as a non-dualistic account of human beings, while also foregrounding non-anthropocentric visions of the world. Posthumanism marks a historical moment 'in which the decentring of the human by its imbrication in technical, medical, informatic, and economic networks is increasingly impossible to ignore' (Wolfe 2010: xvi). A more dynamic conception of the human involves an expansion of the terrain in which it is constituted and its structuration is formed by diverse layers, which can include ecological thinking, as well as reimagining human nature within a more holistic planetary system.

As affirmed by Serpil Oppermann (2016) in an abstract for her article, 'ecocriticism becomes posthuman; post-natural and post-green in the process of critiquing the taxonomy of tensions and links between what it means to be either human or non-human. But how do we interpret synthetic matter that responds to a broad range of stimuli', including more biophilic and humane ethical experiences? This remains a key preoccupation with regards to environmental media and in evaluating its importance while engaging with audiences. Recalling for instance a flurry of postmodern (playful) explorations of identity formation and cyborgs becoming more humane than human, on being hunted down in *Blade Runner* (see Brereton 2005); not to mention more benign evocations of environmental cautionary tales, embedded in Hollywood classics *Wall-E* and *Avatar*. Katherine Hayles most eloquently talks of how such resonant themes 'evokes the exhilarating project of getting out of some of the old boxes and opening up new ways of thinking about what being human means' (1999: 285).

Contemporary environmental media and representations certainly needs to also develop new ways of thinking to help audiences connect with the paradigm shift needed to address our climate crisis. Building up an ethical mindset using the attributes of posthuman thinking as well as ontological philosophising can greatly assist in this educational process.

Posthumanism most certainly criticises anthropocentric humanism and opens its inquiry to embracing non-human life: from animals to artificial intelligence, to other forms of expression such as hyper-objects. From 'deep ecology' to 'dark ecology' (Morton 2016), the affinities with Western posthumanist ethics are explored by many scholars, as a critical discourse which abandons its habitual anthropomorphism and actively brings into consideration the nonhuman elements of the world. The ethics and politics of deep ecology underpin a new type of ecology, which is oriented towards the experience of an 'ecological ego', which supports no harm to nature and respect for all creatures. Such philosophical and ethical forms of deep ecological thinking can help environmental communication relate to a broad range of long-term challenges.

A tremendous amount of moral thinking and feeling around environmental issues can be activated using such postmodern-posthuman theorising and investigation across media analysis. This specifically pertains to understanding humans in the process of watching and engaging with films for instance, alongside all modes of audio-visual entertainment. In fact it is not an exaggeration to say – as already alluded to – that for most people, this is the primary way in which they acquire environmental knowledge, much less developing ethical attitudes within contemporary culture. Drawing on various eco-ethical and posthuman studies (see Brereton 2005, 2016, 2019), students can explore both in scale and theme how conventional and new forms of audio-visual media might creatively address the global problems of our heretofore unsustainable environmental future.

References

Brereton, Pat. *Hollywood Utopia: Ecology in Contemporary American Cinema*. Intellect 2005.
Brereton, Pat. *Environmental Ethics and Film*. Routledge 2016.
Brereton, Pat. *Environmental Literacy and New Digital Audiences*. Routledge 2019.
Hayles, Katherine. *How we Became Posthuman: Virtual Bodies in Cybernetics, Literature and Performance*. University of Chicago Press 1999.
Morton, Timothy. *Dark Ecology: For a logic of Future Co-existence*. Columbia University Press 2016.
Oppermann, Serpil. 'From Posthumanism to Posthuman Eco-criticism'. *Relations*: 4–1. June 2016.
Wolfe, Cary. *What is Postmodernism*. University of Minnesota 2010.

Postmodernism and Climate Change Communication

Postmodernism – as alluded to across previous discussions – is based on scepticism around all the grand theories or conventional metanarratives, such as modernism (not to mention eco-modernism), which ostensibly believes in the ongoing possibility of progress, coherence and the dominance of scientific rationality in solving all our problems. Postmodernist thinking, alternatively attempts to describe and differentiate contemporary human existence from radically different perspectives. It privileges the schizoid personality and favours cyborgs and performativity of selfhood (such as Karaoke style music performance), rather than presuming the presence of a coherent selfhood with fixed human characterisation and representational modalities. Furthermore, from an aesthetic perspective, any notion of originality or coherence within art is jettisoned and instead such stylistic attributes tend to foreground the mixing and matching of generic conventions, using reflexive pastiche and parody, alongside calling on a growing preoccupation with audience's pleasure and breaking down any apparent divisions between popular and high culture – much to the chagrin of so-called modernist and post-Enlightenment thinkers.

Marxists, like Fredric Jameson (1980), together with Jean Francois Lyotard (1979), first coined the term postmodernism, mapping this amorphous and most slippery of concepts as a confirmation of the dead-end of the old democratic routes of progress, which apparently at times became an affirmation of the status quo. One of the most student-friendly overviews of the evolution of this complex multi-strand and often contradictory theoretical phenomenon is explored by Hans Bertens (1995) *The Idea of the Postmodern*. While more cultural and audience-focused critics have helped to unfold and stimulate new openings and fractures within conventional postmodernist discourses, including the breakup of existing stultifying metanarratives, such as Communism, Marxism, and even with some wishful thinking, the totalising pull of Capitalism itself (see Brereton 2001: 136–137).

As a multi-strand academic phenomenon, postmodernist studies was fashionable in Western media and within many new disciplines across Higher Education Humanities from the 1970s onwards. This was a period when the apparent luxury of complex and trans-disciplinary thinking was actively encouraged and served to map the steep rise of reception and audience studies, alongside cross-disciplinary areas like cultural studies. However, it would appear that this whole movement has recently lost some of its potency, as the world has slipped back into more polarising divisions, where for instance 'the other' and anti-Western enemies were demonised through global terrorism – such as those sparked by the atrocities of 9/11. More clear-cut divisions and polarisation between good and evil and less reflexive modes of analysis appeared to come back into the ascendent. The 'enemy' across various fields of study, appeared to be more clearly recognised and demonised within media representations.

Furthermore, as the climate crisis escalated with a huge rise in global migration movements and increasing levels of poverty across several regions of the world, it appears that the luxury of such reflexive identity politics have been called into question as being still a useful, even legitimate, mode of academic engagement. Especially with the rise of the alt-right and growing concerns over fake news, coupled with various prescient cultural wars, alongside recognising the continuing rise of more defined gender and racial 'me too/Black Live Matters' politics, not to mention the huge paralysing effects of the global 2020/21 pandemic, scholarship and debate has tended to shift and polarise around more core defined principles and refocus back to 'traditional' power and equality.

Consequently, there appears to be few devoted followers of what might be characterised as coherent, albeit reflexive ('both-and' rather than 'either-or'), postmodernist environmental analysis of late. One might nonetheless be concerned that the proliferation of identity and cultural wars appears at times to dwarf the more long-term, existential environmental crisis, which has to remain prescient and constantly encourage more reflexive 'both-and' exercises of engagement and analysis, all the while promoting robust and workable solutions. In any case the apparent luxury of such reflexivity within postmodernist thinking does not appear to chime, much less, cross-connect, with the more urgent need for clearly articulated, empirically based reappraisals of globally mediated and ethical ways of living, which encompasses 'either-or' policy driven solutions. This conundrum is coupled with the necessity of reigning in excessive capitalist and commercial activity, as we face a terminal threat, while fighting for our very survival in securing a low carbon transition.

Nonetheless, the mediated pleasure(s) of irony, pastiche and transgressive expression through for instance 'queer green thinking' (see Seymour 2018) are all badly needed by mass audiences to help actively engage with such difficult and challenging material. Such reflexive ballast and support is helpful in the ongoing media struggle to attract a broad range of citizens and audiences, not necessarily enticed by the often preachy nature of much environmental discourse. A broad range of postmodern thinking and most importantly provocative and engaging aesthetic strategies have over several decades of creative expression and scholarship helped to draw more audiences into reflexive engagement. Hence co-opting postmodern thinking can help offset the splintering and disrupting dangers of binary expression across more fundamentalist modes of environmental thinking, which demands unconditional acceptance by all, who do not necessarily conform with such prescribed dogma. New modes of joined-up thinking and critical expression are badly needed to support moving all citizens, especially some jaded audiences, to more pro-active engagement with media and audience pleasures; all the while pivoting to more sustainable behaviour patterns of engagement.

References

Bertens, Hans. *The Idea of the Postmodern: A History*. Routledge 1995.
Brereton, Pat. *Continuum Guide to Media Education*. Continuum 2001.
Jameson, Fredric. *Postmodernism, or, the Cultural Logic of Late Capitalism*. Duke University Press 1980.
Lyotard, Jean Francois. *The Postmodern Condition* (translated 1979). Manchester University Press 1984.
Seymour, Nicole. *Bad Environmentalism: Irony and Irreverence in the Ecological Age*. University of Minnesota Press 2018.

Population Overshoot: Our Ecological Footprint and Loss of Biodiversity – *Downsizing*

According to the seasoned American sustainable environmental scholar Bill Rees, speaking at a June 2020 webinar (details below), teasing out the growing population explosion or over-shoot remains a major problem, which many environmentalists do not want to face up to. Basically, as humans, we are using natural resources and waste sinks faster than we can regenerate, much less assimilate into our over-saturated bio-systems. Greenhouse gasses are accumulating at ever increasing levels and all the while the climate is radically changing for the worse. But as Rees (2020) rightly affirms, we have been hearing about these problems now for 50 years and all the evidence is there, yet little has changed. There has been extensive warnings and a cascade of data available to speak to this dilemma, but unfortunately as humans we tend to ignore this information. There are so many ethical implications in addressing such population concerns, coupled with the ongoing challenge to actively address the excessive levels of over-shooting, limited by planetary boundaries, while striving to deal with our growing climate crisis. Population control advocates tend to focus on so-called developing countries with fast growing populations, but where its citizens consume very few resources and whose carbon footprint tend to be minimal, compared to richer regions of the world.

See for instance Herman Daley's work (1973, 1977) on the ecological footprint and limitations around our global bio-capacity, noting that currently the world has exceeded its total capacity by, approximately, a 68% overshoot. Humans are consuming, dissipating and displacing other species on this planet by a totally unsustainable margin. As many experts explain, we are using the planet as if it was more than 50% larger than it is in reality. Or using the analogy of a bank loan for example, we are borrowing what we don't have and will pay the price with a depleted carbon budget into the future. Everyone is seemingly competing with everyone else for the shrinking bio-capacity of the planet and at the same time (over)consuming the finite 'natural' resources of the earth.

In particular, as affirmed by so many environmental communication experts, the so-called techno-industrial narrative reinforces our species innate expansionist model. The neo-liberal driven global marketplace constantly promotes accumulation of stuff, and at the same time conceives of the resultant system as a definer of all social values. More general ethical and moral breaks and considerations are consequently disallowed. For example, some techno-fix experts (cited in Pamplany et al. 2019) somewhat incredulously claim that we have the technology and resources to feed our growing populations for the next seven billion years. Hence, especially within the right-wing media and even throughout established mass education, it can appear easy to dismiss concerns about the environmental crisis and not take seriously demands for radical economic, social and political transformation.

Mapping Our Human Population History from an Ecological and Environmental Perspective

It took 200,000 years of evolution to reach one billion people on the planet by the early 1800s. However, there then followed a seven-fold expansion and expediential growth to 7.8 billion by 2020 – as superbly demonstrated by David Attenborough's one-off (2020) Netflix autobiographical documentary cited elsewhere. Fossil fuels in all its various manifestations have been the driver and means by which the world has been able to grow increasing levels of production and consumption, facilitating greater population growth over time. Historically, corrections to such dramatic growth are often signalled by famines or disease – ostensibly signalling the need to reduce our populations and not develop so quickly. Incidentally, this feeds into cautionary religious allegories, conceived at a biblical level through Hollywood tales like *Noah* (2014).

Over a relatively short period of time, it has been noted that per-capita incomes increased exponentially in the rich West, while the expanding populations of the impoverished southern and developing regions continue to barely survive, with very low per-capita resource allocations. Hence, as already intimated, the perniciously divisive strategy of blaming increasing population levels across poorer regions of the planet for all *our* climate change problems, remains both ethically inappropriate and certainly inaccurate. In response, contemporary society and governments look to crude levers of efficiency to get the planet off the hook, together with calls for more geo-engineering and techno-fix solutions. In any case, it would appear much of humanity is umbilically tied to the 'growth model' and securing increased acquisition of material wealth, while paying little attention to the scientific and environmental signals we are receiving around global warming and climate change, much less our equally challenging and interconnecting problem of the expediential loss of biodiversity.

Basically, the planet needs to completely decarbonise by 2050, while techno-solutions for food production to help sustain existing growth and secure our long-established food security from being constantly at risk will not be enough to solve our problems. Meanwhile, more equitable redistribution of other natural resources including energy for growing populations does not even seem to be on the table. Saving the environment unfortunately appears more of a long-term agenda and thereby easier to put off, as against more immediate tangible problems like 'saving the economy', upon which most political energy is focused on. For instance, back in 1972 when *Limits to Growth* was first published, such questioning of the sanctity of the growth imperative was heavily criticised; a criticism which has remained prevalent ever since. Unfortunately, the pendulum has not swung in the right direction, in spite of much discussion and re-application of a range of environmental and sustainability principles becoming more mainstream. Many in government and business still believe that efficiency gains and increases in technological innovation will help solve our population and climate problems?

Case Study of Population Control Using the Science Fictional Tale – Downsizing

Downsizing is an innovative and cautionary eco-tale focused on over-population, directed by smart postmodern filmmaker Alexander Payne (2017). The preamble focuses on scientific experiments, which shows the breakthrough that finally enables scientist Dr Jorgen Asbjornsen (Rolf Lassgard) to uncover a way of 'downsizing' humans so that they can become more sustainable within a finite planetary resource model. Especially, the over-population dilemma is solved through an extreme technological fix response. Such a 'creative imaginary' further illustrates a radical off-the-scale fictional solution to the ever-increasing global Co2 emissions crisis, while taking on board growing fears concerning urgent responses to climate change. A few years later this game-changing and unbelievable techno-fix discovery is rolled out at an academic conference, where the Scandinavians literally reveal themselves having achieved this biological downsizing feat. The conference attendees and film audience are introduced to the first cohort of human guinea-pigs, who carried out the experiment and survived. Rolling out this radical solution to the broader maxi-public of course, remains the biggest challenge for such an experiment to also help reduce overall consumption.

In the so-called 'reel world' – as dramatised for a Hollywood story, which in turn serves as a narrative frame of the film – we are introduced to an overworked couple Paul (Matt Damon) and Audrey (Kristen Wiig) who are finding it hard to make their payments on their original house, yet want to move on and secure a nicer and bigger place to live. Representing a typical upwardly aspiring Western couple, they are finally lured by the prospect of getting more real estate space for their buck and becoming rich in the process. This economic trick is achieved by literally and physically downsizing – a phenomenon more usually ascribed to the empty nest syndrome that appeals to older couples, looking for a smaller and more sustainable mode of living accommodation having reared children, who have in turn left to set up their own family units.

On paper at least, what is not to like about this utopian scenario, which most certainly would solve many of our very difficult social planning and even more intractable environmental problems. At the conference a small, black bag is shown to represent the totality of all the waste created by the minia-turised community after many years of experiment. In many ways, echoing the fruits of a circular economy experiment, pushed to its extreme. None-theless, it takes an intoxicated extra in a bar to highlight the obvious eco-nomic and political difficulty that if more people were to carry out this radical experiment, 'normal society' would consequently be greatly affected. In par-ticular, such radical transformation would have a huge effect on (everyday) house prices, much less the volume of tax revenues and the general economic system, and at the same time radically reduce the erstwhile stable 'big wealth' garnered for the majority (full-size human) community to keep 'normal' society functioning.

Such an extreme and unbelievably radical solution, ostensibly designed to address climate change (and increase one's own standard of living and general 'well-being' at the same time) would produce so many unintended con-sequences that need to be recognised and fully evaluated. It might also be perceived for instance by those not willing to take such a radical step, as being a very 'selfish' procedure to go through with, while not necessarily taking into account the greater common good of all. Recalling current cli-mate justice debates and tensions between so-called First and Third World environmental concerns, here again new polarising divisions are created between humans, as either (downsized) citizens, pitted against those who simply are not ready to make such a dramatic but altruistic life-changing decision and jump into the unknown. At a more prescient and realistic level, we can begin to also perceive fissures and tensions between very early adaptors or eco-citizens who are willing to make extensive behavioural change decisions to protect the planet and the common good, as against those who are not for varying reasons.

But of course in this cinematic fantasy, as a consumerist-driven solution, Leisureland – the ultimate Disney theme park – is set up in this new world order as a unique selling point which has it all. Screen audiences get to see how the glamour of 'high living' can still be ecologically and sustainably available for all. Lovely miniature well-designed houses, with ideal, well-planned architectural environments to live in; all having the prospect of achieving the good life for those who live there. While the unfortunate medical business and procedures needed to be undergone for this radical (science fictional) process are recognised as 'difficult', there are apparently few other downsides if one is willing to not think too much. Paul still looks appealingly 'normal' having been shaved from top to toe. Under anaesthetic, all his teeth are pulled out. Apparently, only nodding to basic science and medical anatomy – as his head would blow up otherwise. After the quick assembly line process of being reduced and being fitted with new miniature teeth, he is seemingly good to go.

As in many science fictional storylines, such as the *Jurassic Park* franchise, the actual laws of science are conveniently mangled and massaged, so as not to get in the way of a good story (Brereton 2005). Nonetheless, I would still contend that the 'creative imaginary' and provocative 'what if' scenarios embedded within such science fiction tales can assist audiences in reconceptualising and helping to 'think environmentally' and even stir up more innovative even sustainable thinking into the future.

Eco-citizens ought to be cognisant of the urgent need to develop critical antennae around the dangers of simply supporting a simple greenwashed business agenda, much less embracing such pro-environmental films and narratives like *Downsizing* as uncontentious, productive and provocative. At the same time, such cautionary tales can help to keep such difficult debates firmly in the public consciousness.

References

Brereton, Pat. *Hollywood Utopia: Ecology in Contemporary American Cinema*. Intellect 2005.

Daley, Herman. *Steady State Economics*. W.H. Freeman and Co. 1973.

Daley, Herman. *Steady State Economics*. Earthscan Routledge 1977.

Pamplany, Augustine, Gordijn, Bert and Brereton, Pat. 'The Ethics of Geoengineering: A Literary Review'. *Science and Engineering Ethics* September. 2019.

Rees, Bill. (SCORAI and sustainability) expert speaking on Webinar for IRAS (Institute on Religion in the age of Science) 29 June 2020.

Q

Queer Theorising and Nature: New Modes of Imagining Gender – *Brokeback Mountain*

Queer studies have become a prominent part of gender studies and serves to question the dominance of heteronormative models of cultural expression and representation, which privileges so-called normative male–female relationships, together with so-called nuclear families. Environmental film scholar, Nicole Seymour has highlighted the need for greater use of comedy, pastiche and more innovative modes of irony and parody to be deployed, as a provocative means of addressing a range of environmental issues that are often dogged by preaching and pontificating and not effectively speaking to mass audiences. Such strategies have been appropriated as part of the arsenal of gender politics that has fed into the rubric of queer studies. Co-opting this approach to gendered environmental representation, challenges the frequently recognised and historical disconnect sometimes evident within gender studies and eco-criticism, recalling divergent attitudes and approaches toward nature and the environment. See for instance *Strange Natures: Futurity, Empathy and the Queer Ecological Imagination* (2013), where Seymour provides a useful analysis of a specifically 'queer' understanding and appreciation of nature, emphasising the fractured agency of non-human identities, while calling out various forms of environmental degradation.

So-called queer nature can be defined both as a noun and a verb and can be decoded as

> an ecology that may begin in the experiences and perceptions of non-heterosexual individuals and communities, but even more importantly is one that calls into question heteronormativity itself, as part of its advocacy around issues of nature and environment – and *vice versa*.
>
> (Mortimer-Sandilands and Erickson 2015: 161)

The long history of gender politics and media activism, especially as moderated through queer studies, can help promote more sophisticated environmental and identity connectivity.

DOI: 10.4324/9781003123422-17

Catriona Mortimer-Sandilands and Bruce Erickson in 'A Genealogy of Queer Ecologies' (Mortimer-Sandilands and Erickson 2015: 159–163) focuses specifically on the convergence of nature and queer theory through a reading of *Brokeback Mountain* (2005). Their reading builds on and contrasts with revisionist gender-environmental exposure frequently evident in the heteronormative Western genre that usually privileges an environmental reading of the indigenous native Americans (see Brereton 2005: 91–96). Here, however the two male leads,

> Jack and Ennis's shared refusal to name themselves as "queer" is part of an ongoing narrative strategy, by which the film distances both men from the taint of urban, effeminate – what Judith Halberstam calls "metronormative" - articulations of gay male identity (2005: 36).
>
> (Mortimer-Sandilands and Erickson 2015: 159)

The authors of this critical overview of the film further suggest that the presentation of the two males in this rural-masculine manner has the effect of 'naturalising' their relationship, insofar as their attraction and love can be read as entirely separate and distinct from what have, through much of the 20th century been presented as 'unnatural' or 'degenerate sexualities'. In fact these gendered-environmental discourses 'are an important point of conversation between queer and ecological politics, because they reveal the powerful ways in which understandings of nature inform discourses of sexuality, and also the ways in which understanding of sex inform discourses of sexuality'. Essentially, both trajectories are linked, 'through a strongly evolutionary narrative that pits the perverse, the polluted and the degenerate against the fit, the healthy, and the natural' (ibid.: 160).

At least since the early 20th century in Western art and media, 'wild spaces have been understood and organised in a way that presents nature – and its personal domination in the guise of hunting, fishing, climbing, and other outdoor activities – as a site for the enactment of a specific heteromasculinity' (160). Furthermore, the two protagonists, Jack and Ennis, are both presented as 'shepherds', which in turn locates the film 'in a long history of pastoral depictions of nature and landscape and, indeed, an equally long history of pastoral representations of male same-sex eroticism, noting how the landscape of *Brokeback Mountain* is tied 'to a historical, homoerotic Arcadia' (161).

While this reading remains convincing, much work needs to be carried out towards analysing and pairing of 'queer' with 'ecology' and a number of scholars, including Seymour and others, have sought to uncover new ways of linking them together in more fruitful ways. Certainly, this area of investigation is ripe for further critical development and can draw on an extensive pool of gender and queer scholarship, which can further feed into environmental criticism and help promote active engagement across all sections of society.

References

Brereton, Pat. *Hollywood Utopia: Ecology in Contemporary American Cinema*. Intellect Press 2005.

Mortimer-Sandilands, C. and Erickson, B. 'A Genealogy of Queer Ecologies' (159–163). In Hiltner, Ken. (ed.) *Ecocriticism The Essential Reader*. Routledge 2015.

Seymour, Nicole. *Strange Natures: Futurity, Empathy and the Queer Ecological Imagination*. University of Illinois Press 2013.

R

Regenerative Soil and Overcoming Desertification: Case Study of *Kiss the Ground*

In looking for holistic solutions to our climate crisis, there is none greater than finding solutions to reductions of carbon emissions from agriculture. For instance adapting an older and more sustainable form of mixed agriculture, which is less intensive and uses much less artificial fertilisers, needs to be followed in reducing the environmental ill-effects of factory-type farming. This radical reimagining of agriculture will greatly assist in securing the health of our human population, increase the overall biodiversity of the planet, and most importantly help to sequester more carbon from the atmosphere and thereby support a robust nature-based solution to our climate emergency.

Many of these issues can be illustrated using the provocative documentary *Kiss the Ground* (2020), narrated by the renowned screen actor and activist Woody Harrelson, and supported by a very active and engaging educational website www.kisstheground.com. The documentary streamed on Netflix, garnered a large audience with its coherent and direct environmental message. This format is reminiscent of earlier soil-focused documentaries like *Dirt! the Movie* (2009) in calling attention to the prime importance of organic and regenerative soil to sustain all life. Scientifically and chemically, this is affirmed at the start of the documentary with audiences informed that carbon is our friend in helping the soil. As humans, we are made up of carbon and this precious chemical is essential for the creation of all life forces, including the soil. Yet, some might believe especially on looking at our ongoing climate emergency that carbon is simply the enemy. The positive affirmation of the necessity of carbon for all life processes, is reinforced by the tag-line of the documentary; 'awakening people to the possibilities of regeneration'. This scientific perspective is further illustrated by a number of instructive animations of the potency of sub-soil: 'the solution is right under our feet'.

Similar to our seas and the environmental dilemma concerning over-fishing – critiqued in the controversial documentary *Seaspiracy* (2021), which is also available on Netflix – mono-cultural and intensive farming of soil has become a major problem over the decades, all of which add to the precarious

DOI: 10.4324/9781003123422-18

sequence of environmental crisis we are currently facing. Recalling, for example, the huge levels of desertification witnessed in the American Mid-West during the 1930s and the eponymous Dust Bowl phenomenon, which displaced millions of migrants who had to flee to California and other more stable fertile regions. This exodus produced an environmental catastrophe that was effectively visualised through John Ford's adaptation of the John Steinbeck classic novel *Grapes of Wrath* (1940). More insidious and large-scale human exploitation of the land – primarily designed to maximise consistent and increasing crop returns – was kick-started after World War Two in America (at least), through co-opting research by the German Nobel prize-winning chemist Fritz Haber. Haber had helped develop nerve gasses for the war effort, which coincidentally inspired the use of ammonia for enriching soil, together with nitrogen to help increase grassland production – all of which was subsequently rolled out across the world. (For more details of this, read a *New York Times* article by Wayne Biddle 'Nerve Gases and Pesticides' from 30 March 1984.)

Up to the present day, building on Haber's work, the eponymous 'Roundup' chemical brand has been used for large-scale agriculture, as well as on small private gardens for pesticide control, quickly dominating the global market. Only recently has the product been banned across various jurisdictions, citing its harmful effects on humans. Such chemical abuse has led activists to think back to the roots of the environmental movement in America with Rachel Carson railing against the poisonous effects of DDT on humans – another well-known chemical product, which was extensively used in the 1950s and early 60s as a weed controlling pesticide. Some engaging speakers and activists are filmed in *Kiss the Ground*, while being weaved into this environmental story of the importance and history of soil. These include an agricultural science expert who spent all his life working with farmers, who highlighted the benefits of regenerative modes of tillage, alongside meeting organic farmers who have learned the deep stewardship lesson and can point to strong results from their work. They are linked to celebrity film activists like Ian Somerhalder, fighting in the media for the transformation of agriculture into becoming more environmentally wholesome and sustainable.

The documentary visually illustrates the differences between 'dead soil', which has lost all its bio-organisms because of pesticide over-usage, compared with organic/regenerative farming that looks healthy and alive with the soil not being abused through erosion and abuse of chemicals. But why then is there such resistance to more holistic, regenerative and sustainable modes of farming? Essentially, one could suggest, this is because it remains a precarious business. For intensive farming, using artificial chemicals can secure at least short-term quick returns on land investments, producing intensive high-quantity mono-cultural crops and increasing levels of livestock and milk production. Shockingly, it is estimated, as a result of such intensive agriculture that there is probably only about 60 harvests left in total across much American soil. The worry over desertification and unprotected soil and fears of future 'Dust Bowl' events, remains particularly stark across great swathes of middle America, Africa and even parts of South America, alongside other agricultural regions across the planet. Nonetheless, this very worrying and precarious situation can be reversed, by wholeheartedly applying regenerative models of land husbandry. Displaying the ongoing need for more innovation and the creative reimagining of farming to make it more environmentally sustainable, is actively witnessed and illustrated across every aspect of *Kiss the Ground*.

As cogently affirmed, 'the future is in our hands'! Noting the 2015 Paris climate agreement, the narrator effectively echoes the frustration of concerned citizens, farmers and the ordinary public, recalling the continued slow progress with regards to climate change, with politicians caught up in much fruitless rhetorical discussion. Nonetheless, fresh thinking is demonstrated by a French agricultural Government Minister, who apparently spearheaded and embraced a regenerative soil solution proposed at the Paris Accord discussions. Unfortunately three large states, namely America, India and China, did not sign the agreement on this innovative soil initiative. The documentary asserts that all countries and regions need to be on board in this ongoing struggle, if *we* are to transform the nutritional value of our precious soil and protect our climate future. This is the ultimate 'low tech' solution for our precious soil into the future.

Eating well and valuing good quality food has to be a starting point for such a transformation. Regarding agricultural practices, farming has to move away from intensive monocultural practices with corralled cattle penned in huge enclosures, where they simply stand all day eating grain, alongside huge dairy herds producing ever increasing quantities of milk. Such an artificial mode of agricultural production encourages extensive carbon emissions as a result. Furthermore, this big business food system model constantly needs more fertile land to grow feedstuffs, simply to fatten up the animals, rather than being used for human consumption. This exponential growth model is simply not sustainable as a dominant mode of agricultural practice, while facing up to our climate catastrophe. Bio-diversity loss can be radically improved through adopting older mixed farming strategies, using less intensive methods and having less harmful chemicals being applied to our fragile soils. 'Once our precious soil is destroyed – there is no going back', echoes the abiding message of this provocative cautionary ecological documentary.

Religious Fanaticism and Romanticisation of Nature: Case Study of *A Hidden Life*

Many so-called religious fanatics are often driven by their love of nature and the need for environmental conservation and protection. There remains an ever-present danger however with much 'unadulterated nature idolatry' becoming 'predicated on a utopian wish-fulfilling fantasy' (Brereton 2001: 35), which calls up a number of ethical and related difficulties. For example

German Romanticism 'with its glorification of nature has often been critiqued as a philosophical and aesthetic seed-bed for the evolution of Nazism' (ibid.: 35). While this may be over stating such connections, nonetheless it is worth teasing out tensions between extreme forms of nature idolatry and even fascist ideology.

A contemporary filmic auteur Terrence Malick explicitly calls attention to such aesthetic tensions, using environmental spiritual cautionary tales, framed from a uniquely cinematic perspective. Malick who made *A Hidden Life* (2019) is an artist much written about from an environmental-philosophical and aesthetic perspective, recalling his seminal *Tree of Life* (2011) (see Brereton and Furze 2015).

A Hidden Life ostensibly focuses on the need to stand up to oppression, especially recalling the late 1930s and 40s in the newly occupied Nazi Austria. The tale recalls how a local farmer had to literally take his life in his own hands, while standing up for his deeply felt human values. Based on a true story, Austrian farmer Franz Jägerstätter (August Diehl) faces the threat of execution for refusing to fight for the Nazis. In the movie, audiences are treated to close-ups of the harsh but nurturing habitat of his mountain-farm, as Franz and his resolute family strive to cultivate and make the soil fertile, while in the midst of political oppression. Love of nature and the power of environmental protection, not to mention political injustice, underpin the main protagonist's rationale for putting all his mental and physical strength into embracing environmental and social justice and constantly striving towards 'doing the right thing'. These tensions come to a head during the intense political upheaval of the Nazi era, when many locals either hide their convictions and concerns, or alternatively, as our hero does, stand up for their fellow humans and for nature generally.

The first movement of the film foregrounds the pleasure the couple receive from their blissful, almost Platonic communing with nature, while engaging in various rituals with their children, together with their close-knit community. The young couple are totally and unconditionally in love and this bond secures their faith in life and in facing up to future struggle. In the end, Franz's wife has to accept the stubborn, but pure ethical, stance of her husband towards embracing martyrdom, even if no one else in the community appears to care. The story ends with a quote from George Elliot's classic novel *Middlemarch* (1872), which foregrounds the overall theme and gives the film its title.

> For the growing good of the world is partly dependent on un-historic acts; and that things are not so ill with you and me as they might have been, is half owing to the number who lived faithfully *a hidden life* and rest in unvisited tombs.
>
> (emphasis added)

From silhouettes of mountains and glistening sun sparkling through the Alpine landscape, this otherwise 'hidden life' of ordinary people is brought into the open and illuminated through seasonal change from bright summer light to glistening winter snow. So much explicit evocation of a romantic landscape and nature is captured and echoed through the temporal rhythm of life. Franz's struggle coupled with the very survival of his family makes the sacrifice possible, as he strives to bear witness to the truth and acquire the strength to stand up to such unadulterated evil. Most notably when imprisoned near the end of his journey – and only being able to spy a small bit of sky – Franz takes sanctuary in such pleasures, remembering back to his beloved and expansive mountain habitat and family. He can find sanctuary and sustenance from such small, measured evocations of his love of nature, before having to face the ultimate human challenge and sacrifice, on being executed for his beliefs. Even a glimpse of nature's transcendent essence helps to feed into biophilic aspects of active environmental connectivity, which in turn affords him (and hopefully the audience also) much needed sustenance.

All of this is counter to evoking a purist Fascist nature aesthetic, carrying no ethical responsibility, which was appropriated by the controversial Nazi filmmaker Leni Riefenstahl, for instance towards celebrating a pernicious ideology and heroic mindset, which is evident through the representation of mountain landscapes celebrating the heroic potency of an Aryan regime (Brereton 2001). Malick alternatively co-opts this powerful natural landscape aesthetic for more altruistic purposes while adding a clearly constituted environmental framework and ethic aimed at speaking to all that is benevolent and heroic in the human spirit. The cinematic language used in the film drive a productive environmental agenda, which is both inspiring and productive. Such a creative imaginary continues to speak to contemporary audiences and foreground the ultimate urge and desire to actively fight for environmental protection well into the future.

One could certainly argue that facing up to the challenge of climate change similarly requires, even demands, that everyday citizens actively stand up to the oppression of established social and political conventions that endanger our environment. The struggle may not appear as pernicious, compared with the historical Nazi era, but such heroic struggles ought to be co-opted by the environmental dilemma facing humanity, as embodied by the climate emergency. While such links may at first seem tangential – yet further evidenced through a fuller exploration of the ongoing environmental agenda of Malick's oeuvre (see Brereton and Furze 2015) – this specific filmic allegory helps to illustrate the ongoing struggle to promote radical environmental engagement and protection of nature, no matter what the cost to individuals. For more discussion on the call to become martyrs for the environmental cause, see also the spiritual and environmental reading and analysis of Paul Schrader's *First Reformed* (2017).

References

Brereton, Pat. 'Utopianism and Fascist Aesthetics: An Appreciation of Nature in Documentary/Fiction Film'. *Capitalism Nature Socialism* 12(4): 33–50. 2001.

Brereton, Pat and Furze, Robert. 'Transcendence and the Tree of Life: Beyond the Face of the Screen with Terrence Malick, Emmanuel Levinas and Roland Barthes'. *Journal for the Study of Religion, Nature and Culture* 8: 329–351. 2015.

Hulme, Mike. 'Should Future Investments in Energy Technology be Limited exclusively to Renewables?' (96–108). In Hulme, Mike (ed.) *Contemporary Climate Change Debates: A Student Primer.* Earthscan Routledge 2020.

Renewable Energy Debates and Critiques: Case Study of *Planet of the Humans*

A move to renewable energy is considered by most environmental communicators and policy makers as the only way forward in facing up to the climate crisis. The Paris Accord has put in place a strategy for governments to aim for a net-zero carbon emissions by 2050 and to achieve this target, fossil fuels will basically have to be eliminated. Consequently, there is an urgent demand to ramp up all forms of renewable energy in its place. But like most environmental issues, on the ground there are many related issues to take into account concerning this radical transformation. Some of these renewable debates are critically framed within a very useful student-friendly volume, edited by Mike Hulme (2020).

For instance, in Chapter 7, a debate between Jennie C. Stephens and Gregory Nemet pose the provocative question, '[S]hould future investment in energy technology be limited exclusively to renewables'? Five reasons are suggested around why energy investment needs to be limited to responses that privilege all forms of renewables:

1   The pace and scale of energy systems change requires such a strategic focus
2   Investment in so-called 'clean fossil fuel' or alternatively carbon capture and storage (CCS) are wasteful and provide false optimism for the future
3   Investment in nuclear power is dangerous, uncertain and unnecessary
4   Renewable transformation provides an opportunity to redistribute political power and reduce socio-economic and racial inequalities
5   Renewable energy is sufficient to meet future energy demands (97).

Yet there continues to be a debate around perceiving renewables as a silver bullet for low-carbon transition. For instance, recent solar climate engineering (together with other innovations in wind and new forms of renewable energy sources) creates tension between thinking that humans can (easily) manage the problem of moving from dependence on fossil fuels across the planet, while others discussed below, affirm that such investment further perpetuates the dangerous illusion that a technological fix for climate change is possible. Most environmental communicators nevertheless accept, almost unconditionally, the inherent benefits of a radical move to renewable energy sources, especially wind and solar. However, a recent documentary titled *Planet of the*

Humans calls attention to a broad range of conflictual environmental discussion that was heretofore absent from the broader public debate and certainly all environmental communicators and students need to be fully aware of these contentious issues and be armed in responding to such debate.

Critique of Renewable Energy: Case Study of **Planet of the Humans (2020)**

Since its direct release to YouTube, this has become a hugely controversial environmental documentary, critiquing various forms of green energy and promoting much debate across many environmental communication networks. The well-known, left-leaning filmmaker Michael Moore produced the documentary that was released straight to the free streaming online platform. It offers a fairly brutal critique of some well-known 'clean energy' people and groups (mainly US-based), delivered with Moore's customary brand of outrage. As a film and environmental historian, the opening clip from *The Unchained Goddess*, a Frank Capra TV documentary from 1958, shows, historically, how long media documentaries have been reflecting on various environmental issues; all of which remains highly relevant, taking into account the human-caused climate crisis.

Overall, I found the eco-documentary generally weak, at least from an aesthetic point of view, compared for instance to *Earth* (2019) – an art-house critique of mining and energy extraction (see Brereton 2020). Nonetheless, it remains intriguing from many angles, including clips from Capra's historical documentary alluded to above, highlighting the reality of CO_2 emissions and climate change, which continues to the present day. The messaging, much less the science, has not changed that much over time.

While Moore is simply listed as the executive producer on this documentary, his passion and constant drive towards 'following the money' rationale infuses the storyline. The documentary critiques the unconditional growth and endorsement of all kinds of renewable energy, while at the same time alleging that some environmentalists have been apparently 'turned' by the lure of sponsorship and even securing support from big-business capitalists, a storyline which remains central to the narrative's overall trajectory.

Focusing in particular on well-known political environmentalists like Al Gore and his active embracing of biomass fuels to support 'alternative energy' production, while clearly demonstrating that this process is not as green as was envisaged. Basically, the documentary refers to critiques of the use of biomass, which ends up aggravating environmental problems, by cutting down plants. This is coupled with the burning of trees to facilitate such farming practices, not to mention encouraging the growth of the palm oil industry across South America. (For further critiques of Gore and his environmental credentials, see an analysis of his sequel to *An Inconvenient Truth* in Brereton 2019: 84–92.)

Other big environmental scalps highlighted, include the long-established conservationist American movement The Sierra Club, and most surprisingly the unsuspecting activist Bill McKibben. McKibben remains a well-respected and life-long environmentalist and founder of the 365-movement (see 'Keep it in the Ground'), which was set up to help stop fossil fuel and carbon being released from the ground in the first place. Yet allegedly, according to this intervention, this global environmental organisation is somehow part-sponsored by several oil and/or coal and biomass fuel energy companies. The documentary further infers that in spite of McKibben's strong environmental values, he is somehow compromised by his support for the biomass industry.

A review in Michael Mann's *The New Climate Wars* (2021) is strikingly scathing of the documentaries' downright inaccuracies and feeding into right-wing anti-climate change rhetoric. Mann cites a review by Neil Livingston (2020) who affirms that it is 'inaccurate, misleading and designed to depress you into doing nothing' (141). Meanwhile 'conservative foundations and media outlets loved Moore's film', alongside 'fossil-fuel-funded groups like the Competitive Enterprise Institute and the Heartlands Institute' (Mann 2021: 141).

While critiquing various friends of the environmental movement, the pervasive enemy and target of course remains capitalism; citing big business and especially multi-millionaires, such as globally known figures like Virgin boss Richard Branson, who are apparently jumping on the green bandwagon. The polemical tone of the discourse suggests that such rich business figures cannot do any good, much less apparently can the documentary countenance any inherent benefits around appealing to profit-driven executives or companies; even if they are ostensibly driven by well-meaning green ethical motives and values, while adopting the benevolent sentiments of a strong Corporate Social Responsibility ethos. Such entrepreneurs and business agents are all painted with the same brush and dismissed outright, while ostensibly acting to protect the economic and political status quo. Consequently, using this totalising binary logic and adopting a fixed vision of left-right ideological purity, environmentalists, under no circumstances should 'sleep with the corporate enemy' – otherwise they will get pulled down in the mire with them. This remains an ongoing tension within environmental activism and across the scholarly discipline of environmental communication.

Much left-leaning discourse paints a clear ethical rationale and frameworks for what is intuitively wrong with the dominant ideology of business and growth-driven capitalism. Many environmentalists agree with such an evaluation and prognosis, but are often less forthcoming in suggesting alternative practical solutions. Finding pragmatic ways to help resolve such prevailing and resource-deficit problems, while facing up to the often contradictory range of global, environmental dilemmas, remains extremely challenging. All of which is beyond vague appeals to do the right thing that is constantly tarnishing the active working out of specific social and historical tensions, much less affording clearly articulated experimental solutions.

Most controversially, so-called renewable energy sources and their environmental proponents are highlighted as not being all they are cracked up to be by this documentary. This of course is not new for most well-read energy-environmentalists, but such evidence can provide ammunition for those who want to target the renewable energy sector. For example, it is asserted that solar energy needs scarce and deep-mined products to make so-called 'clean' energy, alongside noting the high levels of raw materials, which are also required to construct wind farms. Yet this quickly outmoded hardware is often simply discarded after a relatively short 20+ years installation lifespan. Furthermore, the documentary illustrates how such alternative energy sources can further end up badly despoiling the habitat they are situated within. This feeds off much academic-focused NIMBY-like criticism, recounting the negative consequences of globally rolling out extensive areas of wind and solar energy projects. (See discussion of NIMBYism and Windfarm in this volume.)

The resource dilemma of renewable energy follows an easy target of a well-meaning environmental music concert, refuting a claim by the organisers that the rock concert was totally powered by renewable energy. Basically, as the camera crew goes backstage at the event, they discover that the small solar panels that are used on the site would barely fire up a toaster. All such claims around the power and potential of renewable energy sources are apparently orchestrated as (greenwashed) smoking mirrors, which are subsequently used to promote or refute (take your pick) the green dream and wishful fantasy of some environmental activists. Furthermore, some of the sponsorship for such environmental events – according to this documentary at least – comes from the oil/gas and coal industries, together with their bankers. In particular, the Koch Brothers are called out, as being the most globally recognised 'hate figures' for environmentalists; apparently they are coincidentally also securing further tax relief, by actively powering up the development of a renewable energy business.

As already alluded to across several entries in this volume; as humans we remain the problem with our over-consumption modes of living, especially across the so-called developed world. By not being good stewards of the planet, we have to face up to our inadequacies and shortcoming, or alternatively simply accept defeat. Basically, it's not CO_2 *per se*, which is the main problem facing us, but our own (over-consuming) species and modes of living, which drives increases in carbon emissions. In spite of all the criticism, this proposition is usefully highlighted in the crude final assertion in the documentary. But such a knee-jerk response probably remains unhelpful in speaking to mass audiences who, as the literature asserts, requires clear propositions concerning the problems and solutions, towards both engaging with and learning from this very complex (wicked) crisis. Media responses to climate change have to balance communicating this difficult process of transformation, while at the same time encouraging the creation of more environmentally literate and sustainable energy citizens.

These limitations and specific aspects of the documentary's diegesis become even more resonant when framed *post-hoc* by a series of televisual interviews with the makers of the programme. Here they try to respond to many environmental critics, who in turn tend to simply dismiss the programme as an anti-environmental documentary. Yet Ozzie Zehner, who is the producer of *Planet of the Humans*, suggests that as a society we are using the wrong model of growth, which is normative at present and affirms how we need to rethink the whole system of values in society. Few if any environmentalists would disagree with such an assertion, much less his overall evaluation of the dilemma.

Capitalism, Consumption and Growth

Meanwhile, Michael Moore suggests that they are *all* environmentalists and how *we* (promoting an inclusive rhetorical communications strategy, while speaking to all strands of environmental thinking) need to have the courage to speak to our friends across the NGOs and other active environmental movements, while highlighting some contradictions in their logic and reasoning. He goes on to affirm how the failure of the (environmental) movement, simply stems from not being radical enough and how by using such established political (and democratic!) tactics, 'we are not going to save the planet. We are in a desperate state – growth is really the death of us'.

Moore is never short of a witty remark and certainly knows how to polarise divisions between various groupings and cohorts, as witnessed on a BBC *Newsnight* interview shortly before the American election in November 2020. Many deep environmentalists, even if they do not agree with Moore's strident critique of environmentalists themselves, might nonetheless albeit grudgingly agree with his assessment of the bigger picture and certainly recognise his dire prognosis around the climate crisis.

Consumption and growth, according to Moore, are still the only words Wall Street believes in and such a system basically requires all businesses to grow year on year, pushing us as citizens to consume more. 'These are the dirtiest words in capitalism. But when is enough!'. Moore perceptively notes the three times in recent years when CO_2 emissions actually fell; during the terrorist attacks of 9/11, the economic crash in 2008, and in 2020 with the global downturn as a result of the pandemic. Of course, he is only commenting on North America and is not reflecting upon the more complex global situation. Certainly, all of these reductions had nothing directly to do with the environmental movement and even goes so far as to affirm how the global movement basically has done little if nothing to address the climate change emergency over the last 30 years. While not drawing attention to the fairness or accuracy of such a major claim, Moore continues that they simply want their documentary to help trigger discussion and raise some key questions within the environmental movement. This media and communications debate is 'bigger than climate change' he contends, affirming that there is more to damaging our planet than simply the over-use of fossil fuels.

Certainly, at least at a macro level, one would have to have sympathy with this polemical steer and even his overall prognosis. But as a scaffolding and primary step or benchmark for effective action; one would have to assert that ending our dependence on fossil fuels remains a good place to start for environmentalists to initially focus their energies. Furthermore, and somewhat less pugnaciously than Moore, the director Jeff Gibbs claims that their documentary is not designed to attack environmental leaders *per se*, but rather looking into the future and recognising the limitations of renewable energy. While not accepting the dangers of conflating issues and wanting it both ways, Gibbs affirms how 'we are not from the fossil fuel industry'. Of course, such rhetorical assertions beg the question, if this make their often dated and unhelpful critiques simply playing to the gallery, or further trying to have it both ways? Recalling Michael Moore's dictum that the first rule of documentaries is 'don't make a documentary – make a movie' (Moore 2014). All the while, such provocative discursive and rhetorical pronouncements are not fully addressing or unpacked across these complex environmental issues and debates.

Somewhat puritanically and self-righteously, Moore goes on to affirm that 'we' (presumably meaning the environmental movement) should strive not to end up working for the Devil (namely all capitalists and corporate America). As if people and organisations were simply characterised as ethically good or bad and can all be clearly tarred with the same brush. At the outset, from a media and communications perspective, it should be noted that most (material) media production is produced and primarily driven through capitalist norms of success and failure, while glibly affirming that the public can 'take the truth'. Somewhat left-field, recalling the effects of the 2020/21 pandemic, Moore most eloquently talks of how 'Mother Nature' has sent us to the 'time-out room', while affirming how we are the ones now in the cages, rather than 'the bats in China'!

In my judgement the most insightful scholarly environmentalist response to the documentary is provided by a blog 'Planet of Some Humans' written by environmental philosopher Adrian Ivakhiv (2020):

> *Planet of the Humans* is a shot launched by the degrowthers against the green new dealers. It's an unfair shot (which makes it a pot-shot) because of its inaccuracies, but it is basically an incendiary device aimed at a close internal competitor (i.e., internal to the environmental movement) that is hoping to draw on a much larger audience to increase its impact.

References

Brereton, Pat. *Environmental Literacy and New Digital Audiences.* Routledge 2019.
Brereton, Pat. 'A Eco-Reading of Documentary/Fictional Narratives'. *Irish Studies in International Relations* 31: 43–58. 2020.
Hulme, Mike. (ed.) *Contemporary Climate Debates: A Student Primer.* Routledge 2020.

Ivakhiv, Adrian J. 'Planet of Some Humans'. 1 May 2020. htttps://blog.uvm.edu/aiva
    khiv/2020/05/01/planet-of-some-humans/
Livingston, Neil. 'Forget about Planet of the Humans' in Films for Action, 24 April
    2020, www.filmforaction.org/articles/film-review-forget-about-planet-of-the-humans.
Mann, Michael. *The New Climate War: The Fight to Take Back our Planet*. Scribe
    Publications 2021. www.scorai.net – see extensive analysis of sustainable consump-
    tion and critique of this documentary.
Moore, Michael. '13 Rules of Documentary Film Making'. *IndieWire*. 10 September
    2014. https://www.indiewire.com/feature/michael-moores-13-rules-for-making-docum
    entary-films-22384/

Risk Society and Climate Change

Ulrich Beck's theory of risk society helps to frame various connections
between the management of risks and survival. In the risk society we live in,
various aspects of financial, environmental, and terrorist dangers are all in
play and not fully controllable, according to Beck's thesis. Back in the early
1980s, the theme of risk was clearly in the air, with the escalation of Cold
War tensions creating a pervasive sense of threat. The campaign against
DDT, given huge prominence by Rachel Carson's bestselling *Silent Spring*,
had heightened awareness of the dangers of invisible chemical pollution.
Furthermore, the American Three Mile Island incident of 1979 brought home
the danger of nuclear accidents. Dealing with global risk, one might suggest
such tensions have come full circle with the 2020/21 pandemic.

A fascinating essay by Adam Tooze (2020) focuses on the importance of
risk theory using Beck's ideas, especially with regards to the 2020/21 pandemic. Tooze recalls how Beck argued that the omnipresence of large-scale
threats that were of global scope, anonymous and invisible, were by all
accounts the common denominator of our new epoch: 'A fate of endanger-
ment has arisen in modernity, a sort of counter-modernity, which transcends
all our concepts of space, time, and social differentiation'. The question, so
vividly exposed by a local crises, such as Chernobyl or the global coronavirus
pandemic, is how to navigate this world. The relevance of Beck's answers are
even more prescient in current times, while dealing with the ongoing difficulties of climate change.

According to Christian Klockner (2015), 'risk communication' helps to:

- Increase the perceived risk in a population that is common both for
  health or environmental risks, which the public often seems to
  underestimate
- Decreasing the perceived risk is often the aim with regards to technology-
  related responses and is mainly driven by companies interested in introducing a new technology. Generally, people tend to overestimate some
  type of risks and at the same time underestimate others (Klockner 2015:
  127).

Basically, the more that is known about a particular risk such as climate crisis, the higher is the overall risk perception. According to Klockner, people tend to downgrade ecological risk that is connected to a behaviour that has strong benefits for humans, especially where the adverse effects on humans and other species are uncertain (Klockner 2015: 129). How 'to communicate uncertainty remains especially relevant for environmental communication', especially around developing effective messaging strategies (Klockner 2015: 134).

Recently, on a Climate Change Masters student webinar by a planning expert based in New York (Ms. Manuela Powidayko) highlighted the need to encourage citizens to realize that an apparently low-level, 1% risk of yearly flooding, accumulated quickly, and becomes significant over the lifetime of a house mortgage for example. Consequently, accumulating rates over the years demonstrates in very real terms how this apparently low-level increase can dramatically affect the overall insurance premium. Making risk both relevant and applicable to general audiences is always a good strategy to adopt in explaining the direct effect of insuring against climate change and to help normalise its ongoing necessity. Overcoming the perception that 2030 much less 2050 appear a long way ahead, regarding key end dates in securing zero carbon emissions, requires a constant appreciation of the need for annual metrics and benchmarks towards meeting these immovable deadlines.

Klockner goes on to cite five major factors contributing to amplification or attenuation of risk; including sources of information, information channels, social stations (which can be translated as social agents), individual stations (which can be understood as intrapersonal processes) and institutional and social behaviour (Klockner 2015: 135). All of these should be used towards developing a matrix for communicating risk factors with regards to all aspects of the climate crisis, drawing on Beck's seminal work on the topic while framing such discussion and debate into the future.

References

Klockner, Christian A. *The Psychology of Pro-Environmental Communication: Beyond Standard Information Strategies*. Palgrave 2015.

Tooze, Adam. 'The Sociologist Who Could Save Us from Coronavirus'. *Foreign Policy*. 1 August 2020. https://foreignpolicy.com/2020/08/01/the-sociologist-who-could-save-us-from-coronavirus/

S

Sensory Big Data and Art: Communicating through the Five Senses

There is a growing movement within art practice to help repurpose sensory big data (usually used to promote big business) to support sustainable environmental messages for mass audiences. While conventional mass media outputs tend to be dominated by sight and sound, (ocular centrism), much innovative art formats can alternatively be applied towards actively promoting all the other senses.

Environmental data in particular, as many eco-arts scholars like Trish Morgan (2020) asserts, can not only be made visible but also audible, tactile and even smelly etc. This feat can be most clearly evident within innovative digital forms of environmental art, which signal new ways of representing and promoting cognitive engagement and even behavioural change. Ecological art tends to be pragmatic and even materialist, while being revealed through sustainable solutions and modes of consumption (Morgan 2020: 12). Furthermore, Linda Weintraub (2012: 3) usefully describes ecological art as a set of practices that run counter to 'the age-old course of human chauvinism'. Hence a form of anthropocentrism that centres on ideas of 'progress' is countered by a radical new ecocentric outlook.

Other scholars like Haynen et al. (2006: 2) focus on the need to embrace political ecology and talk of how 'little attention has been paid so far to the urban as a process of socio-ecological change'. Discussion about global environmental problems and the possibilities for developing a more sustainable future, 'ignores the urban origin of many of these problems'. In many ways political ecology foregrounds the power contexts in which environments are imagined, using all the senses and indeed highlights how they are ordered and managed within contemporary societies. Echoing Robbins observation how 'environmental research that cannot reflexively locate its relationship to power is self-evidently dangerous and has indeed proved truly violent in the world of urgent environmental justice challenges. The pursuit of one seems almost inevitably, to give rise to the prodding of the other' (Robbins 2015: 98).

The communication of environmental and ethical problems and their interconnecting solutions remain one central dimension to societal transformation

DOI: 10.4324/9781003123422-19

(Garnham 2000). While this student-friendly volume tends to focus on more mainstream and commercial audio-visual media and communication, the potential of critical art formats and other non-commercial products to communicate environmental issues – see for example the entry on Museums in this volume – often afford novel, fresh and innovative ways of speaking to the public and should be clearly harnessed. (For instance, there is an exhibition titled 'Eco-Visionaries' (2019) at the Royal Academy London, England https://www.royala cademy.org.uk/exhibition/architecture-environment-eco-visionaries.)

The exhibition includes 21 works of ecological art that calls on a broad range of senses and imaginaries in addressing climate change. Such an exhibition has been critiqued by some reviewers, including Oliver Wainwright, writing a *The Guardian* review (2019), insinuating how:

> We power our future with the breast milk of volcanoes, whispers a seductive voice. On a big screen in the Royal Academy, dreamy aerial drone footage pans across the endless white expanse of the Bolivian salt flats, while a tank of eerie green battery juice bubbles in the corner of the room.

Wainwright's provocative review points out that there is a poetic myth around how the Salar de Uyuni salt plain came into being. According to the Aymara legend, the great white desert was formed by the breast milk and tears that flowed from Tunupa, a goddess in volcano form, who wept when her baby volcano was taken away from her. The mountain might have another reason to weep now. The world's tech companies have set their sights on extracting one of the planet's largest lithium reserves from beneath the salty crust of the Salar.

This strange mix of poetry, science and narrative speculation sets the tone for an exhibition that is thought-provoking and apparently frustrating in turns. Eco-visionaries brings together artists, architects and designers whose work is inspired by our current environmental crisis. Rather than offering scientifically driven critical analysis or other forms of practical measures, the exhibition mostly occupies the realm of fictional scenarios and dreamy futures, veering towards climate emergency, as both engaging and immersive entertainment. Nonetheless, such innovative art-based installations and exhibitions can often serve as a provocative and fruitful means of speaking for and to nature, all the while teasing out the full implications of the growing environmental crisis.

References

Garnham, N. *Emancipation, the Media, and Modernity.* Oxford University Press 2000.
Heynen, N., Kaika, M. and Swyngedouw, E. *In the Nature of Cities: Urban Political Ecology and the Politics of Urban Metabolism.* Routledge 2006.
Morgan, Trish. 'Sensing our World: How Digital Cultural Practices Can Contribute to Changing Social Norms Around Consumption'. *Report 355.* EPA 2020.

Robbins, P. 'The Trickster Science' (89–101). In Perreault, T., Bridge, G. and McCarthy, J. (eds), *The Routledge Handbook of Political Ecology*. Routledge 2015.

Wainwright, Oliver. 'Eco-visionaries Review: The Salt Flats Will Die and the Jellyfish Shall Rise'. *The Guardian*. 21 November 2019.

Weintraub, L. *To Life! Eco Art in Pursuit of a Sustainable Planet*. University of California Press 2012.

Shock Doctrine and Pandemics: As a Precursor for the Climate Crisis

This so-called shock doctrine explores how American 'free market' polices came to dominate the world through the exploitation of disaster, which in turn served to produce global 'shocks' to both people and countries. Naomi Klein's classic *Shock Doctrine* (2007) talks of the use of public disorientation, following massive collective shocks – such as wars, terrorist attacks, natural disasters etc., to push through unpopular economic measures. Along with other left-leaning political and ideological critics, Klein perceives the global rise and dominance of an extreme neo-liberal form of capitalism that in turn helps to legitimate more extreme modes of economic activity. She traces these transformations within America, UK and other Western countries, and goes on to infer almost counter-intuitively how, not facing up to or dealing with our climate crisis is part of this new form of amnesia. In turn, this approach serves as a shock to established systems that crave stability and maintaining the status quo. Furthermore, it also serves to withstand any moves towards more equal redistribution of wealth, much less coping with climate disasters that affect different parts of the world in contrasting ways.

Klein's popular, left-leaning thesis is focused around Milton Friedman's economic model, which is capable of being only partially imposed under democracy, while authoritarian conditions are required for the full implementation of its true vision. For economic shock therapy to be applied without restraint – 'as it was in Chile in the seventies, China in the late eighties, Russia in the nineties, and America after September 11, 2001' – some sort of additional major collective trauma has always been required, one that either temporarily suspended democratic practices or blocked them entirely (Klein 2007: 11).

According to Klein, Friedman devoted his life to fighting a peaceful battle of ideas against those who believed that governments had a responsibility to intervene in the market to soften up its sharp edges. He believed history 'got off on the wrong track' when politicians began listening to John Maynard Keynes, the intellectual architect of the New Deal and the modern welfare state. The market crash of 1929 for instance apparently created an overwhelming consensus view that laissez-faire forms of business had in fact failed and that governments needed to intervene in the economy to redistribute wealth and regulate corporations. During these dark days for laissez-faire economics, when Communism seemed an attractive alternative ideology for many countries, the welfare state was embraced by the West and economic nationalism even took root in the postcolonial Southern regions.

Consequently, embracing any form of the 'common good' much less protecting the environment, was not even on the table for serious consideration with the rise of a pure vision of capitalism. One could further suggest that this level of imbalance continued right up to the global financial crash of 2008, which was ostensibly caused by poor financial decision making, yet ending up with governments bailing the system out. Affirming the proposition that private enterprise and investment banking leverages excessive risk taking, they eventually require state and public governance – who are always more risk averse – to eventually step in and bail the system out when things go wrong.

The notion that market crashes can act as a catalyst for revolutionary change has also had a long history of discussion on the far Left, most notably recalling the Bolshevik theory that hyperinflation, while destroying the value of money, takes the masses one step closer to the destruction of capitalism itself. This proposition explains why a certain breed of sectarian leftists, even some extreme de-growth environmentalists, are forever calculating the exact conditions under which capitalism will reach the pivotal tipping point of 'crisis'; reminiscent of how evangelical fundamentalist Christians calibrate signs of the likelihood of a forthcoming Rapture – as evidenced in the ending of Malick's *Tree of Life* (2011).

Environmental media scholars Lisa Parks and Janet Walker (2020) acknowledge Naomi Klein as a key public journalist and mouthpiece towards helping to frame our global media responses to climate change – see in particular her 2019 tomb *On Fire* discussed elsewhere – and linking this to both economic and political fault-lines across the world. Klein effectively used media to engage the public in resisting what she calls a new 'pandemic shock doctrine'. Environmental lessons around climate justice and building forward better need to be urgently learned in many areas across the world.

References

Klein, Naomi. *The Shock Doctrine: The Rise of Disaster Capitalism*. Penguin 2007.
Parks, Lisa and Walker, Janet. 'Special Issue/stream Introduction, Forthcoming in Media + Environment', July 2020. 'Disaster Media: Bending the Curve of Ecological Disruption and Moving Toward Social Justice'.

Sixth Extinction and Environmental Disasters

As numerous environmental studies assert, the previous historical extinction events include: the Devonian extinction 360 million years ago; Permian-Triassic extinction from 250 million years ago; the Triassic-Jurassic extinction from 210 million years ago and the Cretaceous-Tertiary extinction from 'just' 65 million years ago. In the current geological time period, human society has developed a pattern of expediential growth, which, according to most environmental experts, is leading to the prospect of a sixth mass extinction event.

Consequently, to continue 'business as usual' and destroying more habitats at scale, will continue to degrade our precious planet, producing ever more pollution and excessive carbon emissions into the atmosphere. Highlighting the very real prospect of a sixth extinction certainly focuses attention on the historically global significance of our biodiversity loss and climate emergency. But of course such a realisation can alternatively lead to various forms of fatalistic denial, coupled with heightened levels of eco-anxiety, rather than provide a spur towards mobilising all our considerable efforts to fight against such an undesirable future.

The 2020/21 pandemic – like others before it – helps to illustrate the possibility of future catastrophes to come. Many deep, environmental commentators draw connections with the biblical scale of the outbreak, as corresponding to new modes of 'punishment' for our hubris and our poor stewardship of the earth. But of course, the people who suffer most during pandemics and climate crises are not necessarily those who helped cause the problems in the first place. Some fundamentalist-based religious groupings, as well as more mainstream spiritual leaders including Pope Francis's very influential encyclical 'Laudato Si' (2015) have made various biblical connections between human hubris and frailty in not taking responsibility for our habitats – well before the full effects of the pandemic were felt across the world in 2020. In reality, the COVID-19 virus is simply the latest in a number of novel disease outbreaks, that are thought to be increasing in frequency, and which apparently resulted from human interference with the natural world (IPBES 2020; Almond et al. 2020).

The spectre of a sixth extinction remains a cogent image to communicate the severity of the crisis, which is often visualised in cautionary eco-science fictional tales (see Brereton 2005). Yet such a narrative trope can also backfire in mediating the severity of such global disasters, leading to increased levels of denial/fatalism/eco-anxiety. Furthermore, reflecting on such long term historical time periods, extinction epochs may unfortunately be less successful in mobilising public opinion and behavioural change than one might expect. As governments and politicians, much less businesses, often think in short yearly balance sheets or electoral cycles of four–five years, individuals similarly only think of more immediate concerns around financial and other contingent forms of security. The prospect of a sixth extinction needs to be co-opted and scaled up in several ways by environmental communicators to help mobilise all parts of society across the world towards urgently addressing the environmental and climate crises.

References

Brereton, Pat. *Hollywood Utopia: Ecology in Contemporary American Cinema.* Intellect Press 2005.

Pope Francis. Encyclical Letter 'Laudato Si: On Care for our Common Home'. 2015. https://www.vatican.va/content/francesco/en/encyclicals/documents/papa-francesco_20150524_enciclica-laudato-si.html

IPBES. 'IPBES Report: Escaping the "Era of Pandemics"'. n.d.www.ipbes.net/pandem ics

Almond, R.E.A., Grooten, M. and Petersen, T. *Living Planet Report 2020: Bending the Curve of Biodiversity Loss.* WWFn.d.https://www.zsl.org/sites/default/files/LPR%202020%20Full%20report.pdf

Slow Violence and Poverty: Lack of Equity in Representing Environmental Scholarship

Rob Nixon coined the term slow violence to mean 'a violence that occurs gradually and out of sight, a violence of delayed destruction that is dispersed across time and space' (2011: 2). Rather than the apparent suddenness of a sixth extinction event for instance, it includes gradual acidification of oceans and the incremental horrors of climate change. As affirmed in an interview with Miyase Christensen, Nixon recognises that one of the positive developments has been a movement away from top-down understandings of what it means to live on 'Spaceship Earth' – as one journalist said, 'beware of anyone talking about Spaceship Earth, this idea that we are all equal inhabitants in the spaceship, while those who are directing the spaceship are sitting in Geneva, Washington or wherever'. The emergence and diffusion of environmental humanities in capturing the 'slow violence' of climate justice, building on colonial power structures, which are just one aspect of the decentralisation of voices necessary towards 'defining what constitutes the environment, culturally and politically' (1).

Born in South Africa, Nixon started out as a postcolonial activist and socially engaged writer constantly working for the overthrow of apartheid in all its formats. On leaving his homeland as a political exile, he moved to America where he worked with the very influential post-colonial scholar Edward Said at Columbia university in New York. Since then, according to an interview and review piece (Christensen 2017), he has focused almost exclusively on environmental and public writing, particularly in relation to the struggles for environmental justice in the global South, while questioning much Western-centric environmental thinking, which tends to view the planet and its destruction from a particular hegemonic perspective.

For instance in the July 2021 online conference for the 'International Association for Media and Communication Research' (IAMCR), the Environment, Science and Risk Communication Working Group keynote presentation dramatically highlighted this core imbalance within our ever-expanding Environmental Communications discipline. As further articulated in their co-edited 2020 reader *The Local and the Digital in Environmental Communication*, which outlines the huge imbalance within the Western-centric scholarship across this field and the paucity of investigation across so many other parts of the world. Citing a major literature review study from 2018, published in *Environmental Communication*, the authors found that of the articles in our sample, over half (266, or nearly 53%) examined American-based media messages of environmental issues. Ninety-six (19% articles) examined European nations, thirty-two (6.4%) was all that was published or examined from China. Other major developing countries like Brazil (8) and India (9), appeared in less than two percent of published environmental studies.

(Comfort-Evans and Park 2018: 864)

Such a huge imbalance across the planet in published scholarship has to be addressed, urgently, with much more case studies set up and supporting research from across the world.

Hence a more equitable cross-continental approach is badly needed to address the academic-driven 'slow violence' of not representing or addressing environmental issues and climate crisis from across the world. An urgent challenge certainly, which this volume has also fallen foul of, with a paucity of non-western case studies and entries. But such a radical transformation requires a major transformation of environmental journals, book publishers and research funding organisations to take the lead in reversing this imbalance, by actively funding and publishing more high-quality representative scholarship from across the world.

Back to Nixon's biography and his colonial framing of the violence and injustice embedded within the climate change debate, following the 2003 invasion of Iraq, Nixon focused on the role of depleted uranium munitions in modern warfare. He wrote a short book on the topic, which also involved interviewing Iraq veterans. In turn, this started him 'thinking about slow violence, about invisibility, the absence of spectacle, the difficulty of finding narratives and imagistic forms of communicating profound damage that is diffuse and scattered across time and space and lacks a core theoretical and dramatic focus' (Christensen 2017: 3).

The term slow violence has been increasingly co-opted by the environmental movement to reflect the slow but steady pace of ecocidal destruction and has remained a dominant term in the lexicon of environmental communication studies. Environmental media scholars Lisa Parks and Janet Walker recall the wisdom of Nixon's pronouncements around slow violence or 'the long dying's—the staggeringly discounted casualties both human and ecological that result from war's aftermaths or climate change' (2011: 2–3). Nixon together with many educationalists and environmental scholars calls out the necessity of developing trans-disciplinary research from all corners of the earth, together with encouraging the mass media to take on a bigger role in this all-encompassing environmental struggle.

References

Christensen, Miyase. 'Slow Violence in the Anthropocene: An Interview with Rob Nixon on Communication, Media, and the Environmental Humanities'. *Environmental Communication* 2017.

Comfort, S.E. and Park, Y.E. 'On the Field of Environmental Communication: A Systemic Review of the Peer-Reviewed Literature'. *Environmental Communication* 12(7): 862–875. 2018.

Diaz-Pont, J., Maeselle, P., Egan Sjolander, P., Mishra, A. and Foxwell-Norton, K. (eds) *The Local and the Digital in Environmental Communication*. Palgrave 2020.

Nixon, Rob. *Slow Violence and the Environmentalism of the Poor*. Harvard University Press 2011.

Parks, Lisa and Walker, Janet. 'Disaster Media: Bending the Curve of Ecological Disruption and Moving toward Social Justice'. *Media + Environment* 2(1). July 2020.

Social Media and Climate Change Communication: A Tool for Innovation!

Is social media actively assisting in making constructive climate change transformation, including supporting innovative policy change across the globe? Mike Schaper (in Hulme 2020) alternatively argues that the fragmentation of established news media, brought about by the growing proliferation of social media outlets and the associated prevalence of online echo-chambers, fuel dangerous forms of destructive identity politics and issue polarisation. This makes support for climate policy change harder to break through and often undermines the possibility of a constructive mode of mass deliberative democracy. Alternatively, other scholars like Peter North, focus on the benefits afforded by digital platforms for coalescing and developing radical social movements that can speed up the transmission of counter-cultural environmental values; necessary for both climate mitigation and effective adaptation. Some go so far as to argue that social media platforms can further assist in promoting new forms of climate democracy.

Certainly, more so than so-called legacy media (TV, Print and Film), more extensive behavioural audience research has been carried out regarding the ongoing potency and influence of social media's new digital platforms. Somewhat cynically, one might suggest, this is because it's technically easier to focus investigation on new media, with its (freely available) algorithms and development of database (big data) analysis – drawing on the growing digital potency and range of high-tech computer tools. As a result, behavioural economists in journals like *Environmental Communication* and *Public Understanding of Science* (PUS) etc. have shown that audiences and online users have all sorts of biases, which is further evident through the growth of digital media audience scholarship. Going back to primary psychological principles, it continues to be affirmed that humans are *de facto* emotional creatures and not always logical, much less science-driven in their attitudinal formation and behaviour patterns (Thaler 2015). Consequently, audiences do not automatically accept what 'the science tells them' and subsequently change their behaviour in line with clearly laid out empirical findings. All of which call to mind perennial debates around social media being more influential, interactive and dialogical, while also taking into account the role of mass media as gatekeepers for the framing and disseminating of messages. Such debates are explored in several other entries and references, including behavioural effect theory, fake news and documentaries examined such as *The Social Dilemma* (2020).

References

Hulme, Mike (ed). *Contemporary Climate Change Debates: A Student Primer*. Routledge 2020.
Thaler, R.H. *Misbehaving: The Making of Behavioural Economics*. Allen Lane 2015.

Spiritual Representations of Environmental Agency – *First Reformed*

Many deep environmentalists call for the development of a spiritual sense of reverie of nature as a powerful mode of engagement and cross-connectivity. For instance writing in 2001, Bron Taylor speaks of a sense of 'connection and belonging to nature (sometimes personified as a transparency, if not a transcendental power) which unites' (1), while calling up otherwise competing forms of spirituality. Such co-joining of deep connecting with nature and spirituality is also embedded for example in the call to Christian action, coupled with ethical solidarity embedded in the bible and also evident across other global religious texts and manifestos. We all need to 'stand up for the good of the (global, but often this is reduced to American) community' and do the right thing, as evident across so many powerful narratives.

This phenomenon is brought to a new level of dramatic engagement through the more spiritual-religious agency, using a form of radical environmental struggle, as witnessed for instance in the film *First Reformed* (2017). As the climate crisis worsens, linking religious martyrdom and environmental agency will become increasingly popular among several religious sects. For instance, following on from the use of religious fervour to drive fundamentalist, even nationalistic politics, including more contemporary manifestations of Muslim's jihad and revolutionary fervour, one suspects that new generations of green activists might further draw on the practices of faith systems to help kick-start revolutionary environmental politics.

Directed by Paul Schrader, this small-scale art house, black-and-white movie presents a more hard-line and direct evocation of the need for clerics and citizens generally to actively fight for the protection of nature, as humans face up to the horrors of climate change. The film draws on Schrader's seminal academic study, *Transcendental Style in Film* (2018), focusing on the creative historical direction of filmmakers like Ozu, Bresson and Dreyer. In his latest edition, the author adds a chapter on slow cinema, which certainly encapsulates the specific tone and style of this and other innovative, environmentally focused narratives.

Drawing on a cursory eco-reading of the film, first developed in Brereton (2019: 111), pastor Toller (Ethan Hawke in a stunning performance) portrays a character who is willing to rise above the usual 'business as usual' modalities and recognise the massive intellectual and behavioural transformation that is required in facing up to the challenges of climate change. This tension is addressed head-on throughout this dark climate and religious allegory. Reminiscent of the farming protagonist cited elsewhere in a reading of *Dark Waters* (2019), the pastor's persona also finds the strength, through both the intellectual and personal attributes necessary to imagine taking on the systemic change demanded in making a real difference. This includes moving away from embracing the edicts of his own conservative, religious organisation and taking on the requisite radical vision to face up to the demands for clear environmental regulation, alongside other types of strictures and action; all of which are necessary towards addressing the growing environmental crisis.

Incidentally, an analysis of the film's nature and religious use of imagery must also take account of its application of magic realism effects, especially concerning the levitation scene, when Mary (Amanda Seyfried) needs psychic 'comfort' and asks the Pastor to replicate what she ritualistically did with her late husband. Basically, this performative ritual involved mounting each other fully clothed and face-to-face, while concentrating on each other's very act of breathing. This provides a surrealist image and memorable scene, as they both levitate with transcendental ecstasy – recalling the Oscar winner *The Shape of Water* (2018) and its evocative environmental themed storyline, especially recalling the water-based dancing sequence between two contrasting species.

In an earlier scene Mary's husband Michael (Philip Ettinger) shoots himself in a snow-filled landscape, which he deemed sacred, having requested the Pastor to meet him at this natural site. Michael apparently was unable to face bringing a child into this ecocidal (environmentally dystopic) world and thus signals a broader population control conundrum, exacerbated by the climate crisis. All the main protagonists in their different ways are struggling against norms and prescribed rules, while dealing with external powers and responsibilities in this dark, yet overly mediated world. Apparently, it would seem that taking on the role of a would-be terrorist becomes the only logical strategy for the main protagonist to adopt in facing up to the almost criminal levels of public non-action in response to the insidious and destructive nature of the climate crisis. The greatest challenge facing the planet has unfortunately led to a form of paralysis and inactivity, which in turn equates with a pernicious form of evil – at least as evident in the mind of this very troubled pastor. One wonders how environmental, much less religious, activists might at least concur in responding to such a dilemma and assist in such reframing of our climate crisis. Communicators pulled across the polarising tensions between pragmatic versus idealistic responsibility, not to mention revolutionary environmental transformation, helps to foreground a more radical strategy in dealing with such an appalling climate crises vista. The allegorical story-line invites all viewers, as constituent global eco-citizens, to ponder how to adequately respond to such a dilemma.

A voice-over by the pastor appeals how 'every act of preservation is an act of creation'. How we participate in the creation and acceptance of evil deeds being perpetrated on our planet every day remains an abiding challenge and call to arms. He recites this troubling ethical dilemma, while looking at the polluted seascape, where the suicidal victim, Michael wrote his last will and testimony and requested that his ashes be scattered in this desecrated landscape. Apparently, the pastor has uncovered through the intersession of prayer, radically new forms of active communal engagement, alongside aligning with social, as well as spiritual modes of deep-violent, environmental modes of expression.

Earlier the pastor was accused by his boss Pastor Joel Jeffries (Cedric Kyles), who runs the evangelical Abundant Life Church, of not being situated in the real world and being given over to the 'garden of darkness'. While God is present in all of nature, his spiritual leader affirms, we have many areas to find our authentic voice that in turn help towards uncovering a productive path for the Church. Yet while this pragmatic approach seems appropriate and measured, at the same time in the real political world, the American government, during this period, had sought to actively deny the very scientific existence of the climate emergency. Who speaks for God in such circumstances becomes the abiding dilemma raised by the pastor in this co-joining of spiritual, political and natural forces.

The climax of the movie occurs (please excuse plot details being revealed) where reality and fantasy become co-mingled, as Pastor Toller goes to the ultimate extreme by putting on a bomb vest left by his young charge, as the invited celebratory congregation builds up for its 250th anniversary. Almost magically, or more unconsciously, probably through his dream-like death-wish fantasy, he spies Mary unexpectedly entering the church. Consequently, the Pastor replaces his bomb vest with a Christ-like crown of thorns and proceeds to ingest some type of viscous dark oil – one presumes as a form of atonement for the (climate change) sins of human nature. Nonetheless, in a further twist, the couple's final (fantasy) loving kiss says it all; reaffirming the ever-present utopian ideal that love and faith can inevitably conquer all, once injustice and all forms of corruption are both named and faced ethically.

Many scholars however question the complex meaning of the film's ending. At an eco-critical and spiritual level, a review of *First Reformed* by Alissa Wilkinson in *Vox* (2018) explores how Schrader develops a spiritual film, which takes great strides to take faith (if not also environmental belief) seriously. It's certainly about as far away from today's crop of 'faith based' (and one could certainly add environmental) films as you could get, and its use of style and its restrained tone is a big reason why this is the case.

In a revealing interview with the director, Schrader affirms that just because you put Jesus Christ into a Hollywood melodrama doesn't mean that it's a spiritual, much less a divine nature film. Discussing the state of the Christian church in the United States, the director affirms that there are two types of church these days:

There's the traditional church of devotion and mediation and then there's an arena-based, entertainment-based church. Of course there are Christians in both. But my preference is for the devotional. In the arena-based church, you get the same hit as you would at a Taylor Swift concert or a football game – that emotional bump you get from being in a crowd, all believing the same thing and saying and doing the same thing.

Basically, according to Schrader, mediation (and probably one could add, at least the residue of some deep mode of environmental engagement), needs 'the slow experience' rather than the more immersive big budget Hollywood spectacle.

Some eco-film and *avant garde* scholars like Scott MacDonald (2015) would agree with regards to environmental messaging and the need for a more distancing and reflexive format to speak to such environmental issues. While I believe it's certainly not clear-cut whether it's best to choose commercial and/or art-based media, both modalities, ranging from high to low cultural expressions can assist in their different ways with the ever-pressing environmental communications agenda.

Schrader incisively continues how

St. Augustine taught us that suicide is a sin, but the death of Sampson (a Biblical figure who brought down a building to kill a group of wicked people as well as himself) is not a sin. That's a martyrdom.

So after Michael kills himself because he is unable to accept the responsibility of bringing new life into the world, what Toller finds is

the cloak of martyrdom that he can wrap around himself and turn its sinfulness into redemption. That's the virus he catches. It's a pathology of suicidal glory. The pathology that I can affect my own salvation through my own suffering.

(cited in Wilkinson 2018)

So whether he's an environmentalist or a jihadist is not clear – according to Schrader at least. The drive towards such extremist environmental activism has a long way to go before even beginning to have such dilemmas addressed, much less recognising the weight of our environmental culpability and ever-growing crisis of conscience.

A key scene underpinning this environmental reading that foregrounds the benevolence of nature, occurs later in the film when Pastor Toller rediscovers the everyday pleasures of life and living. The cleric apparently had not cycled for 20 years, but finally rediscovers the simple and active power of exercising in nature. It's God-given, he pontificates, while the camera focuses on the leafless trees above and reinforces the therapeutic (or biophiliac) pleasure of movement in nature with his companion Mary, who currently is with-child – further reinforcing allegorical comparison with the biblical mother of God.

Recalling other classic transcendental cinematic works by Andrei Tarkovsky or Ingmar Bergman, not to mention Terrence Malick explored elsewhere, the (back)story remains ostensibly about the passion and commitment of an environmental activist Michael Mensana (Philip Ettinger) who commits suicide, but who by any measure could not be classified as religious. Essentially, as earlier affirmed, not wanting to bring a child into the world and face them later on with their innocent hope and optimism appears to be his dominant concern, as the world becomes worse and worse due to increasing populations, loss of biodiversity, runaway pollution and general, human-induced climate disasters. Over the course of some cursory exposition around this troubled character, audiences are provided with several 'mini-lectures' on his existential dilemma, while being shown images of how bad things really are in the environment and recognising the worrying prospects and signals of future catastrophic disaster.

Linking Environmental Action and Martyrdom – Calling on Religious and Racial Justice

Meanwhile, the iconic church building – which remains the focus of identification in the film and symbolises religious expression, not to mention embodying an index of deep environmental belief, is framed front and centre from the start in a long, slow, tracking shot, which kick-starts this austere black-and-white slow chamber movie. Prophetically, we learn later that the sacred timber building was used as a stop-off and safety haven during the dark period of slavery, with various pastors over the years protecting the innocent in this sacred building. Now, unfortunately this sacred space has become misused and abused as a tourism site and tax-haven for a big industrialist to help salve his conscience, not to mention affording a greenwashed comfort-blanket for the exploitative and extractive industrial corporation that is actively engaged in polluting the landscape.

But nobody appears to be doing anything about it. An extreme case of political or religious, not to say environmental amnesia or greenwashing. Consequently, the director is forcibly posing the question; can the church again inspire hope for the future and help face up to and fight the pernicious and wicked dangers of climate-change emissions and global pollution, while at the same time supporting the tenets of equality and supporting a 'Just Transition'? *First Reformed* concentrates on developing a spiritual and religious mode of articulating active agency in dealing with our climate crisis.

A extreme form of environmental creative imaginary focused around activism might at least be inspired by such performative and narrative excess. Such dramatic tensions are displayed more frequently through national political and war-like fervour – see for instance an eco-reading of Mel Gibson's 2016 anti-war tale *Hacksaw Ridge* (in Brereton 2019: 111). But learning the lessons from fundamentalist animal lovers for instance, who have often adopted a militant stance, to more mainstream democratic political activity, while at the same time marrying more middle-class environmental activism, as illustrated by *Women at War* discussed elsewhere, all such approaches have an important role to play. Certainly, in this extreme manifestation of environmental conflicts and tensions, taking a concrete stand in the struggle for radical transformation leads to many difficult ethical dilemmas. The film goes to great lengths, recalling both a mainstream filmic tradition, alongside an *avant garde* and fundamentalist religious perspective, to powerfully highlight the full implications of our climate crisis on personal agency and responsibility, while posing a provocative faith-based ethical response.

References

Brereton, Pat. *Environmental Literacy and New Digital Audiences*. Routledge 2019.
MacDonald, Scott. *Avant-Doc: Intersection of Doc and Avant Garde Cinema*. Oxford University Press 2015.
Schrader, Paul. *Transcendental Style in Film: Ozu, Bresson, Dreyer, With a New Introduction*. University of California Press 2018.
Taylor, Bron. 'Earth and Nature-Based Spirituality From Deep Ecology to Radical Environmentalism'. *Religion* 3(2). April. 175–193. 2001.
Wilkinson, Alissa. 'Paul Schrader on First Reformed: This is a troubling film about a troubled person'. *Vox*18 June 2018.

Sustainable Communication and Environmental New Media Research

Sustainable development became central to the public agenda through the auspices of the 1992 Earth Summit, alongside being foregrounded through the development and codification of the United Nations driven Sustainable Development Goals (STGs). There are growing levels of research around developments in sustainability, linked with all forms of environmentalism and communication of these values (see Geiger and Fischer 2018). Early scholarship in sustainable communication, according to environmental expert Alison Anderson, tended to focus on localised conflicts over environmental issues and mostly examined legacy or print media case studies across Western countries. More recently in the last decade there has been a greater focus on the growth and sustainability of digital media, which she argues at the same time can 'lead to digital overload and cognitive dissonance' (Anderson 2021: 31).

All types of media across all platforms can play a major role in communicating the importance of environmental sustainability, by helping to shape public awareness and political agendas. Yet it must be recognised that sustainable development is perceived as biased towards the interest of northern (developed) countries (Barkemeyer et al. 2013), rather than the poorer developing regions, which needs development to take them out of the poverty trap.

Most certainly mass media can and will play a critical role in measuring and achieving success around the Sustainable Development Goals (SDGs) over the next critical decades.

Alternatively, research has also suggested that social media outlets, such as Facebook and YouTube, not to mention Twitter, have played significant roles in promoting right-wing conspiracies that encourage aspects of climate denial, rather than supporting sustainability (see Murdock and Brevini 2019). A major challenge therefore is to make all aspects of sustainability more tangible and personally relevant for all citizens and stakeholders and connecting the local with the global environmental challenges facing our planet.

In particular, Anderson calls for new ways of visualising sustainability, alongside all aspects of environmental and climate change issues that offer the potential to increase active and holistic engagement with these prescient issues. For instance, there are good opportunities to involve young people as agents of change, tapping into self-curation of personal images, using new storytelling mechanisms and also calling on less-visible marginalised sections of society, which embraces citizen journalism/bloggers and social influencers (Anderson 2021: 45). By all accounts, new digital-born media players, such as Vice and BuzzFeed are experimenting with innovative and interesting ways to engage their young audiences, including through immersive journalism (ibid.: 46). Environmental communication scholars and students need to always analyse their use of online media and tap into audience pleasures, as they uncover new avenues and protocols for speaking to the challenges of our climate crisis (Philo and Happer 2013).

Sustainable Development Goal 12 – Responsible Consumption and Production

Goal 12 of the SDG's focuses on 'ensuring sustainable consumption and production patterns', and therefore is aimed at both the consumers as well as the producers of goods. SDG12 consists of 11 global targets, which are accompanied by 13 indicators to monitor the targets' progress. These include:

- support developing countries to strengthen their scientific capacity
- develop tools to monitor impacts (such as sustainable tourism)
- rationalise inefficient fossil-fuel subsidies
- achieve sustainable management of resources
- halve per-capita food waste
- achieve sound management of chemicals
- reduce waste through prevention, reduction, recycling and reuse
- encourage adaptation of sustainable practices
- promote sustainable public procurement
- ensure people have information to live in harmony with nature.

References

Anderson, Alison. 'Sustainability in Environmental Communication Research: Emerging Trends and Future Challenges' (31–50). In Weder, Franzisca, Krainer, Larissa and Karmasin, Matthias (eds), *The Sustainability Communications Reader: A Reflective Compendium*. Springer 2021.

Barkemeyer, R., Figge, F. and Holt, D. 'Sustainability Related Media Coverage and Socioeconomic Development: A Regional and North-South Perspective'. *Environ Plann C: Gov Policy* 31(4): 716–740. 2013.

Geiger, S. and Fischer, D. 'Measuring What Matters in Sustainable Consumption: An Integrative Framework for the Selection of Relevant Behaviors'. *Sustainable Development* 26(1): 18–33. 2018.

Murdock, G. and Brevini, B. 'Communications and the Capitalocene. Disputed Ecologies, Contested Economies, Competing Futures'. *Polit. RCon. Commun* 7(1): 51–82. 2019.

Philo, G. and Happer, C. *Communicating Climate Change and Energy Security: New Methods in Audience Research*. Routledge 2013.

Sustainability Accounting (Dr Aideen O'Dochartaigh DCU)

Sustainability and accounting seem initially unlikely partners, but with just 100 companies responsible for 70% of greenhouse gas (GHG) emissions (Carbon Disclosure Project 2017), learning to account for, and hold companies accountable for, their social and environmental impacts is of vital importance. Accounting was previously a fairly narrow concept, which only considered an organisation's financial interactions, but through sustainability accounting it is also broadening out to incorporate its social and environmental interactions. There are two elements to sustainability accounting – counting the organisation's internal costs and benefits (environmental management accounting) and reporting them to stakeholders (financial accounting), who in turn influence what issues companies engage with.

Environmental management accounting is relatively straightforward for organisations with the will and the resources to implement. Using traditional accounting tools like costing and budgeting, organisations can account for their physical inputs, such as raw materials, water and energy, and outputs, such as greenhouse gas (GHG) emissions and waste. Various tools have been developed to measure and record data, such as the Environmental Profit and Loss (P&L) account used by Puma, or the Natural Capital Accounting framework, which allow organisations to produce an environmental balance sheet. For example, in Ireland the bogs owned by energy company Bord na Móna or the woodlands owned by forestry company Coillte, become assets on the company's environmental balance sheet.

Social interactions are more challenging to account for, so organizations often rely on a stakeholder approach to identify issues to engage with. This means selecting the groups of people, besides its shareholders, that have the greatest interest in the affairs of the organisation, and the greatest power to impact it negatively if the relationship deteriorated. This approach is popular for a very good reason: it links sustainability with organisational strategy and most pertinently for many managers, with its financial bottom line.

The 'business case' for sustainability has framed much corporate engagement with social and environmental issues for the last 50 years (Walley and Whitehead 1994). For senior management to support an initiative there must be a business case – how will this help the company? However, what is good for business is not always good for sustainability. For example, 'eco-efficiency' (using fewer resources to make a product), can be cheaper for the organisation, but these resources are typically channelled into producing more units of product, so absolute resource use – and environmental impact – ultimately increases (Dyllick and Hockerts 2002).

In this context it is not surprising that a gap is often observed between corporate talk and action on sustainability. Claims of environmental distinction from highly polluting companies, such as this ad from Exxon Mobil, and you thought we just made the gas, rarely reflect the reality of its business operations (Exxon produces 3.6 billion barrels of oil or oil equivalent per day). Unlike financial reporting, sustainability reporting is largely open to interpretation, with individual companies free to cherry pick the issues where they perform best. This ambiguity opens the door to greenwashing explored elsewhere, where organisations' reports of their environmental purity prove to be greatly exaggerated. Such practices can take several forms, from the relatively benign tactic of exaggerated claims, like airline EasyJet claiming that its flights have a lower carbon footprint than driving in a hybrid car, to the more sinister technique of casting doubt on the severity of the problem, where companies fund front organisations to spread misinformation on a particular topic and undermine scientists or campaigners (Laufer 2003).

Significant advances have been made in sustainability accounting in recent years, however, particularly in relation to carbon accounting, as companies become increasingly aware of climate change. Companies are lining up to set 'science-based' targets for GHG emissions reduction, with varying success (Dahlmann et al. 2019) and researchers are developing ways of linking company and sectoral emissions to global ecological indicators (Bebbington et al. 2019).

With the escalation of interlinked ecological, societal and economic crises, it has never been more important to understand how organisations can contribute positively to ecological resilience and social justice, and to develop the structures to support corporate accountability to society. Sustainability accounting will certainly play a crucial role in helping Environmental Communications students and citizens in general to appreciate and evaluate the importance of business and accounting in facing up to climate-change challenges.

Authored by Dr Aideen O'Dochartaigh
(DCU Business School, Dublin City University, Glasnevin, Dublin 9)

References

Bebbington, J., Österblom, H., Crona, B., Jouffray, J.B., Larrinaga, C., Russell, S. and Scholtens, B. 'Accounting and Accountability in the Anthropocene'. *Accounting, Auditing & Accountability Journal* 33(1): 152–177. 2019.

Carbon Disclosure Project. *The Carbon Majors Database - CDP Carbon Majors Report 2017*. Carbon Disclosure Project. 2017.

Dahlmann, F., Branicki, L. and Brammer, S. 'Managing Carbon Aspirations: The Influence of Corporate Climate Change Targets on Environmental Performance'. *Journal of Business Ethics* 158(1): 1–24. 2019.

Dyllick, T. and Hockerts, K. 'Beyond the Business Case for Corporate Sustainability'. *Business Strategy and the Environment* 11(2): 130–141. 2002.

Laufer, W.S. 'Social Accountability and Corporate Greenwashing'. *Journal of Business Ethics* 43(3): 253–261. 2003.

Walley, N. and Whitehead, B. 'It's Not Easy Being Green'. *Harvard Business Review* 72(3), 46–51. 1994.

T

Tipping Points Around Climate Change Transformation – Audience Research

Reaching an unstoppable tipping point where the planet's climate cannot recover echoes much of the more provocative doom-laden media coverage around climate change in recent years. Expediential changes occurring through global warming are becoming irreversible, as temperatures rise, pollution increases and overall levels of biodiversity are reduced to critical levels. Such a prognosis can unfortunately lead to fatalistic responses and a growing belief that it's probably too late to reverse, much less stabilise the situation. Such worrying patterns around carbon emissions and general, climatic activity remain of ongoing concern.

Meanwhile, within environmental communications and behavioural analysis research, much time is spent on estimating the relative percentage of a population that is required to kick-start radical behavioural change to help turn around the global population and meet these challenges. Estimates vary between as little as 10% of a population functioning as 'early adaptors' in kick-starting more sustainable ways of doing things, while other studies put this figure at over 25% of the total population, before even beginning to envisage such a major transformation. The Annenberg School of Communication at the University of Pennsylvania in America for example carried out research on this issue in a 2018 project led by Damon Gentola and Joshua Becker. Participants in the project were financially motivated to start off a specific behavioural-change experiment and record how this began to influence others in the experiment. Of course, it is very difficult to prove retrospectively how many citizens it might take to 'start a revolution'; a live future-looking experiment might help to estimate the power of such innovative potency. Overall, the experiment found that influential texts and pro-active story telling can potentially serve as an effective tipping point towards promoting radical change. With its more targeted environmental media production, designed to promote long-lasting 'creative imaginaries', such a tipping point towards environmental change and transformation can be further kick-started in the very near future. By all accounts this signals the need for more environmental communication research in this area.

DOI: 10.4324/9781003123422-20

In another study on this topic, postcolonial scholar Rob Nixon (2013) argues that the world is drowning in data, statistics and so much empirical scientific data. Instead, he suggests, together with many environmental communicators that the engaging power of storytelling is needed to promote environmental awareness around climate transformation. Some theorists together with activists from environmental action groups like 'Extinction Rebellion' are dedicated to publicising the dangers of climate change going out of control. By so doing they hope to stimulate the emergence of radical new ideas/attitudes and to ensure that new environmental politics achieve greater legitimacy and hopefully become the norm.

Case Study – Tipping Point in Media Coverage of Climate Change: Audiences Analysis

Media coverage of international science-based climate-change conferences for instance can influence general public opinion, alongside various other forms of engagement (Flora et al., 2014). Nonetheless, media power and its effects remain a contested area of investigation and is generally considered highly dependent on individual predispositions or psychological motivations (Nisbet et al. 2013). In particular, personal ideological and political differences seem to coincide with a variation of beliefs about climate change (McCreight and Dunlap 2011). Such cognitions, alongside more general value orientations have been found to determine levels of scepticism in the population, but also can signal more active engagement with climate-change concerns (Corner et al. 2014). Climate-change scepticism across many studies has been identified in particular as a strong barrier towards securing support for mitigation policies, alongside carbon-reducing activities (Engels et al. 2013).

According to Wonneberger et al. (2019), factors that help distinguish and categorise American beliefs around climate change, include foregrounded attitudes and bespoke behaviours relating to such concerns, alongside inherent global warming beliefs, issue involvement, policy preferences and, of course, recognising audiences on the ground and evaluating their explicit behaviour patterns. The type and strength of motivation in response to climate change has often been found to vary, especially due to individual differences and contextual factors (e.g. Flynn et al. 2017). For instance, marrying strong attitudes with high levels of knowledge and involvement can trigger defence motivations, which help reinforce these predispositions (Strickland et al. 2011). Alternatively, negative forms of issue engagement can trigger defensive motivation, leading to a disconfirmation bias (Kunda 1990).

Furthermore, as uncovered in other behavioural studies, part of the less engaged, young or student cohort, much less many other sections of society, might not change their beliefs, attitudes, or intentions, or at least do so in a negative direction (Flora et al. 2014). All of these tensions serve to indicate a mix of indifference and reinforcement of pre-existing negative attitudes towards environmental issues (Wonneberger et al. 2016: 179).

As a rule of thumb, comparing information seeking behaviour across climate-change issues, audiences segments has revealed that more engaged segments of the population tend to be actively looking for information about climate change (Metag et al. 2017; Roser-Renouf et al. 2015). Nonetheless, the less engaged may also unfortunately be the least inclined to pay attention to media coverage about the issue, rendering potentially effective situations of high exposure to climate-change information less likely (Wonneberger et al. 2016: 180). Based on the theory of motivated reasoning, Wonneberger et al. concluded that the extent of such media effects may differ for more or less engaged audiences segments. Their unsurprising findings further indicate that media effects are clearly segment-specific and also that exposure to event-specific media coverage mainly evokes defensive motivations. These tendencies appear to confirm the common-sense view that media coverage of climate change mainly reinforces pre-existing attitudes and do not necessarily produce a tipping point for transformational change (e.g. Wonneberger et al. 2016: 187).

Still much of the behavioural research supports clear and balanced solutions that dramatise the long-term greater good for *all* citizens, as we strive to tackle our global existential climate crisis. Note, ongoing assessment of the relative influence and power of media alongside explicit communication campaigns, together with assessing behavioural responses, preoccupy a number of entries across this student-centred volume.

References

Corner, A., Markowitz, E. and Pidgeon, N. 'Public Engagement with Climate Change: The Role of Human Values'. *WIREs Climate Change* 5(3): 411–422. 2014.

Engels, A., Hüther, O., Schäfer, M. and Held, H. 'Public Climate-change Skepticism, Energy Preferences and Political Participation'. *Global Environmental Change* 23(5): 1018–1027. 2013.

Flora, J.A., Saphir, M., Lappé, M., Roser-Renouf, C., Maibach, E.W. and Leiserowitz, A.A. 'Evaluation of a National High School Entertainment Education Program: The Alliance for Climate Education'. *Climatic Change* 127(3–4): 419–434. 2014.

Flynn, D.J., Nyhan, B. and Reifler, J. 'The Nature and Origins of Misperceptions: Understanding False and Unsupported Beliefs about Politics'. *Political Psychology* 38: 127–150. 2017.

Kunda, Z. 'The Case for Motivated Reasoning'. *Psychological Bulletin* 108(3): 480–498. 1990.

McCright, A.M. and Dunlap, R.E. 'The Politicization of Climate Change and Polarization in the American Public's Views of Global Warming, 2001–2010'. *Sociological Quarterly* 52(2): 155–194. 2011.

Metag, J., Füchslin, T. and Schäfer, M.S. 'Global Warming's Five Germanys: A Typology of Germans' Views on Climate Change and Patterns of Media Use and Information'. *Public Understanding of Science* 26(4): 434–451. 2017.

Nisbet, E.C., Hart, P.S., Myers, T. and Ellithorpe, M. 'Attitude Change in Competitive Framing Environments? Open-/closed-mindedness, Framing Effect, and Climate Change'. *Journal of Communication* 63(4): 766–785. 2013.

Nixon, Rob. *Slow Violence and the Environmentalism of the Poor.* Harvard University Press 2013.

Roser-Renouf, C., Stenhouse, N., Rolfe-Redding, J., Maibach, E. and Leiserowitz, A. 'Engaging Diverse Audiences with Climate Change: Message Strategies for Global Warming's Six Americas' (368–386). In Hansen, A. and Cox, R. (eds) *The Routledge Handbook of Environment and Communication.* Routledge 2015.

Strickland, A.A., Taber, C.S. and Lodge, M. 'Motivated Reasoning and Public Opinion'. *Journal of Health Politics, Policy and Law* 36(6): 935–944. 2011.

Wonneberger, Anke, Meijers, Marijn and Schuck, Anderas. 'Shifting Public Engagement: How Media Coverage of Climate Change Conferences affect climate change audience segments'. *Public Understanding of Science PUS* 29(2): 176–193. 2016. https://journals.sagepub.com/doi/full/10.1177/0963662519886474

Transdisciplinary Research (TDR) and Environmental Communication

Transdisciplinary Research became popular from the 1970s, focusing on the integration of knowledge from different science disciplines and (non-academic) stakeholder communities to help address complex societal challenges. In particular as a result of the pandemic of 2020/21, science from every angle was used in the fight against the virus. Scientific data, information and expertise from different domains and different countries needs to be integrated and unified to help actively inform and drive global policy makers. Of course, as global economies ebb and flow or go into meltdown, difficult choices have to be made that balance public health together with economic imperatives. At its most basic, trust between science, policy makers and citizens remain critical in assessing these often difficult choices and TDR can be considered as an essential tool for building and maintaining trust, while ensuring the longer-term suitability and effectiveness of mitigation measures.

As an OECD report (OECD 2020) affirms, TDR provided a powerful mechanism for combining different branches of knowledge and practice to develop the social and technological solutions that were used during the extended 'response and recovery' phases of the global reaction to COVID-19. Such transdisciplinary initiatives are needed even more for the greater challenges of our climate emergency.

Furthermore, the Executive Summary of this OECD report reiterates this conclusion, citing the impacts of global warming, biodiversity loss, natural disasters, economic migration and health pandemics. All of these concerns are manifest at multiple scales and constantly require both technological and social innovations. In order to achieve such a multi-lateral response, different scientific disciplines, including natural and social sciences, alongside humanities (SSH) need to work together and fully engage with other public and private sector actors, including of course policy makers, to both map out and uncover workable solutions. Most certainly, finding solutions to complex societal challenges, such as those embedded in the Sustainable Development Goals (SDGs), cannot to be generated or based solely on isolated disciplinary research, but require a broad approach to addressing very difficult scenarios while planning for a precarious future.

Challenges remain around how to select and effectively engage with so many disciplinary actors, while ethical considerations concerning managing such broad-ranging engagement continue to dominate debate. This 2020 report lays out some useful recommendations for governments who in turn ought to promote transdisciplinary and multidisciplinary research and provide resources to maintain various long-term connections, alongside working with research funders, universities and other stakeholders. Addressing societal challenges, using co-creation of research and knowledge, calls attention to new modes of best practice, which are becoming an essential framework in facing up to major environmental challenges, especially involving the wicked problems of climate change.

References

OECD. 'Addressing Societal Challenges using Transdisciplinary Research'. Policy Paper, no. 88 June 2020. https://www.oecd.org/science/addressing-societal-challenges-using-transdisciplinary-research-0ca0ca45-en.htm

U

Utopian Environmental Messaging: Lessons from Hollywood and Guides to Young People

Utopianism can be broadly defined as the desire for a better way of living expressed in the description of a different kind of society which makes possible an alternative and more positive way of life. In *Hollywood Utopia: Ecology in Contemporary American Cinema* (2005), I argued for the power of utopian narratives to speak to and for an environmental agenda. Focusing on science fiction, westerns, road movies and various other forms of nature-based representations, I suggested that especially within so-called 'feel-good' utopian storylines, individual heroes and protagonists strove to 'do the right thing' for the environmental common good. The potency of an ecological agenda shone through and helped audiences to recognise a dream of human nature in harmony with the environment, which was both therapeutic and, in many ways, educative, instilling a renewed love of nature (biophilia) and a greater sense of environmental literacy. As Bryan Norton affirms, such audio-visual modes of environmental learning seek to educate the public 'to see problems from a synoptic, contextual perspective' (1991: xi).

This early study of utopian narratives in film together with later eco-filmic scholarship has contributed to a strategy of building bridges and creating cross-connections between other academic disciplines, including Literature, Geography, Philosophy, Anthropology, Feminism and Cultural studies. So much criticism of utopian evocations of environmental agency concentrates specifically on the dangers of excessive idealism. Of course utopian representation is frequently dovetailed and contrasted with its dystopic alternative; as evident within environmental readings of science fictional tales from *Dark City* (1998), *Blade Runner* (1982), *The Fifth Element* (1997), *Jurassic Park* (1993) and *Waterworld* (1995), to more contemporary tales such as *Avatar* (2009), all of which are extensively analysed, from both an environmental, utopian and dystopic perspective (see Brereton 2005).

Uncovering hope, much less utopian values from within the complex environmental climate crisis is certainly challenging and environmental messaging has to be careful not to indulge simply in new forms of greenwashing

DOI: 10.4324/9781003123422-21

or idle dreaming, when so much heavy lifting around political, economic and social change making is badly needed. Recalling for instance the struggle for race equality – remembering back to the iconic Martin Luther King's 'I have a dream' speech (1963) – one can suggest that to effectively mobilise public opinion, audiences crave positive hopeful messages, which ought to be balanced of course with the urgent reality of our climate crisis. This is evident within various documentaries and other media artifacts highlighted in this volume, ranging from David Attenborough's oeuvre, to more positive messaging for young people, such as Damon Gameau's 2019 utopian environmental parable *2040*.

Greta Thunberg's short biography *I am Greta* (2020) and so many other mediated iterations of her environmental struggle also dovetails with her well-considered but stark (utopian) dream calling on us all to face up to the challenges of the environmental crisis, while pronouncing 'our house is on fire'. From young people's Friday Marches, to Extinction Rebellion, together with other environmental activist movements that have come to the fore in the last few years, a hopeful revolution and transformation of global movements and thinking appears to be in the ascendent. Utopian dreaming is often mixed up with real, hard-edged polemical critique, while at the same time helping to encourage (young) people to stand up for their environmental rights. By any measure, doing the right thing concerning the whole planet has to be the number one priority.

Utopian dreaming is certainly not just in the clouds, as evidenced by a very useful new volume for younger children by an Irish fictional writer Oisin McGann, titled *A Short, Hopeful Guide to Climate Change* (2021). Its blurb on the back announces:

> It's a story about our civilisation and our environment, about wildfires and glaciers, war and wilderness. It's about tiny ocean creatures, giant machines and teenagers protesting on city streets. It's about climate change and the millions of people who are already taking action to do something about it.

This very well-conceived and up-to-date volume does not in any way patronise its younger audiences with saccharine pronouncements concerning our inherent love of nature. It pulls no punches with regards to the importance of agriculture for Ireland for example. McGann affirms,

> because food and water and the land that provides them are so important, nations put a lot of effort into keeping control of them. And when there's a shortage of these things, well … that's when we start fighting over them.
>
> (2021: 116)

After laying out all the major environmental issues in a logical and coherent manner, the book concludes with a short chapter titled 'Reasons for Hope', highlighting the huge innovations humans have made with regards to travel and the eradication of smallpox, not to mention the hole in the ozone layer, and the very quick and efficient introduction of vaccines to protect humanity against COVID-19.

McGann concludes, 'you are part of this story' and affirms:

> We are part of a thin skin of life around a ball of rock, floating in space. Our control over our environment made us powerful; it allowed us to become the most advanced creatures on the planet. But for too long, we've been getting ahead of ourselves, charging forward so fast that we can't see where we're going. Now it's time to recognise what it took to get us here, the price the Earth has paid, and to start putting more thought into our futures.
>
> It's time to take better care of our world. It's fragile, complicated and majestic…
>
> And it's the only one we have.

(213–214)

Utopian, much less simply pro-social polemical messaging across all media, including audio-visual storytelling, as well as young people's teacherly texts, have a part to play in helping humanity to face up to the enormous challenges of climate change, while at the same time keeping all our dreams alive.

References

Brereton, Pat. *Hollywood Utopia: Ecology in Contemporary American Cinema.* Intellect 2005.

McGann, Oisin. *A Short Hopeful Guide to Climate Change.* Little Island Books 2021.

Norton, Brian. *Towards Unity Among Environmentalists.* Oxford University Press 1991.

V

Veganism and Promoting Environmental Values Through Celebrity Endorsement

Veganism involves people eating no food derived from animals, including meat, fish or dairy products, while vegetarianism simply involves eating no meat products. Both forms of food consumption are better for the planet and tend to result in less carbon emissions overall. The lifestyle involving green food consumption is however less prevalent than one might think. For instance, it is estimated that in the UK, less than 1% of the population are vegan, with 2% vegetarian (The Vegan Society 2014). Meanwhile, in the USA approximately 2.5% of the population are vegan and 2.5% vegetarian. One would hope such figures are increasing and it should be noted more adopt a partial vegetarian diet. Of course, many so-called developing large nations like India and African countries maintain a more vegetarian-based, sustainable diet. From a Western perspective especially, to adequately address our climate crisis, more people need to move to a vegetarian or a vegan diet, supporting the future sustainability of our planet. Furthermore, varying diets has become an issue in populous regions like China and other developing parts of the world, where the more affluent classes are adopting a meat-based Western diet.

Achieving such a transformation in diet remains an uphill struggle, as Cole and Morgan (2011: 5) for instance reveal in a powerful set of anti-vegan discourses that routinely frame vegans as self-denying, ridiculous, faddish and hostile – a reflection of the hostility that vegans regularly encounter from non-vegans. The researchers also found that women are the targets of both anti-vegan and sexist discourses, using tactics that present vegans (and women) as over-sensitive and even somewhat irrational. This regressive mode of stereotypical gendering responses is similar to that of vegetarianism, where for instance eating meat is equated with (full-blooded – excuse the pun!) heterosexual masculinity (Nath 2011). Vegan food consumption certainly has an uphill struggle, both perceptually and in mobilising support on the ground, towards building global consensus around a move to encouraging fewer meat-eating diets across the world; an environmental struggle, which the most

DOI: 10.4324/9781003123422-22

powerful farming industries, as expected, would lobby against, since it pulls against the continuous growth of dairy and meat production.

Nonetheless, somewhat surprisingly, it was announced that 'high-end vegan cuisine' became one of the Top Ten food trends back in 2013, marking a shift in media representations of vegan food from dull to desirable. Supporting this slow building trend is the rise in the number and profile of celebrities who have adapted a vegan diet – including Al Gore, Bill Clinton, Ellen DeGeneres, Natalie Portman, Mike Tyson and for 22 high, media-profile days, Beyonce and even Jay-Z. Such high-profile celebrity endorsement, according to analysis by environmental scholar Julie Doyle (2016), needs to be ramped up further and can signal how central emotional appeals are targeting viewers' self-interest, together with their moral sense of social and ecological responsibility for the planet.

Probably the most famous documentary example supporting non-meat eating remains *Cowspiracy* (2014), which was funded via personal and crowdfunding sourcing. Picked up by Netflix due to the involvement of Leonardo DiCaprio, it became highly successful online and across the world (see Brereton 2019: 66–68). Furthermore, see also Kip Anderson and Keegan Kuhn's vegan advocacy film *What the Health* (2017), which can be viewed on Netflix, while Jonathan Safron Foer's book *Eating Animals* (2009) is frequently cited as a cause of lifestyle change in eating patterns for many people in the Western world.

But of course there are numerous problems with celebrity endorsement, as highlighted by Doyle, who explores the celebrity culture logics, which make it more marketable with new forms of lifestyle practices, all the while recognising the over-gendering of veganism as a predominantly female preserve. Elsewhere, environmental literary scholar Alexa Weik von Mossner, recognises a clear utopian preoccupation within many vegan films like Marc Pierschel's *The End of Meat* (2017) and Liz Marshall's *Meat the Future* (2020), both of which look forward to a better time when consumers no longer need to torture and kill animals, but instead can keep eating our beloved (albeit cultured GMO) meat. Her analysis affirms that such films appear a little naïve in their approach and probably the researcher is correct in calling for more irony and irreverent humour across all levels of environmental representations, to more effectively speak to a wider strata of the general population and society.

Meanwhile, Doyle affirms how veganism offers an important critique of unethical and unsustainable food productive practices, yet at the same time illustrates how vegans have been historically stigmatised in mainstream media as being 'too extreme or even [seen as] terrorists'. Given the recent prominence of celebrity vegans, one might question how the cultural intermediary work of vegan celebrities might make the ethical practice of veganism more accessible. Doyle brings together philosophies of ethical veganism and ecofeminism with various literature on ethical (food) consumption and celebrity culture, to help analyse the educational campaigning work on veganism.

Overall, it is affirmed that such ethics end up being reworked through the 'commodity logic of celebrity culture to make it more marketable and thus consumable as a set of ideas and gendered lifestyle practices, where the individual choice is designed to be healthy and kind' (Doyle 2016: 777).

Public celebrities frequently present veganism as a diet and lifestyle choice that foregrounds an ethics of care, compassion, kindness and emotion that is consistent with ethical veganism (cited in Doyle 2016). Nonetheless, this general individual behavioural approach is reworked through the 'commodity logic of celebrity [and] is exploited as a mode of production in the service of marketing ends' (cited in Driessens 2013). Hence, celebrity culture expects a return on their investment, which of course often remains the bottom-line rationale. Such investment can sometimes however backfire and not necessarily assist the overall environmental movement, as suggested through a cogent critique of the American celebrity Ellen DeGeneres (Doyle 2016: 16).

Reminiscent of all aspects of celebrity endorsement of climate-change issues, relying on celebrities to promote a vegan or vegetarian lifestyle, can unfortunately end up being counter-productive and not necessarily increase overall public transformation. I would nonetheless suggest that at least putting such sustainable modes of consumption and environmental issues on the media agenda remains a good start – as further illustrated in the Green-washing Lite entry cited elsewhere – while striving to pivot towards greater awareness around vegetarian or vegan food consumption, in striving to achieve a low-carbon food and sustainable resource-based future.

References

Brereton, Pat. *Environmental Literacy and New Digital Audiences*. Routledge 2019.
Cole, Matthew and Morgan, Karen. 'Vegaphobia: Derogatory Discourses of Speciesism in UK National Paper'. *British Journal of Sociology*. 2011.
Doyle, Julia. 'Celebrity Veganism and the Lifestyling of Ethical Consumption'. *Environmental Communication* 10(6): 777–790. 2016.
Driessens, Oliver. 'The Celebration of Society and Culture: Understanding the Structural Dynamics of Celebrity Culture'. *International Journal of Cultural Studies* 16 (6): 641–657. 2013. https://core.ac.uk/download/pdf/19578455.pdf
Nath, Jemal. 'Gendered Fare? A Qualitative Investigation of Alternative Food and Masculinities'. *Journal of Sociology* 7: 261–278. 2011.
The Vegan Society. 'The Vegan Society Anniversary Ripened by Human Determination: 70 Years of the Vegan Society'. 2014. https://www.vegansociety.com/sites/default/files/uploads/Ripened%20by%20human%20determination.pdf
Weik von Mossner, Alexa. 'Screening Veganism: The Production, Rhetoric and Reception of Vegan Advocacy Film'. In Wright, Laura. ed. *Routledge Handbook of Vegan Studies*. Routledge 2021.

W

Water Documentaries as Public Service Announcement (PSA) – Irish Water Conflict

As a growing body of literature illustrates, there are increasing tensions over the best or the most appropriate way to effectively communicate complex environmental risk scenarios, coupled with taking into account their economic implications. Potential tensions and obstacles broadly range from the dangers of preaching and pontificating, as against striving to promote more interactive and dialogical modes of address, where sometimes the message, revolving around water security, or any form of waste for that matter gets constantly diluted by the media machine.

By all accounts there often are deeply engrained tensions in communicating messages around conservation and water in particular; ranging from considering water as a scarce and precious commodity, or alternatively as being a natural right for all to have free and open access to as part of a basic human right and a part of global citizenship. These somewhat contradictory values and understandings, recalling the essential nature of such life-giving liquid, varies across the world, depending on whether water is defined as an essentially scarce resource that needs to be fought over, or alternatively is perceived as being free and easily accessible across the regions.

All of which serve to affect our varying understanding and (political) appreciation of various types of natural resources from soil to water. The necessity for instance of nationalising such essential natural resources have become a big decision, and is against favouring the privatising and monetising of water supplies, albeit promoting extreme forms of neo-liberal and corporate governance. Alternatively, embracing water as a precious natural (and free) resource, but one which needs constant resource management and support is also open to dispute. This remains the preferred approach of many environmentalists across the political spectrum, whether its dealing with water, energy or any other natural resource for that matter, all of which are essential for the maintenance of human life.

Water remains a primary source of life on planet earth and is a focus for much environmental communication. In certain parts of the world, both the

DOI: 10.4324/9781003123422-23

quality and quantity of water is poor and inadequate for human survival, while in other regions water and rainfall is less of an immediate problem, while sometimes leading to flooding and other related disturbances. How to communicate these various environmental tensions, while effectively creating messages around how water is an essential element for human survival, remains an ongoing conundrum. Highlighting the central importance of water, short, dedicated documentaries designed as Public Service Announcements (many of which have been developed by water authorities across the world) have become popular with mass audiences and are frequently uploaded onto freely available platforms like YouTube for audiences to discover and enjoy.

In a specific exploration of Ireland as a case study, a region usually has abundant natural precipitation, investment in water infrastructure unfortunately has been severely lacking over the years. Furthermore, water security and long-term development of infrastructure has remained a very difficult environmental debate, which has been complicated by specific local historical contexts. Most notably, an EU-driven edict to monitor and tax water supplies to Irish homes backfired, in part because of a communications failure (Clinch et al. 2018). This cautionary environmental case study ought to be fully examined and appreciated by students from across the world, while striving to address the environmental and educative agenda around securing and managing precious water resources into the future (see Bresnihan et al. 2019).

Polling data from the 2016 Irish General Election, highlighted how the introduction of such controversial water charges had a huge impact on voter behaviour at the time. The poll showed that water charges surprisingly was the fourth highest issue influencing first-preference votes amongst those polled. Basically, the previous government attempts to introduce water charges as part of a range of austerity measures that was backed by the European Union, following the global financial crash of 2008 was not accepted by the majority of the public. The subsequent water charges demonstrations created a major social movement, which succeeded in mobilising resistance by large numbers of people from across the socio-political spectrum.

The success of this movement in fighting the introduction of water charges can probably be explained by the failure of the government at the time, coupled with the unfortunate timing of events. A 2018 academic report by Peter Clinch and Anne Pender cited a number of broadly based reasons for failure. These included conflicting beliefs regarding perceptions of water as a human right and reduced levels of public trust in government and public institutions, both internationally and in Ireland, while being damaged by the fallout from the economic crash; personal values of water consumers; as well as how the charges were alternatively framed by government and protesters, and most notably the unfortunate timing of the charges coming on the back of a long period of economic austerity following the financial crash.

Water charges were first mooted during the so-called 'Celtic Tiger' era when there was major economic growth and expansion back in 2002; a period when everyone appeared to be in a 'credit bubble frenzy' and conversations tended to be about the value of domestic property and going on more foreign holidays. However, to even envisage introducing such charges, after the 2008 financial crash was by any measure a high-risk strategy. Basically, it was (rightly) perceived that the general public were forced to bail out the banks, who helped cause the crisis in the first place and thereby had to take on so much austerity for years to come. Consequently, calling for another water charge/tax, especially one that was being insisted on as part of an EU edict, was regarded by many as simply too much to swallow. Like much policy and tax innovation across government, much less dealing with the cost of the climate emergency, timing unfortunately is everything.

Direct address and full explanation of such issues need to be mediated, developed and extended at all levels, while announcing such a contentious political and environmental issue. In particular the resultant focus on austerity in Ireland and elsewhere, encouraged the framing of all forms of politics, including those around the development of water charges, as pulling against the well-formed ethical principle of the polluter, paying for their natural resources, and most especially any unnecessary waste was called into question. Meanwhile, such charges and their justification were endorsed by many environmentalists on the ground. Such well-founded environmental logic however did not appear to chime within this difficult political and economic period. By any measure, this was 'the straw that broke the camel's back' and appealing to raw civil rights and injustice became a popular refrain in fighting against this so-called environmental tax. Consequently, the governmental communication machine was at odds with the media process of narrating and explaining the unexpected popular response against any form of water charges. Furthermore, the somewhat irrational negation of the 'polluter pays' principle that underpin much environmental belief, was by all accounts out of kilter with the public mood and was perceived as a lost cause.

All of this very local conflict over water charges provoked extensive and well-organised demonstrations, leading to the majority of elected politicians caving into public disquiet and all but concurring with the proposition that citizens should not have to pay separate taxes for water, as mandated by EU regulations. Some activists have argued that this remains a victory for democracy, nonetheless the under-invested water system has to be paid for somehow (see Bresnihan et al. 2019). Alternatively, across the rest of Europe and elsewhere, it would appear that citizens more readily support separate taxes for water treatment of all kinds and even appear to have a greater acceptance of various forms of balanced environmental regulation.

By any measure the aborted introduction of water charges in Ireland was a communications disaster and the government's strategy and policy proposal, as deployed initially at least, was certainly not fit for purpose. The outdated Public Service Announcements (PSA) approach discussed below of providing public information using a 'science deficit' model of communication and outlining a clear rationale for its implementation did not work towards mobilising, much less legitimatising, public buy-in, together with the growth of a much needed consensus for water protection and security. This followed a constant backfooting strategy used simply towards justifying the decision that was already made (in Europe). As already insinuated, political researchers have explored how the (radical) Left successfully mobilised public support using the water charge debacle with great success. While other critics question if more conspiratorial influencers were deployed throughout this hugely influential grassroots movement, resulting in a complete turnaround by the political establishment, following the 2016 General Election.

In any case, the government appeared to have been out-manoeuvred by a collective grassroots effort in mobilised support for resistance across all socio-economic and political classes. The clear message is that environmental issues and their media communication – be that paying for water resources, or some other environmental initiative for that matter – has to be always married with and underpinned by an economic and social justice rationale. Meanwhile, all of these tensions and apparent conflicts have to be carefully communicated and messaged appropriately, if citizen consensus is to be mobilised and hopefully secured.

Water remains essential for human and all forms of life, yet safe drinking water shockingly remains a very limited resource, as evident across many so-called developing countries in particular. Critical to fighting the global water crisis are public awareness campaigns, including public service announce-ments, which assist in calling attention to a number of these related environ-mental concerns. While for instance the YouTube platform that currently houses so many promotional water documentaries has become a popular medium for disseminating such prosocial content, environmental commu-nication efforts embodied in these short presentations and campaigns remains largely under-investigated and not always analysed with regards to their overall effectiveness (Krajewski et al. 2017: 1).

Most crudely, environmental communications students can see how this global water crisis is conceptualised as two distinct, yet interconnected envir-onmental difficulties and problems, namely those related to water quantity and water quality. Regarding quantity, on a global level people use freshwater at twice the population-growth rate overall, resulting in a critical shortage of the supply necessary to meet current needs (Solomen 2011). Regarding quantity, thousands of children die daily from waterborne diseases (WHO/ UNICEF 2015). Yet nearly 10% of these global diseases could be prevented by simply improving sanitation infrastructure and using better management of water resources (Barry and Hughes 2008).

Environmental communication research most specifically highlights the important role that mass media play in shaping public understanding of environmental issues, including most importantly the growing need for water (Ho et al 2013). Furthermore, water's global environmental importance stretches further than its biological functions, referencing gender equality, economic progress, social well-being, and national security and political strife, which are all underpinned by water (Bigas 2012). Some of these debates and tensions can be further explained through an examination of information-driven water documentaries.

Case Study – Water Public Service Announcement (PSA)

Short promotional and informational documentaries are frequently found as part of a growing repository on the YouTube platform. So-called PSAs are defined as short (30 seconds to 2-minute) televised advertisements sponsored or produced by governmental agencies and non-governmental organisations 'to draw attention to important social issues and promote socially desirable attitudes and behaviours' (Kononova and Yuan 2015; Waters and Jones 2011). Promoting prosocial behaviour through PSAs are especially advantageous because of their ability to efficiently disseminate messages to widespread audiences, similar to extended advertisements across the media spectrum (Bator and Cialdini 2000).

Scholarship however is unfortunately limited in the area of media content analysis and especially with regards to an examination of attitudinal impacts on audiences and consumers of such on-line media. Searls (2010) for instance found that emotional appeals significantly influence the environmental attitudes of PSA viewers. While only one study specifically addressed environmental PSAs hosted on YouTube, concluding that the congruence of PSA messages with surrounding advertisements was associated positively with video recall, but negatively with attitudes towards the videos (Kononova and Yuan 2015 cited in Krajewski et al. 2017: 3). Unpacking and extending such tentative findings which have implications for all forms of audio-visual environmental media requires more empirical and longitudinal audience investigation across this growing area of media production and analysis of online reception.

The YouTube platform provides PSA producers, among other media providers, free access to billions of viewers from around the world, without the time, cost implications or forward planning required for mainstream media distribution. Consequently, to effectively transmit environmental messages through an open access medium and portal, this mode of transmission ought to be fully recognised and embraced as part of a broad environmental communications media strategy. As the global water crisis continues to get worse, even in so-called advanced economies where investment in water infrastructure has been under threat, more concerted efforts need to be taken by environmental communicators to raise awareness of this ongoing crisis and ultimately help persuade politicians, stakeholders and citizens generally to step up and take appropriate action.

Specifically, calling on the need for environmental communicators and mass media to support tipping points for change and transformation, one can take comfort through examples such as those which have highlighted the proliferation of plastics polluting our oceans. In a popular episode of *Blue*

Planet 11 (BBC, originally broadcast on November 2017), the doyen of environmental communications and nature documentary David Attenborough, (who single-handedly commands bigger audiences than the most successful reality-TV programme on television), devoted a small section of an early episode in the series to addressing the long-term consequences of plastics being literally dumped in our oceans, while outlining the catastrophic effects this is having on our fish and ocean habitats generally. There was an immediate and global response to the issue, which continues to the present day, with various political and policy initiatives been developed in its wake. For instance in the UK 'Waitrose and Partners' (Siddique 2018) talk of an 800% increase in questions from customers about plastics, which they believe can be directly linked to the documentary, not to mention various other PSAs dealing with the topic. Certainly more low-key new imaginaries and visualisations of water abuse and pollution can over time further assist in influencing audience awareness and promoting greater environmental (water or plastic) literacy, hopefully leading to behavioural change.

Krajewski et al. (2017) suggest that current water-related PSA's often do convey our susceptibility to the water crisis, but would benefit from more efficacy-based messaging to ensure viewers' acceptance of the overall message. While of course such PSA's can never be considered in isolation, much less construed as a silver bullet, constituting a total communication strategy or package, nonetheless together with nature documentaries and other audio-visual media output, PSAs can provide a useful spark in the ongoing struggle to promote water awareness. Such nuanced messaging formats and protocols need to be culturally and regionally coded and modulated, helping to take into consideration the broad range of diverse stakeholders, cultures and communities that often display different levels of water concern for the future, across different countries and at the same time call upon variable levels of knowledge and engagement with such perennial issues.

Describing a lack of message certainty, viewpoint diversity, together with scientific evidence, Hurlimann and Dolnicar (2012) concludes that newspaper reportage, for instance, in Australia may 'work against public engagement in water issues and undermine the public's understanding of and confidence in water management measures (6497). While other studies across the globe have criticised the lack of water-related newspaper and press coverage, much less further audio-visual coverage, except during times of severe weather crisis (Altaweel and Bone 2012). It would appear that globally there is a shortage of corresponding scientific expert opinion, much less a concerted mediated space for promoting greater forms of 'water literacy' within this coverage (Wei et al. 2015). YouTube and other online platforms can assist at least in some ways to fill this dangerous vacuum.

Assessing how such media reporting dovetails or transfers onto the audio-visual and narrative-driven portals of YouTube, while at the same time avoiding the danger of top-down scientific delivery of information – echoing the so-called 'Deficit Model' of communication – remains subject to investigation. Emerging health and general science communication research has recently begun to focus on exploring the use of online videos and examining their content, sponsors, characteristics and effectiveness, alongside their use of health and behavioural strategies (Briones et al. 2015). But much more communication analysis is needed to uncover the most effective aesthetic strategies required towards promoting effective environmental communication, drawing on work done on health and other areas of investigation through these short vignettes together with more conventional audio-visual documentaries.

Most explicitly it would appear there is a prescient danger of 'over-stressing fearful messages'. Scholarly research is given over to explaining conflicting findings in the literature around fear appeals (Witte 1992). According to many scholars, to be effective a message using fear needs to have information addressing four components: severity, susceptibility, self-efficacy, and response efficacy. Susceptibility is the likelihood of being at risk, simply for a negative consequence. Research shows that people are most likely to adopt recommended behaviours to protect themselves against a threat, when perceptions of both threat and efficacy are high (Witte and Allen 2000). If a message however elicits a higher perceived threat than its perceived efficacy, message rejection can occur (Witte 1992). For instance, when audiences did not expect global water crisis, PSAs designed to exclusively contain fear appeals can consequently become valuable in supporting a variety of emotional appeals (Lewis, et al. 2013).

Most notably some other studies illustrate that visual representation of data, especially when integrated with text through infographics, can promote increased active engagement. Such research thereby calls into question studies that relegate visual cues to simply facilitate peripheral processing only. Nonetheless, all of these approaches are important to take on board when evaluating the inherently visual nature of documentaries, including these water videos posted on YouTube (Krajewski et al. 2017: 5).

Coincidentally, a larger study of climate change messages by O'Neill and Nicholson-Cole (2009) found that such messages help capture attention and generate a sense of issue importance by using dramatic, shocking, or scary images of water shortage. At the same time – as the literature demonstrates and is further outlined in an analysis of behavioural media entries in this volume – this approach can exacerbate feelings of helplessness due to a lack of solution-focused elements. These complex and often contradictory research findings make it difficult however to make clear communication judgements, regarding the most effective strategies to implement across various scenarios.

In conclusion, the average American, alongside other populations across the broadly defined Western world, all appear less immediately concerned with water, much less with longer term worries over climate change, as they (unconsciously at least) believe that it will probably more directly affect the poor and marginal communities in developing regions, living within precarious habitats and inadequate infrastructure. Meanwhile, again at least unconsciously, richer and more mobile citizens and communities, who have greater financial and other resources at hand, believe that they can escape from the ill-effects of flooding, as well as heat, together with the devastation caused by hurricanes and freezing temperatures.

Essentially, because many citizens only need to turn on one of the multiple water taps (faucets) in their home for unlimited access to safe, clean drinking water, many wonder why all the fuss! Consequently, environmental communicators recognise that there is a distinct lack of appreciation of the environmental dilemma, much less motivation for individuals across the so-called 'First World' in particular to even think about water, much less change their current broadly unsustainable (and very wasteful) habits.

Hence, the common use of scientific metrics around scarce resource management of water and other natural resources, which are also used in climate change scientific media coverage, coupled with fear tactics regarding environmental concerns, often fail as an effective communication strategy, especially across wealthy middle-class and privileged stakeholder communities. Environmental communication efforts to bring a number of vital concerns and long-term natural resource tensions and tipping points around climate change to the forefront of world consciousness, does not appear to have been successful in the main. Consequently, it is more important than ever to continue to uncover novel and effective ways to communicate across current and new mass media platforms and apply this knowledge to help improve all aspects of environmental communication into the future.

References

Altaweel, M. and Bone, C. 'Applying Content Analysis for Investigating the Reporting of Water Issues'. *Computers, Environment and Urban Systems* 36(6): 599–613. 2012.

Barry, M. and Hughes, J. 'Talking Dirty — The Politics of Clean Water and Sanitation'. *New England Journal of Medicine* 359(8): 784–787. 2008.

Bator, R. and Cialdini, R. 'The Application of Persuasion Theory to the Development of Effective Proenvironmental Public Service Announcements'. *Journal of Social Issues* 56(3): 527–542. 2000.

Bigas, H. (ed.). *The Global Water Crisis: Addressing an Urgent Security Issue.* Papers for the InterAction Council, 2011–2012. UNU-INWEH 2012.

Bresnihan, Patrick, Garavan, Mark and O'Donovan, Orla (eds.). 'Special Issue on Water, anti-privatisation struggles and the commons'. *Community Development Journal* 54(1). 2019.

Briones, R., Nan, X., Madden, K. and Waks, L. 'When Vaccines Go Viral: An Analysis of HPV Vaccine Coverage on YouTube'. *Health Communication* 27(5): 478–485. 2012.

Clinch, Peter and Pender, Anne. *Water Policy Report September 2018. 'You don't miss the water till the well runs dry': An Inquiry into the factors influencing the failure of domestic water charges in Ireland.* https://www.ucd.ie/apep/t4media/UCDReporton theFailureofIrishDomesticWaterChargesFinal130918.pdf

Ho, S.S., Scheufele, D.A. and Corley, E.A. 'Factors Influencing Public Risk–benefit Considerations of Nanotechnology: Assessing the Effects of Mass Media, Interpersonal Communication, and Elaborative Processing'. *Public Understanding of Science*, 22(5): 606–623. 2013.

Hurlimann, A. and Dolnicar, S. 'Newspaper Coverage of Water Issues in Australia'. *Water Research* 46(19): 6497–6507. 2012.

Kononova, A. and Yuan, S. 'Double-dipping Effect? How Combining YouTube Environmental PSAs with Thematically Congruent Advertisements in Different Formats Affects Memory and Attitudes'. *Journal of Interactive Advertising* 15(1): 2–15. 2015.

Krajewski, Joanna M.T., Schumacher, Amy C. and Dalrymple, Kajsa E. 'Just Turn on the Faucet: A Content Analysis of PSAs About the Global Water Crisis on YouTube'. *Environmental Communication* 13(2) 255–275. 2016.

Lewis, I.M., Watson, B. and White, K.M. 'Extending the Explanatory Utility of the EPPM Beyond Fear-based Persuasion'. *Health Communication* 28(1): 84–98. 2013.

O'Neill, S. and Nicholson-Cole, S. '"Fear Won't Do It" Promoting Positive Engagement With Climate Change Through Visual and Iconic Representations'. Science Communication30(3): 355–379. 2009.

Searles, K. 'Feeling Good and Doing Good for the Environment: The Use of Emotional Appeals in Pro-environmental Public Service Announcements'. *Applied Environmental Education and Communication* 9(3): 173–184. 2010.

Siddique, Haroon. 'Waitrose Steps up Action to Remove Plastic Bags'. *The Guardian*. 15 September 2018. https://www.theguardian.com/business/2018/sep/15/waitrose-steps-up-action-to-remove-plastic-bags

Solomen, S. 'When the Well is Dry…Water Scarcity Requires Drastic Solutions'. In *Global Water Issues: A Compendium of Articles*. US Department of State, Bureau of International Information Programs. 2011. http://photos.state.gov/libraries/amgov/30145/publications-english/Global_Water_Issues.pdf

Waters, R. and Jones, P. 'Using Video to Build an Organization's Identity and Brand: A Content Analysis of Nonprofit Organizations' YouTube videos'. *Journal of Nonprofit & Public Sector Marketing*, 23: 248–268. 2011. doi:10.1080/10495142.2011.594779.

Wei, J., Wei, Y., Western, A., Skinner, D. and Lyle, C. 'Evolution of Newspaper Coverage of Water Issues in Australia During 1843–2011'. *Ambio* 44(4): 319–331. 2015.

WHO/UNICEF. *Progress on Drinking Water and Sanitation. Joint Monitoring Program Update 2015*. World Health Organization 2015.

Witte, K. 'Putting the Fear Back into Fear Appeals: The Extended Parallel Process Model'. *Communications Monographs* 59: 329–349. 1992.

Witte, K. and Allen, M. 'A Meta-analysis of Fear Appeals: Implications for Effective Public Health Campaigns'. *Health Education and Behavior* 27(5): 591–615. 2000.

Weather Documentary Scholarship: Mediating Climate Change Effects and Public Opinion

Weather media scholarship is a growing area of investigation, which feeds into developing environmental communication strategies around climate change. Recalling for example the proliferation of a growing number of so-called 'once in a generation natural disasters' like Hurricane Katrina, which have been extensively investigated by environmental media scholars. Note for instance *Extreme Weather and Global Media* (2015), edited by Julia Leyda and Diane Negra, which sets out to challenge what might be characterised as apparently a-political or neutral environmental weather representations, while critically assessing mediated documentary weather reports across international sites including India, Germany, and Japan. Contributors to the volume address key questions about the kinds of weather information that media outlets circulate, the relations such outlets have with government and non-governmental organisations, and how their coverage shapes public perceptions of and responses to disasters. These and other media studies projects call out the complexities and narrow-mindedness of much weather media, as a kind of gathering ground for structural analysis of the differences and ever-expanding inequalities in the ways that people and non-human beings are impacted by atmospheric dynamics, seismic activities and wildfires, as forces that might seem natural but are profoundly social and political in effect.

Writers from many disciplines have discussed the importance of recognising how social, political, and economic factors have enhanced the impact of hurricane-force winds in the media (Squires and Hartman 2006). These climate events have often impacted disproportionately more on lower income groups. For instance, African Americans in pre-Katrina New Orleans, Louisiana, constituted over 50% of the population, yet bore the brunt of the tragedy, as highlighted by serval media studies. In her influential collection *Old and New Media after Katrina* (2010), Negra opens with an emotive assertion that

> representations of Hurricane Katrina cannot be read outside of a neo-liberal context, marked by "New Economy" market fundamentalism, state-supported assaults on the environment, intense anti-immigration rhetoric [and] the withering role of state care for the vulnerable and various other perversions of democracy that have flourished in recent years.
> (2010: 1)

Other film and media scholars like Jennifer Fay in her book *Inhospitable World* (2019) demonstrate that weather and war have always served as foundational, yet sometimes also simply as a backdrop topic in the process of filmmaking. Drawing on examples ranging from the films of Buster Keaton to China's Three Gorges mega dam, to Antarctic exploration; Post-Katrina documentaries offer a critique of the racialised social ecological contours of disaster. Spike Lee's *When the Levees Broke: A Requiem in Four Ac*ts (2006) and the sequel *If God Is Willing* and *da Creek Don't Rise* (2010) remain affecting cases, illustrating racialised tensions embedded within environmental crises. The systemic problems these environmental documentary series also expose and focus on what researchers consider the insufficient and unequal allocation of federal funding for hydrological engineering projects, alongside the lack of federal aid for rescue operations. All of which occurred during a natural crisis when people were stranded in the flooded city of New Orleans without food or water for days and this even continued into the rebuilding phase after the catastrophe, with uneven access to health and homeowner insurance benefits, making the crisis worse for many disadvantaged communities.

Meanwhile, in another more rarefied volume *Weather as Medium: Toward a Meteorological Art* (2018), Janine Randerson explores weather driven art projects in this time of climate crisis, harkening back to works by Aotearoa-New Zealand kinetic sculptor Len Lye and Fluxus performance. The study echoes the art-based response to climate change and recalls aspects from the *Museums and Curating Exhibitions* entry in this volume. This study draws on contemporary art pieces, critiquing the way mainstream cinema has fostered humanity's perception of its own centrality and importance. 'We need to learn how to live and die in an unpredictable and increasingly inhospitable world' (11).

Weather certainly remains a touchstone for everyday conversation, which can speak to a range of contentious environmental issues. Mediated representations of weather can both mobilise and reflect these tensions and can be effectively used to garner support towards pro-active environmental action into the future. Environmental studies certainly need to learn from both the symbolic and everyday real power of weather forecasts in speaking to mass audiences and learn especially to demand more long-term climate forecasting and warnings from such a pervasive generic staple of audio-visual media.

References

Fay, Jennifer. *Inhospitable Worlds.* Oxford University Press 2019.
Leyda, Julia and Negra, Diane (ed). *Extreme Weather and Global Media.* Routledge 2015.
Negra, Diane. *Old and New Media after Katrina.* Palgrave Macmillan 2010.
Randerson, Janine. *Weather as Medium: Towards a Meteorological Art.* MIT Press 2018.
Squires, Chester and Hartman, Gregory. *There is No Such Thing as a Natural Disaster: Race, Class and Hurricane Katrina.* Routledge 2006.

Westerns Reflecting Deep Environmental Issues and Nature's Revenge – Wild River

The Hollywood western genre has long been interpreted as an explicit format that foregrounds debates around the 'tragedy of the commons' and dealing with scarce natural resources, especially with regards to land and water (see Brereton 2005). While the genre has become less popular of late, film scholars insinuate that it has morphed into science fiction, addressing new forms of colonisation, by opening up new frontiers – see for instance the *Star Wars* franchise. To illustrate its ongoing potency, some contemporary rebooting of the genre, witnessed in *Wild River* (2017), call attention to the Western's perennial power in speaking explicitly on an environmental agenda, which incidentally was also alluded to in a reading of *Brokeback Mountain* discussed elsewhere.

Written and directed by Taylor Sheridan, this modern-day western narrative is located in the permanent winter of snow and apparent silence of rural Wyoming USA. The story highlights the struggle to survive and face up to base 'animal instincts' and locals who apparently have nothing to do, but take drugs or carry out various forms of extreme violence, including rape. Cory Lambert (Jeremy Renner) is a modern-day hunter, who helps to kill the dominant animal predators like wolves who are worrying the domesticated sheep, as well as pumas and lions. Such alpha-animals of course are only doing what they do naturally, essentially training their young to kill for food. Cory accidentally discovers the body of a young native Indian girl Natalie Hansen (Kelsey Chow), who after being viciously raped, attempted to escape her tormenters by running barefoot out into the winter snow. The expert hunter has to adopt his skills to hunting human protagonists, who are breaking all the natural laws of nature.

The opening shots of the film capture the unfortunate victim *in media res*, running barefoot across the frozen and inhospitable landscape. Later, we learn how she somehow found the energy to run away from her attackers for up to six miles, before succumbing to extreme cold and exhaustion. This scene of endurance in the cold, snow-covered landscape is filmed in moonlight and appears both beautiful and eerie at the same time – similar in ways to the 'magic hour' lighting perfected in *The Revenant* (2015). The cinematography and imagery dramatises the crisp sensation of snowfall and its elemental beauty, while in the background the camera portrays the eternal majesty of the snow-covered landscape; all of which is offset by the primal human struggle for survival.

Helping to solve the enigma of the girls' death, is a lone FBI agent Jane Banner (Elisabeth Olsen) who is called into the region and does not appear to be a good fit for the job, not least having no suitable weather attire to cope with the elements. But she quickly adapts to the situation and realises that Cory is an necessary ally in their quest to hunt the killer. Probably the most clunky and jarring of scenes in the movie is an expositional one, where Cory tells of how his own daughter died, affirming that parents can never let their guard down for a moment. His personal grief with the loss of a child remains ever-present throughout the film. Nonetheless, he must re-live such traumatic experiences and engage with his relative Martin Hansen (Gill Birmingham) – who incidentally has a leading role in *Yellowstone* discussed elsewhere – and who also cannot cope with the loss of his daughter. Nonetheless, Cory coaches Martin that he must accept the pain and even embrace it if he is to retain all the memories of his beloved child. The tale revolves around an emotional saga on grief and revenge in dealing with the pain of losing a child so tragically, while also foregrounding an ecological allegory on nature's role in this tragic chain of life.

The unnatural violence of these young males, coupled with their difficult living conditions remain a most visceral mediation on cruel and vicious poverty, which takes the viewer to the edge of human experience. While nature documentaries show how lions/pumas and their cubs learn to act instinctively; the alpha predator animals in this fictional film, albeit based on real events, are similarly portrayed as almost gentle, protecting and family-loving. In turn this provokes a form of therapeutic and anthropomorphic endorsement of benevolent human values, which is evident across a growing cohort of nature programmes. Meanwhile, as in so many generic westerns focusing on human protagonists, retribution and justice must be carried out when innocent victims are attacked by fellow human beings. Revenge is the only ethical human principle or law of nature that apparently works towards bringing back balance within the generic western worldview. Having avenged a violent death, in the concluding scene Cory sits with his Indian relative, Martin and father of Natalie, in his blue and red 'death face paint' – both of them spending time grieving for their children.

Questioning such native myths and the apparent (right-wing) human need for revenge, Slavoj Zizek draws a comparison between *Blade Runner 2049* (2017) and *Wind River*. The underlying problem in both films, according to Zizek, is that of a ritual of mourning that enables us to survive such an unbearably traumatic loss. The glimmer of hope provided by the ending of the film is that Martin and Cory will be able to finally cope, through engaging in the minimal ritual of just sitting silently together (Zizek 2017: 7). The illusion around the human benefits of 'immersion into a native culture' is especially evident within such storylines. When we progress from

> the naive immersion in a ritual to its utter dismissal as something ridiculous; all of a sudden we find ourselves back in the same ritual, and the fact that we know it is all rubbish, in no way diminishes its efficacy. Can we imagine something similar taking place between a human and a replicant? A situation in which the two invent and participate in a similar empty ritual?
>
> (Zizek 2017: 8)

Wild nature (much less cyborgs or replicants, to which I would include wild animals) continue to be used and allegorised, while assisting its human inhabitants cope with the violence of life. While Zizek has a point, probably this tension is to be expected within such genres. However, if it helps sooth human pain and anxiety, while at the same time keeping the power of nature and its need for protection in the foreground, then some form of environmental learning and engagement is probably still taking place.

Facing up to climate change, at least allegorically, is reminiscent of facing up to the violence of family bereavement, which in turn cannot be cured through revenge and retribution, as Zizek and others suggest. Nature always strives to find a way, as James Lovelock and his Gaia theory illustrates.

Audiences, I believe, can pick up on the order and balance of nature that needs to be maintained for greater harmony to be restored. If the climate crisis is to be fully recognised as a real and present danger, the allegorical influence of such Western heroes, functioning as stewards and protectors of their habitat ought to be constantly co-opted by the environmental movement as a trope of pro-active learning and engagement.

References

Brereton, Pat. *Hollywood Utopia: Ecology in Contemporary American Cinema*. Intellect Press 2005.
Zizek, Slavoj. 'Blade Runner 2049: A View of Post-human Capitalism'. *The Philosophical Salon*. 30 October 2017. http://thephilosophicalsalon.com/blade-runner-2049-a-view-of-post-human-capitalism/

Wind Energy: Storytelling, Renewable Energy and Community Adaptation

Wind farms on land and most recently at sea are becoming a growing investment proposition across the EU and many parts of the world, as technological innovation and set-up costs come down. This in turn calls up tensions between the instillation, as against the more difficult public acceptance of wind turbines, alongside the adaptation of solar energy. Seeing wind energy, alongside solar power, as part of the future imagined landscape – which of course younger generations have grown up with and generally support – has taken some time to be realised across various (especially high-value tourist) regions of the world. Renewable adaptation remains a necessary trajectory for the growth of new energy landscapes, helping to secure our long-term, low-carbon transitionary future. Such renewable technologies need to be creatively integrated in the landscape and positively contrasted with more unsustainable modes of fossil-fuel production.

Extensive literature reviews across a range of disciplines – including Psychology, Media aesthetics, Environmental Science and Politics – all focus on representing various aspects of alternative energy, stimulated by the demands of facing up to radically reducing global carbon emissions. Engaging with this literature is an important first step for students towards shaping and framing a communications research agenda that supports sustainability and ensuring the future survival of our planet (See studies by Hulme 2019; Pasqualetti 2011; Weintrobe 2013).

The role of social sciences and humanities especially through communications in framing the issues and signalling effective solutions to the climate crisis cannot be underestimated. While the interrelated concerns of climate change, fossil-fuel usage, and the general drive towards low-carbon transition, is often considered as the preserve of science, technology, engineering and economics, there is a growing recognition in the academy and society generally that responding to climate change requires an equally difficult, but necessary shift in the overall human mindset and communications strategy. Determining how humanity addresses the existential risks created by its own actions, cannot be left to so-called hard sciences and engineering alone. While STEM research can develop understanding of the environment and devise new geo-engineering technologies and instruments to reduce reliance on fossil fuels, moving to a low-carbon future demands a social and political act of human transformation, as this volume constantly affirms. To address this transformational mindset, we need to recognise and call upon the power and influence of mass media to help promote such a sustainable environmental agenda, alongside beginning to understand the individual and group psychology of audience perceptions, as well as appreciating the attitudinal and behavioural triggers necessary to undertake such a radical approach to trans-global environmental adaptation.

A repivoting in the academy around all aspects of climate change mitigation and adaptation is echoed for instance in a Scottish low-carbon research project (Sterling University n.d.) focused around the centrality of storytelling in the Humanities, which provides the common denominator to base much interdisciplinary thinking, while supporting and encouraging citizen buy-in. The humanities and communications in particular recognise the pervasive power of narrative and storytelling as *the* most powerful tool in its arsenal, which can address a multiplicity of publics and potentially help change people's thinking, shape their identity, motivate action and hopefully serve to predispose the latent potential of citizens across the world to actively influence future events. Recent scholarship within climate change and eco-film study for instance has endorsed the notion that extending our imaginative capacity is crucial towards devising more effective ways of representing, understanding and even promoting action (see Brereton, 2019). Through a broad range of promotional and powerful narratives – across various media formats, including journalism, broadcast media, film, as well as the proliferation of online platforms – complex environmental issues can be brought into focus and pulled together in ways that have deep social and cultural resonance. Furthermore, such narrative structures can assist by becoming more concrete, meaningful, accessible and resonant for decision-makers and ordinary citizens alike. This phenomenon is exemplified through analysis of renewable energy projects and their mediation, as explored in textual analysis projects such as 'Irish Energy Landscapes' (Brereton and Barrios O'Neill 2021).

Close interdisciplinary collaboration with STEM research is needed especially to bring together differing understandings of key environmental themes, using enticing meta-narratives for global audiences to connect with. Evaluating for instance how different Irish stories present the core environmental issues involved in making the transition to a low-carbon society, which in turn can contribute towards teasing out how best to inform, educate and influence public attitudes, as well as facilitating long-term transformation. By exploring textual, spatial and longitudinal transitions in this way, humanities and social science can help tease out the primary triggers necessary to spark fruitful public debate and build consensus, all the while educating a more critical and environmentally focused and attuned citizenship.

Certainly, effective public (media) engagement remains a prerequisite towards promoting Low Carbon Energy Transition and helping towards informing debate around all forms of sustainable productivity. Consequently, communications research ought to focus on exploring effective methods for mobilising behaviour change. Yet critics claim such ongoing environmental initiatives – which could be dismissed by some as a form of environmental greenwashing and PR – often end up promoting instrumental modes of societal acceptance, while failing to address the deep emotional, ethical, political and other aspects of engagement needed to promote and secure successful transition pathways. Essentially, long-term transitional processes remain multi-faceted, involving choices between social, technical and financial solutions; all of which have consequences for the trajectory of future environmental sustainability.

Case Study: Communicating a Renewable Energy Strategy for Low Carbon Transition (LCT)

At the outset, the process of moving from a carbon-intensive environment to one that is more sustainable, while always promoting energy transition, remains well behind schedule and under pressure across many countries. Many stakeholders support the idea of change and the urgent need to move to a post-carbon economy, yet there remains a lack of public engagement and especially commitment concerning the measures necessary to fully activate this transformation. The globally slow progress has appeared to improve however with the Biden Presidency in America, alongside the EU Green New Deal and measures laid out by China, India and other countries, all of which place climate change mitigation and adaptation firmly on the political agenda. Yet a key objective of ongoing environmental media research, across the volatile political landscape throughout the world continues to be centred around exploring how to mobilise public opinion to recognise climate change as the 'global challenge' of our century.

For instance from an Irish context (which is replicated across many countries) building on current advertising and promotional campaigns, spearheaded by government agencies, research can help examine the relative success and effectiveness of various environmental communication campaigns and related climate strategies. In particular from an Irish perspective, such research can assist in analysing the relative success of various renewable energy wind farm projects, especially those situated on forest lands (Coilte), as well as on other state-owned properties (Bord na Mona), and tease out how effective such organisations are in communicating the importance and necessity of these sites for adopting alternative energy projects. Helping to carry out extensive online media and developing a series of audience studies to gauge such responses has to remain a major preoccupation for much environmental communication research into the future.

Such environmental research draws on a number of core concepts and strategies including:

- The need for new knowledge around *citizen engagement*
- The need to develop media/citizen *environmental literacy*, drawing on a comprehensive range of cross-disciplinary areas, including social science, literary studies and arts practice, town planning, engineering, geography, environmental science, communications and other related areas of study. Finding a fresh language and an evolving mode of environmental literacy remains essential in helping inspire new generations to become critically engaged and responsive to the environmental challenges ahead, especially with regards to radically innovative energy solutions.
- Constructing a clear demonstration of the most productive and useful range of media approaches to help normalise energy or other forms of transition. Environmental sustainability in particular underpins a model for effective campaigning into the future.

Producing case studies and evidence of *best practice* across audio-visual mediated fictional and documentary environmental narratives remains a core preoccupation. Teasing out the environmental communication challenge in general, while taking into account the complexity around our climate emergency and affirming the preferred strategy needed remains essential. Furthermore, increasing understanding and appreciation of how low-carbon transition narratives can be distilled, to facilitate engagement and active public debate remain an important ongoing strategy. While some studies give preference to the 'Deliberative Democracy' engagement model (Dryzek et al. 2018; Devaney et al. 2020), most others promote a range of more mixed-methods approaches. One should probably not simply endorse a 'one size fits all' response to the challenges of environmental communications, much less appear to preach down to audiences, with off-the-shelf prescribed solutions. As affirmed at a webinar for a Dingle Community Energy project in Ireland (November 2020) outlined elsewhere, audiences, citizens and communities want to help 'write the book' of their future and not just read the finished product. Certainly co-creation of solutions is essential, as environmental communicators strive to secure a long-term sustainable future for all.

By all accounts, several studies show that a dogmatic strategy around engineering environmental solutions does not work, at least not on its own, especially with regards to modifying overall behaviour patterns. New research and environmental investigation has to strive to contribute to and foster interest in the protection and enhancement of our natural and built environment, while focusing on how the audio-visual industries can catalyse debate and support a range of productive environmental transformations.

Such projects attempt to frame a template for a comprehensive communications model of environmental media production, designed to effectively engage citizens and encourage behavioural change, rather than simply reverting back to a top-down and 'scientific-deficit' approach. Alternatively, it is important to help mediate fruitful debate between the various stakeholders and publics. From tool-kits, to working models of effective communication and flows of pro-active engagement, all of these various strategies need to be taken on board and modified, while being evaluated as fit-for-purpose, both at a micro level and most especially as all types of communities strive to face up to the dire need to achieve a low-carbon future.

References

Brereton, Pat and Barrios O'Neill, Danielle. 'Irish Energy Landscapes on Film'. *Journal of Environmental Media* 2(1): 101–115. 2021.

Brereton, Pat. *Environmental Literacy and New Digital Audiences*. Routledge 2019.

Devaney, Laura *et al.* 'Deepening Public Engagement on Climate Change: Lessons from the Citizens' Assembly'. Report published by *Environmental Protection Agency* (EPA). No 314. 2020.

Dryzek, John and Pickering, John. *The Politics of the Anthropocene*. Arnold Press 2018.

Hulme, Mike. *Why We Disagree about Climate Change: Understanding Controversy, Inaction and Opportunity*. Cambridge University Press 2019.

Pasqualetti, M. 'Social Barriers to Renewable Energy Landscapes'. *The Geographical Review*. The American Geographical Society of New York 2011.

Sterling University. 'Connecting with a Low Carbon Scotland'. n.d. https://www.stir.ac.uk/about/faculties/arts-humanities/our-research/centre-for-environment-heritageand-policy/projects/connecting-with-a-low-carbon-scotland/

Weintrobe, S. 'The Difficult Problem of Anxiety When Thinking about Climate Change'. In Weintrobe, S. (ed.). *Engaging with Climate Change: Psychoanalytic and Interdisciplinary Perspectives*. Routledge 2013.

World Bank (The) and Developing Effective Financial Environmental Communication

The World Bank began back in 1944 and was set up to deal with building up Europe and the World after a devastating global war. On a webinar for our Climate Masters (28th October 2020, Dublin City University), a climate change specialist Ms. Celine Ramstein spoke of how there was several hundred employees working specifically on climate change issues at its Washington headquarters. The global organisation basically gives low or no interest long-term loans to low-income and so-called middle-income countries across the world. As might be expected, the African continent receives a large percentage of all loans, with strict environmental and social security safeguards built into them. Such loans tend to be focused across a range of global problems, including protecting cultural heritage and helping indigenous peoples, as well as securing a range of dedicated climate change measures. The World Bank's overall and ambitious goal is to end poverty and boost the basic income of the bottom 40% of the worlds' population.

While focusing on the energy sector in particular, Ms. Ramstein talked of how environmental communicators need to speak the same language as stakeholders like Engineers and Government officials. Especially in low-income countries, it is important to get energy supplied in a secure and most especially through an affordable manner. This bottom-line necessity presents a major challenge, as many local officials do not think long term or sustainably, especially if it involves extra costs needed to kick-start adopting and using renewable energy infrastructure. This short-term approach can unfortunately become the norm, even if savings can be made over time, not to mention taking into account the global benefits of lower carbon emissions.

Such economic considerations also apply to lower income families, who find it very difficult to secure more efficient heating and other environmentally sustainable resources in the short term. In many developing countries, even if eventually these larger populations are put onto the electric grid, poor people are unfortunately often not able to pay the service fees demanded to stay connected. So at all times, regulators and environmental policy makers and communicators need to think outside the box and through a more holistic systems approach, while striving to be sensitive to and connected with all these various issues across the world. The global message is to strive towards building resilience and use varying often local – even if not necessarily per-fect – strategies towards addressing and hopefully solving both short and long-term environmental difficulties that in turn help to address the longer term climate crisis.

Unfortunately, the 2020/21 pandemic posed a further major global chal-lenge, with over 40% of the poorest people in the world living in 'fragile states' across the planet. Ms. Ramstein spoke in general of the need to effec-tively mainstream climate change strategies and concerns within organisations like the World Bank. This process involves the development of climate risk screenings to help make countries more resilient with regards to how they grow and develop their economies. Of course this remains a major challenge which has to be agreed at a global level and is very much on the agenda for the delayed UN Climate Change conference COP-26 in Glasgow (November 2021). This approach can be assisted by seeking out various 'co-benefits' in securing climate change wins, which remains essential, as various poorer countries strive to raise their standards of living. Talk of 'greening the recov-ery' – particularly after the COVID pandemic of 2020/21 – has had varying meanings and sometimes negative connotations for many developing coun-tries, where outright poverty continues to be a major concern. Many global environmental communication scholars remain hopeful however that what the World Bank pronounces on will help frame the agenda and actively encourage and influence global environmental debates, leading to more effective and resilient climate justice solutions for the whole world.

Reference

Ramstein, Celine from World Bank in the USA presenting at DCU's Guest Lecture Series for Climate Change Masters Students (28 October 2020).

The Future of Environmental Communications
Overcoming Anxiety

Overview: The Great Derangement

Amitav Ghosh's *The Great Derangement* (2016) critiques the limitations of the literary novel, which aims to exhibit the vagaries of 'individual moral adventure'. Apparently, devoid of ethical purpose, the future is forfeited to the whims of the market, ceded to the nihilisms of economic growth. For some critics, the turn inwards across modern fiction mirrors the turn towards commodity fetishism. In a review by Alexandre Leskanich (2017), the novel – together I would contend with much audio-visual and new media – often uses narrow scales of time and space that rarely exceed more than a human lifespan. Such a limited timeline does not allow the climate to violently intrude upon the habitual routines and ordinary concerns, which most stories prefer to portray. Ghosh therefore calls for a heightened imaginary response to addressing climate change. Although some scholars question whether fiction, including all forms of media communication alluded to in this volume, can do much to remedy this situation, not to mention various forms of political and economic intransigence. Nonetheless, mass media has a major role to play, at least in keeping such environmental questions centre stage and embedded within public consciousness, while encouraging both creative imaginative responses, alongside active engagement in facing up to the global environmental challenges of our times.

For instance, calling attention to the pervasive nature of water and weather narratives, as well as the 'tragedy of the commons' in the misallocation of land and other finite resources; all of these and more essential concepts besides, help to clarify the broad range of such an open-ended investigation. By any measure, the broad scope of audio-visual media exemplified in this student's primer, helps to tease out a range of ethical and environmental tensions and agendas that need to become part of mainstream communication discourse and hopefully can help kick-start a move towards a just and more sustainable low carbon future.

There are so many contested and problematic terms, concepts and theories, both alluded to and constantly addressed in this volume, which are all but impossible to bring together in a comprehensive manner. Nonetheless, the

DOI: 10.4324/9781003123422-24

short volume has tried to map out some of the most pertinent and provocative concepts in the field, while also providing illustrations of such debates, using extensive audio-visual textual analysis where possible. As media and environmental academics, we strive to navigate the ever-growing theoretical–practical divide across our interconnecting disciplinary fields, which constantly throw up so many challenges, while trying to somehow link all these fields together. Not surprisingly, such a synthesis approach has ongoing echoes of perennial conflicts and tensions within media/communications; especially between so-called instrumental and practical development of communication skills, as against more open-ended, cross-cultural, critical and theoretical debates. All of which gets mobilised within a field that continues to morph and evolve all the time. Most scholars and environmentally aware citizens might agree on the specific problems that need to be privileged and kept in the foreground, if not always accept the timescales needed for action. All the while, coming up with agreed solutions and problem-solving communication strategies remains an ongoing challenge. But at least in striving to imagine a series of protocols and modes of thinking that will help create a greener, more sustainable and climate justice future, half the battle is facing up to the urgent requirement to secure a low-carbon transition.

Incidentally, *Don't Look Up*, written and directed by Adam McKay, who made *The Big Short* (2015) and *Vice* (2018), was a big hit for Netflix for Christmas 2021. With a roll call of star names including Leonardo DiCaprio, Jennifer Lawrence and Meryl Streep playing a 'Trump-like' American president, there is much for audiences and environmental media students to engage with well into the future. Surprisingly, the parody of an 'end of the world' scenario has divided reviewers and critics, with many (rightly) suggesting that it does not fully hang together as a cautionary tale, yet several environmental scientists and activists have endorsed this imaginative response to the climate crisis. Most certainly it will serve as a catalyst for discussion, which is important.

Realos vs Fundis: Green Growth vs De-growth

The ongoing tensions between so-called 'Realos' and 'Fundis' can be characterised as encapsulating 'Green growth' versus 'De-growth' (or post-growth, as defined in Tim Jackson's 2021 study) and this helps to map out where scholars and teachers fit into this apparently polarising schism. Environmental communicators strive to consciously and objectively tease out and provide some form of constructive dialogue across this never-ending debate. For instance, here in Ireland at the time of writing in 2020/21, the Green Party like many other environmental organisations, is currently grappling with sharing power in government, while trying to function through a difficult pandemic, not to mention a (late)capitalist or neo-liberal economic model of political expediency and praxis. At the same time, this relatively small political party is dealing with so many internal tensions and disruptions. As a fractured organisation, similar to the environmental movement generally, it is struggling to deal with many apparently contradictory values and belief-systems, while trying to manage its social, political and most importantly green political agenda.

Likewise, across the world, the environmental crisis is being mobilised in various ways and is certainly not owned by Green political parties. Effective strategies and workable solutions calls on *all* politicians and governments – both on the Left and the Right, as well as all in between, to strive to grapple with such a long-term and ever-challenging climate crisis. This is where balanced and effective media and communication interventions remains essential, in helping to build consensus towards co-creating long-standing solutions, with regards to both mitigation and privileging various forms of adaptation.

It should be recognised that committed environmentalists, including NGOs and activists of all colours and hues across every part of the world, do not necessarily have all the answers and certainly need to work with and across the full range of stakeholders within every nation and society to help ensure that climate action becomes the number one political, social and even cultural issue and concern that has to be faced up to and urgently addressed. Helpfully, in Ireland at least, the demand for strong political action is assisted by a Supreme court judgement, mandating the government to take direct responsibility towards achieving its EU climate targets. But of course legal censure remains of little use, if all sections of society don't come together to make difficult decisions and unflinchingly face up to the challenges ahead.

In a website published in the lead up to COP 26 in Glasgow (November 2021 https://transform21.org/), the opening blurb affirms that the global pandemic threat has shown that governments can act swiftly and resolutely in a crisis and that people are ready to change their behaviour for the good of humanity. Mary Robinson – Former President of Ireland and Chair of the Elders (made up of retired political dignitaries from across the world) affirms how '[W]e need countries to raise their ambitions for their nationally determined contributions in order to limit global warming to 1.5 degrees by 2050. The time for this level of higher ambition is now'. In this ever-fluid global situation, this primer can never be fully up to date. Still one hopes that environmental communications students and academic scholarship generally will continue to lead the way, by uncovering clean and effective ways of mediating and pivoting towards a low-carbon future, as well as helping to ensure reduced pollution and increasing biodiversity, all of which are essential in promoting our holistic planetary future.

Environmental Communications and the Future

With regards to justice, equality and power politics, media and environmental communications, alongside several other disciplines, including several strands within Social Sciences and Cultural Studies, have been grappling with many of these (Left/Right) concerns and issues, as well as more resonant green political tensions and norms for a long time now. From an educational media studies perspective, this has been forged by a broadly Gramscian, Foucauldian, not to mention a Habermasian and even a postmodernist agenda, while at the same time framing a range of complementary and sometimes contradictory intellectual agendas. The mega-discipline of media/communication studies in particular, using the lens of environmentalism, strives to appreciate and address various aspects of audience pleasures, coupled with dealing with identity issues around gender, class and ethnicity – as explored through several entries in this volume. There is also a growing focus on the political economy perspective and the ever-increasing material footprint of the media and communication industries themselves; as all strands of the media industries are brought together while striving to promote more productive and sustainable modes of green messaging.

Only recently has environmental politics and behavioural psychology come into this debate and most directly into public consciousness, with its own particular set of questions and ways of engaging audiences using effective argument and frames. But the challenge remains in uncovering how to link existing long-established theorising, together with audiences' behaviour, while calling on environmental and communication debates towards striving to tackle the challenges of a Just Transition. All the while, students grappling with all these disciplinary areas need to keep focused on the minefield around sustainability, ensuring long-term environmental security.

Here in Ireland the work of environmental scholars and activists, like Peadar Kirby who helped set up the Cloughjordan eco-village, remains instructive on the ground, especially in espousing the radical thinking of Karl Polanyi's '*The Great Transformation*' (1944). Such scholars shine a light on various possible futures and help to tease out explicit tensions within green politics. New identity and environmentally driven politics are certainly needed for the island, together with the rest of the world. A broad range of positions and political expressions are essential to take on board, as students strive to square academic complexities around environmental debates, while dealing with the ongoing on-the-ground practical realities for citizens and stakeholders in their local communities. Perhaps the possibility of full dialogue and consensus between so-called Realos and Fundis, much less those citizens not necessarily engaged in environmental dialogue is not fully possible across such wide-ranging discourses, where many in turn do not wish to be pigeon-holed in one camp or the other. Yet, by any measure, the primary role of environmental communication is to provide the most effective glue and even suggest a range of robust tools to help to develop and sustain such a necessary dialogue.

One could also go so far as to assert that such labelling, demonising and reductively categorising of well-held positions (all of which has long been part of the Left–Right ideological discourses for centuries, much less recalling nationalistic and fractured identity politics within the academy) are continuing at a pace with the growth of green and environmental thinking. The process of debate and discussion needs more than ever to develop critically engaged and road-tested responses, rather than an un-reflexive drive toward polarisation and crude labelling of particular green positions, which is not helpful towards uncovering a coherent, much less workable solution for the major climate change problems of our age. These extend into debates and tensions around what has been categorised as eco-modernism, sustainable models of development, as well as all the other aspects embedded in this complex arena that deal with global equality and justice. Environmental communication platforms can certainly provide an open forum where robust debate can take place.

For example here in Ireland, eco-modernism appears to be used as a constant critique of mainstream (Realo) Green politicians and such a label is used to support a fixed position that pulls against any critique of de-growth etc. Crudely, yet respectfully, I would assert that its relatively easy for tenured academics like myself to be positioned as appearing more radical within and across the green spectrum, while at the same time acknowledging the inherent benefits and necessity for activists, critics and scholars of all hues to have the safety and security to think outside the box of conventional thinking and practice. Such debate and sustained analysis certainly helps lay the groundwork for student learning, while outlining future models and always striving to engage with practical approaches for active environmental communication.

But, as illustrated by decades of ideological analysis within media and communication studies especially, looking into the long-established, but fractured, movements across Europe and America in particular, there are no easy solutions, much less a clear formula for effective environmental praxis. Adding to the mix, a broad range of other disciplines, drawn from Business, Social Sciences and the Humanities makes this struggle even more difficult to manage.

How to marry such scholarly and political tensions across the very different drivers of public enterprise and business practice, together with the need to create various forms of sustainable employment, alongside productive engagement with the global industrial–stakeholder community, remains an ever-present conundrum. All the while striving to highlight a pathway for radical transformation towards future environmental justice and equality, always remain a major challenge and objective. Surprisingly, it would appear from experience over the decades that some of our undergraduate students tend to be more conservative and less radical than their tutors, as evident from a recent audience research project using Higher Education students (see Brereton and Gomez 2020). Nonetheless, such conservative-leaning students are frequently the least vocal in class, compared with more left-leaning students, who tend to be embraced within a liberal orthodoxy.

Furthermore, many environmental communication students simply want to acquire a set of skills and pragmatic toolkits to help them secure employment into the future, on witnessing the expediential growth of sustainability management and greening of businesses. While more adventurous students tend to crave radical transformation of social and environmental norms and expect the academy to afford them the space and critical tools to reimagine this potentially utopian future. Such a crude (journalistic) breakdown of the student profile and their motivation coincidentally appears to coincide with theoretical and practice approaches to both environmental and communication academic programmes, where many of these students similarly want to use their educational experience for learning and critical reflection, if sometimes in contrasting ways. Meanwhile, others simply expect such sustained critical engagement on programmes to assist in securing and/or at least augmenting future prospects for employment.

Of course some of our best environmental students also use learning and research primarily for altruistic reasons, as they eke out a precarious living within various NGOs and back-room political organisations. Yet, many more remain sanguine and at least unconsciously instrumental in their thinking, especially regarding their long-term desires and expectations. How might tutors and the ongoing development of a general environmental communications curriculum, best frame and co-opt such apparently contradictory tensions and assist in meeting the ever-expanding desires and (real) needs and motivations of students, without simply degenerating into consumer clientelism or instrumental modes of teaching and learning? This remains a major challenge for all concerned and all my colleagues are actually engaged in this dilemma.

Anecdotally, I witnessed such tensions first-hand, while being requested by an ex-student, who was working in the airline business to encourage our environmental masters' students to get on-board (excuse the pun) and help witness and observe an eco-sustainability project that they were facilitating. At the outset, such a project could easily be dismissed as an exercise in blatant PR marketing and even greenwashing. Nonetheless, at least privately, some students were more than happy to become involved with the project, raising questions around the role of educators, as both gatekeepers and arbitrators of so-called 'best practice' across environmental communication and pedagogical practice. As illustrated in *Environmental Ethics and Film* (Brereton 2016), environmental and ethical red lines are not as clear cut, as they might first appear.

Furthermore, how to build bridges with younger radical environmentalists while acknowledging the slow rate of political transformation and recognising the so-called 'democratic deficit' permeating most western political organisations and policy-based institutions? The dominant political apparatus in particular remains very slow towards promoting, much less rolling out, climate change policies, as the apparatus strives to enact political, alongside social and cultural transformation. Unfortunately, such political activity does not always take into account the dire need for urgent and radical change to adequately address the ever-growing carbon crisis. One wonders incidentally, as raised numerous times in this volume; if the 2020/21 global pandemic – which has been an ever-present spectre in writing many of the entries – might help constitute a cautionary fore-warning and serve as a concrete model regarding the need for efficacy and coherent action throughout such a period of radical transformation. Could such a traumatic and deadly virus and its ongoing effects on global society be usefully repurposed as an effective template in transforming a reluctant citizenry across the world to face up to the climate emergency? As evidenced across several entries in this volume, the general public often espouse change, but when it comes to practical actions that affect their day-to-day living – especially concerning climate change – they appear most reluctant and almost by default espouse a 'business as usual' lethargic form of behaviour. In any case, professional and academic environmentalists are probably expecting too much of the pandemic in showing the way forward. As a French philosopher Bernard Henri Levy at the end of a wide-ranging discussion and in a throwaway comment on BBC's *Newsnight* (BBC Newsnight 2016) asserted, such a pandemic has no agency at all – it is just a 'virus'!

Demonising the other, whether it is right-wingers or rural protectionists, not to mention farmers, multinationals, or the super-rich, including media celebrities, can unfortunately become a media circus or game (even sometimes a witch hunt) that does not necessarily produce effective results in mobilising global behaviour change from the top down, much less from the bottom up. As human beings, we love to blame someone else, which often begins with the assertion often left unsaid: if only *they* just stopped producing or consuming so much, the environment would be better off. Consequently, environmental communications as an academic discipline urgently need to carry out various modes of engagement and persuasion on a global scale and not just succumb to blaming others, while balancing restrictions and culpability in dealing with the ever-growing developing world population, which is badly affected by (climate-based) poverty and global injustice. Effectively dealing with various forms of environmental insecurity remains a major challenge towards 'building back better' and securing a low carbon future that we all can be proud of and wholeheartedly embrace.

Furthermore, recalling Joseph Schumpeter's notion of 'creative destruction' (Kopp 2021) and how various forms of conflict can nonetheless lead to some productive results. By all accounts such a conflictual strategy and approach remains a high risk one, with the possibility of many unintended consequences and certainly should not be the only solution to be privileged in responding to our unstable future. Finding the appropriate scapegoat or enemy, as already noted, often remains a media sport and is frequently indulged in by academics (and even Green scholars) – while constantly appealing for radical change within various ongoing political struggles. But how to build bridges and forge long-term and grounded consensus through co-creation of solutions, remains much harder to seed and grow. Yet this approach appears necessary in forging transformational and environmental changes and securing a robust low carbon future. Pivoting and reprioritising across various political, social and communal norms remains essential, while ensuring all planetary citizens are treated justly and equally; all the while recalling the somewhat glib political mantra of 'leaving nobody behind'. This struggle remains a huge challenge and no expert has the full picture or the complete answers on how to cope with these difficulties, especially as the various faulty political even democratic systems strive to muddle through with their short-term election cycles, meanwhile a majority of industrial global systems still support naked self-interested (capitalist) wealth production. A robust media and communication network can however support the seismic shift necessary towards ensuring consensual engagement, in addressing all aspects of our climate crisis.

Most interestingly, on a more practical and future-facing trajectory, journalists like Caroline O'Doherty (2021) sheds some common sense and light in reviewing areas of hope for the future with regards to climate change. O'Doherty outlines several climate change reasons to be positive, as against some ongoing concerns and worries:

- There are green minds in the White House, with the election of Joe Biden and the end of the reign of a global climate denier. Green leadership helps to foreground environmental messaging.
- The huge success of Greta Thunberg and the Friday School Strikes with the ongoing passion of the youth in fighting for climate change. This new form of active agency has been foregrounded in several entries in teasing out how climate change communication can help address the issues most effectively.
- The national commitments to meeting and extending the Paris Accord. For instance China has set a new target of becoming carbon neutral by 2060. America now aims to reach this milestone by 2050, with Japan and other countries including India, being even more adventurous. Certainly, the role of China is central to this challenge around climate change, yet much more is needed by students to fully assess the growing global importance of such ever growing power blocks and regions. Meanwhile, the signs are also looking a bit better with regards to the active engagement of big business. As O'Doherty rightly affirms, whether 'it's to keep up appearances or avoid future fossil fuel shocks – or maybe even because it's the right thing to do – growing numbers of multinational manufacturers, service providers and investment houses are making public commitment to climate action and divesting from fossil fuels'.
- Pushing climate change legislation, alongside rolling out carbon budgets and 'climate proofed' legal changes in behaviour and practices to reach carbon neutrality.
- Knowledge and science is growing in power; in many ways; we now have detailed insight through precise language and linguistic tools of the communication necessary to explore how nature works and how to keep carbon in check through oceans, forests and bogs etc.

- Coupled with other more hopeful signs, including more local, community, regional and national, as well as international, engagement with this ongoing emergency.

But of course, as various commentators, including professionals and scientific environmental experts like David Attenborough reported on within this volume constantly affirm, there are equally major issues and increasing environmental difficulties facing the world.

- The maths and environmental science is so bad; many wonder if we can make the radical change in time. The IPCC Report (August 2021) certainly makes grim reading.
- Progress continues to be equated with the crude measure of GDP, so increasing wealth and insatiable consumption remains the measure of success.
- The political climate – the slow pace of democratic politics and the constant rise of populism highlight how it becomes difficult to get real long-term transformation.
- Loss of biodiversity – according to several estimates, only 35% of the planet's wilderness is left, which over the years has served as an effective cushion and carbon sink for our planet.
- It's the economy stupid. Economists have put a natural capital value of 100 trillion a year on the services nature provides for humans. 'But nature never sent an invoice and mankind never wrote a receipt'. With the European (and the American) Green New Deal for instance – everyone asks what it will 'cost'! But if we don't address the problems in the first place, what will be the final cost for the planet? By all accounts, environmental communications and their evolving (journalist) specialist media skill-set need to be co-opted more effectively in addressing these ongoing crises and help turn around all regions of the planet we live on.

This student guide has drawn on a full range of global environmental debates, including Eco-Modernism, Eco-Socialism, Green New Deal, Green Idealism, Platonic Green Spirituality, Frugal De-Growth, Intergenerational and Youthful rebellion among others. While related concepts and examples, particularly pertinent to this study include, 'best practice' approaches across environmental journalism alongside all forms of audio-visual media production that need to be constantly updated and critically evaluated from both an aesthetic and thematic perspective. Such positions, theories, principles and debates embody laudable aims and objectives, even constituting workable frameworks in themselves. But how to link each of these desperate areas with practical political, social and cultural responses, while promoting an efficient and economical use of time and resources, as part of a time-limited Environmental Communications curriculum, remains an ongoing challenge.

A green European politician and environmental scholar Dirk Holemans (2020), for instance calls for a paradigm shift in thinking and systemic development and this in turn calls out a well-honed challenge for all environmental and media communicators to get this message across. Such a call to action can help create new and more effective modes of resistant adaptation across so many areas of society and the economy, alongside the mass media and communications eco-system in particular. In turn, he argues, this can help humanity uncover the necessary levers to instigate major radical changes that are required to address the urgent and multiple threats to life, instigated by our ongoing climate crisis.

Finally, it must always be highlighted, as noted in Michael Mann's *The New Climate War: The Fight to Take Back our Planet* (2021), that the big fossil fuel industries were inspired by those in the gun lobby, the tobacco industry and alcohol companies, while basically shifting responsibility for climate change from corporations to individuals. Most of the heavy lifting in the climate crisis has to be achieved from the top down and especially by those citizens who have the most resources at their disposal. Furthermore, as alluded to in several entries, the news media often need conflict to survive and sometimes remain overly preoccupied with feeding various forms of doomism – the notion that climate change is just too big a problem for us to solve – as well as using arguments like the cost of change is too much for society to bear.

But essentially as we also have witnessed with the 2020/21 pandemic, the opposite argument remains true. The cost of *not* facing up to climate change or any other global challenge is far greater than simply ignoring it or leaving it for another day. Mann most pointedly urges environmentalists to spend time communicating with those who are 'reachable, teachable and moveable' (2021: 262) and always look to hopeful solutions. Certainly environmental communication students fit into this category and all future investigation and scholarship needs to draw on various forms of hope and constructive learning for the future.

This short A–Z volume only scratches the surface, while always drawing on so many disciplinary areas for students to investigate. Hopefully by encouraging students and scholars to read more widely, the short primer goes some way in helping to hone their critical and practical skills for the future. The climate crisis needs all aspects of environmental communication and student learning to be at the top of their game in the ongoing struggle to address so many inter-related issues and environmental concerns.

References

BBC Newsnight '"Europe Might Be Dying": Bernard Henri Levy - BBC's Newsnight' 24 March 2016 https://www.youtube.com/watch?v=0M48_xWT-CM

Brereton, Pat. *Environmental Ethics and Film*. Routledge 2016.

Brereton, P. and Gomez, V. 'Media Students, Climate Change, and YouTube Celebrities: Readings of Dear Future Generations: Sorry Video Clip'. *ISLE: Interdisciplinary Studies in Literature and Environment* 27(2): 385–405. 2020.

Ghosh, Amitav. *The Great Derangement: Climate Change and the Unthinkable*. University of Chicago Press 2016.

Holemans, Dirk. 'Resilience under Shock: Time for a Paradigm Shift'. 2020 https://www.greeneuropeanjournal.eu/resilience-under-shock-time-for-a-paradigm-shift/

Jackson, Tim. *Post Growth: Life after Capitalism*. Polity Press 2021.

Kopp, Carol M., Boyle, Michael J. and Costagliola, Diane. 'Creative Destruction'. *Investopedia* 23 June 2021. https://www.investopedia.com/terms/c/creativedestruction.asp

Leskanich, Alexandre. Review of *The Great Derangement*. *LSE Review of Books* 2017.

Mann, Michael E. *The New Climate War: The Fight to Take Back our Planet*. London: Scribe 2021.

O'Doherty, Caroline. 'Climate Change: Five Reasons to be Cheerful and Five to be Fearful'. *Irish Independent* 2 January 2021.

Printed in the United States
by Baker & Taylor Publisher Services